FIFTH AVENUE:
A *VERY* SOCIAL HISTORY

KATE SIMON

A
VERY
SOCIAL
HISTORY

Fifth Avenue

A HARVEST/HBJ BOOK
HARCOURT BRACE JOVANOVICH   NEW YORK AND LONDON

Grateful acknowledgment is
made to The New York Times
for permission to quote from
the article by Olin Downes
which appeared on March 30,
1934, © 1934 by The New
York Times Company.

LIBRARY OF CONGRESS CATALOGING IN PUBLICATION DATA
Simon, Kate.
Fifth Avenue: a very social history.

(A Harvest/HBJ book)
Bibliography: p.
1. New York (City)—Streets—Fifth Avenue.
2. New York (City)—History. I. Title.
F128.67.F4S55   1979   974.7′1   79-11996
ISBN 0-15-630712-X

First Harvest/HBJ edition 1979

A B C D E F G H I J

CONTENTS

LIST OF ILLUSTRATIONS

Reservoir
Fifth Avenue and 42nd Street

Consuelo and William K. Vanderbilt
Carnegie Mansion drawing room

Fifth Avenue and Broadway
Madison Square Park, 1876
Madison Square, 1895

The Flatiron Building

Fifth Avenue and 44th Street
Mansion at Fifth Avenue and 126th Street
Metropolitan Club

Sherry's French Garden

The Waldorf Astoria
C. K. G. Billings' Horseback Dinner

H. C. Frick
James Hazen Hyde and Rejane
The Belmonts and Caroline Perry
Mrs. William Astor

The Scene today

ACKNOWLEDGMENTS

I should like to express deep thanks to Dr. James J. Heslin who introduced me, long ago, to the many charms and uses of The New-York Historical Society where he is director. Many thanks, also, to Miss Sue Gillies of the Society's library and her assistants, and to Miss Wendy Shadwell of the Society's Print Collection for their ready, knowing help.

To Miss Esther Brumberg of the Print Department of the Museum of the City of New York, my gratitude for her amiable, expert assistance, and to Miss B. Holly of the gift shop at the Museum, my thanks for efforts in my behalf that she didn't have to make at all.

This might be the time and place to settle an old debt: many, many thanks to two opinionated, amusing and wordy ghosts, Philip Hone and George Templeton Strong, without whom where would we writers on New York be?

And by no means last in the line for thanks, the polite, anonymous voices that patiently unsnarl knotty little research problems when one phones the Brooklyn Public Library Telephone Reference Division.

FIFTH AVENUE:
A *VERY* SOCIAL HISTORY

CHAPTER 1

RACE MEET

September 25, 1866, was a glorious day. Three commanding high livers, August Belmont, Leonard Jerome and Jerome's partner, the wit William R. Travers, were prime movers of that particular day, the day the American Jockey Club held its first meet. Racing was not new to New York; expensive trotters had been tried out at hot speeds and high betting on Harlem Lane, now St. Nicholas Avenue. There was racing, too, on Long Island tracks, but those were centers for hoi polloi, its petty touts and flashy ladies. The city had, however, bred enough bon vivants, gentlemen acquainted with the royal sport in European centers, to merit its own aristocratic club and a track that would run blooded horses under gentlemen's rules.

The *Times* reported that the city, up to Fourteenth Street, was bustling with preparations, the streets lined with equipages—four-in-hands, single spans, stylish turnouts. Two of these were the conspicuous carriages of Jerome which, although the *Times* didn't say so, were probably trilling and brimming with the prettiest unfettered women in New York—those that Belmont had not cadged. Burnished harness was buckled on the silken horses, liveried grooms placed generous picnic hampers and then helped settle the ladies behind the gentlemen charioteers, who drove in white hats and dogskin gloves. Before noon, everything and everyone was in place, and the carriages began to leave the doorways of the houses that lined Fifth Avenue from Washington Square to Madison Square. The carriageless remainder of thousands of enthusiasts rode off to the races in improvised vehicles provided by the Harlem Railroad Company. The *Herald* reporter compared them to cattle cars that sprayed flying coal into the mouths and eyes of the passengers. The *Times* man, out for fun, sustained no insult or injury, and in the spacious, Dickensian style of the day described the train ride as "orderly as a country funeral, as jolly as a first-class picnic party, as genial as Knickerbocker Christmas." *Harper's Weekly* was pleased that New York had established an "American Derby" at last, and lavished a good deal of space on the effulgent carriages and the Victorian chinoiserie stand for judges and reporters. At Jerome Park, the papers sang, the ladies of the *haut ton*, leading off a thousand "ladies of fashion, ladies domestic, ladies professionally literary, ladies of birth and culture, ladies of dress and ladies of more quiet taste," felt as protected in the elegant clubhouse as in their own drawing rooms.

Sportsmen from all over the country came, bankers and clerks, members of society and Tammany—not immutably separate groups—theater people, including the famous Madame Ristori who was playing *Medea* and Schiller's *Mary Stuart* in Italian. There were pickpockets and policemen on foot and horse, and a brothel keeper or two, sedate in their discreet dress and carriages. There was John Morrisey, the Tammany gang brawler, pugilist, gambler, sportsman and Congressman; and his boss, the big Boss, William Marcy Tweed. There were the horse-loving Vanderbilts; the chic, limpid beauty, Mrs. August Belmont, a woman of singular charm; and fat Jim Fisk, vulgar, gross and mistress-laden. General Grant was there and roundly cheered when he appeared with Leonard Jerome on the grandstand after the first race. Later he was flatteringly mobbed by the crowd that had laced its pleasure with refreshments from their hampers. "The atmospheric vapors became laden with congenial cognac, gay old rye, cool claret, bully Burgundy, cold biscuit, appetizing tongue, cut chicken, apple pie, old and lively cheese—not to forget champagne and cigars," chortled the *Times*.

The race meets of the American Jockey Club were to continue as highlights of the social and racing season, but there might never again be quite so jolly, bibulous and gay a mixture of financiers and hackmen, the elite and the adventurer, civic-minded aristocrats and corrupt profiteers, the "Old" New Yorker money and the New. The latter, launched on a swing of financial and social mobility, would, if it held on, place the diadem of "Old" on the heads of its scions and their steely, ambitious wives.

Fifth Avenue, from Washington Square to Madison Square, was now the place for money to live and show. Tourists were directed to its distinctions: the carved façades and shining, ornate metals at the doors of the brownstone houses; indoors, rich paneling and, as Harriet Beecher Stowe complained, rarely a good kitchen and, more rarely, a bathroom. This was soon to change, though many New Yorkers were repelled by the immoral "French" fittings of bathrooms installed in some new Madison Square mansions.

Critics were deploring, in the immortal New York plaint, the rapid rise and decay of buildings, and doubting the longevity of the houses rising on Fifth, because we lived like nomads and our finest brownstone houses were basically tents of changing materials. The houses kept marching on, promising soon to line the Avenue to Forty-second Street and making tentative darts into the Fifties, to sit in the slow-growing shadow of St. Patrick's, whose cornerstone had been placed in 1858. The salubrious air and soaring property values in the streets near Central Park, now that its dismal squatter colonies had been replaced by silky leas and romantic groves, were luring

purchasers. Those merchants who hadn't the money or faith
for Fifth Avenue property took their families to Brooklyn and
the Jersey shore, abandoning their once fashionable lower
Manhattan neighborhoods to a vast immigrant population
which comprised, early in the 1860s, almost half of the city's
people. The poor who could not accommodate themselves in
the dreadful lodging houses that surrounded the Bowery, the
infamous Five Points, the lower edges of the East River, and
those chased from the swamps and garbage of Central Park,
moved as squatters to Dutch Hill, at Fortieth Street near the
East River, while others put up their shacks and lean-tos along
the Hudson from Fortieth Street to Eightieth.

Summers, the obscene crowding of the slums increased the
incidence of cholera and yellow fever. Very few of the rich—
who were rapidly becoming infinitely richer with the ownership of vast stretches of city land leased to slum landlords—
concerned themselves with the plague pits they owned. Nor did
the city fathers, a body of "lower and blackguard scum than
any in Western Christendom, or in the world," according to the
diarist George Templeton Strong, one of the few to admit that
disease did occasionally cross class lines. "The epidemic is God's
judgment on the poor for neglecting His sanitary laws. It will
soon appear as His judgments on the rich for tolerating that
neglect—on landlords for poisoning the tenants of their unventilated, undrained, sunless rookeries. . . . We are letting them
perish of cholera and . . . they will prove their brotherhood
and common humanity by killing us with the same disease."

The deepest pit of pestilence, as of depravity, dissolution,
vice and drunkenness was Five Points, the meeting of Baxter,
Worth and Park streets, not noticeably changed from the place
Dickens had described in his *American Notes* in 1842. In the
eighteenth century it had been a marshland that encompassed
a pond where pioneer experiments with a steamboat took place.
A public-works program to relieve unemployment caused by
the depression of 1808 drained the area and it became a work-

ing-class common. The draining had been poorly done, the land began to sink and its unsteady houses and pubs were taken over by freed slaves and the poorest of immigrants. The neighborhood became one of New York's attractions (at all times the city has shown a perverse pride in its blackest holes) not only for foreign writers but for visiting ministers who found it difficult to believe, as they walked in the area, that New York had any claim to be a Christian city. They described the loose women who filled the sidewalks and beckoned from the windows, the fighting and drunkenness, the vermin in the lodging houses, the shameless entertainment in the theaters. There was no Sunday and no policemen to tamp down the jollity. The police were afraid to mingle with the murderers and thieves who lived in these streets and afraid of the ward heelers who warned them to stay away. The most colorful rookery was "Old Brewery," exclusively the lair of prostitutes and thieves a number of whose friends lived in a one-room coeducational unit that slept seventy-five men and women and swaggered under the name of "Den of Thieves."

The presence of such a citizenry, though small in the swelling population of skilled laborers and merchants, was a constant dim threat. The passions of the draft riots of 1863 had been terrifying and as an act of propitiation and an effort to prevent other such demonstrations the civic-minded were prompted to establish industrial schools, the Children's Aid Society, missions and clubs and health services. The hope was that such institutions would divert the slum boys from their gangs, the girls from their swarms of pubescent prostitutes, and reduce the high rate of infanticide that was the slum's solution to one of its many problems. A Citizens' Association (which included the giant slumlord, Astor) had quickly formed after the riots, and sent a group of physicians to examine the slums. They found disease, polluted milk and water, walls that crawled with vermin and, said one inspector, rats who were plumper and livelier than the children in the crowded, airless rooms.

As in medieval hospices, the hale were bedded down with the diseased and the only privies were uncared for boxes in the backyards. From the investigation grew a Board of Health, valiantly and vigorously led, but too young in age and concept and too hampered by a corrupt city government to be effective. A Tenement Act was shortly passed that required more space between buildings, more windows in each apartment and ruled that cellars no longer be used for human habitation. The owners of the properties, with venerable, respected names like Fish, Jones, Rutherford, Schermerhorn, Goelet, paid no attention to the ruling. It was their contention that the houses were fouled by the dissolute Irish savages who inhabited them and that all improvements were consequently a waste. Although a few papers called them pithy names, no one could force the owners to improve their properties. Fernando Wood, who had been the Tammany mayor before and during the Civil War, was now a Congressman, still a power in Tammany and devoted to the Astors who scorned him socially. Under the Tsardom of William Tweed, which had begun in the 1850s and would last into the 1870s, the inner Tammany Ring controlled every aspect of city legislation including tenement laws, and although moneyed power found itself uneasy with him, Tweed was a useful friend. He assigned the moneyed to sit on committees formed each time another public voice was raised in outrage over the city's slums, the stench and smog of increasing industrial plants, the effluvia from inadequate sewers and the abundant supply of manure from horses, goats, and pigs, and the human urine that made slick ice on cold days. In this one sense, New York in the mid-1860s was a completely democratic city: it stank for rich and poor alike.

Burglaries and daylight robberies were on the increase and there was talk of citizens' vigilante committees. Fires—resulting from rotten timbers in the slums, from the new gas lamps that ignited the curtains of fine houses, and from the vanity and eccentricity of volunteer fire companies and their boy groupies

—constantly gobbled up houses and streets. A professional fire department had to evolve and it did in 1865. The population was about nine hundred thousand, in 1866 the value of the city's real estate approximately four hundred million dollars and rising rapidly. Strangling traffic prompted plans to open a transportation tunnel under Broadway from Warren to Murray streets, the first attempt at a subway, abandoned and not revived until 1900 because property owners were slow to see the advantages of underground railroads. A trial trip of an experimental elevated railroad on Greenwich Street from the Battery to Cortland gave promise of a reasonable solution to traffic congestion and of access to expanding city distances and thus led off a swift proliferation of elevated lines. Foot traffic along Broadway, the shopping center, was so heavy and crossing so hazardous that a footbridge was thrown across Broad Street at Fulton. Merchants on both sides of Fulton complained that the bridge shadowed their windows and displays; the bridge was removed.

Though the streets were hazardous and inadequately lit, the carriages that crowded Fifth Avenue became increasingly commodious and regal and gravid with the weight of jewelry and furs and small mobs of liveried footmen. The middle class continued to establish its houses across the waters and northward in outlying areas served by ferries, horse-drawn streetcars and elevated lines. The Hansom Cab Company sent out its conveyances to help clot the chaotic traffic, insupportably noisy with the rusty groan of thousands of iron-rimmed wheels and the strike of iron horseshoes.

This complex of ills, described by the New York *Post* in 1867 as making New York "the most inconveniently arranged commercial city in the world," didn't impede the city from launching out on a wild drive to gigantism, spurred on by Civil War profiteering. Beside being "the most brilliant assemblage ever seen on a race course in this country," the first American Jockey Club meet might be considered a symbol of the watershed dividing the old intimate city of stalwart merchants and responsible financiers from the new gilded thieves' den of uncontrolled financial sleight of hand. It was precisely this thieves' den quality that impelled Leonard Jerome to withdraw from Wall Street because, he said, it had fallen into the hands of highwaymen. More and more markedly the capital of the country was becoming New York, with Washington a devoted and well-paid servant: the nomination of Grant for the presidency was designed and successfully sponsored by A. T. Stewart, William Backhouse Astor and Cornelius Vanderbilt. The transatlantic cable finally, after several disappointing tries, began to work reasonably well. Telegraphy was chattering deals across the country, meshing it to New York. Political scandals grew more floridly monumental, part of the gestation of the Big City.

About 65 percent of the nation's imports came through New York and heaped the spanking Broadway shops with French laces, English woolens, rare objects to fill the larger and larger Fifth Avenue drawing rooms with costliness. Shipping, shopkeeping, banking and real estate, for which New York was the nation's center, were the prime moneymaking occupations. A considerable amount of manufacturing, the garment industry an important element, went on as well, earning a million and a half dollars in 1860. Bank deposits had almost tripled between 1861 and 1865. Between 1860 and 1870, real estate doubled in value, reaching an estimated worth of one million dollars.

New York entertainments were becoming more numerous and varied. The theater flourished, as did the concert saloons and their pliant waitresses, available for a bit of extracurricular activity. Balls grew more extravagant, laced with longer and longer strings of pearls and diamonds. Money was still for loud public spending, some of the showiest displays put on by rough China traders who let it be known that they could afford to spend five hundred dollars for a bouquet of flowers. There

were, of course, the dangerous pleasures of the Bowery and the
Five Points district, and the safer joys of parades. Crowds
gawped constantly at increasing numbers of foreign celebrities
and their entourages who made stately, exotic displays on their
way up Broadway and Fifth Avenue. There was always Barnum's Museum, too. His "200,000 Curiosities" included white
whales, albino children, a fat woman, a distorted human featured as "What is it?" and tableaux of Moral Spectacular
Drama. For those who favored classical theater, tickets were
available in florist, drug and fruit shops. Less demanding theater could be found at Leon and Kelly's Minstrels on Broadway,
and vaudeville at the Fifth Avenue Theater at Twenty-eighth
Street. Circus aficionados filled the New York Circus opposite
the Academy of Music on Fourteenth Street. Those who
weren't dashing around among public entertainments or seek-
ing the popular tensions of séances, stayed at home to wonder
over the depth of pictures viewed in the new stereopticon or
discussed the virtues of a remarkable sewing machine that
could gather, hem, ruffle, shirr and tuck, all for the price of
$5.00.

One of the best and cheapest entertainments of Old and
New City was millionaire-watching. The August Belmonts entertained frequently in their lower Fifth Avenue houses, first
at 72, at Thirteenth Street, and later 109, at the corner of
Eighteenth Street. At no cost one could examine the superb
carriages that filled the street and admire the red carpet (actually owned by the Belmonts, not rented, as was the habit) rolled
out for the feet of honored guests. If lucky, one could catch
glimpses through the open door of the naked Bouguereau lady
whom the cosmopolite Belmont chose to hang in his entrance
hall. Commodore Cornelius Vanderbilt and his son William
Henry could be observed in Central Park and along Third
Avenue exercising the horses they prized more highly than
their women. It was one of the pleasures of Leonard Jerome,
Winston Churchill's grandfather, to shock churchgoing crowds

with bravura Sunday displays of horsemanship as he drove his glittering carriage, loaded with a mini-harem of beauties, along Fifth Avenue.

There were of course other occupations for prosperous citizens: financiers and politicians to manipulate, frauds to design and watch out for, astute wheeling and dealing; but they were not quite yet the later gigantic forms of chicanery that gained and lost monumental sums in maneuvers so complex they required a man's full and wary attention. There was time for impromptu racketing around and spending money in innocent shamelessness, unmoved by the feeble criticism of discontented labor and the "low" press. While the men took their pleasures, some of their wives were busy with a delicious literary scandal touched off by an article by Harriet Beecher Stowe, published in the *Atlantic* and titled "The True Story of Lady Byron's Life." Byron, dead since 1824 but still exciting, was undergoing considerable reappraisal. Fault was increasingly pointed at Lady Byron, who was judged too harsh in her reports of her errant husband. To defend her friend, Lady Byron, also dead by this time, Mrs. Stowe let it be known that Byron had carried on an incestuous affair with his half sister, Augusta Leigh, conveniently dead as well. The uproar was caused in some quarters by the fact itself, if fact it was, and in other quarters by the bad taste Mrs. Stowe had showed in exhuming a matter whose protagonists could not speak for themselves.

That scandal was dim, limited to the comparative few who cared about Stowe, Byron et al., compared to the roars of revulsion that issued from Dutch patroon families when Tom Thumb, Barnum's masterpiece, who sang and danced and kissed the ladies for a thousand dollars a day, and Lavinia Warren, also about three feet tall, were married in 1863, attended by intense curiosity and excitement, in fashionable Grace Church. (Its sexton was Isaac Brown, fat and arrogant, coarse and unscrupulous. Hostesses were dependent on him to

distribute invitations, which he often passed to seedy young
men whom he introduced as foreign gentry. He was patroniz-
ing, given to extravagant flourishes, the power who could ruin
or sponsor a break into society. As a side line, a lucrative one,
he conducted a carriage-hire business.)

Women's Rights was showing its monstrous head, its pro-
ponents reviled by the male populace as "female pests" and
"loathsome dealers in clack" recently become uncommonly
loud and offensive, about on a level with the whores of Leonard, Church and Mercer streets. To the three "infatuated"
girls who applied to Columbia's law school, one trustee's response was, "No woman shall degrade herself by practicing
law, especially in New York, if I can save her." The vast majority of women agreed that such ambition was outrageous;
the female domains of nursery, kitchen, drawing room and
benevolent endeavor were quite enough. The only weapon of
the society woman was the snickersnee that hung over guest
lists. The "Old" Schermerhorns, Brevoorts and Stuyvesants,
and the newly old Astors were welcomed to lavish dinners and
theatricals in houses on lower Fifth Avenue, on Stuyvesant
Square and Lafayette Place; but the foulmouthed, vulgarly
rich Vanderbilt was excluded as, for a time, was the "Oriental"
(euphemism for Jewish) Belmont before he overwhelmed society with the Rothschild money he represented and his beautiful, Southern-belle wife. Jerome and his wife were rarely
invited but he didn't care, cherishing the freedom such exclu-
sion offered him.

A thriving New York merchant or banker tried to keep
his wife contented in a house equipped with the latest commodities: hot water from the taps, gas lighting and, if she insisted, a bathroom. His furniture was a stylistic mess called
"Renaissance," anyone's Renaissance. This "style" took on
baroque weight, rococo trills, and Oriental flourishes from the
newly opened East; Elizabethan England left its mark as well,
and so did the French Louises. There were the inlays in metals,

woods and porcelain that the Empress Eugenie liked and the eclectic charmers introduced in Victoria's London Crystal Palace Exposition, brought to New York's Crystal Palace in 1853. It was ponderous stuff, maddened by arabesques, curlicues, carved fruits and flowers, animal claws and human busts as support and ornament. Red velvet and dark satin hung at the windows and covered plump sofas and chairs. The clutter was thickened by embroidered footstools and little tables and cabinets that held darling porcelain animals and goose girls and, in a place of honor, the Victorian gathering of asphyxiated birds and flowers imprisoned in a bell jar. It all cost a good deal and that was the point.

The householder stocked his cellar with rare French wines that cost as much as twelve dollars a bottle. He bought his wife a cashmere shawl whose price was one thousand dollars, the latest in French bonnets and gloves from A. T. Stewart's and jewels from Tiffany's, whose agents scoured the earth for gems that would bring whatever sum they chose to ask. He readily agreed that she could order antique brocade to cover the new chairs and put a marble "Niobe and Her Children" in the entrance hall and yes, he would dress up for a forthcoming gala, curly wig and all, as Charles I to match her Queen Henrietta dress ordered of a Paris workshop. Once out the door, he was usually his own man, chasing where and what he liked, leaving his wife to endure with forbearance and prayers. When those gave out, she went off to Europe on the tactful excuse that she wanted her children to grow up in cultured surroundings.

Although talk of an art museum had been in the air for some time, a few dedicated collectors had difficulty finding homes for their treasures. Most art and antiques dealers were selling mediocre European paintings and fakes to fill the private galleries that were being tacked on to houses invariably reported as "splendid mansions." There was also a brisk market in contemporary American painting. Thomas Cole (who ran newspaper ads as "landscape and historical painter," 1 Wall Street, in the 1820s) died in 1848, leaving a good number of naturalistic American landscapes; but the public found more impressive the allegorical series he called "The Voyage of Life," "The Course of Empire" and an unfinished "Cross and the World." His pupil and successor, Frederick E. Church, painted strong American landscapes and supplanted Cole's allegories with the wild romanticism of South American scenes. His immense "Heart of the Andes" sold for ten thousand dollars in 1859, the highest price paid for an American painting up to that time. The Hudson River School retreated to the modest clarities of local landscapes. Much of it was selling, particularly the work of Asher B. Durand.

The middle class was buying the cheery prints of Currier and Ives that proved (when they were not depicting ships' disasters) they were living in the best of all possible worlds, exemplified by seven thousand versions of idealized history, beaming family reunions, the innocent graces of sleighing and ice-skating, a world of peach-cheeked, dimple-armed children. For sculpture the middle class went to John Rogers whose studio was at 212 Fifth Avenue. Rogers produced about eighty homey genre and patriotic groups, three-dimensional versions of Currier and Ives sentiments worked with the fine detail and touches of humor that appealed strongly to the general taste— and still appeal, for their workmanship and as nostalgic views of a serene, affable world. The growing taste for art impelled a number of New Yorkers to turn from Phineas Taylor Barnum's freaks to the copies of famous paintings he hung in his "American Museum," or to Cooper Union where Thomas Jefferson Bryan, a pioneer collector, showed a large group of Old Masters in the hope that they might be the base of a national gallery. Or, there might be a show at the Studio Building at 51 West Tenth Street, headquarters of the Artists' Fund Society, the place where William Backhouse Astor began to collect in his youth.

Other institutions were formed more swiftly than the
hoped-for art museum, lost for years in sporadic talk and general indifference. The Free Academy, founded in 1849 by the
Board of Education against strong opposition, became, in 1866,
the College of the City of New York, housed on East Twenty-
third Street where a branch of the College still stands. By 1866
Peter Cooper's "Union," on the site where his store had been,
was already well established as free libraries, reading rooms and
day and evening classes for working people. The multilingual,
striving city, a potential cosmopolis erasing the gay small town
it was before the War, was judged vulgar by some, in constant
disarray, uncared for and shrieking, the brownstone mansions
depressingly monotonous. Mark Twain, returned from prospecting and reporting in Nevada and California, found New
York irritatingly crowded and big; it created an unwholesome
restlessness in him. Walt Whitman, like a bearded baroque
angel, flew in ecstasy over the city, singing its "splendor, pic-
turesqueness and oceanic amplitude." (And one must remem-
ber that it was then, and for thirty years to come, Manhattan
only.) As ever, New York was anything anyone chose to em-
brace, reject, love, hate.

Lauded and loathed, the city went on its omnivorous way,
the shrewd money consuming, for speculation or later building,
northerly stretches of the city. In spite of active building, housing was scarce. Young couples found it difficult to settle; they
hadn't the money for houses nor always their parents' conviction that a house was a basic essential. Their needs and changing values inevitably produced the first apartment house, built
by Rutherford Stuyvesant on East Eighteenth Street, much admired for its efficient coziness. A house, though, particularly on
Fifth Avenue, was yet the laurel wreath that crowned financial
success, the costlier the better. In late September of 1866, the
Herald Tribune, among its long lists of "board and lodgings
wanted," ran an ad that offered an elegantly furnished brown-

stone, west of Fifth Avenue on Forty-seventh Street, for thirty thousand dollars, the same price asked for a four-story brick house on the Avenue itself, unfurnished.

The *Herald Tribune* featured other ads, ordinary matter like notices of theater and concerts, objects for sale, with a fair concentration on horses and secondhand pianos. However, the ads that compelled most eyes and elicited Puritanic howls concerned themselves with two sturdy perennials, spiritualism and abortions.

Kate and Margaret Fox, a couple of Rochester girls from whom had issued remarkable other-world rappings (done with their strong and obedient toes, it was later revealed) and written communications from Benjamin Franklin, were on the wane in New York, floating away on alcohol. But there were many replacements; clairvoyance was an earnest, exciting preoccupation and, to more than a few, a substitute for rational Trinity and stylish Grace Church religion. Of greatest interest was the newspaper's listing of "doctors as private Medical companions" to married women, adept at curing "certain" diseases. A few of the doctors gave addresses without names. A Madame Restell, confident enough to reveal her name, claimed to cure in one interview at her office at 64 West Thirty-fourth Street, "married ladies, from whatever case" with or without medicine. In another notice she was more explicit: her Infallible French Female Pills (as in wines, bonnets and cuisine, "French" was *the* persuasive word) were of two types. Number One sold for one dollar and Number Two for five. Neither ever failed, both were safe and healthy and could be bought at the Thirty-fourth Street office or at a druggist's on Greenwich Street. By 1869, Madame Restell, long established as the city's leading abortionist, had achieved the status of a spacious brownstone at the northeast corner of Fifty-second Street and Fifth and had become an encyclopedic repository of dangerous secrets. Others might guess but she knew that Mr. X had brought her his

simpleminded, nubile daughter who had slipped away from her
fashionable school to play with the boys; she knew how much
Mr. Y had paid for the treatment of a winsome little actress
who might not be half so appealing, and become a threat,
behind a belly. Madame was rich and awesome, a dread figure
shadowed by rumors of illegal deaths (the death of Marie Roget
in Poe's story was attributed to her) from which she protected
herself by a judicious distribution of large sums of money. She,
her house, her liveried carriage and stylish wardrobe were a
blot on the Avenue, her customers said. She was shunned, ver-
bally abused as Madame Killer, whose cellar floor covered thousands of fetal bones. Her business, nonetheless, lasted as an
unacknowledged essential for many years.

Although some of Madame's neighbors were dreaming of
marble dress for their conservative brownstones and the elaborate ducal fantasies that would line Fifth Avenue ("two miles
of millionaires") before the century was out, one good house
was still enough. That, the Grand Tour, a year or two in a
foreign university and the purchase of Barbizon paintings were
the entrenched habits of prosperous lives in the 1860s. Not too
long after were to come the shooting lodge, the country estate,
the marble cottage of one hundred rooms in Newport, the
Paris pied-à-terre, an historic French chateau, the English estate complete with heirlooms and deer park, yachts like ocean
liners, private railroad cars with solid-gold fixtures, lissome
beauties rescued from the stage, horses that could compete at
Auteuil and Ascot. For daughters, soon, noble titles and distorted lives. For sons, in some instances, great art collections
and reputations for probity; in others, lassitude and gaudy multiple divorces. And, crown of crowns, the palace on Fifth Avenue in the Fifties or above.

The tentative income tax imposed during the Civil War
was repealed in 1872 and did not again appear until the eve
of World War I. In the interval, the millionaire came closer to

billionaire; his wife and children grew more unhampered, imperious and esoteric in their tastes. They became the royal families, the heroes and heroines of the United States, the founding fathers of the "idle rich," the makers of the swift great fortunes from steel, oil, railroads, cattle kingdoms, mines, and monumental corruption. "These were," in the words of Stewart Holbrook, "tough-minded fellows, who fought their way encased in rhinoceros hides and filled the air with their mad bellowings and the cries of the wounded; while their determined womenfolk badgered them into erecting monstrous houses that were much like the ennobled bathrooms of ancient emperors. The men were as magnificent in their piratical wars as they were pathetic in their dude clothes, trying to eat with a fork, wondering how best to approach a chaise longue. They were a motley crew, yet taken together they fashioned a savage and gaudy age as distinctly purple as that of imperial Rome, and infinitely more entertaining."

The analogy that links the money empire that grew from Civil War to 1900s with the Roman Empire is irresistible, thus frequently reached for. But does it work? Carrie Astor a Messalina? Alva Vanderbilt an Agrippina? The scandals of Guggenheims, the complex divorces and half-divorces stalemated as bigamy of latter-day Astors, the parades of everybody's mistresses matched against the inventions of Tiberius and Nero?

An analogy does suggest itself: Fifth Avenue as gold, diamond, ivory crest of the American money empire rose about as swiftly as the Roman Empire did, in something under a century. There the analogy ends. Rome held on and on, while Fifth Avenue, almost before her century was out, was already making room for her Huns and Visigoths. But while the going was good and tax-free—the money pouring in unspendably fast, tastes gloriously vulgar and startling price tags fluttering like confetti through the air, and on the public presses, photography eagerly recording the grotesque grandeur—Fifth Avenue was a stupendous Roman circus. It was, as well, a version of Olympus, inhabited by mythical creatures who believed in their own myths, to a considerable degree enhanced by lesser, poorer people who saw in these creatures their small schemes, their yearnings and illusions come to dazzling fruition.

CHAPTER 2

IN THE BEGINNING:
WASHINGTON SQUARE

The ceremonial beginning of Fifth Avenue, at Washington Square, was announced on July 1, 1826. The New York *Evening Post* of that date listed the order of events of a Fourth of July celebration at the new Washington Parade Ground, part of the jubilee commemoration of the nation's fiftieth birthday. "First, the horse artillery will fire a national salute at 7 A.M. Second, his Honor the Mayor of the Committee of arrangements of the Corporation will be received at two o'clock at which time a return salute will be fired by a detachment from the sixth Brigade of Artillery. Third, at half past two, the Declaration of Independence will be read. Fourth, at three o'clock two roasted oxen and other refreshment will be served up for the citizens and the military under an arbor decorated in the appropriate manner for this glorious anniversary."

On July 5 it was reported that high officers, led by Governor De Witt Clinton and Honorables named Van Rensselaer, Van Courtland, Fish, Bogardus, had marched up from the Battery to the newly cleared square for the ceremony that named it "Washington Military Parade Ground." Then on to the arbor and the oxen. Four hundred feet of tables laden with beef and hams and garnishments, "moistened by a plentiful supply of ale," were provided to feed most of the ten thousand assembled. The explosions of fireworks fizzled and sputtered because of rain; otherwise it was a great day. There was no mention of the deaths of John Adams and Thomas Jefferson both of whom died that day. News took a leisured pace in 1826.

Fifth Avenue was actually born fifteen years earlier, in 1811, as a line on the Commissioners' Map. The line broadened to roadway rapidly: to Thirteenth Street by 1824, to Twenty-first Street by 1830, to Forty-second Street in 1837. It had reached as far as One hundred twentieth Street by 1838. The map was fleshed out with the names of farmers who held the pieces of land that crossed or abutted the Fifth Avenue line, the farms' borders arranged to share the Minetta Waters, which had two sources, a brook that rose at Fifth and Twenty-second Street and another at Sixteenth and Sixth. The trout-filled waters joined at Twelfth Street, flowed into the middle of Fifth Avenue at Ninth Street, continued on to Eighth, then veered westward to join the Hudson in the vicinity of Charlton Street. Later covered over—as were a multitude of city streams and ponds that supported trout, otter, beaver, and watered berries, trees and garden crops—the Waters insisted on rising, flooding lower Fifth Avenue cellars, confounding and molesting subway and water-main and gas-line engineers.

A map folded into a guidebook of 1833 shows surrounding streets fairly well populated along Eighth Avenue and its tangents up to Eighteenth Street: on the east, the map indicates thickets of people and their houses as far as Twelfth Street, thinning out at Union Place. The area south of Washington Square is heavily shaded in, joining the density of the lower city. The square itself is shown as a faint shadow (sparsely occupied) moving from Waverly Place toward Eighth Street. *New York As It Is in 1883 and Citizens' Advertising Directory* (a small book, pocket-sized) explains that Washington Square is "the first of the series of open squares laid out within the last seven years, in the upper part of the City," and, according to the author's precise figures, apparently an expensive proposition from its very beginnings. Although the old potter's field that became the square had been city property, its expansion required purchases from individual proprietors that amounted to $77,946.42. In 1828 the city treasury disbursed another $2,876.28 for a wooden fence around the square. "During the present year, 1833," the book continues, "a range of superb private residences has been erected on the north side of the square and the name of the street, on the petition of the owners of those buildings, changed from Sixth Street to Waverly Place in honour of Sir Walter Scott."

In its dim past the city plot later known as Washington Square Park had been a gallows field, becoming in subsequent years a potter's field. Burial ground for the poor, the formal parade ground to which that was changed, and adjoining strips of Fifth Avenue developed from a patchwork of farm sections acquired from several people and put to several uses. Early records show a farmer named Minto as the owner of twenty-one acres of land that ran from Washington Square to Tenth Street, from Fifth Avenue to the Bowery. Late in the eighteenth century a large piece of that property was bought by Captain Thomas Randall, the apogee of whose colorful career was the time he acted as coxswain of a crew of thirteen ships' captains who rowed George Washington from Elizabethtown Point to his inauguration in New York City. The captain had been a freebooter, working in and out of New Orleans, but retired to a life of probity as merchant and property owner, and left his son Robert quite rich, with the means to buy more of the Minto land. Robert Randall died in 1801, leaving an extraordinary will that might be viewed as a compound of guilt and sentiment. With the help of the prominent lawyer Alexander Hamilton, he left bequests to relatives and servants; and he left land that dipped into potter's field and stretched up to Eighth Street on Fifth Avenue and toward the east to worn-out sailors who had found no snug harbor as his father had.

The Sailors' Snug Harbor Estate, then worth twenty-five thousand dollars, drew large incomes from the houses that filled the area within a few decades, to reach a value of fifty million dollars at the beginning of the twentieth century.

The Randall land, as mentioned, encompassed only a small portion of potter's field. A much larger section of the area had been, in the late eighteenth century, the property of Elbert Herring. At that time the city was in need of a new burial ground for the poor since the communal graveyard to the north (Madison Square) was crammed to its edges with accumulated victims of the yellow fever and cholera that rotted the city's summers well into the nineteenth century. In 1797 Mr. Herring agreed to sell the city ninety acres of his land and the dead poured in, those who died of yellow fever wrapped in yellow shrouds. A few streets to the west, near the Hudson River, lived the summer families who moved each year from the pestilential airs around their Battery and City Hall Park houses to the salubrious breezes of the village of Greenwich. Summer annexes of commercial houses formed the Village's still extant Bank Street; the buildings returned to ordinary domestic uses when the plagues abated and the city engulfed the village. Not only bankers' and merchants' families began to stay through the year—shaping neighborhoods of good houses and gardens and the neat solidity that remains on a few streets near the Hudson—but the men who worked on the river wharves, the craftsmen and the small shopkeepers as well. They took their free hours to stroll under the trees that shaded the indigent dead as their forebears went to be entertained by an occasional hanging.

Washington Square was a busy field and economically used, until it too became overfull and property owners eager to improve the area stepped in. A new potter's field was opened far uptown (Bryant Park), and the square at the base of Fifth Avenue was flattened, tombstones ripped out, rows of trees planted, to produce the orderly Washington Parade Ground.

A contemporary observer, skeptical of the magics popularly practiced in the city, reported with satisfaction that the last tombstone to be pulled up was that of a devotee of Mesmerism who vowed that its powers could overcome the plague and who died, nevertheless, within a few days of the onset of the disease.

While Captain Randall was still raking in booty in New Orleans, a Dutchman, Henrick Van Brevoort, was acting as alderman in a city, which, though nominally English, still was comfortably full of thriving Dutchmen like the Van Rensselaers, the Stuyvesants, the Schermerhorns, the Rhinelanders and the Roosevelts. In 1714 Henrick acquired for the sum of four hundred pounds land that straddled Fifth Avenue for a short distance and ran eastward to the Bowery and then took a long stretch northward. The family sold portions off at great profit, holding on to a section below Eleventh Street where they meant to stay. A later Henry Brevoort, of the 1840s, guarded his farm, his kitchen gardens, his pet bear and his tavern with high passions. Behind a blunderbuss he refused to let the city drive Eleventh Street through his land for access to the new Grace Church, in spite of the fact that the architect was the esteemed James Renwick and a relative. (The street, incidentally, was never cut through. Its sign on Broadway points straight into a shop window.)

Another Henry Brevoort built a spectacular house at 24 Fifth Avenue (Ninth Street) in 1834 with the proceeds of Wall Street investments based on real estate sales. The house was almost square in a faintly Palladian manner, the doorway supported by fluted columns, the roof ornamented with runs of Greek key, the spacious rooms introduced by a graceful stairway. It was in these rooms that a masked ball was held which put a halt, for a time, to this form of "continental" entertainment. One of the guests was Miss Matilda Barclay, the daughter of the British consul; another was the young man she loved, a Southern gallant, all manner and little substance, of whom Matty's parents did not approve. The masked lovers stole away and were married early on the morning of the ball. Masked balls were obviously hazardous and it was decreed that anyone who offered such divertissements would be fined one thousand dollars, the fine reduced to five hundred dollars if a host confessed to having staged such an entertainment and avowed he was very sorry. It was inevitable that the confession fee would be collected among friends in *advance* of the balls, a system that evolved as subscriptions. Always in the forefront of fashion, it might easily have been the Brevoorts who first served dinner in the newfangled, disconcerting French style where, instead of the usual everything-out spread, like an indoor picnic, the table bore only ornaments when one sat down. Then dishes were handed around, one course after another, confusing because one didn't know how much to take, what was coming next or how much of it, and conversation was hampered by the dishes constantly thrust between table neighbors. The Brevoorts were also the first family to allow a reporter—a reporter of the scandalous *Herald* at that—to witness a ball. It was better than having an event described by an overactive imagination as a "true account" of society excesses that might inflame an unruly public.

Henry Brevoort had built his house at number 24 during a welter of building in his immediate neighborhood caused by the same factors that would drive houses northward and farther northward along Fifth Avenue. Values were such that a contemporary of Brevoort sold his downtown house, which had cost twenty-five thousand dollars in 1821, for sixty thousand dollars in 1836, the site to be converted into shops with a hotel above them. "Almost everybody downtown," he said, "is in the same predicament, for all the dwelling houses are to be converted into stores. We are tempted with prices so exorbitantly high that none can resist, and the old downtown burgomasters, who have fixed to one spot all their lives, will be seen during the next summer months in flocks, marching reluctantly north to pitch their tents in places which, in their time, were orchards, cornfields, or morasses a pretty distance from town."

While a few old burgomasters were still vacillating between money and inertia, James Boorman built a house on the square and, as well, at 1 and 3 Fifth Avenue, whose adjoining stables ultimately became Washington Mews. New York University, whose first buildings were erected between 1833 and 1837, was a chaos of dissension and money woes, and as it filled the east side of the square became, also, the partial cause of a riot. The university building committee and a number of local builders had negotiated with Sing Sing for stonecutting by its prisoners, cheaper than the rates asked by city stonemasons. A large group of irate masons gathered to march on the university building but were held back by the militia. The ensuing riot and the slow dispersal of the men frightened the neighborhood sufficiently for the militia to stay on the parade ground for four days and nights. Were it a unique labor demonstration, the terror might not have been so great, nor the militia been called out; labor demonstrations and strike parades were indigenous to the city. This was a menacing show of strength by sophisticated unionized "Workies" who held meetings to protest wages, the high cost of living and the incarceration of the poor in debtor's prison. They called for equal and universal education, and some went so far as to demand a socialistic division of property.

After the frightening pause, the houses continued to fill the periphery of the square. William C. Rhinelander, of the family who held long leases on extensive sections of Trinity Church land and the rights to the waterfront that edged those lands, put his house on the western corner of Fifth Avenue and the square. It was designed by the architect of Trinity Church, a handsome house soon to be accompanied by other equally handsome houses of red brick and white stone in the Greek Revival style. In ten years, Fifth Avenue and its tangents was filled with such houses, as far as Twentieth Street, but the oldest were still considered the choicest. These were the twelve houses called "The Row" that occupied the north end of the square from Fifth Avenue to University Place. Their doorways were stately, their front gardens engagingly neat in the English style, and they displayed a harmony of exterior design imposed by a plan that decreed uniform height, similar window lengths and roof details. A number of the houses had cisterns, but water for washing was carried from a pump in the square; the pump water had properties laundresses insisted were "soft" and consequently good for household linens. The long back gardens were graced with grape trellises and romantic arches. These and the row west of Fifth Avenue were the houses that Henry James, who was born near the square, and Edith Wharton, who was born into square society, knew intimately well before they went into exile to write of them.

An important witness and recorder of the city and the square's rapid growth was Philip Hone, mayor of New York for one year, commission agent and auctioneer of foreign and domestic goods, connoisseur of food and wine, friend of Washington Irving and Fanny Kemble, lover of Italian opera and the works of Sir Walter Scott, staunch pillar of the Whig party and ardent clubman. Hone kept a diary of his small, seething city, from 1828 to his final illness and death in 1851, whose viewpoint is from the piano nobile window of a mansion (emphatically conservative and snobbish as if to dispel Hone's working-class origins). All his Irish are rough, destructive, brutish and ignorant; he warns that no important finance should be entrusted to the hands of gentlemen whose Biblical names—Isaac, Solomon—betray their origins in "that nation"; inflated prices must surely be too high for poor people, but these must not be permitted to display their desperation in demonstrations; slavery is not altogether just, but Abolitionists are extreme, hysterical and dangerous. Among reports of large parties in new, always "splendid," houses, there is frequent conjecturing about the potential wealth of William B. Astor, the son of old John Jacob and heir to his uncle Henry Astor's fortune, and fulminations against the Treasury Department for the constant leak of funds. Hone records abominable performances—"stale, flat, and unprofitable"—at the fashionable Park Theater and a familiar litany of complaints indigenous to the city in all its decades. The city was too rapidly tearing down and building, he said; there was rubble and dust constantly in the streets. He decried the speed and carelessness that cause buildings to collapse and the corruption that had judged them safe. He echoed a favorite city pastime of exchanging stories of buildings that fell and shattered like egg crates, crushing inhabitants or the people working in them, or of crusty bachelors who tipped chairs against walls in their lodgings and crashed through into the apartment of a neighbor, invariably a testy spinster.

The population, which had grown fairly slowly until 1800 when it reached 60,500, shot to 300,000 in 1837. (At that rate of increase, it was prognosticated that New York would have more than two million people by 1880 and, by the turn of the century, six million.) The base of the population was still of Dutch and English descent, though increasingly overshadowed by an international variety that jammed the streets and houses. Though the flood of Irish immigrants who came to settle in New York and Boston is usually attributed to the potato famine in Ireland a decade later, conditions for Irish peasants had for a long time been unendurable and by 1837 there were more Irish in New York than all other foreign groups combined. They constituted the major part of the labor force of the city and of the begging poor and the dissolute, who elicited from gentlemen like Philip Hone resentment that New York was becoming the "almshouse" for Ireland.

The cost of living rose by 33 percent in the mid-1830s and even the middle class was finding it difficult to maintain its families. Prosperous bachelors became wary of marrying: the old institution of the bachelor's ball on St. Valentine's Day, when a good number of young men were pulled out of celibacy, was falling into disuse and the resistance to marriage became worrisome to members of the Massachusetts and New York legislatures who urged bachelors to marry. The response was floods of letters which said in various tones, "Mind your own business." There was no danger of a diminution of population however, as long as New York and its promise were so attractive to immigrants and smart Yankee country boys.

Since housing was scarce and expensive, many young men and young couples and a majority of the twenty thousand annual visitors lived in boarding houses and ate most of their meals at inexpensive "refectories" open all hours. The thirty hotels—concentrated on lower Broadway, close to ships, merchants and banks—were too few for the constant stream of newcomers and out-of-town businessmen, and it was common to see luggage carried from hotel to hotel in a search for lodgings, the bags carried by black men whose generic name was "Sambo."

New York clung to its reputation for being the dirtiest of the major cities but once in a while there was a general cleanup as during the summer of 1832, an especially catastrophic cholera year. It was reputedly the first time that the streets were thoroughly cleaned and ancient filth carted away. A primitive sanitation force, the "Scavengers," who were hired during the epidemic, stayed on with their inept shovels and brooms. These men and a few street inspectors were considered a sufficient force by the city aldermen, who were reluctant to spend more money on cleaning up; they thought the city pigs were doing a fair job of it.

The troubled 1830s expressed its woes and angers in riots. The Abolitionists—gentle Christians or strident zealots depending on one's sympathies—found themselves in the center of a riot on the Fourth of July of 1834. Their celebration of the holiday was a meeting to expound on the Declaration of Independence as the document which established that black and white were free and equal. An anti-Abolitionist mob invaded their chapel, formerly a theater, ran up to the tiers of boxes and the gallery, raining everything they could let fly, including benches, on Abolitionist heads. After they broke up that meeting, the mob attacked other Abolitionist houses and churches, among them that of a black congregation. It went on for three days, belatedly quelled by an extemporized police force (there was not yet a steady organized body) ordered out by the mayor and the city corporation.

The winter of 1837 was a time of outrageously expensive bread and flour, known to be held for higher prices by a number of speculators. The newspapers published articles, thundering with the full-blooded words of the time, about the avaricious, greedy, cruel merchants who were feeding off the blood of a populace that was weak with starvation and blue with cold. After an orderly mass meeting at City Hall, a group of militants broke into a leading storehouse, rolled out casks of flour and wheat and threw their contents into the roadway, enough to cover the street to a height of two feet and more. The mayor arrived quickly with a group of constables armed with long sticks. A mouthful of flour stifled the placating speech the mayor had planned and the crowd went on to destroy another flour storehouse and its contents.

While many were rioting—for bread, against Abolition— another group of young men spent its time in peacock displays. They called themselves "dandies," a term borrowed from the English exquisites. Some worked a bit, some borrowed and others lived off doting female relations. They were numerous enough to belong to three orders. The "chained" dandy wore a gold chain around his neck, sometimes attached to a watch, often not—watches were expensive items. The second group were "switched" or "caned"; they carried a small switch of metal with an ivory head and a tassel of silk kept in constant motion. The "quizzing-glass" dandy wore on his neck chain a monocle for supercilious fixing on passing strangers, par-

ticularly females. The most luminous dandy had the combination—glass, watch and switch—the triple Grail for thousands
of the city's boys.

More serious thinkers were absorbed in the new science
of phrenology while the general populace brought its curiosity
and excitement to balloon ascensions, gala departures and ar-
rivals of rival steamships, the drunken noise of July 4th, watching engines rattle and pant as they dragged long trains at the
incredible speed of twenty miles an hour.

Those who had the means spent their summers in Rock-
away or the inns of Whitestone. The rest of New York took
its ease in Battery Park, an agreeable place for walking and
admiring passing steamships and fishing smacks, for sitting in
the cooling touch of sea breezes. A favorite time for walking
was Sunday after church when everyone was out. Though some
members of the upper classes stayed away because they found
it offensive to be on the same promenade with Irish maids
carrying little Irish flags accompanied by ditchdiggers, the
Sunday airings remained, until the opening of Central Park,
one of the strongholds of egalitarianism in the city.

Ferry service took holiday makers, especially Sunday gentlemen whose wives spent long hours in church, to the pleasure
grounds of Hoboken, a "picturesque" Eden with a winsome
merry-go-round, a small wax museum, an optical machine that
was one of the precursors of the camera and a modest railroad
built in 1826, the first railroad in America, Hoboken claimed.
In the nature of such places, it soon decayed into coarse prowling grounds that sheltered gangs and into "groves of Venus"
that sheltered prostitutes. Not even a buffalo hunt which thousands of New Yorkers attended could revive Hoboken's earlier
good clean fun.

Fires were an endless source of diversion. Alarms were
heard at least once a day, sounded on the advice of spotters
on tall beacon towers who frequently mistook the smoke from

an unclean chimney for a serious fire. Boys called false alarms for the joys of helping pull the engines or, better yet, to watch the fights between rival fire companies. There were sixty-four companies of twenty-six men each. Their only pay for seven years of service was exemption from military service in the state of New York. These volunteers had volunteer assistants, apprentices who had none of the privileges of the masters except that of sharing the imperious group pride which prompted one gang to let a block of buildings burn in protest over an indignity suffered by their chief. These young mechanics and clerks—tough, strong, quick, well-connected politically and when skillfully organized capable of swinging elections or blocking rescues—left the vulnerable city terrified of potential disaster. It came as the Great Fire of December 1835. The fire burned out a square quarter-mile, densely filled with the best stores and warehouses, four and five stories high; it burned out Paternoster Row, the periodicals publishing center of Fulton Street; it destroyed houses tucked among the business buildings. The losses were, it was estimated, greater than those suffered in Moscow during the Napoleonic Wars. In all, nineteen blocks comprising 674 buildings and merchandise valued at somewhere between twenty and forty million dollars were gone. Philip Hone, with the usual sour eye peeled for the rabble ("Irish"), reported that they were prowling among the ruins guzzling fine imported liquors and drunkenly shouting, "Ah! They'll make no more five percent dividends! This will make the aristocracy pull in their horns." He was more calmly graphic about "cloths, silks, laces, prints of the most valuable kind dug out partly burned and nearly all ruined. A mountain of coffee lies at the corner of Old Slip and South Street. The entire cargo of teas arrived a few days since—lies in a state not worth picking up, and costly indigo and rich drugs add to the mass of mud that obstructs the streets." The commercial center of the city was wiped out, insurance companies hadn't enough money to cover losses and those property owners with some resources left looked to rebuilding to the north.

The water supply came from several sources. There were free pumps on almost every corner of the city that poured saline water, often "physic" in its effect. Those who could afford it had better but not-too-potable water pumped in from the Collect. The most palatable water was drawn from the Tea Water Pump at Pearl Street and Park Row, carried through the streets in hogsheads and sold for a penny a gallon. Legislation was stirring for Croton water to be brought from upstate and stored in huge city reservoirs in the next decade.

A substantial proportion of New Yorkers rarely bothered with water, or they made it more friendly by lacing it with drams from the grogshops—as numerous as the pumps, approximately one for every thirty male New Yorkers—where three cents bought a snort of rum, gin, brandy or whiskey. In the clubs and sophisticated houses, madeira, port, sherry and claret were drunk, while the blades concentrated on champagne, often paying champagne prices for disguised cider. Encouraged by doctors who had little else but alcohol and opiates to work with, everyone resorted to the bottle to cure malaise and illness. The cure for the common cold was a ritual of rubbing the nose with mustard, smoking cigars, drinking infusions of catnip tea fortified with cayenne pepper and, on a starvation diet, consuming spirits and spirits and more spirits. It may not have cured a cold but undoubtedly made it easier to endure.

New Yorkers spent considerable amounts of time reading. They took a broad variety of magazines and had a choice of fifty newspapers—fourteen dailies, eight semiweeklies and the rest weeklies. Ten were large "sixpenny" papers (the term sixpence was still commonly used to represent six and one quarter cents). Distribution of the smaller "penny papers" was the major source of income of the city's poor boys. The most notorious and influential of the new penny papers was the *Herald*, established in 1835 by James Gordon Bennett ("ill-looking and squinting"), who became famous and infamous, along with his son, in the annals of New York journalism. With the advent of the penny press, everyone read. Hone, once more: "A carter may be now seen sitting on his cart; a barrow-man on his barrow; and a porter at his stand; each perusing a penny paper, while waiting for the job." They read that ferry fares were twice as much as they should be because of collusion among owners, that the horrifying number of deaths resulting from fires and boiler explosions on steamships were the result of an indifferent and powerful monopoly of pilots. The penny papers were accused by the older, larger sheets of being rabble-rousers, liars and liberals, charges which the ac-cused enjoyed for the publicity and the fact that they could often keep hot matters boiling which increased newspaper sales. Reasonable citizens, often shocked at the contents of the penny press, nevertheless defended it because it gave diversion and education to workers who might otherwise spend their leisure and pennies in saloons.

The city was in its protean way, many things to many people, each view colored by the rosy beam or the dark mote in the spectator's eye. Liberals liked the egalitarianism, were surprised and pleased to see the "air of consequence" of well-dressed free blacks (there were no slaves in New York after 1827) strolling down Broadway or the Bowery with their frilled and satined ladies. They enjoyed the fact that maids preferred to be called "helpers," that waiters and public servants were neither too obeisant nor too truculent, that the city's workers were quite well dressed. Unhappy others warned that excessive egalitarianism made rude and insolent workers who would be-come monsters to be put down, inevitably, by force.

Fanny Kemble, the actress, who had enjoyed high social and professional success in the United States, reported on her return to the neat old squares of London that New York was an inept stage set with no design or pattern. Her compatriot,

Mrs. Frances Trollope, who had failed to conquer the savages of Cincinnati with her French imports and her *Musical Fantasia*, loathed America and Americans. New York City was, however, not America to Mrs. Trollope. She had fallen deeply in love with the "lovely and noble city" with its "various and lovely" objects. Broadway could never, of course, be compared with Bond or Regent Street, but it was splendid, even "noble." She had never seen anything more beautiful than the harbor of New York and, supreme accolade, doubted that the pencil of the great Turner could do it justice, "bright and glorious as it rose upon us." Venice was no more magnificent than New York, which lived in its own, special, golden light. Hudson Square (between Hudson and Varick streets) was the equal of the best London square; the ice water served in villas on the river was a sign of a civilized people; the bonnets on the ladies in well-kept churches were "like beds of tulips, so gay, so bright, so beautiful"; the Hudson River was a stream of Paradise. "In truth, were all America like this fair city—I should say that the land was the fairest in the world."

To a degree, the contrasts, the nervous changes in this "devilish lively community" affected Washington Square and lower Fifth Avenue. A few of the householders were dazzled, as their downtown friends had been, with offers pressed on them by eager purchasers. For the respectable sum of fifty-seven thousand dollars, Henry Brevoort of the classical house sold it in 1850 to Henry de Rham (the ennobling "de" was taken on by a Swiss ancestor when he hit these impressionable shores). By the time the de Rhams took over, there were two churches in the immediate vicinity, the Church of the Ascension (Episcopal), at Tenth Street, consecrated in 1841, and the First Presbyterian Church, between Eleventh and Twelfth streets, that began to welcome worshipers five years later. Hardly had it settled in when the Church of the Ascension was the scene of a stirring marriage. On June 26, 1844, Philip Hone reports in his diary that John Tyler, "accidentally become an unworthy occupant" of the presidency, "flew on the wings of love—the old fool—to the arms of his expectant bride. . . . The illustrious bridegroom is said to be fifty-five years of age and looks ten years older and the bride, Julia Gardiner, is a dashing girl of twenty-two." A younger diarist, George Templeton Strong, wrote: "I've just heard a rumor that old John Tyler was married to one of those large, fleshly Miss Gardiners of Gardiners Island. Poor, unfortunate old jackass." Miss Julia, incidentally, was hardly a shy, retiring maiden and knew full well what she was doing. She was one of the first prominent ladies to lend her looks and position to advertising. A department store distributed widely a picture of her in fur-trimmed velvet over a cascade of lace, carrying, in lieu of a large reticule, a sign advising that she preferred shopping at Bogert and Mecamly's on Ninth Avenue because their goods were both beautiful and astonishingly cheap.

James Boorman, whose house led off the Row, turned 1 and 3 Fifth Avenue over to his sister to use as a school for upper-class young ladies. Her successors were two Misses Green from intellectual Massachusetts, and later the Misses Graham. Among them they created a favored institution for educating the daughters of banking and mercantile leaders, one of them Jenny Jerome, the mother of Winston Churchill. In a time that spoke of the education of women as a Pandora's box that released monsters, the school produced few, if any, bluestockings. It assured, however, a moral tone by hiring teachers from the nearby Union Theological Seminary and by trying to involve a parent or two in the welfare of the school.

It wasn't easy to snag fathers. One of the enduring gifts England left New York was the gentlemen's club, which prospered and grew splendid along with the fortunes and houses of its members. By midcentury, when Fifth Avenue was built up almost to Madison Square, the clubs moved onto the Avenue as well. Each had a solid core of interests: the arts; politics conservative or politics liberal; a membership kept carefully exclusive or an inclination to welcome an actor or two or possibly a journalist. The Union Club, a gathering of four to five hundred merchants, bankers and politicians, was the first to move, in 1855, to a three-hundred-thousand-dollar brownstone at Twenty-first Street and Fifth. It was shortly split by severe dissension: the resolutely Republican, pro-Lincoln members broke away as the Union League Club. The Manhattan Club, the stronghold of Democrats, took over a former residence at Fifth Avenue and Fifteenth Street while the calmer, more intellectual Atheneum settled on Fifth Avenue at Sixteenth Street. The Lotos Club, literary and artistic, as was the Arcadian, came to stay for a while between Washington Square, the nearby Academy of Music and promising Madison Square. They were joined on the Avenue by the New York Club, the Travelers and the Knickerbocker Club, another offshoot of the old Union Club. The Knickerbocker, spurred on by John Jacob Astor, III, had decided to create a sanctuary for descendants of early New York families and for that purpose bought a house for $180,000 at the corner of Twenty-eighth Street.

Clubs, the Hotel Brevoort—opened in 1854 and especially hospitable to English ships' captains who might influence custom its way—and nearby entertainments helped solidify and make especially pleasing the lower Fifth Avenue community. Among its merchants and bankers, there were a few who were unusually civic-minded, ambitious for New York and New Yorkers. At number 8 was the marble house, the first of its kind, built in 1856, of John Taylor Johnston. A fortune made in railroading bought him one of the best collections of his time, including a Turner, generally judged powerful but lunatic. Johnston established in his former stable the first gallery that was open to the public, on Thursday afternoons. Once a year the gallery was used for a merry, bibulous artists' reception. In spite of such unusual practices and a turn in fortune that lost him his collection, he was chosen to be the first presi-

dent of the Metropolitan Museum of Art, established in its new
building in Central Park in 1880 after a number of peripatetic
years. Isaac M. Singer, whose little machine liberated millions
of women and spurred the fashion industry in New York, lived
at number 14. Most of the early householders considered themselves quite rich with fortunes of about one hundred to three
hundred thousand dollars, not taxed and yielding steady returns. There were exceptions. James McBride, an outstandingly
prosperous merchant, was reported to have seven hundred
thousand dollars, and Robert L. Stuart, a Scottish immigrant
in 1805 who had made with his brother a fortune as sugar
refiner and candymaker, had the means to gather an art collection.

On the death of Mr. Stuart, his collection was left to the
Lenox Library with the stipulation that the paintings not be
viewable on the Sabbath. The injunction was Mrs. Stuart's
who said she would also withdraw the gifts she had given the
Metropolitan Museum if *it* stayed open on Sunday, although
the ostensible purpose of Sunday hours was to divert the working class from its usual Sabbath transgressions—too much drink
in the company of light women. The Lenox of the library was
James, who lived at number 53. Suspicious, dour, stingy and
a dedicated bibliophile, he was one of the richest men in New
York, the inheritor of a prodigious fortune that reached into
several million.

And then there was August Belmont, the subject of con-
tradictory legends, who first lived close to the square and
then established himself at Eighteenth Street and Fifth Avenue.
He walked with a slight limp, the result of a pistol duel in
which a bullet was driven into his hip. The result of a youthful
scrap, a romantic matter of honor, he implied; because he had
been called a Jew, the gossip said. As head of the Democratic
party, as a representative of Rothschild interests, he would see
that the country was safe financially; the country was unsafe
with one major party led by so sly a man; moreover, with ex-

ceedingly strong European ties. He spoke several languages fluently, some said; he massacred them, said others. He was an evil man with a tortuous mind and an outrageous womanizer; he led a blameless private and public life, free of scandal at home or in politics. He was a Rothschild bastard; he was a gifted German boy, born Schoenberg, whom the Rothschilds found and trained to handle papal monies at an early age. He was too suave, too elusive and altogether too rich to be accepted comfortably. George Templeton Strong, who was critical in the late 1840s of Fifth Avenue houses that plundered the earth for show at their soirees and tables, grew mellower, or simply richer, or had a crush on the lovely Mrs. Belmont, in 1860. He extolled her grace and charm as she entertained crowds of millionaires and foreign dignitaries in her most splendid house with its distinguished picture gallery and "gorgeous" ballroom. Her husband remained loathsome to him, a "foreign money-dealer [who] had made himself uncommonly odious," "a cosmopolite adventurer," an insult to the public good.

At number 10 lived Amos F. Eno, who would set the spark that later kindled Madison Square. Just off Washington Square lived two considerable gentlemen, one very much approved of by the society of lower Fifth, the other shunned—and he didn't give a damn. The first was William H. Aspinwall of College Place, a merchant shipper who had built up the Pacific and Latin American trades and earned several million dollars in the process. He was civic-minded, spoken of as an "Old-style New Yorker" by his contemporaries, and although that usually meant a man who conducted himself modestly, it was his house that was for a time *the* palace of the city, a place of kingly velvets and marbles. The other, who lived at 10 Washington Place with extensive stables behind the house and grounds ample enough to allow for a small racing track, was Cornelius, the Commodore, Vanderbilt. Of a family of industrious farmers, Cornelius made a deal with his mother to work several acres of the farm for a cash wage, one hundred dollars a year. This he spent, aged seventeen, on his first primitive ferry. It was 1811, and though the city was small, it had begun some time before establishing homes across the rivers. Cornelius's shaky boat came in handy and so did the additional two ferries he shortly owned. Then on to brutally hazardous steamships which earned him half a million dollars while he was still fairly young. In his riper years he turned to equally ruthless operations of railroad systems that expanded his fortune to numerous millions.

He was crazy about horses, whist, money—he soon outdistanced Aspinwall financially and kept on accumulating—and found his wife a drag. On the grounds that she nagged him and was not cooperative and complained of having to move out of their rural mansion on Staten Island to suffer the confusions and snobbery of the city, he had her committed to Bloomingdale Asylum for a while. In his seventies, already the richest man in the United States and remarkably adroit at skirting the law which was too slow and cumbersome for him, the Commodore began to fend off decay and death with methods orthodox, experimental and mystical. Two mystics found their way to him: Victoria Woodhull, née Claflin, and her younger sister, Tennessee Claflin, a pair of versatile, attractive young women who knew how to heal cancer, call up spirits, tell fortunes—and were not averse to a bit of prostitution for pleasure and profit. Guided by a father who had taught them a good deal of their wisdom and accomplishments, and urged out of Pittsburgh by angry clients and neighbors, they came to New York and found their way to the famous millionaire. Victoria became his mystic healer while the lusty, less clever and more beautiful Tennessee supplied mysterious waves of strength through physical contact. This old King David kept his Shunammite maid to warm his brittle bones for over a year while Victoria and her lover planned more lasting favors from the Commodore than Tennessee was extracting. They established a brokerage firm, Woodhull, Claflin and Company—with Vanderbilt's cooperation, although the girls never acknowledged this. They managed a businesslike office in spite of constant invasions of the curious and amassed seven hundred thousand dollars in three years, mainly on railroad stock maneuvers and inside early information from their good friend. A new young Mrs. Vanderbilt got in their way; she had firm objections to mystic healing and lady friends who might just be making some of their money on brothels. The Woodhull, Claflin, Vanderbilt ties were severed, or seemed to be.

After the Commodore's death his will gave rise to hectic dissension in the Vanderbilt clan. It practically denied his nine daughters (no Vanderbilts, the old man said) and his dissolute, epileptic son, Cornelius Jeremiah, who had been forced out of the house and ultimately committed suicide in a hotel to which he had been exiled. After minor rearrangements, William H. Vanderbilt emerged as chief beneficiary, Tennessee got a painting of *Aurora* which the Commodore had promised her and, in partnership with Vicky, the trusteeship of a sum with which to promote spiritualism. The sisters let it be known that they were owed a great deal more for stock market business they had arranged for the old man; gossip said they claimed over one hundred thousand dollars and were ready to sue for it. There was no suit, but the girls, shortly after the will was settled, began to splash around in money—jewels, furs, trips with trails of servants, a house abroad—like the inheritors of a neat fortune.

A stone's throw from the Vanderbilt house, from New York University and the square was a house of the most demanding standards kept by Madame Josie Woods. She was always magnificently dressed, beautifully poised, handsome and an unrelenting snob, limiting her guests to the very best people as rigidly as did the Stuyvesants and Brevoorts.

It is quite conceivable that Belmont, whose reputation included satyriasis—families warned each other to keep their daughters out of his reach—was a customer and recommended friends and potentially valuable business associates to Josie, who insisted that all newcomers be introduced by a member client of her well-run house. Less conceivable was the improbable patronage of his neighbor, James Lenox, who rarely entertained or permitted himself to be entertained—certainly not among Josie's pretty girls and their jaunty friends. Nor would he have tolerated the luxurious furnishings (his tattered drapes were a neighborhood shame) or the presence of an English butler, the status symbol supreme, or the prices Josie demanded for the services of her girls. According to the not always reliable but entertaining Lucius Beebe, the girls paid Madame one hundred dollars in gold for their rooms and received fifty dollars from each man entertained privately. At that rate they didn't have to work very hard, an unrushed courtly atmosphere could be maintained and long intervals of coquettish conversation over a steady flow of champagne brought in a good return. Stately Madame Woods disassociated herself and her charges altogether from the cheap, rough women of Greene Street nearby. Hers was a dream of an exquisite harem in the delicate, graceful style of Persian prints and the liquid gestures of Japanese art, of the clusters of lovely, pearl-like ladies in the courts of Charles II. So distinguished a place was hers that, like her Fifth Avenue neighbors, Josie kept open house on New Year's Day to receive her respectful customers.

Long before an axe cut into the first elderly tree on the future Washington Square, well-informed real estate speculators—Astors, Goelets and Schermerhorns in the lead—had bought property to the north. The block between Sixteenth and Seventeenth streets, from Union Square to Fifth Avenue sold for $197,000 in 1836, the lots that fronted on Fifth Avenue were valued at $57,000 each. Union Place had been, early in the nineteenth century, an exclusive suburb for the country

villas of Goelets and Roosevelts whose town houses stood near
the tip of the island. Their park was surrounded by a massive
iron fence which lasted until 1870, when the Place became the
Square, already part of the flourishing theater center that had
forced out the country houses. The combined opera house and
ballroom named the Academy of Music had established itself
on Fourteenth Street near Irving Place, at the side of a stubborn farm. Irving Hall provided less exalted entertainment at
Fifteenth Street. The small eighteenth-century shops of Cherry
Street and Catherine Street that had swelled and moved to
larger and more fashionable quarters on Broadway were now
beginning to ring this upper square. Tiffany moved its five
hundred craftsmen and sales people into a new iron building
at Fifteenth and Broadway—"hideous," some thought the style,
which was tolerated by others because it found use for the
excess iron and ironworkers left unemployed at the close of
the Civil War—and Brentano's very literary emporium came
to rest for a while at 33 Union Square.

Delmonico's, which for a considerable time had lived on
William Street, made its first move uptown in the late 1860s,
taking over the seigniorial Fourteenth Street house of a clipper-
ship merchant, Moses H. Grinnell, a house with a history that
returns to the Brevoorts. In 1762 they sold a piece of their
property from Fourteenth Street northward to John Smith
who had made his money in the slave trade. He built his
country house on the choicest segment, the center of Fourteenth Street immediately west of the Avenue. His widow
stayed on for some years after his death and then sold the
land for $4,750 to Henry Spingler who placed his barn at
the southwest corner of Fourteenth Street at Fifth. A Spingler
granddaughter, married to a Van Buren, inherited the farm
and maintained a portion of it; on another section she built
herself a fashionable brownstone just like her neighbors'. Her
property rose to the irresistible value of $200,000 and in 1845
it was cut up, along with another piece of land stretching from

Eighteenth to Twenty-first streets (once part of the large farm of Sir Peter Warren, a freebooter in the Caribbean, and sold to an Isaac Varian for $3,000 in 1791), to be sold to several moneyed New Yorkers, among them Grinnell.

By the time Grinnell's spacious rooms were serving terrapin, canvasback duck and champagne as New York's leading restaurant, with ballroom windows on Fifth Avenue and a renowned seraglio next door, Union Square had established itself as meeting ground for public demonstrations. In October of 1860, a huge crowd gathered to watch a torchlight parade under a sky full of exploding rockets and Roman candles to prove its dislike of Abraham Lincoln while the bands played "Dixie." Here in the Metropolitan Fair building, decorated by Richard Hunt, were organized and run successfully a variety of entertainments and the sale of goods contributed by foreign countries for the benefit of the Sanitary Commission established during the Civil War. Here a large sober mass meeting in support of Grant and a pro-Lincoln rally. Here jets of fireballs, red, white and blue, exploding above the heads of the great rejoicing crowds come to celebrate Sheridan's victory. One reporter prognosticated that "Perhaps Union Square will be held a classical locality by our grand-grand-grandchildren and awaken historical associations," a fairly valid prophecy, though fulfilled with not quite the coloration he envisioned.

On Washington Square, in spite of its settled quality, changes were taking place. The former school at 1–3 Fifth Avenue became a house for a member of the Delano clan which melded with the Dutch-born patroons Roosevelt. Later yet (1920), it was bought by Rodman Wanamaker of the family that had purchased and renamed for itself the famous A. T. Stewart shop—the greatest store in the country, nay the world, its effulgence dimming mercantile Paris—that stood on Broadway between Eighth and Ninth streets.

Immediately above 21 (where Mark Twain spent several

unhappy, elderly years) there was a house owned by a Major General Daniel E. Sickles. He was a Civil War veteran with one leg and reaching into his nineties, permanently angry over his dimmed glory and reduced finances. In 1912 he decided to lease the second floor of his brownstone at 23, on the northeast corner of Ninth Street, to Edwin Dodge and his wife Mabel. They were both rich, she driven by yearnings to live fully every moment, a fashionable philosophy in her time, encapsulated by her contemporary, Edna Millay, in the famous image of a candle burning at both ends. The Dodges had lived in Europe for some years and there Mabel had experimented with dress to suit her uniquely poetic personality and settled on a nimbus of floating silks, something Isadora Duncan, something the drowned Ophelia, something Ariel, something Ottaline Morrell and misty Pre-Raphaelite ladies listening to sad, distant tunes.

The quality Mabel most cherished in herself was her genius for penetrating, sharing and serving the deepest thoughts and souls of others, particularly creative people.

After ten years abroad Mabel had no wish to live in the States; she was back only to find a school for her son. But her new neighborhood was beguilingly Old World. The street was tree-lined, its houses taking on an anachronistic charm, a few tacky, most proud and well-kept. Immediately to the south was the Washington Arch, reminiscent of Parisian and Roman triumphal arches. (It was designed by Stanford White as a temporary ornament to help celebrate the centenary, 1889, of the first inaugural of George Washington. A few years later, $128,000 was collected to have White rebuild it as a permanent enhancement to the square.) On the south side of the square, an Italian campanile soared over the Judson Buildings, also designed by White. Southward and to the west, a small international city of Frenchmen, Irishmen and Italians living in cheap houses and tenements that attracted writers and artists as well. To a cosmopolitan eye the Village then held the combined allure of the Place Furstemburg, the Via Margutta, a bright dash of Trastevere and the cafes of the 5th Arrondissement. The stage was set for a new branch of Dodge-style Bohemia. All it required was a cast of creative characters to eat at Mabel's opulent table and bask in her mysterious powers. She found an abundance of intellectual and artistic life around her, stirred by the ferment of the times. The sculptress Gertrude Vanderbilt Whitney was showing the works of new American artists she sponsored in her MacDougal Street studio. Social strictures were falling away, poetry had begun again to sing, a militant left was making itself heard, the lines of parading Suffragettes were becoming denser and longer, the old phoenix, Free Love, which had flamed and guttered in New York for over half a century, rose once again. The young flocked to the Village for the unfettered life of no legal ties, no rigid habits, no Grand Rapids oak, no corsets physical or emotional.

The zeitgeist and Mabel were obviously right for each other but Mabel wasn't sure at first. To lighten her dark spirits she covered her apartment in white—walls, ceilings, draperies, fireplace and rug. The white was brightened with furniture in pastel blues and yellows and a burst of color in a Venetian chandelier that was a porcelain aviary of multicolored birds and flowers. Though Carl Van Vechten the novelist, then a music critic, found her house a bower of enchantment and infused it with life, Mabel was still depressed. Then came Jo Davidson, the sculptor, who was delighted with the lovely, generous house and the eager responsiveness of his hostess. He brought his friends in droves and Mabel's luminous white salon with its Marie Laurencin touches shook with the thunder of revolution in society, in art, in manners, as she listened, entwining her soul with those of her rebels.

She met Alfred Stieglitz and learned avant art in his "291" gallery at that address on Fifth Avenue. With him and his cohorts she helped organize the landmark Armory Show. Prompted by the muckraker Lincoln Steffens, by the proponent of free love and anarchism Hutchins Hapgood, and the young journalist Walter Lippmann, she staged Evenings. The food was Lucullan, the vintage wines flowed, the noise rose to deafening decibels; Mabel Dodge's evenings became a symbol of the Village and were the Elysian Fields of the artistically and intellectually advanced. Mabel stood apart, silent in her romantic veils, but visitors reported that she exerted a morbid influence that heated passionate quarrels, particularly during those Evenings that were planned around a speaker, general discussion to follow. Roaring poets stamped out while another read: during a Magazine Evening, conservative editors were thrown to howling young wolves of writers, hungry and scornful; an infuriated exodus was caused by a lecture on Freudianism by Dr. A. A. Brill, one of the first public discussions of psychoanalysis in America. Birth control and propaganda for extreme social reform, via revolution preferably, blazed Mabel's pastel room. The press saw to it that the Evenings were conspicuously reported, especially when the anarchist Emma Goldman, whose lover Alexander Berkman had tried to assassinate Henry Clay Frick, and Big Bill Heywood, the head of the Wobblies (IWW, the Industrial Workers of the World), lectured. Not always a good press, but press Mabel had, and the satisfaction of nurturing that essential to the enlightened life, "understanding."

In the course of a conversation with Bill Heywood she learned that he could get nothing into the press about the working conditions, the inadequate pay and the police brutality that caused and maintained the historic silk weavers' strike in Paterson, New Jersey. Mabel suggested that public sympathy might be aroused by a reenactment of the strike, complete with goons, police, workers and leaders, in Madison Square Garden. In the group that evening of 1913 was John Reed, a young god, a successful writer, confident, beautiful, fun-loving and courageous in rebel causes. He offered his services as writer and producer and with Mabel's money and the power she poured into him the show presented to an audience of fifteen thousand was a stunning, moving success, reported finally by the city's press. Working closely and constantly together in the shaping weeks, Mabel and Reed, who was ten years younger than she, fell in love and after an idyllic sojourn at her Italian villa, returned as the most glamorous of the free lovers to 23 Fifth. (Mr. Dodge had removed himself from the brouhaha of 23 some time before.) Reed became an Evenings star—when he was around. His Paterson fame as speaker and writer earned him the job of reporting on Pancho Villa's activities in the Mexican Revolution. His brilliant articles made of him a celebrity, poised for wandering among troubled, exciting places. Mabel could not relinquish him to the world; she moaned and clung. He, the golden rebel and king of reporters while still in his twenties, wouldn't be held. He moved fast and Mabel had to give up following him. She tried a liaison and marriage with the painter Maurice Sterne, another divorce, and then moved on to New Mexico. There she became a member of the quarrelsome coven that worshiped the Great D. H. Lawrence, and then settled into a final marriage with an Indian of the area, Antonio Luhan.

Mabel's brilliant Village was fading as she moved away from it. During World War I repressive measures were taken against radicals and the leaders were dispersed, to prisons, to Europe, to the suburbs. The prickly, lively *New Masses* stopped publishing; John Reed, observing the Revolution in Russia, was shortly to die, at thirty-two. The Cafe Brevoort, a relic of the old Hotel Brevoort, succumbed, too, to Prohibition. It had been the place where—because of an article sold, a showing announced at a gallery, the return of an old friend with a little cash—parties were held that rivaled those in the cafes of Montmartre. The food was continental, the wine cellar responsible, the atmosphere stimulating and remembered with teary pleasure by octogenarians who had sharpened their young tongues on the assembled wits, gawped at Village Aphrodites and wallowed in la vie Bohème far from the staid halls of Yale. From the "A" Club at One Fifth Avenue where women's suffrage had been heatedly discussed; from Polly's restaurant where they had been insulted by her consort-cook-waiter, the anarchist Hippolyte Havel; from the Liberal Club on Mac-Dougal Street; from the studios and cold water flats, they came to the Brevoort. It was at the Brevoort that a generous Village girl, inspired by the presence in the hotel of Belgian soldiers brought to America to whip up enlistment fervor, felt it her patriotic duty to "do solace," as the Arthurian legends so prettily put it, to all the soldiers so far from home. She was cheered on and money collected for her subsequent accouchement, according to a favorite Brevoort legend.

The wake on the last night before Prohibition set in was a memorable Saturnalia, or at least remembered so by misty participants. All the liquor in the Brevoort cellars was brought up and sold to the guests at nonprofit prices. Drinking as much as they could in situ, the habitués then dragged their bottles to the square and proceeded to become heartily drunk and raunchy. The shrilling girls stripped and danced and jumped into the fountain; the howling fauns chased them around trees and through bushes. To judge from nostalgic reports, it was a scene from a Pompeian panel of gleeful rites led by Dionysus and his son Priapus.

The companion Hotel Lafayette, immediately to the east, took over fervent discussions and chess games, civilized post-Prohibition drinking, foreign luminaries and an aura of legend; but things were never quite the same around the square, though locals insisted that, at least up to Twelfth Street, the neighborhood had remained its old-fashioned, well-mannered self. They swore that homesteaders were too attached to their houses and memories to decamp. There was mention of a couple of business offices and apartment houses but these were passing clouds, they said, and emphasized the trees and remaining front-yard handkerchief lawns as bits of immortality. But number 60, near Twelfth Street, once the house of Thomas Fortune Ryan, was resold and resold, to become book publishing offices and then the home of *Forbes* magazine. The Salmagundi Club, devoted to unadventuresome art, is a survivor of the old brownstones, quite tired now. The de Rham property lasted a long time, until 1921, when it was sold for $450,000 to George F. Baker, Jr., soon to succeed his father as the head of the First National Bank. A few years later, he resold. The house was demolished and a new version of an earlier Fifth Avenue Hotel put in its place. In recent decades much of the Square and its vicinity has been absorbed by New York University or sunken into the cement and brick of apartment buildings, several shops and restaurants with the taint of doom on their glass faces; and near Fourteenth Street, where for many years Hearn's rivaled the Thirty-fourth Street department stores, a few office buildings and stores that don't quite know what they are or will be.

The decline of Union Square began earlier and was more precipitate. The last decades of the nineteenth century saw the good houses and respectable boarding houses change to minimal stores and warehouses. Delmonico's was preparing to move to Madison Square; the shopping area west of Union Square took up new quarters near Twenty-third Street west of Fifth Avenue. Tiffany's left Union Square, and so did Brentano's, which went uptown to 225 Fifth Avenue. Above Twelfth Street, the Avenue became a dreary sequence of empty lots of demolished houses, the streets bared of trees. As far north as Twenty-third Street, there were spurts of small factories and wholesale offices. The few mansions left on Fourteenth Street became, at the turn of the century, painters' studios, and in the nearby streets grew the tenements of garment workers who supplied the neighboring manufacturers. Union Square began to assume the role it played into the 1930s as workers' forum;

Fourteenth Street restaurants—except Lüchow's—and theaters turned to the shoddy. Ohrbach's and Klein's, which supplied generations of working-class women and students with inexpensive clothing, were the pillars of the square until Ohrbach's defected, leaving Klein's large, alone and ultimately defeated. With the same frequency that improvements for Central Park are announced, come projects for taking the square away from its derelicts, giving it order and consequently uplifting Fourteenth Street, where nothing much has changed for a good while. Hot dogs and hamburgers still vie with *pasteles*; the shops bristle with wondrously high heels; the movies speak Spanish, the record shops thump Afro-Caribbean rhythms. The essence remains what it has been for years, colorful, cheap, spritely and tough.

CHAPTER 3

THE FLY-EYE
OF NEW YORK

s Washington Square settled
back behind its pediments and pil-
lars, in this "very considerable rum city, a pretty tolerably well-
hoaxed city, a city abounding in foul streets, rogues, dandies,
mobs and several other things," Madison Square, a mongrel of
lowly beginnings, was coming to incandescent life.

The first bloom of the sporting, "go-ahead" center, the
vortex of vivacity and high life that O. Henry would call "the
fly-eye of New York; spin it on a pivot and you would see the
world," was the Roadhouse, or Madison Cottage, of a Corporal
Thompson, unfailingly referred to as "genial." Set among cattle
exhibition yards, the tavern became a favorite well for cattle
dealers, coaching parties and gentlemen riders. Additional custom came from a group of sportsmen, the Knickerbocker Club,
who used the large square early in the 1840s to play a variation
of an English ballgame, rounders. Their unique manner of
hitting, running and chasing balls—the "New York game"—
spread through the country rapidly and changed its name to
baseball. Madison Square as the game's birthplace was hotly
contested by Cooperstown, where Abner Doubleday claimed to
have invented it in 1839. The dispute, muted over the years,
still rises feebly now and then.

The site was first recorded as part of thirty acres extending from Twenty-first to Twenty-sixth Street, from Broadway to Seventh, granted in 1670 by Sir Edward Andros, the governor of the province, to Solomon Peters, a free black. A century later the land had become the property of John Horn, who built a farmhouse in the center of Fifth Avenue immediately south of Twenty-third Street. When the Avenue was cut through in 1837, the house stood awkwardly in the way of thickening traffic and was moved to the northwest corner of Twenty-third Street and Broadway. The land to the east of Broadway, from Twenty-third Street to Thirty-fourth Street, was common lands, cleaned up and adorned as parade grounds late in the eighteenth century. An urgent need for a communal graveyard for almshouse dead turned the southern end of the grounds into the potters' field later moved to Washington Square. The rest housed a powder magazine that was joined, in 1808, by a U.S. arsenal. The arsenal beat its arms into ploughshares to produce an orchard that bordered on the Society for Reformation of Juvenile Delinquency, the first of its kind in America, founded in 1824. The parade grounds retrenched to the present limits of the square as Fifth Avenue dug its way northward, the land between Twenty-seventh and Thirty-fourth streets becoming commercially interesting.

The pioneer youth shelter lasted for fifteen years and then was destroyed by fire. The alarm had been sounded quickly enough to save all the youngsters, but there was no fire-fighting equipment and no action until an ex-alderman dashed up on horseback and rounded up enough spectators to form a bucket brigade. Only a section of the building was left when a platoon of voluntary firemen finally arrived. Simultaneously with them came gangs of toughs—from Corlears Hook, the Five Points, the gashouse district—to molest the firemen. When the fire brigade and spectators protested, the gangs tightened ranks and, with fists, sticks and rocks, attacked everyone in sight. The riot soon fizzled out with little help from the frightened constabulary, in the late 1830s still an improvisation of porters, stevedores and cartmen. The building was never restored; the institution moved elsewhere.

Although Fourth Avenue up to Thirty-first was developing a city look, the area to the west stayed reasonably rural for a while, with its Cottage Tavern, the lowing of cattle and, not too far away at Nineteenth Street and Broadway, the old-fashioned rural house of one of the real estate Goelets who kept quail, golden and silver pheasants, and peacocks in his big front yard. When rumor of riots came his way, he had his coachmen pluck out the showy tails of the peacocks so they might look like working-class fowl.

It was with the official opening of Madison Square Park in 1847 that the neighborhood began to turn urban, and quickly. By 1852 the tavern had become a stumbling block on a valuable site. It was razed. In its place at the meeting of Broadway with Fifth and Twenty-third Street rose the first of several local amusement palaces, one the joint enterprise of a group of showmen who called their new wonder Franconi's Hippodrome. It was a fanciful brick building that enclosed an oval ring which measured three hundred by two hundred feet, within the ring a racetrack forty feet wide. Ninety thousand feet of canvas was required to roof the arena and one thousand gaslights to light it. Elaborated with spreads of greenery, illuminated fountains and monster vases of flowers, it could seat ten thousand and provide standing room for three thousand. Turrets fresh and proud, banners flying, the Hippodrome staged its grand opening on May 2, 1853, admitting a full capacity crowd, reported to be the largest crowd yet gathered in the city. There was the usual characteristic scramble for seats, the usual bruised sides, feet and shoulders, and, in time, the settling in for entertainment and edification provided by one hundred and forty human performers, thirty of them women, by dozens of horses and monkeys, a pair of elephants, several deer and camels, and a gaggle of ostriches. The ostriches competed in steeplechase races, the monkeys rode racing ponies; horses danced in the manner of the Spanish Riding School of Vienna, sturdy ladies competed in chariot races. The dashing and racing and comic effects slowed to the stately pace of a medley of medieval and Renaissance pageantry that included a tournament yclept "The Field of the Cloth of Gold." Henry VIII was there, portly and resplendent, and the sly, elegant François I, along with a retinue of historically uncertain but glittering attendants. They strutted around the arena, stopped for trumpet flourishes and then regrouped to watch, along with the enthralled crowd, knights having at each other with lances, broadswords and battle-axes. A knight in black armor who had managed to unseat all rivals was awarded a prize bestowed by the "Queen of Beauty" and the trumpets rang out again. Calm returned with a float carrying Ceres surrounded by the Muses. As her ornate cart made its progress around the arena, the Muses revolved on their pedestals and the Bountiful Goddess sowed golden grain to the right and to the left.

In spite of such glories, the Hippodrome lost enough money to fold up two years after its grand opening. It was erased and gave place to the more durable and legendary Fifth Avenue Hotel, the creation of the Amos F. Eno who had come to New York as a young New Englander and grew rich enough to do his planning in a house on Fifth Avenue very near Washington Square. Because Twenty-third Street was too far uptown to be successful, the hotel was generally referred to as "Eno's Folly." Undeterred, Eno caused the white marble of his most modern and luxurious hotel to rise to six stories, ready to open in September 1859 and reveal its many wonders, among them the first passenger elevator, known as a "vertical railroad." (The "first" was not quite true. There had been other such machines, erratic and unreliable, until Mr. Elisha G. Otis installed one with workable safety devices in a store at Broadway and Broome Street in 1857.) The state entrance of the hotel was a columned portico, adjoined by fine shops. One of them, Knox the hatter, devised an adroit publicity scheme; it gave

brand-new hats to famous statesmen—Lincoln was one of them
—and kept the old as part of an historic collection. Another
shop was Maillard's, the retail outlet for the Michelangelos of
bonbons who won important commissions and prizes for their
edifices of sweets. For one centennial exposition they sent a
fifteen-foot spire adorned with historical figures—the Pilgrim
Fathers landing, George Washington and entourage on the
Delaware, Sitting Bull, General Custer and a good number of
momentous others—that formed a populous and sticky imitation of Trajan's Column.

The hotel was slick and expensive and, to the surprise of
skeptical heads, a great success. The grand entrance hall was
supremely grand, 160 feet long, 27 wide, rising to a height of
15 feet above the marble floors. The deep, plumply upholstered
sofas that concealed couples intent on concealment became
nuggets of city gossip, then city folklore, then served fiction.
The "Amen Corner," a downstairs sitting room, was the agora
of leading Republicans who clustered around the boss, Senator
Thomas Platt, to say Amen to the orders and benefices he
pronounced. The Fifth Avenue was the hostel of Presidents and
potential Presidents; it was here, at a political dinner, that
plans were made which produced the scandal-ridden years of
Grant's occupancy of the White House. The contested election
of 1876 might have gone to Samuel J. Tilden if the Amen
Corner, inspired by the persuasive William C. Whitney, had
not dedicated itself to an electoral vote recount that gave
Rutherford B. Hayes the presidency, in spite of the fact that
his opponent had won 51 percent of the popular vote. Under
the guidance of its lessee and manager, Colonel Paran Stevens,
the hotel became a significant stopping place for processions
jubilant or solemn; and although the big money of the Age of
the Dinosaurs was yet to come, staying at the Fifth Avenue
Hotel or gambling in one of its suites or arranging a banquet
there were telling signs of having arrived.

The first major foreign luminary to stay at the hotel was

the Prince of Wales, Victoria's son, a slender boy who was to age and expand as the Belle Epoque's bon vivant, Edward VII. The youngster, only nineteen in 1860, was welcomed by deafening cannon blasts and roaring bands and thousands on thousands of New Yorkers. They hung from windows and roofs, mobbed the sidewalks, carried signs that welcomed "Victoria's Royal Son" and prayed that "God Save the Queen." They waited for hour after hour in front of the hotel, calling for the exhausted prince to appear at his balcony, and for hours longer to see him acknowledge the serenade arranged by the Caledonia Club. They hung around the next day, waiting for a glimpse of the royal youth as he made his dreary official progress from one dull institution to another. That night the populace relinquished the prince to the aristocracy which had planned a Grand Ball at the Academy of Music on Fourteenth Street. The crowd was so great that the floor gave way, but was quickly repaired under the supervision of Isaac Brown, sexton of Grace Church. The disaster averted, the gala swooped and swayed on, its full effulgence recorded by numerous engravings. The festooned tiers, the pillars and their supporting caryatids were painstakingly rendered and, possibly as gestures of homage to the prince, the artists modeled a number of the gentlemen on Prince Albert while the young ladies resembled Queen Victoria in one of her early portraits, flowerlike head and smooth shoulders rising from a coquetry of ruffled lace and billows of embroidered silks.

The city wallowed in Anglophilia for days and the newspapers recorded the prince's every step—from Brady's photographic studio, to Barnum's museum, to big shops and lordly homes, and, at night, to a torchlight parade of five thousand firemen and their bands. The *Tribune* issued bulletins at ten-minute intervals, to the effect that at 11:20, he descended from his carriage; 11:30, he entered Stewart's department store; 11:40, he examined a French fan. The diarist George Strong, growing tired of it all: "What a spectacle-loving people we are.

Shops are closed and business paralyzed. Wall Street is deserted.
I begin to weary of the 'sweet young Prince.' The Hope of
England threatens to become a bore. In fact he is a bore of the
first order." When the boredom threatened to become general,
a breathless report that the prince had disappeared during the
night. He reappeared, easily tracked down to a refulgent pleasure parlor nearby.

The torchlight parade and chalky blare of calcium light
were revived for General Grant's encounter with a grateful
people at the close of the Civil War. The reception at the hotel
began sensibly and exclusively; one hundred leading citizens
each subscribed one hundred dollars for the event. Then it all
flew apart, mismanaged and unmanageable. Invitations were
issued indiscriminately, tossed around like windswept scraps of
paper. A mob of ten thousand came at the general like a tidal
wave. Half of the three thousand people rushing the supper
rooms for oysters and champagne couldn't get in; the other
half couldn't get out. The fervent mob shouted to the general
that they were praying for him, ambitious mothers pushed
forward their precocious children, complainers bellowed, ec-
centrics posed unanswerable questions. Battered in the dis-
order, the dignitaries slated to be introduced to the general
were labeled with the wrong names by the official in charge of
introductions. November 20, 1865, was, for the hotel, for the
general, for business and political leaders, a shambles to be
blotted out by clearer organization and vigilance in later celebrations.

By the time the Fifth Avenue Hotel had become a major
social lodestone, it was neighbored by a good number of houses
—and more to come—that were in class and style echoes of those
on lower Fifth Avenue. Washington Irving, Chester K. Arthur,
Horace Greeley, Peter Cooper, and a branch of the numerous
Roosevelts who produced Theodore lived in the area. Samuel
F. B. Morse, painter, experimenter in telegraphy, professor at

New York University, head of the Know-Nothing Party (which held that only native Americans should hold governmental office and demanded that newcomers not be granted citizenship until they had been in America twenty-five years), founder and president of the National Academy of Design, lived at Twenty-second Street near Fifth Avenue. To house his academy, he built a Doge's Palace, in the approved Ruskin style, on astonished Twenty-third Street and Fourth Avenue. Yet another font of art was the house of Catherine Lorillard Wolfe. Her father had been a rich merchant of metal household objects; her mother's money stemmed from Lorillard's Snuff and Tobacco, which earned an enormous fortune "by giving them that to chew which they could not swallow." Catherine, without siblings, became the richest spinster in the world when her parents died. Several of her millions went to charities for children and a fair portion into safe, sweet French paintings which on her death in 1887 went to the Metropolitan Museum.

Delmonico's followed its clientele and set up a pretty, gay-awninged house. Other hotels sprang up with admirable speed: Holland House, the Albemarle, the St. James, the Victoria regularly patronized by Grover Cleveland, and the Brunswick—the latter two singularly ugly piles. The Hoffman House outdid them all with its *sportif* atmosphere, the bar decorated with twenty-five thousand dollars' worth of Bouguereau nymphs gamboling with satyrs and a Pan leaping with heated bacchantes in a spacious ambience of textured ceiling, cut glass, fancy pilasters and shining top hats.

As Civil War money poured down on the tricky, the tough and those already well embedded in banks and fast-growing industrial empires, the stakes rose in gambling and casinos grew more splendid and exclusive. Morrisey's was a lavish place at 5 West Twenty-fourth Street, within a few paces of the Fifth Avenue Hotel. August Belmont, the continental bon vivant and sinister power who moves darkly as Julius Beaufort in Edith Wharton's *The Age of Innocence*, was said to have lost

sixty thousand dollars in one night. His consolation was a supper of two canvasback ducks. At thirty thousand dollars per
fowl, this was probably the most expensive meal in history.

Morrisey's rise to fame, fortune and politics never quite
erased the fact that he began as a slum gang leader. He and his
gambling rooms were under frequent attack and, worse still,
he and his wife were excluded from established society. The
iciest snubbing numbed them when they ventured to pierce a
fortress of Old Society, the Academy of Music on Fourteenth
Street. Morrisey remembered, and to celebrate his second election to Congress, he bought for his wife *the* supreme pair of
opera glasses ordered of *the* leading Paris jewelers. The lenses
were surrounded with lyre-shaped frames of diamonds and
sapphires for which the bill, ubiquitously publicized, was
seventy-five thousand dollars.

Morrisey's was hardly the only gambling den of deep carpets, splendid plate, choice wines and rare dishes. There were
several such places in the locality, the "old" rich habitués joined
in increasing numbers by the new rich, characterized by a cen-
sorious visitor as recently gilded "porters, stable boys, coal-
heavers, pickers of rags, scrubbers of floors and laundry women.
Coarse, rude, uncivil, and immoral many of them still are."
Adjuncts to the gaming were expensive "parlor houses" that
required their customers to wear evening dress and order only
the finest champagne at ten dollars and more a bottle—standards set by an establishment that occupied a row of brownstones on West Twenty-fifth Street. By greasing the palms of
desk clerks, the house found out which prosperous visitor had
checked into what hotel and sent him a sedate invitation on
good paper to taste of their wares.

Gambling and political clubs, curvaceous Delmonico's and
livelier hotels began to outshine the Fifth Avenue Hotel, which,
nevertheless, lasted into 1909, witnessing many Madison Avenue events and changes, and the establishment of potent competitors—the Waldorf, the St. Regis, the Plaza—uptown. It had

watched a series of celebrations of Civil War heroes; one inspired a statue to Admiral Farragut in Madison Square Park, a monument, unlike most park effigies, more alive than dead. The sculptor, St. Gaudens, had the wind blow and pull at the Admiral's jacket and forced his legs into a wide, planted hold as they might stand on a heaving deck. For the sculpture Stanford White devised a lyrical art nouveau base of gentle sea creatures in watery veils. Farragut was soon joined in Madison Square by the immense amputated arm and torch of the Statue of Liberty, begging for money so that she might buy a pedestal on which all her several parts could gather and rest. It required the help of public donations unceasingly urged by Pulitzer's *World*, before she could take her place on Bedloe's Island.

During Liberty's humiliating stay on Madison Square, in 1866, she had, at least, a cheerful neighbor. It was an exuberant structure, with deeply framed oriels and busily windowed roof slopes, somewhat in the French style of the Second Empire. It stood at Madison Avenue and Twenty-sixth Street, the house of Leonard Jerome. First came the eighty-thousand-dollar stables, fitted with walnut paneling and rich carpets. Above that a ballroom and a theater with tapestried walls that held six hundred guests. Then, housing for Mrs. Jerome and the little Jerome girls.

Stables, ballroom, theater and domestic quarters were the setting of a festive life. The horse-loving triumvirate of Jerome, August Belmont and William Travers enjoyed not only themselves but each other, setting up and pursuing gaudy and expensive rivalries. Travers made no attempt to match his friends in the showiness of carriages or the quality and cost of horses and mistresses—in those fields they held absolute mastery. He could, though, challenge them to contests of gourmet dinners catered by Delmonico's. Travers' extra gift to his guests was the pleasure of his witty company and bon mots to take home as souvenirs. Jerome and Belmont preferred the more substantial gift, in a society tradition that later reached its apogee as cigars wrapped in hundred-dollar bills. The ladies at Jerome's parties often found jeweled gold bracelets wrapped in their napkins; Belmont gave his guests finely worked trinkets of platinum.

Jerome and Belmont brightened the New York social scene with their battles over the woman of the hour; the weapons masses of flowers, jewelry, career advancement (they both, but especially Jerome, liked and fostered singers), financial advice and rides in handsome carriages drawn by satin-smooth horses. The competition was probably more heated for Jerome: Belmont was richer and had the best of everything.

One of the most conspicuous prizes of their contests was the singer Adelina Patti who at seventeen had startled New York with a stunning performance in *Lucia di Lammermoor* late in 1859. She became the idol of idolatrous New York. Although Jerome and Belmont both lavished attention and gifts on her, gossip granted the triumph to Jerome. He had a jewel-box theater she could use for rehearsals; he had an engaging manner which Belmont lacked; he was an openhanded charmer who glistened with scandal—an irresistible sun for an ambitious young singer to turn her face to.

The next songbird was American Minnie Hauk, only fifteen when she sang to an astonished dinner assemblage. Both men were patrons of the Academy of Music and saw to it that she had a debut there. Belmont took care of the girl's musical education but Leonard had something of an edge again. It was rumored (and he himself may have been the mischievous source) that she was his illegitimate daughter, born of a liaison with the chaste Jenny Lind, whom he had adored—the man reacted to singers as if he himself were a bird in a frenzy of mating song—and who permitted herself to say publicly that she found Jerome extremely handsome.

The lady who most skillfully played the Belmont-Jerome game for a long time was Mrs. Pierre Lorillard Ronalds, a well-born, courageous and sly beauty with, inevitably, a reasonable

singing voice and a good knowledge of music. Newly separated
from her husband when she swam onto the gentlemen's hori-
zon, she was still managing to dress elegantly and live stylishly,
entertaining with musicales in her house and soon singing for
charity at Jerome's little theater.

She was one of the grand cocottes, smooth and skillful,
moving suavely among a number of admirers, the list headed
by Belmont and Jerome, engaged as usual in getting the best
thing in New York at no matter what cost. Fannie Ronalds, a
stylish skater, dancer and horsewoman, accepted gifts from
both as well as from other friends. She was shrewd enough to
visit with Clara, Mrs. Jerome, and play affectionately with the
little Jerome girls, probably to build a barricade of respectability against gossip, especially fervid about her riding frequently
with Leonard Jerome, ostensibly to learn from him the more
arcane points of horsemanship.

After they had known each other for some years, Mrs.
Ronalds mentioned to Jerome that she would like to give a
ball but lacked the means. In the well-mannered style of his
time, he asked for a sparse sum that he might invest for her
and returned, several days later, with enough money for lavish
entertainment. Long in advance of the ball she sent out invitations to the crème, who eagerly accepted. (She was more
amusing than Vanderbilts, certainly more decorative and, in
any case, it was a good idea to keep an eye on Fannie, hold her
in the light.) Guests had ample time to order their costumes
from Paris and she to ponder menus and make enchanted
flowery dells of her salons. On the night of the ball she appeared as Music in a white satin gown embroidered with musical notes, on her head a harp-shaped crown illuminated by tiny
gas lights fed from containers concealed in her hair. Startling
enough the Paris crown of flickering lights, but the riveting
sight was her little red boots hung with bells, not only because
they showed a forbidden inch or two of ankle, but because the
girls of a famous house wore just such tinkly red shoes and

enough of the assemblage recognized their provenance. Audacious Fannie was doing a little *épater*-ing of a society that was choking on its own dustiness, one of the reasons it welcomed this free, playful spirit.

A postlude to the memorable party: some years later Jerome and Belmont were speaking ruefully, nostalgically about Fanny—who might, at the moment, have been entertaining the bey of Algiers. Harking back, comparing a detail here and there, the men discovered that they had each paid generously for the ball, including the famous Paris headdress and the little red shoes.

In the Madison Square house she had yearned for, waiting and waiting for Jerome to alight, Clara continued her regimen of bracing exercises and a busy schedule of lessons for her girls; for her new status—she hoped for acceptance into Society which never came—she stuffed her house with brocades, gold fringe and heavy silks on convoluted woods. Leonard kept pacing the lively steps of his rigadoon, now with Commodore Vanderbilt in a variety of railroad ventures, then with a trader in racing horses, always finding time for a few figures with the ladies. Unfettered, optimistic and eager to be in the national forefront, he lent himself to a wild scheme during the Civil War. Rich Union supporters planned to send blacks, who had been freed by Lincoln, to colonies in Latin America or Africa—a solution to the race problem. Jerome's company raised the money to ship five thousand ex-slaves to a barren island whose source of supplies of water and food was the black republic of Haiti, an uncomfortable distance away. Since the costs were enormous and the scheme held in contempt by many Americans, it was abandoned. The firms involved lost a large sum of money, most of it recovered in railroad stock games, not too difficult for the skillful Jerome.

Clara's iron fortitude cracked; she had had too many songbirds and had lived too long in clouds of gossip. Clara's publicly stated reason for picking up her girls and their black mammy was the usual: to settle in Paris so that her daughters might be brought up in a cultivated atmosphere. Leonard stayed on as a prominent member of the New York Yacht Club, as head of the American Jockey Club whose headquarters were his house on Madison Square and as the controlling factor of the successful Pacific Mail Steamship which he had cornered in the opening year of the Civil War. He got rid of his mansion (taken by the University Club and then the Manhattan Club, which used it well into this century) and began the transatlantic commuting that would continue for the rest of his life. Europe held his lively, musical, extravagant trio of daughters climbing to social peaks; the singers whose European careers he promoted; fabled horses to buy; and, wherever he was, a sunlit bank of charming young women. In New York there were yachting races; the ridiculous spectacle of powerful old Vanderbilt hanging on for life via Mesmerists and magicians; and, through Jerome's influence on the *New York Times*, the pursuit and defeat of the long omnipotent Boss Tweed.

One of the trips he made to England was to greet his first grandchild, Winston Churchill. Family annals insist that he evaluated the child in racing terms: the baby should have pace from his father and staying power from his mother. Being a grandfather did not raise his degree of domestication, though. "The Father of the American Turf" continued examining horses and reacquainting himself with the charms of Mrs. Ronalds, who had settled in England. But even a Jerome life had to slow at some time. A report published in 1884, when he was past sixty: "His is no sere and yellow leaf, but, having lived his life, he now stands quietly by and watches the new generation live their lives, amused by their mistakes and tolerant of their blunders." The Jerome girls were dazzling London society; his wife was writing worried letters about his health and he was feeling less and less a Titan. He returned to England. Made fearful by his obvious decline and the uncertainty of his acceptance into heaven, a relative gave him a Bible to read on his deathbed. A witness reported that he found the Old Testament personae a distasteful bunch, closed the book and died, in 1891, unreconstructed.

Until his final journey to England, Jerome stayed a citizen of Madison Square, his favorite post-mansion address the Brunswick Hotel; it had his kind of action. The Brunswick was the starting place for the New York version of the English coach meet which took place on the last Saturday of May. Gaily adorned four-in-hand coaches lined up at the hotel, dashed up Fifth Avenue into Central Park and northward to Mount St. Vincent (between the present Conservatory Gardens and the Harlem Meer), tore down to Washington Square and back to the Brunswick for an ample, winy dinner. The horses were gallant, the drivers resplendent in bottle-green cutaways with brass buttons and tall white hats, the ladies charming under frilly parasols. The families of the riders, in their best silks and jewels, cheered their men and horses on from the windows and balconies of the Avenue.

The almost unceasing late-nineteenth-century parade of Fifth Avenue spectacles reached one of its numerous peaks at Madison Square with the 1899 celebration of Admiral George Dewey's triumph at Manila Bay. In the style of the welcomes to Titus and Constantine in Rome, Admiral Dewey and reigning dignitaries, Governor Theodore Roosevelt, high naval officers and distinguished citizens led off in their carriage, followed by long lines of minor heroes. They marched and the thousands cheered. Seats in stands along Fifth Avenue went to the chosen, rich and political. One room in a Fifth Avenue house near Twenty-sixth Street cost five hundred dollars for the afternoon; one window jammed with dozens of faces took in three hundred dollars and a four-story building with a spread of windows on the Avenue collected three thousand.

The parade came down Fifth Avenue from Fifty-ninth Street to a gleaming white triumphal arch placed at the juncture of Fifth Avenue and Broadway. Dewey's apotheosis took place in the center of the arch surrounded by the might of fluted pillars, convoluted Roman capitals and bellicose figures surmounted by the time-honored rearing horses bearing a Winged Victory. Under this imperial splendor, Dewey stood for four hours, reviewing the procession, meticulously responding to thousands of salutes.

The Dewey celebration might be considered a farewell gesture to large-moneyed Madison Square. Politicians still used the Amen Corner but wider-flung deals were staged uptown. The beauties of the demimonde soon searched for donors of bigger and better baubles in the Waldorf's Peacock Alley uptown. The Brunswick Hotel had lost its class customers by inadvertently admitting to its dining rooms a party led by a notorious tough and gang leader. But the eating there was still good and Madison Square was still having and making fun. While some ladies left, other gifted ladies moved in. Sarah Bernhardt held court at one or another of the local hotels and so did Anna Held. Mrs. Leslie Carter, who appeared in *Du Barry* in 1901, spent her leisure hours at the Fifth Avenue Hotel and from her suite issued tremulant, dewy-eyed interviews explaining that she had not only studied Du Barry but *was* the incarnation of that pretty plaything of nobles, a king and the guillotine. There were still a number of careful restaurants, there was drinking with the nymphs at the Hoffman House, there was varied shopping along Twenty-third Street, Broadway and nearby Sixth Avenue. For grisly amusement one could visit the Chamber of Horrors in the Eden Wax Museum at 55 West Twenty-third Street. For being wafted to faraway romantic places, dancing girls, flower girls, cigarette girls and just girls in an "Indian Palace" restaurant at 325 Fifth, reputedly managed by the son of an Indian potentate and proud to announce that his were the first public rooms in which women might smoke. A jolly repertoire, but with big money going, the listlessness of abandonment and disuse threatened. To the rescue, the most beautiful and notorious of a series of Madison Square Gardens.

When the Vanderbilts' old New York and Harlem Depot at Twenty-sixth Street and Madison Avenue was abandoned, Barnum took it over as his Hippodrome. Later refurbished, with Barnum still in control, it became Gilmore's Gardens, large enough to attract an enormous crowd that came to be frightened and cleansed at a great revival meeting conducted in 1876 by the leading evangelists of the time, Moody and Sankey. It also housed shows of glossy horses and boxing—the latter not strictly legal, but, described with the useful words "demonstration" or "exhibition" and given a nod from Tammany, not strictly illegal. Under the name of Madison Square Garden the building was shortly torn down to return a glorious phoenix a decade later. The money for the new project came from a curious conglomerate, among them the combination of Phineas T. Barnum and J. P. Morgan, who hired the firm of McKim, Mead and White for the job. The building is generally attributed almost exclusively to Stanford White, who had made a substantial financial investment in the project.

In 1890 there rose on the block between Madison and Fourth avenues, between Twenty-sixth and Twenty-seventh the joyous and fun-loving building, as much the architect's pet toy as his girls, kindling like a favorite beauty constant attention and lavish spending. White had surmounted graceful welcoming arches and roof colonnades with pretty tempiettos and among them placed a tall, graceful tower (whose studios and apartments were White's special domain) inspired by Seville's Giralda which served as pedestal for a Diana who danced with the wind, by St. Gaudens. The cost of the building was three to four million dollars, not too much, it was generally considered, for such an adornment to the city and the building's unique purpose. It was the first large building in the country devoted solely to entertainments: it held a huge amphitheater, cafes, a large restaurant, halls for meetings, shopping arcades and a roof garden. It took quickly. "There is no other building in the world . . . that houses one-half the gaiety and energy, or half the variety" was the general pleased judgment.

Here William Jennings Bryan accepted the Democratic nomination for President; vestiges of the Wild West rode and shot here; Adelina Patti sang here. The summer roof garden served up concerts, vaudeville, comic opera, fantasies of Japan complete with geishas and thin Japanese song. The circus came and went, as did billiard champions and wrestlers. Madison Square Garden was the place for cat shows, dog shows, poultry shows, meets of jumping, dashing, riding in the aristocratic horse shows and the clash and roar of faked battles. A six-day bike ride was an annual favorite as was the Sportsmen's Show which brought in real trees and improvised streams of a landscape inhabited by waterfowl, fish, fishermen and appropriate flora. And as often as possible the popular exhibitions of the art of boxing.

In spite of occasional claps of moral thunder from the clergy, the blithe tunes sang on, the blithest sung by the ringmaster Stanford White himself, a busy architect and leading decorator at a time when that meant scouring Europe for opulent rarities and earning immense commissions on the purchases. White was a well-educated man, knowledgeable in the arts and antiquities, a combination of aesthete and sybarite with ready, imaginative responses to female flesh. He walked in a cloak of gossip which he wore lightly. His gifted partners, left in the shadow, probably didn't mind because his notoriety augmented their lucrative practice. One tale that wound its way quickly around town concerned a party he gave in his studio in Madison Square Garden to honor Diamond Jim Brady, whose aesthetics were limited to the beauties of gems, Lillian Russell and mountainous meals. The supper party for a dozen gentlemen culminated in a huge birthday pie which streamed ribbons, a red one for Jim and white for the others.

Brady reeled in a darling nude. Not to disappoint his other guests White had ushered in from behind closed doors a group of similarly unencumbered girls, one for each guest.

Like other gentlemen-about-town, White had a seat close to the stage for every performance of *Floradora*, mainly interested in the famous sextet who appeared fully dressed but were of such tantalizing beauty that each made highly profitable connections. These were often arranged at the favorite marketplace for pulchritude and gaiety, Rector's champagne palace on Broadway. One of the ambitious girls of the *Floradora* cast, not one of the goddesses, however, was Evelyn Nesbit, whose mother knew early that she had a good property and groomed her willing pupil for a career as star-courtesan with diamond-studded prospects. White found her and kept her and, in the keeping, acted out with the teen-aged girl (already well schooled as model and companion of elderly rich men) scenes from underground Edwardian novels. Like Swinburne and Whistler and others of his era, White was inspired by the look of nubile innocence to tender, delicate inventions, the most famous improvisation the enchanting red velvet swing in which he put her nightly and naked.

The unique entertainment was not quite enough for Evelyn, and marriage was safer. Evelyn married a maniacally jealous, sadistic drug addict, the Pittsburgh millionaire, Harry K. Thaw, who begged her to tell him over and over again about the exciting indignities of her three years with Stanny. She obliged fulsomely. On the night of June 25, 1906, Thaw made his way to the roof garden of Madison Square Garden and shot White dead, closing a sparkling life and releasing long, broad bands of scandal.

In 1902, several years before White was killed, the great odd-shaped tombstone that prophesied the end of Madison Square as the center of diverse pleasures was erected. The Flatiron (Fuller) Building rose to its startling height quickly in spite of one stubborn impediment: a tenant of the Cumberland hotel which the Flatiron displaced who refused to leave until bricks and laths loosened by demolition threatened his life. The new building, one of the tallest in New York at the time, was an example of a new principle in architecture, ex- terior walls and floors supported by steel frames and thus capable of growing to an impressive height of twenty-one stories. It immediately became a famous structure that ap- peared on myriad souvenir items and its site fabled as the corner where winds blew strongest and drove skirts highest, a viewing post for crowds of loafers who stood around to observe while police tried to shoo them away. From this melange of wind, ankles, loafers and cops, social historians say, the expres- sion "twenty-three skidoo" rather obscurely emerged.

The age of the skyscraper had come; the "Old" Fifth Avenue Hotel was preparing to retire; the most reputable shops were moving uptown; the Garden began to reduce its ranging repertoire to a few sporting events, with emphasis on now legal boxing. The many-faceted fly-eye was scarred and dimmed, the brilliance faded to the ordinary dun tones of working streets, the park a haven for the unwanted.

CHAPTER 4

ASTORLAND

oward the end of the eighteenth century a farm that encompassed Fifth Avenue from Thirty-second to Thirty-sixth Street became the property of John Thompson at the price of 482 pounds. When Thompson was ready to sell his land, he advertised that it was "fertile, partly wooded and well watered," capable of yielding produce "profitably disposed of to the opulent families of the city." He also pointed out to the reader that the value of the lots would rise rapidly as the nearby villages of Greenwich and Chelsea grew and the city moved up to meet his farm.

In 1827, William Backhouse Astor bought a half interest in the farm, his portion of the strip that held Fifth Avenue, for $20,500. William Backhouse, a quiet, respectful son, was slated to become the major heir of the fortune amassed by the first John Jacob, since the first son, John Jacob II was retarded or insane—certainly intractable—and therefore sequestered in a tall-fenced house of his own with a doctor-companion. Old J. J. was an early example of rags to riches, arriving as a German immigrant boy in 1784, dying in 1841 as the richest man in America. He liked to say that he became a rich man because he worked hard and went to bed early. There was more to it: his unblinking ruthlessness and fierce devotion to money, and the boundless opportunities open for the courageously greedy.

After a stay with a brother in London he arrived in New York equipped with five flutes and five English pounds and a knowledge of the music business. Neither musical instruments nor the cakes and cookies he tried to peddle on the streets paid enough. He took a job beating dirt and minor fauna out of fur skins and baling them; it paid two dollars a week and board. On a mission to trade with the Indians in northern New York State, he found that a few strings of beads, cheap implements, bundles of tobacco and bright strips of cloth bought piles of otter, beaver and muskrat pelts, the same skins he cleaned and fluffed. Learning that these skins were sold at a profit of 1,000 percent in London, John Jacob went into business for himself. The woman he married became a fur expert and ran the business capably when he ventured out for more and more pelts. It was a stinking, uncomfortable and hazardous trade but the money rolled in, enough to spare seven thousand dollars for a piece of Manhattan land bought from brother Henry.

Alluring wildernesses of fur land, too great for Astor to travel alone, forced him to hire agents who set up trading posts, pushing farther and farther into untracked country. By 1800 Astor had accumulated a quarter-million dollars, some of which he used to compete in the lucrative China trade, expanding from partnership in one vessel to ownership of a fleet that took out furs and brought back valuable silks, spices, tea, rare woods. In his ravagings, Astor almost wiped out the rich-coated otter and stripped Hawaii of most of its sandalwood trees. Like many of his competitors, he made a foray into the opium trade but found that it wasn't sufficiently profitable. He concentrated instead on his furs, his growing New York properties, the China trade and outwitting all events and people who got in his way.

As the Lewis and Clark Expedition opened new areas beyond the Great Lakes, Astor established trading posts of his American Fur Company along the Missouri and Columbia rivers and the streams that fed them. The two expeditions he launched were plagued by catastrophe, as often as not induced by cruelty to the Indians and the stupidity that sold them weapons and whiskey, and finally by the British takeover of "Astoria," the proposed capital of Astor territory. In spite of the setback, and with his China trade profits to back him, Astor continued to expand his fur empire, which spurred the opening of the West and the destruction of the Indian. The grab of land, animals and Indian lives was facilitated by Astor's political friends. The governor of the Michigan Territory which teemed with fur-bearing profits was listed in the carefully kept Astor books for a gift of thirty-five thousand dollars. Competing U.S. government trading posts were closed and loopholes in the law that prohibited the sale of liquor to Indians were opened by bribes in Washington and substantial loans to officials all the way up the ladder to the President. (The story goes that when Monroe became ex-President, Astor quickly asked for the return of his money.)

When Astor disposed of the American Fur Company in 1834, he had accumulated in the fur trade alone two million dollars. It was time to beam his money and influence on additional New York real estate and profits which came to him in various ways. When Aaron Burr needed money to flee after he had killed Alexander Hamilton, J. J. gave it to him in exchange for a large chunk of Greenwich Village. City officials made it their business to see that new city roads were driven through Astor property, thereby increasing its value. Another official owned by Astor arranged to have waterfront property filled and docks built, the ensembles sold to Astor at a minimal price. As he conquered the fur trade, shipping, real estate and politicians, J. J. pushed his way into society, an essential field to conquer for the completely successful life and for exposing his children to possibilities of satisfactory marriages. The best people could rarely afford, for too long, to reject this repository of influence and money, avenging themselves on the buccaneer in feeble gossip. One hostess reported that a nouveau "dined here last night and ate ice cream and peas with a knife." These frontier manners were widely attributed to J. J., fat, ugly (he had Gilbert Stuart repaint his portrait because the first was too naturalistic) and coarse, but too powerful to be disregarded.

On the southwest corner of Thirty-fourth Street and Fifth Avenue, part of the land that son William Backhouse had bought in 1827, William built a red brick house which he didn't use—the family stayed in the colonnaded row of Lafayette Place—but later willed to his son, the second William Backhouse. William's brother, John Jacob Astor III, placed his house on the northwest corner of Thirty-third Street and that one was inherited by *his* son, William Waldorf Astor. The short block became a busy arena of social competition between branches of the family; the fiercest and most durable competitor, Mrs. William B. (née Caroline Schermerhorn), clawed her way to the apex of society as *the* Mrs. Astor. But that came later, and later still the conversion of the two Astor houses, 338 and 350 Fifth Avenue, joined (some said carefully separated) by a garden, to become the first Waldorf-Astoria Hotel in 1890.

In the meantime, Alexander T. Stewart (of the celebrated A. T. Stewart's store) had been watching the houses of the other rich moving onto Fifth Avenue. He had amassed enough New York property to vie with the Goelets and Astors and could afford to build on the northwest corner of Thirty-fourth Street, where once stood the $100,000 house of a patent medicine king, "Sarsaparilla" Townsend. The new Stewart house was imperious, virile, with strong columns and emphatic accents around the doors and windows. Indoors was a sea of real marble rising to classically stormy ceilings created by platoons of imported Italian craftsmen. It had the essential picture gallery, one of the most imposing of its time, and grand halls and drawing rooms and was the most splendid house in America—as it should have been, since it cost two million in 1869 dollars. Stewart was condemned for the extravagance, particu-

larly since he had no children to leave it to. Nor did he entertain society in his marble halls. Most of society still considered
him an immigrant peddler and the less exigent, like Barnum,
who lived on the Avenue at Thirty-ninth Street, just didn't
like him; Stewart had neither charm nor warmth. If the house
gave him pleasure at all, it was not long-lived. Stewart died in
1876 and was buried in the graveyard of St. Marks in the
Bowery, which lost his remains to body snatchers. An obscure
chronicle dug out an explanation for the crime: Stewart had
given a group a five-year loan to maintain a church and
graveyard on Wooster Street with the promise that he would
not foreclose but would extend the loan period if necessary.
When the five years had passed and the loan was not completely
repaid, Stewart converted the church to a stable and dumped
the graveyard remains into a pit. It was a Wooster Street dele-
gation, or their hired hands, who had bound and gagged the
two men guarding Stewart's grave and taken off with the corpse.
The ransom price was twenty thousand dollars, and although
Mrs. Stewart had inherited an estate worth thirty-eight million,
as well as the house, the body was two years in the returning.
The delay was not so much the result of Mrs. Stewart's re-
luctance to pay as the fact that several sets of "authentic"
remains showed up, and how to choose among them? The
macabre events proved not only that graveyards must be more
carefully guarded (as the Vanderbilts did their Staten Island
mausoleum) but that building in marble was an unlucky thing
to do.

    Recovered somewhat from her grief and shock, Mrs.
Stewart had the house photographed, and appalling it must
have been—the hall peopled with dead white statuary menaced
by a heavy metallic octopus of a chandelier. Mrs. Stewart's
bedroom photo showed off stuffing and tufting; the Siva-armed
chandelier again; a huge, dark and heavily carved bed; drapes
elaborately swagged, and swagged once more; and tables burbling with dozens of fancy little things. The house was the

first of a row of mansions on what was then "upper" Fifth
Avenue, houses that began to apply themselves seriously to
suffocating decor and ultralavish entertainments. Mrs. Stewart,
incapable of joining in the social fray, stayed in her house alone
with only servants for company and as she grew older and
witless, paced the cold halls, talking and bowing to the guests
who never came. (Pacing and bowing to absent guests was a
piece of apocrypha attached to the demise of several society
queens, a rough judgment that insisted rich old ladies go crazy
as, apparently, poor old ladies do not.) When she died, the
Manhattan Club took over tenancy. By 1915, the corner had
changed shape and purpose to a squat temple of heavy capitals
on fluted columns with the classical overhang deemed suitable
to responsible finance, the Columbia Trust Company.

These were quiet and mainly dignified changes. What
went on in the James Gordon Bennett house, four streets to the
north, and in the Astor enclave on the street below, was marketplace raucous.

In the spring of 1835, a penny newspaper, the *Herald*,
radically different from the polite newspapers New Yorkers
were accustomed to, assaulted the public. The prose was racy
and colloquial, murders poured gore, scandals were explored
in clinical detail; colorful, punching reports on the profligacy
of the rich, on the dishonesty of Wall Street, on anything that
might interest and irritate the ordinary populace, was its appealing matter. It was the creation of a Scottish immigrant,
James Gordon Bennett, then aged forty. As if life weren't real
unless headlines confirmed it, Bennett published rapturous
accounts of the young woman he was courting and subsequently
married. But marriage did not mean companionship to Bennett who was disdainful of society and dedicated to his work,
and the young Mrs. Bennett found herself distressingly isolated
in her house on Fifth Avenue at Thirty-eighth Street. She took
her young son, James Gordon Bennett, Jr., off to Paris where
she spent most of her life. The boy lived half the year with his

mother, who never said no to him, and the other half with his father, who was usually indifferent to him.

The boy had learned exquisite French, learned the pleasures of good champagne and, still in his teens, had accumulated an impressive knowledge of Paris brothels. He was on the way to being a drunkard and roisterer, arrogant, disdainful, destructive of anything, anyone who got in his way. In New York, he learned to be a host, albeit an erratic and drunken host, and how to have fun with Jeromes, especially big, playful Lawrence, a brother of Leonard, who was a member of the crew that won young Bennett a much acclaimed and expansively feted transatlantic yacht race. He was also learning, in the hours he could spare from racing and drinking, the newspaper business. He observed his father's *Herald* bring in more Civil War news, by more reporters in the battlefield, than any other paper, and witnessed the *Herald*'s pioneer publication of speedy international news after the Atlantic cable finally decided to hold. By the time he was twenty-six and had been working at the newspaper fairly steadily, Bennett Junior decided that Senior was redundant; he dropped his father's name from the masthead and named himself publisher and editor in chief. Senior objected and Junior had to be contented, for the time being, with the title of managing editor. Not for long: the old man, tired, and tired of life with Junior, turned over to him, before the young man was twenty-seven, the complete control of the *Herald*. He made it an extraordinary paper, adventuresome, carefully edited and with the imagination to foster quixotic enterprises that would attract and hold readers. It was the *Herald*, with Bennett as instigator, that sent Sir Henry Stanley to look for David Livingstone in Africa, probably the most famous of Bennett's journalistic exploits.

The end of Bennett's New York social life came when he was in his mid-thirties. He was notorious for being an alcoholic (his biographer, Richard O'Connors, records that he often rode a bicycle around and around the block where his house stood, drinking at each return from a bottle of brandy held by his butler), imperiously willful, immediately responsive to his own impulses no matter how stupid or damaging—he lost several distinguished newspapermen who would not live with his insults——a frequenter of the houses of demimonde. Yet a Southern belle, Caroline May, was willing to be courted by him. He had, after all, a great deal of money, and she was accustomed to spoiled Southern gentlemen who lived in clouds of whiskey. One day he came to see her, already quite drunk and foulmouthed. He rapidly grew drunker and more abusive. In the presence of several guests, he unbuttoned his trousers and urinated in the fireplace (some say the grand piano). Caroline called the engagement off; Bennett was horsewhipped by her brother, Fred, and invited to a duel which left brother and ex-fiancé unscathed.

Bennett went off to Paris, clanking through his accustomed routes in a coat of chain mail in case Fred May came gunning for him. May was no longer interested in him, however, so the armor was cast aside, to be replaced by the utter freedom of nudity at the reins of the coach he drove with great speed through amused Paris. He was the favorite customer of wine merchants, his account the largest in Paris. He was very welcome at Maxim's where he liked to whip tablecloths to the floor and hear the satisfying tinkle of fine plates and stemware —for which he paid generously. He acted as rescue team for Lawrence Jerome, whose wife tried to restrain him from the carefree life. The story is told that a messenger came to the Jerome house to say that Bennett was in a hospital and dying. The nurses turned out to be extraordinarily beautiful, the hospital a famous bordel, and a good time was had by all, with Mrs. Jerome none the wiser.

It was Bennett's pleasure to give away or destroy large sums of money: a bundle burned in a fireplace, a four-thousand-dollar tip to an attendant in a train, buying and handing over to a waiter a restaurant whose owner displeased him.

Along with these sporadic gestures of largesse, there were favors sprinkled on déclassé royalty, titled bums whom Bennett, for arcane reasons, admired. The greatest favor he did this tacky crowd was to publish in his Paris *Herald* full and detailed information of "international society," which flattered them and raised their value in the eyes of American heiresses whose movements, whether on the rue de Rivoli or in the spas of central Europe, were as avidly recorded by *Herald* men.

The *Herald* was for a while overwhelmed by the new journalism of Hearst and Pulitzer, particularly during the Spanish-American War which they had heated up—almost invented. Bennett assigned Richard Harding Davis—the clean-cut, strong-jawed male ideal who matched the clean-cut, strong-jawed Gibson girl—and a few other gifted reporters to the front, and the paper recovered to bring Bennett more of the forty million dollars he spent on women, wine, waste and yachts. One of his yachts, the *Lysistrata*, included a suite for himself on each deck —in case he forgot the way home—and quarters for the raggle-taggle gangs that danced to his tunes.

The fall of the *Herald* was caused by a wave of purity that hit the city in the mid-1890s abetted by the vigorous campaign of Dr. Charles Parkhurst and a competing Hearst paper. The earlier ads for abortionists had expanded into several pages of profitable notices of cheerful companionship, svelte figures, pretty smiles and pliant ways in houses with or without Turkish baths and massage. For a year Hearst, who ran the same sort of ads in his other papers, had a troop of reporters investigating and drawing out a fulsome series on the *Herald*'s iniquities. Bennett was charged with and paid substantial fines for using the mails to carry obscene matter. The ads stopped, the *Herald* lost readers, advertising and good reporters, driven away as Bennett's irascibility mounted to cruelty.

After decades of devoting himself to his own legend, Bennett stopped drinking, stopped splashing money around and settled into a comfortable, elderly marriage with the widow of

Baron de Reuter. On his death at seventy-seven it was expected
—he had said so—that the *Herald* would become the property
of his employees. The last Bennett slap had, through several
peaceable years, been held in reserve: the employees were left
nothing. Frank Munsey bought the papers for four million
dollars and resold the *Herald* and the Paris edition of it to the
widow of Whitelaw Reid and her son Ogden at a satisfying
profit. The rest of Bennett's remains lie under a Paris tombstone guarded by carved owls, the magic totems which he kept
—alive, stuffed, painted—with him always, the gods who protected the long, insolent life that might have been cut short at
several points, for several justified reasons, by several persons.

The Bennetts, always eager to serve their readers spicy
social tidbits, had their neighbors, the Astors, watched and
reported. They turned out to be a rich lode. The major Astor
inheritor, John Jacob III and his brother William B., Jr., had
yet another brother, Henry, who was left a small sum of money.
He was tetched, like one of his uncles, but not desperately, nor
was he desperately poor, because his grandfather had left him
a nice piece of land, on Broadway in the Forties. He built a
country estate complete with racetrack and—reports had it—
silver dollars in close rows embedded in the floor of one room.
He was a robust man, a heavy drinker like his brother William,
given to alternating between alcoholic furies and corrective
sermons delivered in ecclesiastical dress. In his isolated kingdom he had only himself to please. No Fifth Avenue heiress
wife involved him in social battles; he had chosen the gardener's daughter, of whom the world heard little. Not so her two
sisters-in-law. In 1847, John Jacob III married Augusta Gibbes
of a family that claimed King John of the Magna Carta as an
early ancestor, with imposing hieratic stops on the way. Augusta
exercised her aristocratic prerogatives intelligently, with style
and imagination. It was at Augusta Astor's that one met the
leading literari—noted actors and actresses, an established
painter or two—and, on Mondays, joined in literary "causeries,"

an exchange of poems and little essays and critiques in the
French manner. On occasional evenings Augusta would invite
several hundred people to her ballroom at 338 and just to show
that she, too, had them, blazed her way among her guests in
three hundred thousand dollars' worth of jewelry. One ate well
at the house of J. J. III though he, a remote man, was not the
most affable of hosts; and society women could work with
Augusta in one of her favorite charities, the Children's Aid
Society, which sent some of the swarms of homeless boys who
wandered the city streets to rural foster parents, each boy
equipped with a Bible.

Her sister-in-law next door, at 350, found Augusta's social
life too eclectic and egalitarian, without real standards. Caroline Astor had been born into a large mercantile family which
negotiated solid marriages for its children, the big star in their
escutcheon a lineage back to the Dutch patroons wreathed in
exclusivity by time and legend. In Moses Beach's *Wealthy
Citizens of New York*, published in 1845, Caroline's father,
Abraham, was listed as having the admirable worth of five
hundred thousand dollars. The family wealth increased pleasingly in the next decades when they too became major New
York landholders. Caroline was stoutish, with a bulbous nose
and a heavy jaw, and disinclined to cultivate charm. Nevertheless, when she was twenty-two, the families managed to join
her with twenty-three-year-old William B., Jr., a bright, pleasing young man who had been a competent Columbia student,
had cultivated tastes and was well-traveled. Whether it was
Caroline's forceful character—she even insisted that he drop his
cherished vulgar middle name, Backhouse—or the life she designed or a psyche stained by the fact that his father obviously
cared more for his brother John J. III, William abandoned as
soon as he could the role of homebody. He remained long
enough to father four daughters and one son, then ordered an
immense yacht and, except for occasional appearances—a trip
with Caroline to sustain the charade of a happy marriage, a

family crisis or nuptials—stayed away, finding pleasure with lightweight friends. He became one of the prototypes of the playboy millionaire, a type that would proliferate in numbers and notoriety as the generations came on.

Not too far from forty, with children whose matrimonial prospects still had to be looked to, Caroline found herself in need of guidance by a social expert. Her Pygmalion-Svengali was Ward McAllister, a humorless Southern gentleman with one pervasive need: to be leader of any social set he might encounter.

Before he joined forces with Caroline Astor, McAllister had New York society well boxed off from the importunities and vulgar shows of post–Civil War money made in all sorts of ways by uncouth people with no form and a distressing lack of background. He organized a group of twenty-five top-drawer gentlemen, "Knickerbocker families" preferred, and entrusted them with expanding and solidifying their circle. These aristocrats were to arrange subscription balls to which each might invite four impeccable ladies and five gentlemen. Since McAllister had tolerantly decreed that in newish America it was reasonable to consider four generations enough to create a gentleman, it should not have been impossible to find 225 men who could meet the required standards. But it was not easy. Lists and lineages were searched and searched again and found to need a bit of leeway here and some latitude there (except in the case of Catholics and Jews, never admitted). A widely circulated tale of the time had it that August Belmont, on finding himself excluded, threatened to ruin the financial community if he wasn't invited to their next exclusive ball. The invitation came. No one appeared the night of the ball but Mr. and Mrs. Belmont. (Like that of the mad old rich ladies wandering their halls peopled by ghosts, this story is also attached to a number of millionaires, among them an early Vanderbilt and the Philadelphian Stotesbury.)

On his schemes and her money, McAllister and Caroline

filled her life with grandeur and romance, the glamour symbolized by the name he gave her, "Mystic Rose," a name that
evoked the songs of the troubadours and the gracious manners
of the courts of love. Together they conducted the decorous
figures of a strict pavane, courtiers and ladies kept attentive and
under sharp surveillance; a misstep meant banishment from the
court. There were several arenas for pacing the ornate steps:
the Patriarchs' Balls of the 1870s held at various mansions and
later at Delmonico's, junior partriarchs' dancing classes to insure that mating rites among young partners got off to a proper
start, the opera season at the Academy of Music. The important
night at the opera was, for a long while, Monday, and it was
vulgar to appear before the opening curtain was well up. After
the opera, the court retired to Delmonico's for supper or went
on to one of the grand balls. Lesser afternoon levees at Caroline's house assuaged some of the strivers shut out of the post-
opera fetes; no point in cutting out altogether a potent mass
who threatened to take over the financial and—possibly, in time
—the social world, and there were those daughters to marry
off.

None but the crème was invited to the weekly Mystic Rose
dinners, served on gold service reputed to cost three or four
hundred dollars a piece. (They were actually gold-plated, it was
later discovered, but good enough.) McAllister, who did the
ordering, insisting that only the best was tolerable, banked the
rooms with forests of roses and orchids held in brackets and
golden bowls so many and heavy that tables had often to be
reinforced. Dinner was called at the continental hour of eight
—McAllister had studied such fine points—and went through a
costly and indigestible progress of "French" cuisine (more or
less), the menu spelled in French (more or less). A required
opener of the ten-course feast was a soup of the rare *tortue*,
followed by the tortue itself as terrapin, or sometimes by imported salmon; the sequent courses were beef larded with
truffles, a confection of sweetbreads, pâté de foie gras, the in-

dispensable canvasback duck, these accompanied by elaborate treatments of asparagus, mushrooms and artichokes imported from remote places. Then, a sorbet to ease and cool the stomach and on to French cheeses and baroque bombes, bonbons and gateaux. Each step of the way was anointed with French wines and, after the three or so hours the feasting absorbed, the gentlemen retired to seasoned madeira and cigars, the ladies to conversation conducted by Mrs. Astor. There was no censorship of topics; there didn't have to be. The ladies knew what the rules were: no controversial subjects, no gossip, no politics—simply chitchat about the social doings of their peers.

The capping triumph of King Ward and Queen Caroline's efforts of the 1880s and early 1890s took place in January, the month of her great ball, the Thirty-fourth Street castle glowing, the masses of flowers grown to fantasy jungles. In the drawing room, as regally implacable and glittering as the Empress Theodosia in the Ravenna mosaics, stood Mrs. Astor, under a life-size portrait painted by the stylish portraitist Carolus Duran. Her dyed raven hair (in later life it was a wig) was held in a tiara blistered with diamonds, her gowns of satins and velvets threaded with gold and looped pearls. Stomachers, one attributed to Marie Antoinette, and trellises and big studs of gems shaped a cuirass that all but covered the upper section of her Worth creations. Under the portrait, devised to include Mrs. Caroline Schermerhorn Astor in the world of Van Dyck queens and Kneller court favorites, she gravely nodded to her guests as they proceeded to the ballroom, actually the extensive picture gallery. It was the size of this room, according to one theory, which could hold no more than four hundred guests— and all of them distinguished—that determined the quality and number of those who were truly Society. After the restrained dancing—a universe away from the uninhibited shrieking and show of legs in the dance halls almost within earshot—*souper* on the golden plates in the baronial dining hall.

The gallery-ballroom also served as stage for major family

splashes. In the late 1870s, Orme Wilson, of a family which concentrated on advantageous marriages (one sister married Ogden Goelet of the real estate clan, another became a Vanderbilt), began to court young Carrie Astor. He was looked on by Mama as a fortune hunter until the Wilsons guaranteed a reassuring marriage settlement. The celebration of the wedding was immensely successful; among the distinguished guests was General Grant, still riding high in some quarters as ex-President. The value of the gifts reached about a million dollars according to the estimate of the knowing guests who viewed them, according to the tribal custom described by Edith Wharton in her *House of Mirth*. "They had paused before the table on which the bride's jewels were displayed, . . . the milky gleam of perfectly matched pearls, the flash of rubies relieved against contrasting velvet, the intense blue rays of sapphires kindled into light by surrounding diamonds: all these precious tints enhanced and deepened by the varied art of their setting." Some years later, Caroline's son, John Jacob IV, was introduced to an expanded Society (eight hundred), in preparation for his marriage with a Philadelphia heiress whose ancestry went back to roots more ancient than Augusta's; the girl was a fruit of the tree of Alfred the Great, at some point entangled with the twigs of the kings of France. Another daughter married James Roosevelt Roosevelt, strengthening the bonds with the First Families of New York. Her sister, Charlotte, however, cut a scarlet path through the even family progress. She was Mrs. James Coleman Drayton and the mother of four children when she fell in love with Hallett Alsot Borrowe, reported to be a fortune hunter, which, as vice-president of the Equitable Life empire, he probably was not, and handsome, which he undoubtedly was. She wrote him impassioned love letters and they both grew less and less circumspect until the widespread gossip reached her shocked and worried parents. They tried persuasion and threats but Charlotte ran off with her lover to Europe, leaving a husband whose ranting challenges to duels blasted across the ocean fruitlessly. Some say it was Drayton's ultimate revenge, some say it was Borrowe himself who did it but, by one means or another, the New York *Sun* got hold of Charlotte's outpourings and published them. Father William chased around trying to get her back and, as a last resort, cut Charlotte out of his will. The affair and the clamorous scandal went on for some years, only somewhat dulled by the divorce decree granted Drayton in 1896. Instead of marrying Borrowe, however, Charlotte turned to someone new to take for a husband. Her mother, Caroline, usually pictured as a lifeless mummy in the most magnificent of cases, was a devoted mother throughout. After her husband's death she rearranged matters so that the wayward daughter received some of the inheritance and, when Charlotte returned to New York, insisted on inviting her and her husband to exclusive functions.

As the young took social prominence, rivalries between the Astors stiffened. When Augusta's son, William Waldorf, installed himself and his young wife in one of the most extravagant of Newport mansions, Beaulieu, Aunt Caroline had her printer eliminate the name William from her calling card; she was *the* Mrs. Astor and mail was to be addressed to her in that fashion. However, William W., as competitive as his aunt, insisted that his wife receive her letters as "Mrs. Astor, Newport." "Mrs. Astor" had become a title worthy of royal conflicts and papal schisms. The older Mrs. Astor won out—hers was the greater tenacity—and William W., in any case, was directing himself to thoughts of becoming an English aristocrat when the time was ripe. Autocrat he had been for a long time, from birth. He was of imposing physique, well-educated, capable, snobbish and disagreeable. The business life, although it eventually yielded him eighty million dollars, was not for him; politics promised greater power and prestige. Although they were not nominally of the same party, he had help from Tweed in becoming a member of the New York State Assembly. Disdainful as he professed to be of the real estate business, he tried to push a bill through that would reduce from ten cents to five the fare on the New York elevated railroads—then controlled by Jay Gould and partners—so that Astor lands in the Bronx might become more accessible and valuable. Gould, Russell Sage and Belmont were quicker and had more persuasive friends in Albany; the bill failed. He tried again, this time to have the Croton Reservoir, too public a place and too near his his house and properties, filled. There, too, he was defeated and consequently made it his business, it was said, to defeat any measure, no matter what its merits, introduced by any assemblyman who had crossed him. Congress didn't want him either when he tried for it though he spent freely on electioneering and buying votes, according to the newspapers.

Escape from the country he hated, its institutions and disrespectful newspapers, came when he was appointed minister to Italy by President Arthur. He was in his element, in an ambience that suited princes and Waldorf Astors, a magnificent historic palazzo and great paintings. He studied the lives of powerful Renaissance dukes to whom he felt closely allied and used them in writing historical romances which earned him no encomiums as a new literary star. Defeat again, as with politics and Caroline, and once again, when he hired genealogists to prove that Astors were descendants of noblemen. The experts he hired produced a seventeenth-century Frenchman named d'Astorg and before him a Crusader, Pedro d'Astorga, killed in the Holy Wars early in the twelfth century. A nasty newspaper followed up with its own genealogical study, which traced the family back to a Jewish doctor, Isaac Astorg.

William Waldorf Astor was brought back to New York by the election of Grover Cleveland in 1884. Unfortunately this was one of the periods of vociferous complaints about slum conditions. He managed to have himself appointed to an investigative and reform commission and the public roared with rage. He was infuriated by this act of lèse majesté but did unload a large block of his foulest tenements. He bore it all like an English gentleman: the hated cousin, John Jacob IV; his Aunt Caroline; his torpid wife who preferred good works to social competition; his political defeats; the sniping by newspapers. When his father died in 1890, leaving him immensely rich, he announced that he was going to live in England, the only place a civilized man could live, and where his children's lives would not be threatened, as they were in New York. He was on his way, slowed by initial English resistance, to becoming an English baron and then a viscount. He was to be the owner of Cliveden and Hever Castle, the latter once a property of Anne Boleyn's family and given, after her head rolled, to a later wife, Anne of Cleves, by Henry VIII. More importantly, he would in time control an imposing segment of the British press.

Before William Waldorf settled overseas, however, there were a few matters to take care of in New York. He had the masterly notion of razing his father's house and overshadowing his aunt's four stories with the massive size, turrets and bubbled finials of the Waldorf Hotel. His incensed aunt hung on under the vulgar cliff for a year, then she moved to one of the last of the Hunt chateaux, at Sixty-fifth Street and Fifth Avenue. Her son, John J., thought of reviving an old trick he had tried on a synagogue that sat next to one of his properties—put stables on his grounds and stink the Jews out. The state legislature passed a bill to stop him but the friendly governor returned his right to him, by which time he was bored with the idea. But wouldn't it be fun to demolish his mother's house now and put stables there, to stink up William's resplendent hotel? But since they were in business together—their joint fortune estimated at two hundred million—John thought again and decided to join his cousin in the hotel business. They relegated competition to the splendors they hung on their wives, to their literary prowess —John Jacob was a dabbler in science fiction—and to nasty public statements about each other. John wanted to name his adjoining hotel Schermerhorn for his mother but William wouldn't have it, so they called the new, taller section "Astoria" for the dream city John Jacob I had hoped to develop as part of his fur-trapping empire. The contract signed by the cousins stipulated that the connection between the two hotel units could be sealed off and made separate should the alliance become insupportable.

The money flooded in; profits from the bar, despite the gargantuan free lunches, were great enough to carry the total overhead. From the beginning, the thousand bedrooms were fully booked, the ballroom radiant with the glory of the fifteen hundred guests it was designed to hold. The hotel had, for its time, a wealth of bathrooms, many ample suites and a generous variety of public rooms. Some of the furnishings had come from the demolished Astor houses; for much of the rest, agents armed with three hundred thousand dollars had scoured Europe. The total cost was trumpeted as a million dollars. "The largest hotel in the world" and one of the most expensive—potent phrases— took unto itself the functions and show that had been earlier limited to Madison Square.

Gambling salons lost some of their trade to the gaming establishment set up in one man's Waldorf suite—the twenty-thousand-dollar apartment of "Bet-a-Million" (John W.) Gates. He was a coarse man who was adroit at devising trust combinations, his peak achievement the plan for the United States Steel Corporation, which combined the might of Frick, Carnegie, Rockefeller and Morgan holdings to make a billion-dollar monopoly. In spite of his usefulness Morgan loathed him and was influential in having him frozen out of the New York Stock Exchange. Gates could always console himself by gambling, on the comparative speed of two bits of paper being blown across the street, on the duration of a rainstorm, on the potential of stock issues, as well as on the classic games of chance. As much as a million dollars a night crossed the tables in his apartment. Poker stakes ran to a thousand dollars in an atmosphere that was private and relaxed with late suppers provided by a chef who

earned ten thousand dollars a year. Delmonico's lost some of
its custom to the Waldorf's Men's Bar, large, comfortable and
superbly stocked, where, after the Stock Exchange closed, the
lords of industry—Frick, Morgan, Gary, Guggenheim, Whitneys
—consolidated their control of the country's economy.

Considerably before it was ready for use the hotel was
heavily publicized by the Philadelphia hotelier George C.
Boldt, whose key word was "exclusivity." Functionaries had
to be clean and smooth-shaven, an edict that brought him into
conflict with the unions and produced welcome publicity. He
won that battle, and the right to hire desk people who could
understand and respond in French and German as well as
English. To dine in the most resplendent of the hotel's restaurants, guests were required to wear evening clothes. Since many
of the most spectacular evening robes and jewels were carried in
by goddesses of the stage accompanied by their rich protectors,
"exclusivity" took on flexible meanings. The atmosphere was
heady, spicy, laced with whispers that ran in the wake of silks
and furs.

Henry James, who visited the Waldorf on his return from
England in 1905 and reported it in *The American Scene*, saw
the hotel as a triumph of publicity and organization. "Here is
a world whose relation to its form and medium was practically
imperturbable; here was a conception of publicity as the vital
medium organized with the authority with which the American
genius for organization, put on its mettle, alone could organize
it. The whole thing remains for me, however, I repeat, a gorgeous golden blue, a paradise peopled with unmistakable
American shapes, yet in which, the general and the particular,
the organized and the extemporized, the element of ingenuous
joy below and of consummate management above, melted together and left one uncertain which of them one was, at a given
turn of the maze, most admiring."

The imperial thumbs up–thumbs down gesture was the
privilege of the maître, Oscar, a now faded legend who had

learned all the gradations of social discrimination in a studious career at Delmonico's and the Hoffman House. The especial kind of resolute snob only a maître can be, he was also a practical man. If really big money, no matter what its provenance, confronted him, he usually gave it the approving nod as he did the Bradley-Martins of no remarkable origin (Troy, New York) but freighted with sacks of gold and given to displays of it that convinced even Mrs. Astor to disregard their lineage and recognize them. The Bradley-Martins—the hyphen was a Big City acquisition—inspired by the hunger and despair of a city immobilized by the depression of 1896, decided to give a charity ball. The Astoria was not yet ready but the Waldorf would do for magnificent entertainment that would provide hundreds of people with jobs. Well in advance of the event Mrs. Martin had her social staff send out twelve hundred invitations requesting that her guests, dressed for the court at Versailles in the time of Louis XV, appear on February 10, 1897. Well before the ball took place it was a significant public event; the hosts saw to that by sending frequent bulletins to the newspapers. The moralists of the press, politicians eager for the popular ear and the clergy castigated the hostess and her friends for their widely published expenditures, the cost of costumes, of decor, supper, wines, service. The street-floor windows of the hotel were boarded, detectives were hired to appear as guests ready to guard the others against theft and political violence. A large platoon of police, directed by the head of the New York City Police Board, Theodore Roosevelt, watched for sounds and gestures of outrage among the spectators massed on the streets to observe the parade of carriages and the descent of complex coiffures, diamond-buttoned brocades, beauty patches on powdered faces, the silken hose and high-heeled shoes of the friends of Louis.

The guests entered a dell of roses falling in showers, of chandeliers dripping orchids, mirrors and pillars garlanded with yet more roses and orchids—five thousand orchids in all.

Surrounded by the dainty curlicues that stood for Versailles, Mrs. Martin, with the stolid face of a tough peasant, sat on a throne on a lofty platform dressed like a queen, the wrong queen. She had decided to become Mary Stuart. Her jewelry, however, was closer to the prescribed period and place; it included a ponderous ruby necklace that had once adorned the neck of Marie Antoinette and a handful of diamonds that Louis XIV had sprinkled over himself. Her compliant husband dressed as Louis XV, but some of the seven hundred guests had other notions. Mrs. Astor came in a costume designed by Worth that resembled her Durant portrait, herself seemingly the only royalty worth representing. One gentleman decided to come as an Indian in full feathered headdress, carrying a dangle of scalps. A Belmont appeared in full armor, making no secret of the fact that it had set him back ten thousand dollars. After a liveried attendant had called up to the hostess on the dais the name of each guest, his assumed identity and his place in history, the ball opened with quadrilles and cotillions which took weeks to rehearse and hours to perform. To sweeten the hard work, the guests were given goodies of jeweled favors. An enormous supper and hundreds of bottles of wine served by waiters in powdered wigs and knee breeches were worked off with more impromptu, less courtly dances. When the three bands which contributed nonstop music and the guests finally put on their wraps and left in the four hundred carriages their hosts had supplied, the rest of New York was rising for its twelve- and fourteen-hour work day, if it was working at all.

Much to Mrs. Martin's surprise her benevolent gesture (Hadn't hundreds of seamstresses profited from weeks of costume making, hadn't the hairdressers hired to see to the guests' coiffures been well paid and tipped into the bargain? The extra waiters, the musicians, the employees of the hotel which had charged her nine thousand dollars for rooms and help, hadn't they all benefited?) misfired. New York didn't look kindly on her charity. Nasty reports and sharp satire followed closely on the outrageous extravaganza. Then the city decided that the host's taxes should be doubled. Moralists enjoyed saying that the Bradley-Martins were hounded out of New York City by the combination of taxes and opprobrium. Not quite hounded, nor fleeing in shame, they took the time to stage a farewell dinner at the newly opened Waldorf-Astoria, limited to eighty or so friends whose fortunes ran to tens of millions. The feast was supervised by Oscar at a cost of over one hundred dollars per person, a fact not hidden from the public. The Bradley-Martins then took off for England to swing handsomely and unabashed in Europe, helped by a daughter who had captured a title.

Subsequent balls were, for a while, more circumspect and a curious public had to satisfy itself with keeping an eye on the hotel's Peacock Alley, theater and nonstop fashion show, which was a high-class meat rack of sleek, eager-eyed ladies and school to the many poorer girls who studied their dress and techniques. The hotel claimed that an impossible twenty-five thousand people sauntered through the Alley every day under the surveillance of an entranced and wordy press—no entertainment, no gathering of notables unheralded. The Waldorf-Astoria was the court that fed America its fantasies of the good life. Not many American families could serve fat clusters of perfect grapes in February, nor import nightingales to sing on the branches of imported trees; nor could they spend two hundred fifty dollars per person for dinner, as was done at a party for forty Tammany leaders. But there are social historians who insist that the Waldorf improved cuisine in ambitious houses or, at the least, inspired experimentation.

The hotel, in the vanguard of minor female emancipation, admitted women without escorts and closed its eyes to ladies who smoked in the public rooms. In time it had to shift again the meaning of exclusivity. Money was, in any case, moving to uptown hotels, and the Waldorf began to welcome the bizarre, the artistic and literary who kept its memory brightly sweet with reminiscences after the demise of what they liked to call a "colorful caravansary." In that caravansary was one unique, strident and still beautiful international gypsy, Isadora Duncan. She had married the Russian poet Esenin in 1922 so that he might come with her to the United States which would not otherwise admit him. They moved into the Waldorf, an extraordinary choice of housing for a child of the Russian Revolution and, for that matter, his considerably older wife—she was in her mid-forties to his twenty-seven—who considered herself as well a child of that Revolution. They unfurled and waved the red flag literally and figuratively wherever they were, in newspaper interviews, from the hotel, in Carnegie Hall, in Boston's Symphony Hall, calling "Long live Bolshevism!" He was already half-mad and obstreperous, she as often as not drunk and given to lecturing her audiences about real beauty, baring a breast or two in the process, insistently exhorting them to follow the red star. A good portion of her audience came to see an exhibitionistic madwoman, the rest were offended. Engagements were canceled, the money ran thin and they moved on, he to total madness and suicide, she to a macabre death a few years later.

As the inevitable reverse alchemy, gold into dross, took the environs of the Waldorf-Astoria, the dependent cafes and the art galleries, the sybaritic restaurants and gaming houses moved on and up, leaving vacuums for eager merchandise to fill. Altman's, which had occupied Astor lots on Sixth Avenue, one strand of the "Ladies Mile," led off the rush. Still an Astor lessee on its new site diagonally across from the Waldorf, Altman's built solidly, with a dignity that suggested a temple. That was in 1906. In 1907, Oppenheim Collins came to Fifth Avenue across from Altman's, and soon after, Best and Company settled at the corner of Thirty-fifth Street. Tiffany's followed to occupy number 409, at the southeast corner of Thirty-seventh Street, designed as a Venetian palace by McKim and Mead. On the southwest corner of Thirty-sixth Street, a more subtle and graceful Italianate building designed for a competitor, Gorham, by the same architects. The land rental they paid the Astors was thirty-six thousand dollars a year.

The southeast corner was bought by George Boldt, the martinet hotel manager of the Waldorf-Astoria. He paid $1,200,000 and within a short time sold it for $2,000,000. He had been urged to buy the property, obviously in a booming area, by the Astors, an act which points up a curious conservatism in the family. Both William in England and John Jacob in New York were aware of the explosion of land values; there was ample money and credit for expansion and great profits in selling. But the Astors didn't trade much anymore; they held on to what they had, increasing rentals as leases expired, rather than engage in the turnover of land that made many real estate speculators very rich, particularly after subways were opened in 1904 and stretched the dimensions of the city. Had they the ancestral boldness and imagination, they might have nudged Morgan out of the running for first billionaire. It was predicted in 1908 that the Astors would be worth eighty billion dollars by the year 2000, a prophecy that overlooked the tricks played by chance and nature which produced a few remarkable—in several senses of that word—later Astors.

CHAPTER 5

THE FORTIES

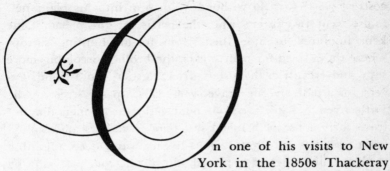

n one of his visits to New York in the 1850s Thackeray made a "long voyage" from his club near Washington Square to a famous country estate on Thirty-seventh to Thirty-eighth Streets near Fifth Avenue. The stylish suburban-Gothic villa whose distinctive portrait appeared in contemporary periodicals was built, in the mid-1840s, for W. Coventry Waddell, a close friend of Andrew Jackson who had made a fortune as financial consultant to the Jackson administration. Placed on high ground that cost something over $9,000, Mr. Waddell's house was a collection of crenellated turrets, slotted towers, gables and bay windows that was described by a Waddell relative as a caster of mustard pot, pepper bottles and vinegar cruet. A winding staircase led to a tower that gave views of the city to the south, the farms and lines of cattle to the north and the Hudson and the East rivers. The house saw distinguished guests and poured good wine until financial reverses struck Mr. Waddell down in 1857. The villa was razed and the newly leveled ground sold for almost ten times the original price.

As the villa disappeared, a conventional four-story brownstone was rising at the northwest corner of Fifth Avenue at Thirty-ninth Street. It was the property of a sour man, John G. Wendel, who had inherited valuable pieces of Manhattan real estate. John G. never parted with a piece of land and was distrustful of agents; he collected his own rents, would never give more than a three-year lease (never at all to a saloon) and made no improvements in his properties; tenants must pay the costs of repairs or do without. With him into his plain new house went two sisters, who, the persistent gossip had it, he kept immured to hide them from fortune-hunting suitors. There they stayed for many years, the brother becoming more testy and eccentric, the sisters drier, dustier, more timid. Except for a dash by one brave sister, Ella, up the street to the Fifth Avenue Bank for household cash, the women did not leave their house of blanked street-floor windows and unused front door. Its only conspicuous luxury was a deep adjoining yard in which their dog played, closed off from passersby by a tall fence. After their brother's death, the old ladies remained in the house, the sole heirs—along with a sister who had managed to marry—of $80,000,000 in real estate. The house was assessed in 1910 for only $5,000; the land at $1,897,000.

Through the rise and fall of the Waddell Villa, and the long purdah of the Wendel sisters, the Croton Reservoir at 42nd Street and Fifth Avenue continued to shine within its high sloped walls, suggestive of truncated pyramid walls, a wonder to admire for its bold style and as prophecy of progress.

On July 12, 1842, the diarist Philip Hone took his wife to see the newly built reservoir. Having admired the "pretty limpid, placid Mediterranean" pool of wholesome temperance beverage, he drank a tumblerful and found it "clear, sweet, soft, well calculated to cool the palates and quench the thirst of the New Yorkers, and to diminish the losses of the fire insurance companies." (Hone was an officer of an insurance firm that suffered severe losses after the great fire of 1835.) He was impressed by the walls, buttresses, towers, gates and the effect "of solid masses of gray granite elaborately finished" and the "wide flagged walk that surrounds the whole which will form a delightful promenade for the millions who will visit in all

future time for centuries after the present generation shall
have passed away." For a man who complained of the constant tearing down and building up in the city, this was a
curious thing to say and certainly proof that the reservoir was
an imposing monument, comparable to the Seven Wonders of
antiquity. The whole city turned out to celebrate its awesome
new possession in perfect order and propriety, Hone said. "The
moral as well as the physical influence of the water pervaded
everything," meaning that there were comparatively few drunks
around. A young reporter experienced water and celebration
quite differently: "Croton water . . . is full of tadpoles and
animalculae," some of the system purportedly used "as a
necessary by all the Hibernian vagabonds who worked upon
it." The celebration was the "usual amount of claptrappery
and stuff and humbug and rowdyism."

Water supply brought in, tadpoles or no, New York was
ready to present the first American World's Fair. The project
took its inspiration from Queen Victoria's Prince Albert who
had promoted a collection of international arts, crafts and
samples of industries, and to house it all, an attractive eccentric building, in reality a gigantic greenhouse, designed by
the gardener of a ducal home. London's Exposition in its house
of glass and ironwork embroidery was a notable success. Why
not arrange such a fair in Madison Square, a potential part of
the city in 1850? Protests from the houses near the Square were
instant and vigorous; a fair would entice too many common
people and their vulgar entertainments. Why not, instead, use
Reservoir Square (erstwhile potter's field, future Bryant Park)
west of the reservoir and free of any significant housing. The
building model was, of course, to be London's engagingly
androgynous Crystal Palace.

A well-connected committee was formed, architects cho-
sen, exhibitors solicited and in July, 1853, the Crystal Palace
Fair was opened with an address by President Franklin Pierce.
As in all such enterprises, commerce was twinned with ideals

of moral and cultural improvement. Subtitles to a flood of engravings that tried to capture the charms of the huge, light cage, spoke insistent leitmotifs of hope: that the fair would put an end to disunion, that riffraff might learn good manners under the influence of the refined exhibits, that slum children would profit from contact with people and things cultivated. Among the reiterated hopes for creating almost instantly a civilized city was an interesting statement of purpose, readying for fruition in England as William Morris and Company: "We would not confine the influence of Art to work purely ornamental, to statues, vases and pictures," but looking forward to an era "when art works are no longer a monopoly, but an everyday possession, within the reach of the mechanic and tradesman as well as the opulent and noble."

The items displayed were hardly all design pioneers but there were, in the vaulting space that sang optimism, the most efficient and newest improvements on machines in several fields—large, well-turned plows, a machine for pressing tobacco more effectively, the latest in Singer sewing machines, a model of Morse's telegraphy instrument, new printing presses, more powerful pumps and a series of valves and coils that produced drinking soda, a recent wonder. There were handsome hardware displays and innovations in furnishings, one of them a sofa for two with a gaming board embedded in the middle. There were beguiling nooks like lacy boudoirs that showed off soaps and perfumes, dreamy niches that enclosed ornaments and silks and, in multitudes, the popular art of the time. Swans and eagles, imprisoned as carvings in furniture or flying free; naked ladies horizontal and vertical, shriven for their nudity by classical names; huge dogs and delicate deer; hundreds of vases in tortured silver; romantic figurines with a harem flavor; timid angels and not quite carefree fauns. The most curious creation, a very popular attraction, was a tight cageful of cupids, some alert and others wasting away, who were an Italian's protest against the destruction of sexual love by Victorian mores.

In the street, no art, no progress, no enlightenment. Surrounding lots had been grabbed up by whiskey stalls, freak shows, gambling, half-hour brothels and, on the north side of Forty-second Street, Warren Latting's tower. A slender cone of braced iron 350 feet tall, it had cost one hundred thousand dollars to build. It held a refreshment parlor and, above, was pitted with thirty-three view landings, the highest—three hundred feet—achieved by an uncertain lift. But the views available from the walls of the reservoir were free and less hazardous, refreshment was available at the tree-ringed Croton Cottage Tavern, a block below, and the Willow Tree Inn, attached to a meat market diagonally to the north. After the first rush of New Yorkers who surged toward anything new, Latting's tower failed. It was sold and burned down three years after its rise; arson, they said.

Its neighbor, the Great Crystal Hope, wasn't doing too well, either. In spite of its wonders, the fair never quite took. Running expenses were high and tickets were not selling; unpaid debts rose and stock value dropped. In desperation, the Fair Association called on P. T. Barnum who might revive it if anyone could. The resourceful showman tried concerts and patriotic celebrations, he advertised imaginatively and vigorously, but even he could not breathe life into the moribund enterprise. Early in November of 1854, less than a year and a half after the grand opening, the New York Crystal Palace, dragging a debt of three hundred thousand dollars, called a halt. There was a flash of activity now and then, a publishers' fair, a reception for Cyrus W. Field when the first transatlantic cable was laid in 1858, but nothing that would sustain the building. On October 5, 1858, with about two thousand people wandering its broad aisles looking at diminished examples of the goods it still held, the palace burst into flames. Although more than two dozen fire hoses streamed water on the fire, the destruction was complete, with losses estimated at two million dollars. Again they said it was arson (the building was heavily insured) and jeered at the promoters who had called the building fireproof. Although few merchants could rescue their goods, the fire was not without some profit: bits of glass fused by the fire and metal distorted by the heat were offered for sale as souvenirs worthy of curio cabinets.

Across from the Crystal Palace and the adjoining reservoir, along Forty-first to Forty-second on Fifth Avenue, there were eleven attached houses in the tight-cheeked, Victorian-Gothic manner of their time, rather more attractive than most because they were more amply windowed and less rigidly cadenced. This was the "House of Mansions" also known as the "Spanish Row," of "cheerful tint and variegated architecture," built in 1856 by a carpet manufacturer. The windows were said to give unrivaled views of the whole island, the spaces and arrangements "suitable to the most fastidious tastes." Those tastes were not quite ready. The site was too far uptown and the project failed although only a decade later Commodore Vanderbilt judged the grounds of the defunct Croton Cottage, a short distance below the Spanish Row, worth the eighty thousand dollars he paid for them. During that decade Rutgers Female Cottage, the first institution of higher education for young women in the city, moved from its quarters on Madison Avenue to the northern section of the House of Mansions and stayed until 1883, more solidly grounded—or luckier—than neighbors torn apart at the start of the Civil War.

Hostilities that had been brewing for many years between pro- and antislavery factions had grown sharper and angrier. Irish immigrants chose not to fight in behalf of "niggers," who would, as free men, threaten their jobs. Nor were they inspired by the knowledge that the scions of prosperous houses might buy, at the going price of three hundred dollars, the services of substitutes. The city was already a tinderbox, in short, when an encampment of Union troops took over the site of Latting's tower in 1862.

Early in July of 1863, draft offices were opened and the names of draftees, chosen by lottery, published. The first draft day, Saturday the eleventh, was quiet. Early on Sunday huge mobs began to organize, according to some observers, on seemingly well-laid plans. Telegraph lines to police stations were cut and railroad tracks ripped up; mobs armed with clubs, knives and guns forced people out of factories and workshops; draft offices were plundered and burned. One group marched on the house of Mayor Opdyke on Fifth Avenue to sack it and were turned away by a persuasive Tweed judge. Several thousand men took over the arms and ammunition of a munitions factory guarded by thirty-five policemen. The police escaped but some of the mob who forced their way into the building to burn it after the sacking were trapped in ensuing explosions. The rampaging thousands beat and kicked soldiers and policemen; a colonel was battered to death, his corpse hung from a lamppost, his head used for target practice. Blacks were hunted and killed, their corpses placed on bonfires ringed by dancing, singing mobs.

One frenzied mass, drunk on triumph and whiskey, accompanied by its women and children, took to Fifth Avenue, destroying Croton Cottage and Allerton's Tavern on their way to the Colored Orphan Asylum which they intended to burn down, orphans and all. The asylum, a large four-story building that occupied most of the block from Forty-third to Forty-fourth Street on Fifth Avenue, had been organized in 1836 by a group of New York women who were granted the land by the city to provide housing and training for homeless black children. In the summer of 1863 the institution held 233 orphans, none over twelve years old and some under two. The local police took all the children they could round up quickly to the precinct station just before the hordes arrived to wreck and loot the orphanage, stealing what it could take away and setting fire to what it couldn't. They found about twenty children and threatened to hang them, with several black men they had picked up, in the garden trees. A party of firemen with the help of several stage drivers of the Forty-second Street line rescued the children and the older blacks and sequestered them in nearby police stations. After destroying the asylum, the gangs moved on the Willow Tree Inn at Forty-fourth Street but left it intact because it was run by a prize ring hero with strong Tammany connections.

Troops were called in from harbor posts and volunteer citizens joined the police force but the pillage and murder went on. Shops and banks were closed; all transportation stopped. The city was a hell of flames and smoke amid the cacophony of fire bells. When their barricades of telegraph poles and heaped wagons were pierced, the rioters climbed up to roofs to thunder down bricks and rocks. The police followed when they could, and threw some of the offenders onto the pavement. On Thursday, July 16, five regiments of New York troops were returned by the Army of the Potomac. By midnight the military and police were in control and held control as more regiments moved in.

On Friday morning, newspapers resumed publication, business began to function tentatively, burned docks and ferry stops were cleared of debris and prepared for reconstruction, damage statistics were gathered and issued. In four days one thousand, two hundred people had been killed. Some estimated a higher number to include many corpses slipped into the rivers and carried out to sea. The vast number of injured was never known. Property loss amounted to at least two million dollars. The military stayed, and one month later, the draft was resumed on the same arrangement as before though the price of substitutes went up. George Strong reports that he hired a sturdy German boy for over a thousand dollars, a boy who would make a good soldier. His uneasy conscience made the diarist record that he had insisted the boy write him

KATE SIMON

if he were wounded or in any trouble that his sponsor might help remedy.

After the Civil War, the Fifth Avenue spaces earlier used by livestock, farm cottages and taverns were filled with brownstones. One of them was the rather simple house at Fortieth and Fifth Avenue that William Henry Vanderbilt, principal heir of the Commodore, inherited as part of his ninety-million-dollar legacy. He had, in his heir-apparent days, picked up American paintings and now, as the master of a stunning fortune, he needed more picture space for more imposing and fashionable art. The house was too small, too ordinary; he had to expand. His wife, quite contented with 450 Fifth Avenue, suggested he add a gallery to the house as a number of his contemporaries had; but that wasn't what he wanted and, as the 1880s arrived, he established the Vanderbilt Kingdom a half-mile to the north. He turned the Fortieth Street house over to his son, Frederick, the "quiet" Vanderbilt, better educated than his brothers, more charitable, less avid for the public eye and immune to pressures for social supremacy. Frederick carefully watched the growth of the colossi of industry and invested the twenty million inherited from his father in oil, mines, tobacco and steel, besides the family holdings in railroads. He died at the age of eighty-one, the richest of the four brothers, with an estate valued at between seventy-two and seventy-seven million dollars before taxes. The Fortieth Street property had been turned over to his wife's niece and, in 1914, to the venerable Arnold Constable department store which had hopped northward from its Pine Street beginnings in 1825, to hang on and hang on until its demise in 1975.

In 1836 the block that became cattle yards and Allerton's northeast of the reservoir had cost Thomas Darling eighty-eight thousand dollars. A much larger piece of property, fifty-five acres that included the east side of Fifth Avenue along Forty-fifth to Forty-eighth streets, was disposed of as common land to Thomas Buchanan for seventy-four hundred dollars in 1805; it was worth twenty million dollars a century later. (Buchanan also bought land along the East River between Fifty-fourth and Fifty-seventh streets, his country seat. After his death in 1815, his holdings came under the control of two Goelets who had married Buchanan's daughters and thus was established the Goelets' fief in that part of the city.)

Shortly after the cattle yards were moved to new railroad sidings on Eleventh Avenue, the Fifth Avenue land was cleared and filled by John H. Sherwood, a pioneer builder of the residential splendor that began to crop up north of Forty-second Street. The Fifth Avenue Bank established itself in the basement of his house, paying a rental of two thousand, six hundred dollars a year, including utilities. Later the bank took over the house of John B. Cornelle at Forty-fourth Street and Fifth, built in 1866, and later still the adjoining house, to become the hushed, legendary bank of courtly manners and elderly furnishings for the comfort of rich old ladies who could maintain a minimum balance of twenty-five thousand dollars in their checking accounts, among them the one audacious Miss Wendel.

The house that stood at the northeast corner of Forty-second Street had several distinctions. It was the property of Levi P. Morton, one of the city's numerous "shrewd Yankees," who had come from clerking in a Vermont country store to a dry goods business in New York, to banking, to a seat in Congress, to the ambassadorship to France, to the vice-presidency, to the governorship of the state. Since his particular congressional field was currency flow and other financial concerns, and he had experience as a banker during the Civil War and after, he managed to accrue a sound fortune that flourished until his death at ninety-four, and after. One of the daughters of the house acquired a title when that became a required culminating gesture of riches. The house was also the setting of a lavish, formal debut for a daughter of a good Madison

Square family, Edith Jones, who would soon become Edith Jones Wharton of Twenty-fifth Street west of Fifth Avenue.

The Croton Reservoir was covered over early in the twentieth century and the New York Public Library began its slow Beaux Arts growth in the white convoluted style made fashionable by the 1893 Chicago Columbian Exposition. Designed by Carrère and Hastings, an architectural firm that ranked with McKim, Mead and White, it was finished in 1911, having absorbed nine million dollars and a great deal of criticism: too much space wasted on show, lumpish with too many heavy details, and so on, in the indigenous New York, instant-connoisseur manner. Some of the criticism seemed justified and Thomas Hastings, after the death of Carrère in 1911, kept trying to redesign the front, a continuously troublesome thing that affected Mrs. Hastings, his widow, as well. Among other bequests, she left a fund for possible alterations to the façade.

The contents of the immensity of white Vermont marble derived from several sources, one a combination of fear and insomnia. Like many rich men of his time, the first Astor was not given to philanthropy; the poor deserved their destitution, planned by God. Fiercely averse to giving, Astor was forced to become a bibliophile by Joseph Green Cogswell, a schoolteacher who came to live with the old gentleman when the children had moved to their own houses and Astor became fearful of being alone, especially through long, wakeful nights. Cogswell used the loneliness as a lever to pry book money out of Astor by threatening to leave—he was once actually on the verge of going to Spain with Washington Irving when the latter became ambassador to Spain. A friend reported that "Mr. Cogswell . . . does not go. Mr. Astor who enjoys his society, has bribed him to remain . . . offered him a permanent salary as librarian of a great public library which Mr. Astor has signified his intention to establish and endow in this city. . . . Maecenas keeps Horace near him and Horace knows when he has a good thing."

Although he did consent to let Cogswell buy books, Astor himself bought only one book, an Audubon *Birds of America* for a thousand dollars, a sum, gossip-history has it, that Audubon had difficulty collecting. The friend reported "Old Astor . . . has become more disposed of late than formerly to give of his abundance. He begins to grow old." And he grew old stubbornly, serving fine dinners that were fed to him as he sat, like an old king, feeble but still sharp, in his ermine cap. According to one biographer of the Astors, Lucy Kavaler, he was tossed in a blanket when he could no longer manage exercise and fed wet-nurse milk when he could no longer tolerate other food. He died in March of 1848: "Bowed down with bodily infirmities for a long time, he has gone at last, and left reluctantly his unbounded wealth."

While Cogswell roamed Europe for books, son William B. furnished the stately Astor Library, on Lafayette Street across from the colonnaded Astor dwellings and the houses of neighbors selected by the Astors so that their property might stay valuably exclusive. The library was opened in 1854 with eighty thousand books to be read there and not by anyone under fourteen. Shortly after, Cogswell, horrified by the "trashy books"—Hawthorne, Dickens, Thackeray, Cooper—that young people were reading, his schoolmaster soul outraged because boys studying the classics copied translations in his library, had the minimum age for admission changed to sixteen. No one, brash boy or serious scholar, was permitted to roam the stacks. In spite of the restrictions and Cogswell's nervous supervision, it was a unique and invaluable library, well-stocked, free and accumulating rarities.

James Lenox, born in 1800, made his money the easy way. He inherited three million dollars and spent little of it except on books. In contrast to the shows of luxuriant "European" tastes and entertainments costing twenty thousand dollars per month in wines alone that August Belmont put on a short distance from him on lower Fifth Avenue, Lenox rarely entertained, except for visits with other Lenoxes. In a neighborhood of luminous Oriental carpets and crystal chandeliers, Lenox kept a careless house with stringy, graying curtains that appalled his house-proud neighbors. He continued to cling to his old house while the trendy moved northward, but for his invaluable books he had Richard Morris Hunt build the sober, dignified Lenox Library on Fifth Avenue between Seventieth and Seventy-first streets on inherited land which he had been told not to sell since the city must inevitably reach it and increase its value manyfold. (Father was right; the farmland he bought for forty thousand dollars in 1820 was worth ten million in 1915.) The library opened in 1875 with eighty-five thousand books and an endowment of more than a half-million dollars, its use limited to scholars.

Eleven years later, Samuel J. Tilden, who had been governor of New York, died, leaving an endowment of two million dollars for a free library. While the major libraries were being established, a group of Grace Church ladies organized a small library open only two hours a week and so overwhelmingly attended that additional places of the same modest kind appeared shortly. With help from the city, they were consolidated as the New York Free Circulating Library and added to the joined Astor-Lenox-Tilden core. These coalitions and the $5,200,000 left by Andrew Carnegie, formed the many-branched New York Public Library system.

Considerably before the libraries big and small were melded, the area around Forty-second and Fifth sported a new exotic bloom. Among the brownstones north of the Rutgers Female College rose the bulbous Byzantine towers of the first Temple Emanu-El, ready for use in 1868. Its congregation, which had had to make do on its hegira uptown with a converted courthouse and two converted churches, consisted of Reformed German Jews. They eschewed the ancient observances of New York's first Jewish colony, the Sephardim who were as resistant to fraternization as Gentiles. Nor were they comfortable with the primitive wailing and ecstasy of the poor eastern European Jews, not yet arrived in great numbers, but their practices an embarrassment to the rational, enlightened Judaism of Germany.

The sumptuous brownstone at 511, sitting in the shadow of the temple bulbs, belonged to the man of the deftest Golden Touch, Boss William Marcy Tweed. He appeared in many New York contexts: Gould's Erie Railroads; cornering the city's printing for his own press; the building of Brooklyn Bridge; with the Astors in manipulating tax rates in their favor and blocking tenement reforms; in attempts to give away, at a price, pieces of Central Park; taking care of his voting poor; clearing, repairing and paving streets and dockyards at shameless profits. It was in this Fifth Avenue house, paid for by part of the two hundred million dollars he and his Ring had stolen from the city, that he was arrested in 1875. The police who came for him were careless, either on instructions or through their own stupidity, and Tweed disappeared into a rear alley that led to his yacht in the East River. He fled to Cuba and on to Spain which proved less safe than he had hoped; he was sent back to New York to die, in 1878, in the Ludlow Street jail.

The volatile society spotlight began to turn, as the century closed, toward the juncture of Forty-fourth Street and Fifth Avenue and rested there for its usual brief while. In spite of the Waldorf-Astoria's nonstop Arabian Nights, a few members of entrenched society clung to the privilege of untouchability and chose the more intimate delights of Sherry's and Delmonico's, for a surprisingly long time in the forefront of exclusive watering holes. After its long trek from William Street to Fourteenth Street to Madison Square, Delmonico's settled into the northeast corner of Forty-fourth Street, in a two-toned building crested with minuscule towers, ironwork frills around the windows and gay awnings that suggested cancan skirts. In spite of Delmonico's enticements, absolute supremacy in luxurious surroundings and provisions was captured by Louis Sherry, formerly of Thirty-sixth Street, who placed his new reception and dining halls and the rooms of a small hotel at 522, the southwest corner of Forty-fourth Street. The decorator was the indispensable Stanford White. Details authentic and inauthentic that recreated the court at Versailles were still the peak of fashion and White obliged, flamboyantly leaving not an inch of ballroom space nude or unfrenchified. Above a bank of long windows, a curlicued balcony and a heroic mural. Between fluted pilasters, large flowery medallions in rococo frames that spilled graceful fronds. In the sloped boxes that curved to the ceiling, grotesques and fancies, plump lozenges and schools of dancing nymphs. To illuminate the swarming fauna and flora, hundreds of winking chandelier crystals. The Sun King, lui même, couldn't have asked for better or more.

The glorious duo was joined by a third, the gaming house of Richard Canfield, which had lived near Delmonico's on Madison Square and followed it up to Forty-fourth Street. Canfield had spent prison time as a felon studying the arts and literature and the evolved life. By the time he opened his exclusive houses in Newport and Saratoga, and now the most exclusive of all, in New York, he was a cultivated gentleman, a discriminating collector of paintings and people. One of his friends, one of the few invited into Canfield's private apartment of pale mahogany touched with mother-of-pearl, a repository of rare books and paintings, was Leonard Jerome, who admired his "passion for the rare and beautiful (that) gives one a feeling that the man is alive, much more so than most clients." The usual client used other sections of the house; new millionaires and those on their way were ushered into public gaming rooms after they were warned that, in the long run, they would lose and must make sure they could afford to. The Whitneys, the Vanderbilts, the multimillionaires like

Bet-a-Million Gates who was known to play two days on end, used private rooms on another floor. No patron's name was ever spoken, only his initial used, and the settling of losses, at times into the hundreds of thousands, was very discreetly arranged in an office whose safe held half a million dollars in cash. As midnight approached, patrons were invited to a lordly supper; gaming houses provided some of the best meals in the city.

Canfield never gambled but grew rich on Wall Street information passed on by his clients and with that money he increased his collections, daring, as other collectors of his time did not, to invest in living artists, a breed he liked and understood. His friend, Whistler, who painted his portrait, was not too unlike himself, sharing contempt for ordinary ethics and morality, clear honesty about himself and his work, and a cool view of patrons. One entertaining group of patrons were the art dealers who paid him extravagantly to teach them the favorite card games of J. P. Morgan that they and their wares might be more pleasing to Il Magnifico. Well-dressed, well-spoken, well-mannered, impeccably honest in his own way and shielding himself from intimacies, Canfield was something of a man of mystery, his death yet another mysterious chapter in a guarded life. He was killed by the wheels of a bus; it may have been an accident, it may have been suicide.

By the time Delmonico's and Sherry's new lights were adjusted for making sallow complexions as sweetly rosy as cherubs' bottoms, Caroline Astor's social mentor had dwindled in reputation to a pale joke. The time had passed when a book like McAllister's sententious *Society as I Have Known It* and the antique rigidities it extolled could be taken seriously. Few appeared at McAllister's funeral in 1895; Caroline Astor didn't bother to cancel a dinner party when she heard of his death. The unrestrained twentieth century, a time for toppling fences, for aggressive court jesters and their uninhibited fancies, had about arrived. The Patriarchs' Balls had disappeared and Mystic Rose, who never before would dine in public, was persuaded by friends to appear at Sherry's one Sunday night in a revealing evening dress of white satin. These Sunday Sherry suppers, novel and chic, were early seeds of the locoweed, café society.

Sherry's was an accommodating place. Not even the exigencies of the aging, still redoubtable Mrs. Frank Leslie who, according to a contemporary photograph, was devoted to ultra clutter in a cluttered age, disturbed its smooth surface. She had always been a woman who knew her own tastes and mind, unafraid of her impulses and convictions. Like other career girls of the eighteenth and nineteenth centuries—Madam Jumel, Victoria Woodhull and her sister Tennessee Claflin, Nellie Bly and Lola Montez—Minnie Leslie made it any way she could out of New Orleans and into the big, promising American world. She was beautiful and clever, with a sharp eye and a talent for reporting what she saw. An early step outward was appearances with Lola Montez, Irish-born dancer and adventuress, who climbed to the court of Ludwig I of Bavaria as his mistress. Other early steps, common among the ambitious girls, led in and out of beds and then into a marriage that seemed promising and came to misery. After her divorce from a drunken madman named Squier, Minnie married Frank Leslie, the publisher of Frank Leslie's *Popular Monthly*, Frank Leslie's *Illustrated Paper* and several other successful publications. She traveled the country, visiting mining camps and Mormon settlements, dens of iniquity and the haunts of society, and wrote about it all. As the wife of the publisher, as writer and editor for Leslie's *Ladies' Gazette*, Minnie dressed extravagantly, always on effulgent show. Between trips they lived in fashionable boarding houses on Fifth Avenue, too wrapped up in their enterprises to bother with domestic details in a house of their own. When Leslie died in 1880, Minnie took over the Leslie publishing empire, continuing to travel in the United States and Europe to report on its fashion, manners and arts. After

nine frenetic years, she sold all the publications, retaining only
the most important and lucrative, Frank Leslie's *Popular
Monthly*. She continued to write, edit, translate where necessary, travel and display her astonishing wardrobe. In 1891
when she was in her mid-fifties, she married Oscar Wilde's
brother, Willie, the marriage celebrated with supper at Delmonico's and soon regretted. He, like her first husband, was
a drunkard and, unlike his brother, not interested in the word,
or anything but his shapeless pleasures. Two years was enough.
She divorced him and concentrated her energies on Women's
Suffrage. She left the movement something under a million
dollars after her death in 1914, aged seventy-eight, her adven-
turous and fruitful life shaping an ideal for women beginning
to reexamine their shackled lives.

Another female rebel Sherry's handled with consummate
poise was Isadora Duncan, who made one of her flamboyant
visits to New York at the end of World War I. The occasion
was a party given in her honor by Paris Singer, the sewing
machine heir and the father of her son, who had given her a
refulgent diamond necklace (one of many rich trinkets she
later pawned) to wear that night. Isadora became quite drunk
and, in her inevitable style, almost immediately amorous. The
magnet of her passion was not her rich protector but rather
a tango artist with whom she danced in unmistakable abandon.
The enraged Paris pulled her from her partner's arms and
pulled, as well, the tablecloth, crashing bowls of flowers and
fine glass to the floor. The unruffled waiters cleaned it all up
and were compensated generously for their trouble, as was
Sherry's for its table setting.

By the time of Isadora's gaudy night, Sherry's was well
practiced in not blinking at the farces and infantile fancies
acted out by clients, including bachelor parties of naked young
girls popping out of pies or a belly dance demonstration by
the noted artiste, Little Egypt. C.K.G. Billings, known as the
"American Horse King," celebrated the imminent opening of

his new quarter-million-dollar stable in 1903 by inviting thirty-six horse lovers to a "Horseback Dinner" at Sherry's. The floor was covered with shaggy, grassy material suitable to horses' feet, the burbling rococo of the walls was covered with large painted drops of rustic scenery, waiters appeared as hunting grooms and the guests greeted each other and raised their glasses from the backs of rented horses—Mr. Billings's racers were too skittish to be relied on.

Hardly had the country scenery been removed from the walls, the gilding retouched and equine odors scrubbed and aired out, when Sherry's returned to Frenchness in preparation for a combination of rarefied chic and yearning for publicity arranged by James Hazen Hyde in January of 1905. It was the first dinner-ball to be photographed, the photographers the Byrons, a family who recorded their times voluminously. The host was a passionate Francophile who felt he was a throwback to the times and manners of one French court or another. He wore the fine-pointed beard and sharply waxed mustaches that said "French" and could allow himself ancien régime affectations and extravagances because, at twenty-eight, he had inherited control of the Equitable Life Assurance Society and the several dozen corporations it controlled. Because of the Byzantine complexity of the organization, it had been shaky for a few years, a situation that in no way impeded the royal progress of the heir.

Dressed in satin knee breeches and as heavily bemedaled as befit a French superpatriot, he greeted his guests in yet another repetition of Versailles, the mandatory setting for feeding on ortolans and drinking the champagne of champagnes poured by servitors in court livery. The sixty tables held rose bushes at the peak of their blooming, masses of orchids frilled the walls. Mrs. Stuyvesant Fish wore a wide, puffed dress crisscrossed with lace and ribbons, her hair powdered and trailing several fat curls. Another guest came as Racine's Phèdre, so heavily hung with metallic cloth and plaques of turquoise that she required two little blackamoors to hold her train. Before they were fed, the guests were entertained by a leading ballerina of the opera and a gavotte performed by a number of young men and women of the best families. The French actress Réjane, then appearing on the stage in New York, took part in a playlet written for the occasion dressed in silks that shone and flickered like sun-touched water, on her head a flirtatious little tricorne. Like the legendary duchesses and comtesses, she was conveyed onto the stage in a sedan chair carried by four bearers. Supper was followed by a poetic recital by Madame Réjane and then dancing to several orchestras. After supper, more dancing, and for those who stayed the course, a full breakfast.

The plethora of published photographs and prose pieces, including Hyde's boast that he had spent two hundred thousand dollars on the ball, evoked the suspicion that the party was paid for by stockholders of Equitable and a clamor rose that its maze of involvements be investigated. Some weeks after the ball, young Hyde was seen to ride out, his equipage and his own exquisite person wreathed in violets, à la Comte Robert de Montesquieu, Proust's Baron Charlus. He was on his way to relinquish the title of "Prince of Equitable," deposed as the result of an inquiry into the affairs of his corporation. Title gone, scepter yielded, he still retained the means that permitted him to lead an exquisite life in France where he shortly settled.

For present-day Americans who have become accustomed to secretiveness in big spending among millionaires—only foundations, grants, gifts of art and respectable public benefices publicized—there is a blatant, farcical quality, a low charm, in the characters and deeds of this time that attached conspicuous price tags to every costume, jewel, flower spry, souvenir, bottle of wine and platter of terrapin that announced the salaries of waiters, sizes of tips, photographers' fees. Money was exalted, ardently celebrated by the select in a Garden of Eden whose brooks ran pure gold and would never dry up. They had not learned shame nor the word "vulgarity" nor were they threatened by high taxes; and like royalty through the ages, Hollywood later, and TV stars later still, they supplied the public with gossip, resentment, dreams, envy, ambition, emulation, a wide gamut of satisfactions.

The most blatant practitioner of "If you got it, flaunt it," reasonably honest, zesty, naive and shrewd, disgusting and funny, was the arch show-off, Diamond Jim Brady. The son of East Side immigrants, bright and ambitious enough to become quickly a ward heeler for Tammany, Jim chose as his career the technical aspects of railroading, about which he became masterfully knowledgeable. As the representative of a railroad equipment company in an industry that was earning prodigiously, and armed with the practical philosophy that anyone who wanted to make money had to have the look of money, Brady spent great sums on himself and on entertaining customers. For out-of-town customers not quite ready to venture the heady air of the Waldorf or sinful Rector's, he ordered enormous meals at Delmonico's and Sherry's. The unbelievable meals, designed to impress potential wheel and brake purchasers with the wealth and power of Brady and his company, were also dictated by his own freakish gluttony. At one dinner which ran through the night and into the morning, fifty guests were provided with ten bottles of champagne each to wash down the ten and more courses served. At midnight, an intermission for the indispensable distribution of favors, finely made diamond brooches for the ladies, diamond-studded watches for the gentlemen. Brady lost no time in reporting that the feast had cost him one hundred and five thousand dollars plus a generous round of tips; the diamond souvenirs accounted for sixty thousand dollars, leaving forty-five thousand for eating, drinking, gaiety and good will.

His private eating—rarely absolutely private since he was

almost always on display—were exercises in gargantuanism. Though accounts differ in detail, there is general agreement that he drank no liquor but consumed one gallon—two, three, four—of fresh orange juice with his twelve full courses, plus three or four extra helpings of the major dishes and a large box of candy to finish up. As a snack between these meals he might pick at six dozen oysters, several fowl, soufflés made of a dozen eggs or more, or six lobsters, a large slab of meat and several portions of rich dessert. He was, not unexpectedly, very fat and florid, with a many-chinned, brutish face, gentled by his genuine good nature and the glow of pleasure his joie de vivre shed. His enormous belly was the cushion for the jewels lying along and around it, as compelling as beacons, as delicate as dew-hung spider webs. It was Brady's pleasure to wear studs, cufflinks, lapel buttons, rings and scarf pins in matched sets of twenty pieces—twenty in rubies, twenty in emeralds, twenty in blue diamonds and so on to a total of thirty complete sets. The most conspicuous was his "transportation" *parure*, big stones set in platinum shaped as trains, bicycles, locomotives—votive pieces to his kind gods.

Accustomed to getting what he wanted for money, Brady did not hesitate to take a dozen bicycles to Tiffany's and order that they be plated with gold, the handlebars injected with diamonds. As purveyors of rubies and emeralds lodged on Fifth Avenue bosoms, as the makers of William C. Whitney's golden plates—and Mrs. Astor's and Mrs. Stuyvesant Fish's—Tiffany's spurned Brady and his crude proposition. According to Lucius Beebe, Jim found an electroplate shop where he installed a tank large enough to accommodate the bikes. Once the wheels shone gold, he had the tank destroyed though it had been costly to build and install. He gave the bicycles to friends, keeping one or two for riding in Central Park next to his especial friend, Lillian Russell, for whom he had ordered a spectacular ten-thousand-dollar machine. It was entirely covered with gold plating, the handlebars mounted with mother-of-pearl incised to allow for jeweled initials, the spokes of the wheels covered with stones that flashed back into the sun myriad little lights with each turn. Dressed in a high-style white bicycling suit, Lillian maneuvered her scintillating chariot, turning her graces to this side and that for her faithful entourage of photographers.

In an unremarkable though commodious house at the corner of Forty-seventh Street, number 579, lived the "most hated man in America," called that mainly because he outshrewded the shrewdest in bilking both the ignorant and sophisticated investor and the government. His taciturn destructiveness, his genius for shady deals, his very presence—slight, dark, private and sickly—made him *the* Mephistopheles of a Mephistophelian financial age. It wasn't that the peers with whom he tangled wouldn't do what he did, that their moral standards were higher; he was quicker. Besides, he was possibly a Jew (not so, say many historians), and everyone knew that by nature they were demonically subterranean, especially in money matters.

Of a family named Gold that settled in Connecticut in the mid-seventeenth century, Jay Gould was, like all robber barons, a boy who knew very early what he wanted—a great deal of money—and, after he had been cheated by a boss in his youth, the power to take and dissolve other people's money. At twenty he was already in charge of a Pennsylvania tannery, one of several owned by former Congressman Pratt. To know more about the leather market he came to New York, observed the larger markets, organized his new information and stepped onto his sinuous path of high finance. With Pratt money he established himself as Jay Gould and Company, a private investment firm. When it was discovered that Pratt's profits had become Gould property, he worked out with Pratt the purchase of the tannery, its site to be known as Gouldsboro. Two of his backers, the prosperous Charles Leupp and his brother-in-law, David W. Lee, would own two-thirds of the tannery for

their investment of sixty thousand dollars. Without their knowledge, Gould used their money to try to corner the hide market.
Several markets fell apart in 1857, with them hides, and Gould
could not cover his futures bought on margin. Demands for
payment came to the reputable Leupp whose credit Gould had
used while he squandered his investment. Not prepared for this
new-style rapacity, humiliated by a twenty-one-year-old crook,
his reputation sullied, Leupp shot himself. When Lee, of
stronger stuff, insisted on getting the sixty thousand back,
Gould agreed to return it over six years at no interest. The
infuriated Lee brought in men to take the Gouldsboro plant.
Militarily, the victory was Gould's but Lee was tenacious and
a lawyer and the legal battles proved too draining. The tannery closed down, and with it a testing time, a learning time,
a practice piece for later forays of greater magnitude.

Wall Street was then in the hands of a few formidable
men, among them Commodore Vanderbilt and Daniel Drew,
who were engulfing railroads, shipping, land speculation and
heavy foreign investments, no controls to impede them. The
Civil War was about to break out and spill its immense profits
almost for the taking. There was a good deal for a young man
concentrated on money to try for. Nominally still a leather
merchant, Gould began to buy into railroads, purchasing shares
low and selling them high, by means fair and mainly foul. It
was said that he knew sooner than other financiers the movements of troop and supply trains because he bribed the war
office—as who wouldn't if he had the means? He made millions
and an awesome reputation, and was ready for a monumental
set-to, the battle for the Erie Railroad, which Commodore
Vanderbilt desperately wanted. Vanderbilt already controlled
three lines that served New York, the New York and Harlem,
the Hudson River Railroad and the New York Central. In
spite of his large investments in Erie stock, he didn't have
control of the line although the stock-buying public thought
so. If he had the Erie, it would mean a monopoly of shipping

from the west and north. One of the contenders for Erie control was old fake-bucolic Daniel Drew whose early self-educa-
tion in chicanery included the inventive notion of amassing
large herds of cattle to whom he fed generous quantities of
salt. As they approached the market, they were encouraged to
drink water to bursting. Sold on the hoof at their augmented
weight, they brought Drew a fortune to spend on railroads.
With shrewd, flamboyant Jim Fisk—"the Alcibiades of New
York," ex–circus advance man, good-natured, illiterate, generous, a womanizer—as partner, Gould made an arrangement with
Drew, whose opening act in the new coalition was to release
over fifty thousand shares of Erie stock. Vanderbilt gobbled it
up, at the same time that he effected an injunction to this sale
and an ensuing additional sale of fifty thousand. The illegal
shares were not withdrawn and Vanderbilt was forced to continue buying to protect his earlier investments. They had him;
not altogether, though. He went to one of his favorite paid
judges and had a contempt action issued against the triumvirate. With just time enough for Fisk to spend a little while
with his mistress, Josie Mansfield (who was to be the cause of
his death some years later), for Gould to say good-bye to his
young family—Drew had no intimates he cared to bother
about—the men took their papers and about six million dollars
in cash across the river to New Jersey by rowboat.

Immured in Jersey, Drew had second thoughts and yielded
to a bid by Vanderbilt that they meet and treat. He took with
him Erie's money but was drawn back to Jersey by Gould's
seizure of his personal monies. It was clearly necessary to freeze
the perfidious old man out. One step was the simple expedient
of joining Vanderbilt without Drew. Fisk and Gould bought
back from Vanderbilt five million dollars' worth of his stock,
at an embarrassing loss to him of a million dollars, more or
less. Gould now had control of Erie and a grudging admission
from Vanderbilt that he was a wizard. After the appointment
of a board of directors that included William Marcy Tweed

came the time to work seriously on Drew. Gould and Fisk increased the capitalization of their line by twenty million dollars, most of it converted to private wealth for both men. They then forced the stock to fall, and Drew with it. As he sold his declining stock in growing quantities, the partners bought it. Suddenly, they pushed the price up and Drew, who could no longer command the money to buy, slipped toward bankruptcy, another Gould murderee.

When Vanderbilt signed a peace treaty, it did not necessarily mean (no more than it would for Gould or Carnegie or Guggenheims or numerous statesmen) that he accepted or acted on its terms. Gould's Erie victory rankled and there were angry hopes for squeezing millions out of him, maybe enough to ruin him as he had Drew. Vanderbilt's New York Central, which had been charging a hundred twenty-five dollars a car for transporting cattle from Buffalo to New York, dropped its price to one dollar a car, a loss Vanderbilt felt he could sustain, particularly if it ruined Gould: who would now use Erie even if its prices fell considerably? Gould's response was to have his agents buy up vast numbers of cattle approaching Buffalo for cartage and ship them on Vanderbilt's New York Central cattle cars at the one-dollar rate. The Commodore lost money and, for a short while, something of his overweening aplomb; his regret at having once more tried to outsmart the smarter Gould was expressed as "never kick a skunk."

Gould, now thirty-two, was at the penultimate climax of his remarkable career, tsar of a financial empire, controller of a key railroad, thoroughly hated; he had a weak chest, no social life except within his own walls, where he spent his leisure as a bookish man with some knowledge of art. He enjoyed—an anomaly for his time and station—being a devoted husband and father who neither drank nor gambled. When he was only thirty-three, he staged one of the most dramatic scenes in American finance, the infamous Black Friday of 1869. Grant was President and although himself medium honest, he had surrounded himself with an eagerly corruptible palace guard, one of them his brother-in-law, A. R. Corbin. To obviate the recurrence of that immortal irresistible, the cornering of gold, the government had established that any such attempt would be countered by the release of gold into the free market by the Treasury Department. In Grant's time a good number of government regulations were relaxed, the prohibition against reaping a full harvest of free gold among them. Gould had been amassing gold. He already owned about half of the fifteen million dollars' worth on the market when he arranged to meet Corbin, offering him the potential increase on one and a half million dollars in gold and to Corbin's sister, Mrs. Grant, the profit on fifty thousand dollars. The assistant treasurer, General Butterfield, also head of the subtreasury in New York, was to receive gains on one million dollars, all this on the understanding that they would cooperate in holding back government gold. That summer Gould began to buy more heavily, accumulating thirty million dollars in gold and gold contracts that guaranteed delivery at the price of the time of purchase. Under Gould's persuasion, Corbin published a newspaper article declaring that the government was not prepared to sell gold, nor even contemplated such an act.

Toward the end of September gold had risen sharply, selling at $140 and up. The pressures on Grant from other financial quarters were increasingly clamorous and he began to ask questions of his money people, finding out in the process about the Corbin-Gould agreement. On September 22, the frightened Corbin showed Gould a letter from Mrs. Grant to Mrs. Corbin saying that the President was outraged over the pact. It was understood that some action would follow and Corbin wanted out, right then, with the hundred thousand that Gould had earned for and through him. Extracting a promise that Corbin would make no move for several hours, Gould began surreptitiously to unload at a high price while seemingly continuing to buy, and since he was the genius to follow, others bought steeply. Gold rose while Grant watched and hesitated, hoping to save the family face and avert panic. The Gould-inspired wave of frantic buying raised the price hourly, to $150, to $160, while ordinary stocks fell, driving several brokers to bankruptcy and suicide. Gould continued to sell secretly at the ballooned prices, neglecting to tell his partner Fisk who continued to buy gold contracts. Foreign and domestic trade were immobilized, merchants' notes were worth nothing and paper money not much more.

At midday of Friday, September 24, when gold reached $164 and all business in the country had stopped, Grant announced the release for sale of five million dollars of government gold. The market price dropped to $133 almost immediately, ruining yet another batch of speculators. (Many of them had no right to walk such high wires, but it was a time, like the late 1920s, when everyone with a few dollars thought of himself as a potential Vanderbilt or Gould. "Rags to riches" was a potent legend with enough real exemplars to hold forth infinite promise.)

Gould was richer by eleven million dollars after the gold debacle and Fisk hadn't done too badly. More suspect and hated than ever, Gould was closely watched and checked by his own former cohorts. When the records revealed that he had milked Erie's resources for his own accounts, he not only lost the presidency of the railroad but was sued by Erie for nine million dollars. He was arrested and freed on a million dollars' bail, for which he bartered property of considerably less value. He then took to surrounding himself more than ever before with toughs to protect him from betrayed partners capable of physical attack and kept gangs at the ready should there be a concerted assault. In his mid-thirties he was worth thirty million dollars, had three babies and a homebound wife; he was in bad health, his life was unsafe, but he couldn't stop. Not while there were tempting swindles to scheme and magnates to harry and destroy.

Still immune to the extravagant shows of other million-aires—that was to come near the end of his life—he moved to a house on Fifth Avenue between Forty-seventh and Forty-eighth streets and kept on making millions, taking over railroads forging their way westward, challenging the powerful Union Pacific that, in spite of its extensive coal-rich territories, was in trouble. Gould knew it; he waited, watched and bought its stock at a low rate until he was close to control of the line. At the same time he so threatened Union Pacific with his com-bination of smaller lines that the larger company bought them up, earning Gould ten million dollars.

When telegraphy became a giant Gould focused on West-ern Union and began to nibble at it. Following a technique he had found eminently workable before, he formed his own com-peting American Union and bought the New York *World* mainly to advertise Vanderbilt's Western Union as the most depraved monopoly, sucking the blood of a victimized public. As Gould's company stretched its poles and wires across the country, reducing its rates to force losses on the competitor, Western Union's stock fell. Gould then had Western Union's lines and poles destroyed, pressing for assent to the merger he had been aiming at right along. In 1881, William H. Vander-bilt called for a meeting with him, succumbing to a merger but no loss of profits, since news of the merger had improved the value of Western Union stock. It was not too long before Gould, his partner and neighbor Russell Sage, and a carefully selected board of directors owned the most important commu-nications system in the United States. Nor was this enough. The *World* attacked the Manhattan Elevated Railway for its inefficiency and contempt for public safety, the prelude to a takeover. A part owner and nominal head of the new company was Cyrus W. Field who, with a fortune made in the paper business, and his promotion of the first transatlantic cable, had become a notable and highly regarded New Yorker. To his chagrin, Sage and Gould doubled the fare from five cents to ten; Field reduced it to five cents again after howls of protest. Field was a nuisance; more and still more inflated Manhattan Elevated stock was forced on him, and its value subsequently deflated. Field went the way of Drew.

In these years, the early 1880s, Gould moved his enlarged family, now six children, to a larger house, 579 Fifth, at the northeast corner of Forty-seventh Street. His vulnerable chest succumbed to tuberculosis exacerbated by insomnia. The newspapers—he had sold the *World* to Pulitzer in 1883—published darkly dramatic portraits of the scourge of Wall Street, the richest man in the United States, nervously pacing the midnight street before his house with a guard, wracked by disease and exhaustion. His wife, socially ostracized and terrified by constant threats to the family, also took refuge in bouts of nerves and depression. The children, quasi prisoners, seemed to flourish, however, some of them with disconcerting exuberance. As if to prove he wasn't ill and certainly nowhere near finished, Gould joined in the game of princely spending. He had built a well-crafted superyacht that cost $250,000 to begin with and required $30,000 a year to maintain. He filled it with rare woods and silks, a riches of bathrooms, the best equipped of galleys and a crew of over fifty. Since he was not admitted to the establishment yacht club, Gould formed the American Yacht Club with other rich outcasts and housed it conveniently at 574 Fifth Avenue. Among them, the Gould family owned a fleet of custom-made cars and several luxurious private trains. Newport was clearly not for the Goulds so Jay bought a country estate, Lyndhurst, in Irvington on the Hudson and expanded it with many rooms, including a picturesque tower to complete the singular Victorian Gothic design of the original house. For his children he built a variety of game rooms and stocked an extensive farm; for himself, the largest greenhouse of any private estate and gardens of tropical plants gleaned from all over the world, including an extraordinary collection of orchids.

George and Edwin Gould were quite grown by 1887 and were taken into the business by their father who had long begun to plan for the consolidation and durability of the family fortune after his death. Edwin was a steady youngster who took his degree at Columbia and learned well what his father had to teach him. George, as if reacting to the concentrated, silent life of his father, couldn't be bothered by school or business. He was for the bright life, for all the privileges and perquisites of the son of an emperor. He loved horses, he loved carriages and yachts, he loved actresses and the gesture of clasping pearls and diamonds around their pretty necks. Among his girls, he found one he was intent on marrying, a lovely young actress, not yet tainted it was generally agreed. Jay made no fuss; his wife fell apart, her recovery slow and never quite complete. After their marriage and a stay in the family house, the couple took a house very close to the nest, at 1 East Forty-seventh Street, not too far from the stables for a dozen and more horses and several carriages that George kept primarily to show off the splendors of his Edith's charming face, her superb, wasp-waisted figure and her costly wardrobe.

While the young were disporting themselves, the parents became increasingly ill. Nevertheless, they attempted one important culminating gesture on their children's behalf, to get them into society. They held a Christmas reception at Lyndhurst in 1891 to which everyone came except the people who most mattered, the Vanderbilts and the Astors. The Gould heirs never did sit in the inner circles of society, but it didn't seem to matter; they had other dances to dance and costly games to play—except for Edwin who stayed on his quiet, independent course. After his father died of a massive hemorrhage in late 1892, George was in control of the family finances as executor of his father's will, which left over seventy-three million dollars (experts insist that the true value of the estate might easily have been double the published amount), to be divided among the six children. George's second son, named

Jay, received a gift of half a million dollars. Helen, the oldest
sister, who took charge of the household during her parents'
illnesses, was to keep with her young Howard, Anna and Frank
until they were mature enough to leave 579, which she had
inherited. The will also provided that only legitimate children
were to be considered inheritors.

Before the younger Goulds could fly in several scandalous
directions (to be observed in other chapters), Edwin began to
raise a family at 1 East Forty-seventh Street, taken over when
George and Edith moved out and uptown. Helen devoted herself to religious works, to bequests to honor her father's name
and to keeping her siblings in tow, with variable success. No
matter what erratic directions they followed, she stayed, resisting invitations to George and Edith's high jinks in their big
house at Sixty-seventh Street and Fifth Avenue. She didn't like
their winy feasting or their guests or Edith's show of half a
million's worth of pearl necklace or their estate in Lakewood,
New Jersey, which in size and luxurious amenities outdid anything in Newport as a complete pleasure dome. Not quite trustful of handsome, playful George, Helen began to look into the
railroad business, taking long trips to see how things were really
done and how they were going. Between long voyages in a
palatial private Gould railroad car, poking her nose into matters George felt were his territory, she was active in female
patriotic societies, assiduously sprinkling religious tracts on
whatever paths she took. She tried to cleanse her father's image
by presenting NYU with one million dollars and two hundred
thousand for its Bronx annex. She gave money to YMCAs and
YWCAs, she gave for the translation of religious matter into
many languages and she gave for women's colleges, if they had
departments strong in religion. Hampered only by the Gould
fear that they might be attacked or assaulted or poisoned, the
result of a youth lived among guards and poisonous whispers,
she filled a spinster life with virtuous purpose. On a journey in
1912 that combined railroad checking and Christian benefices,

Helen met an official of the Missouri Pacific Railroad, Finley J. Shepard, whom she married after a judicious courtship, in a modest, nonbibulous ceremony at Lyndhurst. They and the four children they adopted lived in the old Forty-seventh Street house, which lasted, divested of brownstone neighbors, until Helen's death.

By the time she died in 1934, long honored for her general and Christian public services, Helen had restored some of the Gould name, as did Edwin. He went his own monogamous way, separated from the confusions of the family finances and ensuing legal tangles. He made money on his own and gave sizable amounts of it away to form numerous children's charities, one such notable institution the Edwin Gould Foundation, still active and respected. The family brawls he avoided, the suits, the lush press reports of Gould scandals were of little concern to him. Nor are they, at this moment, to us, since their venue was New Jersey, England, France and upper sections of Fifth Avenue.

CHAPTER 6

XANADU

y 1880 the city had had a new charter for a few years, incorporating Kingsbridge, Morrisania and West Farms. A competition held in 1879 to plan improved tenements resulted in a plague of windowless rooms, or rooms with windows opening on airshafts less than three feet wide. Immigrants were arriving at Castle Garden at the rate of four hundred thousand a year, many buying tickets on sale at Castle Garden for travel to the West. Henry Irving and Ellen Terry made their New York debut and so, after troubled years, did the Statue of Liberty. In spite of earlier protest, plans for Barnard College to be housed on Madison Avenue were going forward, spurred by Bellevue's acceptance of a few female medical students. Brooklyn Bridge, in the building since 1870, was formally opened. The first New York telephone exchange, recently established, issued its first telephone directory, a card of three hundred names. The new roller coaster was providing thrills in Coney Island, a popular excursion spot become accessible with the proliferation of ferry lines. Broadway from Twenty-third Street to Forty-second glittered as the new theatrical strip, soon to empty Union Square of its vivacity.

Everyone who could afford it carried an awkwardly large camera which, in some hands, became an instrument for social reform. It was in the late 1880s that a police reporter, Jacob Riis, and photographer friends took the slum pictures of fetid flop houses, derelicts' saloons, sweatshops and heaps of homeless boys that illustrated the famous book, *How the Other Half Lives*. In response, a spurt of charities and missions, lodging houses for immigrants and homeless children, and industrial schools came into being. 1891 saw the opening of the Educational Alliance which provided gyms, club space, lectures, classes and, later, plays and concerts for the mainly Jewish population in its environs. The Virginia Day Nursery at 632 Fifth Avenue kept a well-run shelter for the children of working mothers, and many such nurseries soon followed. The Salvation Army provided meals and sleeping space on the Bowery; the YMCA on the Bowery conducted classes, nurseries, kindergartens and reading rooms. The first settlement house, the Neighborhood Guild, established an example for organizing neighborhood centers as places of "neighborly and social" spirit. This ancestor of the University Settlement, founded in 1886, commonly known as the Henry Street Settlement, spearheaded civic reform in an effort to further the well-being of the Jewish ghetto.

The new Metropolitan Opera House on Broadway and Thirty-ninth Street, ugly outside and resplendent within, at first had boxes on three tiers but eliminated the third—who wanted to pay for a box so high as to leave one almost invisible?—while the lower became the "diamond horseshoe." The younger nonmusical took their entertainment with wine and friendly girls in the private parlors of hotels and clubs while their less affluent brothers frequented popular dance halls, from the decently decorous to flagrant dives.

New York was then, as before and later, "Fun City" for the visitor, the farmboy, the adventuresome small businessman and the restless village beauties who dreamed of a killing— artistic, amatory, marital—in New York. For their protection and titillation, there was issued in 1879 a publication called

The Snares of New York, Or Tricks and Traps of the Great Metropolis, a glowing advertisement of the dangerous, alluring games that back home could never provide. Each warning was accompanied by case histories and engravings, each leading character a distinctive type: the slick seducer always wore baroque mustaches and a silk top hat; swindlers were the same hook-nosed Jews (never blatantly identified as such) who appeared sixty years later in Julius Streicher's Nazi newspaper *Der Stürmer;* innocence had a broad, small-featured and stupid doll's face; wicked ladies wore tight-waisted, low-cut dresses, sly smiles and invariably showed a bit of leg above their high-buttoned shoes.

Informed that the "number of daily transient visitors to New York City in each twenty-four hours is almost as great as the whole State of Connecticut," the greenhorn is warned against gamblers who ply the trains, particularly females and baggage thieves who counterfeit receipts. Once in his hotel, the visitor must guard against being robbed by the owners of skeleton keys. A walk along the streets opens one to offers of stolen goods, the favorite item an expensive watch which becomes, when the vendor disappears, a carefully wrapped stone. Young women must be careful, on trains and the street, to reject the courtesies of fine-mannered gentlemen who will drag them to houses of assignation, ply them with drugged drinks and violate them. Wealthy merchants and well-to-do foreigners are warned to disregard circulars sent to hotels to advertise exquisitely furnished apartments available at short notice and, if the gentleman wishes, a lady provided for polite conversation and a champagne lunch, on the house. Should he venture, the merchant will be assailed by "thumpers" who will take his money, his watch and ring. Remain very wary when using public transportation. The Third Avenue Railroad abounds in pickpockets, many of them women, and the Fourth Avenue Railroad is even more hazardous because it is used by wealthy citizens. The pickpockets are demonically clever, often working as appealing bootblacks and newsboys who get their training in Fagin schools, the most notorious conducted behind a bar-grocery on Fourteenth Street.

Every corner, every house, every shop sign carries danger: crooked lotteries, crooked racing pools, crooked numbers games, crooked auctions. If you settle in the city, watch out for servants and quack doctors willing to treat "certain diseases" and hired companions for elderly rich aunts who may turn out to be blackmailers. Sweet little girls who come to your door to sell flowers or fruit must be sedulously avoided because they may be sent by parents who will complain that you molested their little virgin and must pay. And take good care of your own women; low-life gangs invade the best neighborhoods to insult ladies with vulgar language.

Don't buy the teeth whitener offered by street vendors; it will destroy the enamel after a few applications and then rot the rest. The belt advertised at five dollars and guaranteed to make you invisible, will not. Put no faith in the ambitious popular book that teaches you to extract good luck and prosperity from the spirits of the dead, to shine beauty on a sallow face, to do without sleep, to become a crack shot, to make a fowl roast itself.

Entertainment is treated extensively. Be warned that places which advertise female minstrels, cancan troops and suggestive improprieties are often disappointing, vitiated by the police. Other, tougher "concert saloons," unafraid of the cops who are afraid of them, offer dirtier, meaner shows and vile, expensive liquor served by pliant "waiter-girls." Should you stay clear-eyed in spite of the poisonous booze, you may observe the ruination of a five-dollar-a-week working girl—plied with wine and thus led astray by a gang leader who struts as he sits. So the book goes on, warning of traps in every stone, on every face, sketching out the Sodom and Gomorrah portrait that gave so much fearsome pleasure to rural America.

While déclassé sections of the city were busy wallowing in

sin, Fifth Avenue was pushing up increasingly elaborate houses
(a number beginning to edge Central Park) in a crescendo of
turrets, swells of bay and swoops of mansard in a lively melange
of styles, nothing as splendid, however, as the Vanderbilt houses
that stretched initially from Fifty-first to Fifty-second and then
beyond. But first there was the distasteful house of Madame
Restell, the abortionist, at the northeast corner of Fifty-second
Street which had to be erased one way or another, since she
refused to sell. A young man wrote to Madame about his poverty and his pregnant wife; another child would utterly undo
them, plunging them into thorough despair. Madame, who
considered herself a public servant as abortionists commonly
did, arranged to see him and gave him the equipment for
terminating his wife's pregnancy. Instead of going off gratefully
he arrested her and revealed himself to be Anthony Comstock,
the ubiquitous scourge of Vice. On the way to prison she offered him an impressive bribe which he refused. She used some
of that money for bail and returned home where she cut her
throat in her expensive bathtub. Consternation to terror shook
a fair segment of the monied male population of the city; the
police had found explicit records and Bennett of the *Herald*
was champing to publish them. They were never made public,
almost certainly destroyed. The articles that appeared in the
papers after her death could hardly say that she was a great loss
but suggested some such sentiment when they turned on Comstock and his crafty, dishonest dealings with her. She would be
missed, obviously, and was commemorated in a cartoon that
appeared in a German periodical which showed Fifth Avenue a
jungle of young children in prams, in countless arms, swarming
on the sidewalk and, not yet hatched, as big female rotundities.

   At the time of the Restell excitement, the "public be
damned" Vanderbilt, William Henry, president of New York
Central and the richest man in the world, after his father
Cornelius died in 1877, decided to build himself a royal de-
mesne. His builders urged marble, the highest expression of

power, but William Henry was afraid of marble; in its cool shine there were evil eyes. Had not A. T. Stewart and William Backhouse Astor died quite soon after their mansions of marble were built? He ordered, instead, three massive brownstone houses, one for himself and two for his daughters, Mrs. William D. Sloane and Mrs. Elliot F. Shepard. In 1881, numbers 640, 642 and 2 West Fifty-second Street were ready for occupancy, having absorbed the labor of more than fifty foreign craftsmen and several hundred American workers. Bay windows made classic with columns, angular balconies girdled with elaborate ironwork, plaster medallions and trills of Tuscan arch were some of the components of these best houses of the city. To enhance the new life and house, William Henry augmented his group of resplendent trotters and moved them to stables at Madison Avenue and Fifty-second Street, and also began to expand his collection of paintings. He now required uptown paintings which were mainly French, a "connoisseur's" paintings, the big refulgent animals of Rosa Bonheur, each mare a Mother Earth, and the glorifications of Napoleon II in vast battle scenes by Meissonier, of whom he bought several canvases, including a portrait of himself, for $188,000. Shortly after the ball that inaugurated the house in 1883, Mr. Vanderbilt issued invitations to a select horde of gentlemen to view his $1,500,000 collection of art.

Both art and house were the matter of a luxuriantly bound book, *Mr. Vanderbilt's House and Collection*, sold to people who mattered and to whom the Vanderbilts mattered. The newly furnished rooms pictured in the book, the quintessence of supreme style, have for the modern eye, a nightmare quality: a general turbulence, a restless combat of pictures and furniture in airless groupings; overwhelming doorways as majestic and ugly as triumphal arches, gilded ceiling curves like sections of Egyptian mummy cases, rugs smothering rugs, wood gouged and tormented; bookcases, mantels and tables—every bit of flat space frenzied with vases, lamps, figurines, boxes and assorted bibelots. (Almost a century later one finds these same objects, in infinitely cheaper versions, as densely cluttering the "tourist goods" storefronts that supplanted Vanderbilts and their neighbors.)

In this typhoon of objects, infuriated by other railroad powers who tried to keep his Baltimore and Ohio Railroad out of New York, William Henry died in 1885. He died with the satisfaction of knowing that Vanderbilts were beginning to move into the nimbus of high society which had never shone on his coarse father, the Commodore; of knowing that he had doubled the family fortune, now worth near two hundred million dollars and that the family mausoleum at Staten Island was guarded by a watchman and a frequently punched time clock to insure that no Vanderbilt corpse would suffer the indignities of Stewart's remains.

The wife of William Kissam Vanderbilt, the second son of William Henry, added another house to the enclave, hers on the northwest corner of Fifty-second Street, meant to outdo every other house in the city and to shatter the confidence of *the* Mrs. Astor sitting on her throne on passé Thirty-fourth Street. Mrs. William Kissam's architect was Richard Morris Hunt who had the training and the agreeable character to follow and fulfill the fantasies of his clients. Hunt was trained in the École des Beaux-Arts in Paris where he worked with prominent French architects. Personable, equipped with high skill and continental manners and (a very important detail, according to historians of architecture) a superior architectural library, Hunt returned to New York where he taught a group of young architects the principles that would become the core of the American Renaissance. Commissions were at first sparse but accelerated with the building boom of the post–Civil War years. His was the first luxury apartment building in New York, followed by an unusual second that repeated the shops, the plump balconies and sloping roofs of Paris. On East Seventieth Street he placed a medieval-Parisian structure to house the Presbyterian Hospital and soon after, the Lenox Library, severe, imposing and imaginative. It was the fancies, though, the rearranged pastiches of Viollet-le-Duc's Gothic Revival and the dramatic spaces of the Italians—the Sangallos, Peruzzi, Palladio —as he revived them in Newport and Fifth Avenue that caught potential clients' eyes. Hunt luxuriated, too, in being the arbiter of taste (interiors were often his as well) who could dip whenever he chose into Nigers of gold for effects he knew his clients wanted—the sense of living in Hadrian's villa or a pink palace in Jaipur furnished with chairs that once bore Gonzaga bottoms and refectory tables that fed Thomas Aquinas. Hunt saw to it that the marble halls and seigniorial staircases were shaped for the feet of gods and that the rare birds and exotic flowers from strange parts of the world would feel at home in their exquisitely wrought conservatories. (Architects more attached to the present and the future, like Louis Sullivan, found the style laughable for the habitats of men of the 1880s, who issued forth from such houses to crowded city streets dressed in dull business suits.)

It was with the commission of 660 Fifth Avenue that Hunt first came into his own as builder for the aristocracy; Vanderbilts had come at least two generations away from their scrabbling beginnings and were now worthy of the ambience of Jacques Coeur of Bourges or the Dukes of Berry. Hunt and the William Kissams left to their relatives the massive brown style and took for themselves creamy limestone in the lilting graces of the Loire valley chateaux, with particular emphasis on the charms of the chateau at Blois, the seat of the most powerful feudal French lords. The mansards rose steeply to frondy crests, their windows laced in Gothic tracery and capped with clusters of patterned chimneys; the balustrades were slim and the plasterwork curlicues tastefully demure. The capping romantic touch was the fairy-tale turret that rose to a slender cone as in the castles of the French Books of Hours.

The dreaming palace at 660 cost three million dollars, a

fair part of it spent on the same Caen marble that had shaped
great cathedrals, silken woods to line a two-storied dining
room, deep rugs and pierced metals for an "Eastern" billiard
room, a music room of dainty French furnishings surrounded
by lissome designs in the boiserie and flights of French cherubs
on the ceiling—all of it the work of a leading Paris decorator.
It was all so stunningly stylish as to make the Vanderbilts—
until recently fairly obscure except when attacked for watering
stock which robbed the American public of at least three million dollars annually—socially inescapable. The house created
as well a reputation for Alva Vanderbilt as a connoisseur of
architecture, decoration and allied arts, a reputation she cherished and fostered.

To say that Mrs. William Kissam Vanderbilt, née Alva
Smith of Mobile, was socially ambitious is merely to say that
she was very rich and fierce in a driving time, a time that gave
an energetic, unhappily married and intelligent woman of
means no other large outlet. Alva's first triumph was hooking
a Vanderbilt. Victory number two was the most fanciful and
expensive house on Fifth Avenue. Victory number three was
an invitation to the annual Patriarchs' Ball. Victory number
four and the knockout blow occurred during the preparations
for the first ball held in the new house in 1883. Its advent
trumpeted long before, like a coronation, it pricked society
into forming a swarming hive around a new queen bee. Troops
of seamstresses were put to work on miles of brocades and lace,
jewelers searched their design books for adaptations from Cellini, carriages were burnished to high glitter. Alva worked
hard. One of the jobs she took on was to rehearse the daughters
of approved houses in the lengthy measures of the quadrille,
earlier introduced to obviate the hopping and stomping that
tended to seep in from hoi polloi destroying the quality of
"court." One of the quadrille cordon was young Carrie Astor,
Caroline's daughter, who, after hours of concentration on the
complex formations, was disinvited by Alva because, as she

explained, Carrie's mother had never called on her so how could she, in all justice and in keeping with accepted social procedure, invite Carrie or her mother? Bowing to Carrie's importunities and the exigencies that beset a mother with daughters to ease into important circles, Mrs. Astor reluctantly unbent and had her footman deliver a card at the chateau portal. The Vanderbilts had made it.

The newspapers were very attentive, happy to record everything about the ball, including the color of the lining of Alva's skirt, copied from a painting of a Venetian princess. The outer layer of the skirt was in luscious brocade shaded from yellow to orange, the millefleur pattern picked out in gold stitching, the gold again used in the embroidery on the bodice of gleaming silk and once again as the frail threads of the gossamer sleeves. The cap glowed with gems arranged as a magnificent peacock in full display. To prove that she was au fond rather sweet and innocent, a small flock of white doves was set to flutter about her when she was photographed in the costume. The entertainment consisted of a smorgasbord of quadrilles: a quadrille in antique German court dress, a Star Quadrille (including Carrie Astor), a quadrille that featured Mother Goose and her intimates, a quadrille of hobby horses. Horses, three blind mice, Dresden shepherds and shepherdesses, all took their carefully rehearsed steps in the immense Louis XV room hung with Gobelins and woods of antique patina wrested from a French palace. A ponderous, costly supper on gold plate peeping from banks of flowers was, of course, served by impeccably trained servants in braid and buttons.

It was the magnificent fanfare that led into a merry dance of Vanderbilts through palaces in Europe and Newport, gaming casinos, yachts of behemoth size, prize-winning horses in splendid stables, alliances and divorces and stentorian whispers of kept ladies, bizarre custody suits, oceans of champagne, an army of servants in maroon livery, the Vanderbilt color, fleets of cars—as many as five hundred in the 1930s—houses on extensive estates whose total value, in the depressed currency of the 1930s, was $125,000,000. One scion, Cornelius Vanderbilt Whitney, had the whole town of Obregón, in Mexico, for his kingdom.

Having reached the top in the early 1880s the clan found themselves in both New York and in Newport kicking down those who threatened their pinnacle. One had to be careful about the climbers with their brassy new mining fortunes and the crude, tobacco-chewing captains of the patent medicine industry; one had to watch those Goulds, the spawn of a destroyer. And one had to show the old money that it was becoming socially obsolete and toothless. Let it exclude Morgans, Rockefellers, Whitneys and Vanderbilts from their decaying Academy of Music on Fourteenth Street; they had their own new Metropolitan Opera, led by William Kissam Vanderbilt. The sharpest threats, those that kept Alva most alert and vindictive, came from her competing female relations. Her troublesome sister-in-law, Alice Gwynne Vanderbilt, also had a Fifth Avenue house, replete with marbles, immense salons and ballroom, and royal French furnishings, between Fifty-seventh and Fifty-eighth Street and the famous Breakers at Newport that rivaled Alva's eleven-million-dollar Marble House at the same resort. Alva then found cause to exclude the wife of her son, Willie K., Jr., who lived at 666 in a chateau designed by Stanford White to harmonize with that of Willie, Sr. Having rid herself of sister-in-law and daughter-in-law, she rid herself of William by divorce proceedings naming as correspondent an adventuresome Fanciulla del West, Nellie Neustretter, "a woman notorious in Europe," according to the full coverage in the March 6, 1895, issue of the New York *World*. Under a front-page head that announced the divorce decree granted Mrs. William K. Vanderbilt were a large picture of the marble palace at 660 Fifth and a quote from Mrs. W. K., "I Don't Want This House." Still on page one, a jab of moral comment: the dozen servants in Nellie's Paris house are probably better paid by Vanderbilt than the brakemen and repairmen on his railroads, a fact that should be of great interest to them. The story goes on to explore the "hunting of big American game on the sunlit shores of the Mediterranean" where for years the Vanderbilt men were to be found amusing themselves, particularly in Monte Carlo, under constant surveillance by the queens of the demimonde. One the grandest horizontals of them all, Liane de Poujy of the famous pearls, had a try at Willie but the prize went to Nellie, who is described in this column as quiet, reserved and the mother of two children, a domesticated type.

Quite another portrait appears on page two. Following pictures of several Vanderbilts, a long story recounting the rise of the family, the social rivalries and Alva's background and works, we reach Nellie again. Now she is a girl who had a liaison with a member of the richest family in her hometown, was sent away to San Francisco, where "she tossed aside her last chance of a good reputation and led a life of open shame." One interval of respectability, marriage to a cigar salesman, was a mistake for Nellie; she left him to become the mistress of a rich New York manufacturer, and on to the top rung of the ladder, Paris and a Vanderbilt. Now she had her own house in Paris, one in Deauville and an allowance of two hundred thousand dollars a year, all supplied by Willie, the subject of a vindictive slap that closes the article: "And a queer figure this newcomer in the lists of degeneracy cuts, with his stolid, florid face, rather ungainly figure, his air of a blundering boy."

To brighten his hours in America, to which he had to return from time to time as chairman of the board that controlled Vanderbilt railroads, Willie slipped up to his Newport cottage, a matter of one hundred ten rooms, forty-five bathrooms and a garage that could accommodate one hundred cars. In 1903 he turned over his interests to the Rockefeller-Morgan–Pennsylvania Railroad combine and was free to pursue his career as sportsman and judge of horseflesh, pausing to com-

plain of the boredom of a rich man who must labor "simply
to add to an oversufficiency." (This sort of protest became increasingly popular as labor leaders and muckrakers pinned
down specimens of the rich for minute examination. The litany
ran to the effect that in spite of the horses, yachts, mistresses,
servants and wines, a millionaire's life rarely included one
happy moment.) Having won the Prix du Jockey Club several
times in France, William K. made the fitting gesture of suffering a heart attack at the Auteuil track in 1920, at the age of
seventy, and dying soon thereafter.

Not too long after her divorce, Alva married Oliver Hazard
Perry Belmont and became the mistress of her second Hunt
house in Newport, Belcourt. Like William, Belmont was an
intimate of horses. He found it essential to live closely with
them and love them, dead and alive, twenty-four hours a day.
He had had Hunt place the stables—where the horses slept in
the gentlest linens embroidered with the house crest—immediately under his living quarters. Two dead favorites, masterpieces of taxidermy, held places of honor with the paintings
and tapestries of his noblest salon. Mrs. B. didn't seem to mind;
she was accustomed to intense horsiness and besides she was occupied with more important matters, namely the social encroachments of Mrs. Willie K., Jr. It was during one of these
contests that she let it be known that no womanly task or
profession was as demanding mentally as running Society. It
may have been Alva whom Ralph Pulitzer had in mind when
he wrote of women "who make of Society a responsibility from
which there is no relaxation, a pastime from which there is no
leisure."

After Mr. Belmont's death, Alva poured her copious
monies and energy into building and building, a female coun-
terpart of the demented Bavarian King Ludwig. Her forces
undiminished by her Master-Builder role, she became a supporter of Emil Coué's cures by self-hypnosis and a towering
suffragette leading parades everywhere, including her bailiwick

and stage, Fifth Avenue, so fired by the cause that she designed
a feminist funeral to follow her demise. She died at the age of
eighty in Paris, and was buried in the usual, man-ridden way,
one of the few times that matters were not arranged as Alva
insisted they be.

The land neighboring the duchy of the Vanderbilts to the
south was in one of its subdued periods, a quiet pause in a
long, often contentious, history. It was and would remain the
property of Columbia University, founded in 1754 as King's
College with a faculty of one, a student body of eight and funds
raised in public lotteries. Graduates of the early years, when
classes were held in the schoolhouse of Trinity Church and the
campus was the church farm, included De Witt Clinton and
Alexander Hamilton, who bridged the time of the American
Revolution which changed the name of the College. The school
grew with the city and its affluence but the going was made
difficult by the state legislature which neglected Columbia in
its distribution of lottery funds to educational institutions. One
undiscouraged faculty member was the influential Dr. David
Hosack, professor of botany and medicine, a leading physician
who was called to attend Alexander Hamilton after his fatal
duel with Aaron Burr. Intent on developing a botanical garden
with emphasis on medicinal plants for the use of his students
and the public, he petitioned the city's Common Council for
the necessary land. For $4,807 plus sixteen bushels of good
wheat annually, or its equivalent in gold or silver coin, Dr.
Hosack acquired fourteen acres of land far to the north, referred to in Columbia documents as the "Upper Estate" which
would become Forty-seventh to Fifty-first Street along Fifth
Avenue and westward, almost to Sixth. Here Dr. Hosack opened
his Elgin Botanical Gardens in 1804 and by 1806 had on show
two thousand species of plants in a large greenhouse and two
hothouses that stood in a flowing, smooth-hilled wilderness of
trees and shrubs.

The Garden flourished, encouraged by showers of the doctor's private funds, but in 1810 he was forced again to ask for help. The state bought the land from him for $74,268, considerably less than he had spent, and turned it over to Columbia as the site of its new college. The trustees were reluctant to build, the area was too inhospitable, too wild.

Discussion went on for years, often spurred and heated by the growth of New York University, Gothicly dominating the fine houses on Washington Square. Finally, a set of plans for Upper Estate building were agreed on and in May, 1855, the trustees ventured uptown to observe the excavating and blasting already going on in the midst of shanties, pigsties and scummy puddles "a mile beyond civilization in any form that can aid the new street lots." The committee ascertained that the cost of digging up and smoothing lots for possible leasing would be several times the ground rent it could expect. No sane man, the trustees agreed, would pay the required fifty dollars for each lot. The few buildings in the vicinity were St. Luke's Hospital at Fifty-fourth and Fifth, the orphan home adjoining a small church (not yet St. Patrick's) across the Avenue and a home for deaf-mutes to the east. The streets in the upper Forties and Fifties were fine for institutions that preferred calm distance from the furies and gaieties of the city. A university, no. The land was too far from the schools for the younger children of professors, the grounds too hazardous for the legs of elderly professors, students might find too many temptations in the semiwilderness and typhus and malaria threatened from the disturbed, excavated earth.

How to recover the losses suffered in digging up the botanic garden and the costs of planning? Selling lots was, as expected, difficult, bidders few and prices offered, low. It was decided to take over the building and gardens of the former asylum for the deaf and dumb on Madison Avenue between Forty-ninth and Fiftieth streets for the college and hold on to the westward land, leasing whenever possible. One visionary thought that leasing should be held off, because work on the projected Central Park might start within a year or two and local land values might rise swiftly. He was overruled; the trustees held pat except for the sale of Fifth Avenue frontage between Forty-eighth and Forty-ninth Street to the Dutch Reform Church in 1857 and, a half century later, the entire block of Forty-seventh Street become an extraordinarily valuable piece of property. The rest of the land yielded comparatively little, its most prosperous tenant in the 1860s Isaiah Keyser who built himself a three-story house and cultivated a large vegetable garden from which he supplied householders of lower Fifth Avenue with produce as well as ice from nearby ponds and meat from local cattle yards. His customers were mainly retired gentlemen who drove out to choose their own vegetables and cuts of meats while they conversed dourly about the frightening new might of the Irish who were planning to display both power and riches in the immense cathedral slowly going up on the east side of the Avenue.

There were other small farms in the neighborhood and a few of the brownstones, "the narrow houses so lacking in external dignity, so crammed with smug and suffocating upholstery . . . cursed with universal chocolate-coloured coating of the most hideous stone ever quarried" that Edith Wharton despised. To one of these, a house looking across to St. Luke's Hospital, came Arabella Duval Yarrington Huntington, one of the camp followers who marched with the conquerors of the West. A lively little widow, as the saying went (often to account for the presence of a child and the absence of a father), she attached herself to Collis P. Huntington, the most powerful of the Big Four who controlled western railroading. His career, like hers, was folkloric American. A young peddler who achieved a store of his own in upstate New York, he joined the gold rush in California to become rich and richer as he acquired railroad and shipping lines. The next inevitable step in the logic of the times was a New York house. He acquired one, too modest for Arabella, "the unofficial Mrs. Huntington,"

who bought another on Fifty-fourth Street a few paces west of
Fifth, enlarged it, renovated it completely, ennobled it with a
grand staircase, stuffed it full of stylish adornments in Moorish,
Renaissance and Victorian style, smothered it in morbid drapes
and soon found it unsatisfactory. She traded it off for nine lots
at the northeast corner of Fifth Avenue and Seventy-second
Street, a deal arranged with John Rockefeller. She toyed with
the idea of building there or on the lots at Eighty-first Street
and Fifth given her by Collis, but both these sites were too
isolated, on the Avenue yet not of it. Before she made any
move, however, she had Collis marry her two weeks after the
death of the official Mrs. Huntington in October, 1883. As one
of his many presents, Collis bought Arabella a house on Fifty-
first Street, very near the Avenue and practically adjoining the
Vanderbilts. That wasn't quite good enough, either, so they
sold it to Andrew Carnegie for $170,000 plus and moved on,
this time to a supremely ugly pile on the southeast corner of
Fifty-seventh Street that had cost $2,000,000. Arabella
crammed this one full of exquisite French furniture à la Alva
Vanderbilt, fields of heroic tapestry, enough stained glass to
illuminate a small cathedral and the undemanding, literal
eighteenth- and nineteenth-century paintings that Collis favored.

Furnishings and arts arranged and the staff readied, Arabella issued invitations to which few that mattered responded.
She was saved from further social embarrassment by the death,
in 1900, of Collis, who left her about $150,000,000, more than
any other woman in the world possessed. Not that Collis ever
protested much, but she was entirely free now to spend wildly,
guided by the Duveens and titled European agents over hills
and dales of art and artifacts. She bought Vermeers, Rembrandts, Reynoldses, as casually as if they were calendar art to
hang on her many walls, including those of a new and spacious
house in Paris.

When she had grown elderly, more harsh and imperious

than ever and victimized by diminishing vision, she returned with some of her lares and penates and the son Collis had adopted to California. There she married Collis's nephew, Henry Edwards Huntington, placed high in the Huntington railroad meshworks by Uncle. Assaults on Society and prodigious collecting, including the complicated acquisition—a matter of daily headlines—of Gainsborough's *Blue Boy*, continued. That, however, is a chapter in San Francisco annals that closed with the death, in 1927, of Henry, whose art collection and library, the largest of any one man in the United States, remain his monument.

Restless Arabella, pursuing art treasures (one catch was Rembrandt's *Aristotle Contemplating the Bust of Homer,* a Duveen purchase) in refulgent New York collections, frequently returned to the "stable," "warehouse," "railroad station," at Fifty-seventh Street. There she died in 1924, the house a repository of Arabella Duval Yarrington Huntington-Huntington tales until its demolition in 1938. One Arabella story has it that, distracted and disdainful of small matters, she left ten or so strings of pearls worth over three million dollars on the desk of her social and art mentor, Joseph Duveen, the Disraeli to her Queen Victoria, the phrase of S. N. Behrman goes. A darker legend repeats that Arabella lived in terror of possible discovery that her son was a bastard and that she had lied about his origins in an early marriage. She paid substantial sums (as did, incidentally, Ryan, Whitney, a Vanderbilt or two, Morgan and others) to the blackmailing publisher of *Town Topics,* Colonel William d'Alton Mann, to avoid the disclosures he threatened. Called to act as a witness against the colonel when he finally came to trial, she chose to disappear rather than be trapped by her oath into making revealing statements.

The house she left early in her career, 4 West Fifty-fourth Street, in the trade with John Rockefeller, matched him in longevity. When he took it over, he inherited some Huntington decor in the advanced taste made fashionable by

Charles L. Eastlake, the painter and critic who had led a short-
lived rebellion against the gruesome imitations of "period"
French and Italian furnishings that were invading new houses.
He called for an "honesty," a "sincerity" that would allow the
grain of wood its dignity, a sofa leg to speak its straightforward
functional piece. Two Rockefeller rooms given by John D.
Rockefeller, Jr., to the Museum of the City of New York, labeled "Eastlake," are engaging examples of decorating honesty
and simplicity in the mid-1880s. The dressing room relies on
rosewood and mother-of-pearl to form inlays of overall patterns; on closets and around the window frame there is a repetition of a comb and hand-mirror motif in mother-of-pearl.
Wiry designs enclose cupids illuminated by milk glass lamps in
the bosomy shapes favored by La Belle Epoque. The bedroom
tends to the Moorish, black and gold arches studded with
bright bits of glass that also shine, like myriad insect eyes,
from the chandelier. Ebony veneer on a mahogany ground with
holly inlays for the ample bed, while the windows and doors
repeat black and gold opulence in designs reminiscent of Morris, Burne-Jones and Company. A difficult room, languid, romantic, salacious, to relate to a wizened old man who drank
mother's milk to stay alive and handed out thin dimes to prove
that he wasn't a robber baron. (A Moorish parlor, incidentally, went to the Brooklyn Museum; the rest was demolished
shortly after Rockefeller's death in 1937.)

Arabella's refusal to settle for less than Valhalla had
brought her successfully among the gods: a lengthening hamlet
of Vanderbilts, a chateau built but never lived in by William
Waldorf Astor, at the northeast corner of Fifty-sixth Street
near his hotel, the Netherland. To the north, on the east side
of Fifth between Fifty-seventh and Fifty-eighth streets, stood
the Marble Row, an early settler of 1871. John Mason, at one
time in his career president of the Chemical National Bank,
bought the land from the city for fifteen hundred dollars
in 1825. In addition he bought common lands from Fifth

Avenue to Park, from Fifty-fourth to Sixty-third Street, part of the estate that was heatedly contested after his death in 1839. Because he did not like the marriages his children had made, he cut them off with small annuities, but there was eventual court restitution of property to the heirs. To Mrs. Mary Mason Jones came the Fifty-seventh to Fifty-eighth Street portion and she used it as she chose, disregarding popular tastes and warnings of isolation so far from the centers of social life. (The Joneses seemed to have been an independent, if not eccentric, lot. One Jones, Joshua, developed the reputation of being the thriftiest and stingiest man in the city. He never used public or private transportation; he walked whatever distances he had to. He spent his life in one room of a dissolving old hotel and never wasted money on firewood, no matter how cold the winter. Of the estate he left, estimated at seven million dollars, one million went to charities, the rest to nieces, nephews, cousins and their offspring, among them the daughter of a cousin, Edith Jones Wharton.)

Mrs. Mary Jones was a fatty, described by an observer at a ball they both attended when she was still quite young as "fat but comely; enough of her to supply a small settlement with wives." She was described in later life by her distant cousin as old Mrs. Manson Mingott, the venerable ancestress of *The Age of Innocence*, whose "immense accretion of flesh had descended on her in middle life like a flood of lava." When gaslight reached Fifty-ninth Street, before she became totally embedded in her own flesh, Mrs. Jones built her Marble Row. An ardent Francophile, she defied the implacable brownstone rule by using pale stone and French mannerisms for the buildings and filling her own house, at the northeast corner of Fifty-seventh Street, with Second Empire frippery of frolicsome Psyches and cupids and leering fauns. Edith Wharton left a masterly portrait of the poised, contented old fat lady and her surroundings: "It was her habit to sit in a window of her sitting room on the ground floor (imprisoned by her obesity), as if watching calmly for life and fashion to flow northward to her solitary doors. She seemed in no hurry to have them come, for her patience was equaled by her confidence. She was sure that presently the hoardings, the quarries, the one-story saloons, the wooden greenhouses in ragged gardens, and the rocks from which goats surveyed the scene would vanish before the advance of residences as stately as her own—perhaps (for she was an impartial woman) even statelier; and that the cobblestones over which the old clattering omnibuses bumped would be replaced by smooth asphalt, such as people reported having seen in Paris. Meanwhile, as everyone she cared to see came to her (and she could fill her rooms as easily as the Beauforts [Belmonts] and without adding a single item to the menu of her suppers), she did not suffer from her geographic isolation."

After Mrs. Jones' death in the early 1890s, the lively, handsome Mrs. Paran Stevens, who had already made her mark on Madison Square as the wife of the manager of the Fifth Avenue Hotel, took over the worldly house. Here she continued her musicales of skilled and unskilled musicians and pursued a lucrative career, not unusual for women who knew everyone, of creating wedges into upper circles through which aspirants, like some Goulds, could slip and, in time, be accepted. She died in 1895 and the house was taken by the Hermann Oelrichs whose money derived from trading in wools during the Civil War and later from shipping as the North German Lloyd Company. The Oelrichs became the apogee of the Gilded Age, he a dashing sportsman and she a vigorous and extravagant social leader who rode out in carriages with silvered fittings, her coachmen dressed in the Oelrich colors, tan trimmed with red. She must have been sturdy as well as vain. "Mrs. Oelrich is never seen in anything but an open trap no matter how cold the weather; with her brilliant coloring and the dark furs she invariably wears she makes a most charming portrait," purred a society columnist. In 1889, Mrs. Oelrich called in her florist to attach thousands of roses to trees arranged as a famous Italian garden. The festivities and the roses were to grace the wedding of her sister, Virginia Graham Fair, to William K. Vanderbilt II, the fun-loving, pioneer motorist son of the house at 660. She brought an imposing *dot* since her father was Senator James Graham Fair, a member of the millionaires' club that was then Congress, once an Irish boy who had made his bit, about fifteen million dollars, out of the Comstock Lode.

It wasn't until seven years later that Virginia and William K., Jr., moved into the house at 666 Fifth, a gift from William, Senior, and by that time they were already irritated with one another. They separated in 1909, he placing himself at great distances from New York by taking part in natural history expeditions to savage places until they were divorced and he remarried. "Birdie," as Virginia was called, kept the house until 1928, when she turned it over to a furrier's establishment and built herself a chateau on East Ninety-third Street. Her sister, Tessie Oelrich of Fifty-seventh Street, continued her frenzied struggle to dominate Newport and ended up certified mad.

On the southwest corner of Fifty-first Street stood the bow-windowed brownstone of the Darius Ogden Millses. Like many eastern boys, Darius joined in the gold rush and, like a number of his shrewd contemporaries, left the lonely, hazardous exploring with pan and donkey to the only occasionally lucky fool. He made his fortune more surely by selling tools and guns at the usual unconscionable markups. He bought mining stock with the profits and control of timberlands and waterways, rose to banking in Sacramento and, at the peak of many millions, established his Bank of California in San Francisco. At the age of fifty-three he was ready to spend $450,000 on the interior of a Fifth Avenue house, and to take on the role of donor to the Metropolitan Museum and the New York Botanical Gardens, and to perform an act of charity

that probably derived from his memories of the West, establishing the famous Mills hotels for indigent men.

Daughter Elizabeth married Whitelaw Reid, an Ohio journalist who had made his mark as correspondent with the Union army during the Civil War. With his skills and ambition and California gold behind him, Reid managed to take over the *Tribune* from Horace Greeley and ultimately made his way to the Court of St. James as American ambassador. His son, Ogden Mills Reid, took over the paper as managing editor and publisher in the years before World War I, and proceeded to cut a wide, tall, superb and inebriate swath through New York. Ogden married his mother's social secretary and when unsavory gossip about her spread by a Mills relative returned to him, he made the disdainful gesture of dropping the money name, Mills, and continued, without the relatives, to lead a shining life uptown.

Meanwhile, back at the Vanderbilt homestead and its urge to grow, Eliza, a third daughter of William H., had married Dr. William Seward Webb thereby so displeasing her father that she was obliged to wait until the age of thirty before she inherited the ten million dollars that included 680 Fifth Avenue. The portion numbered 684 came to another sister, Mrs. Hamilton McKown Twombly. Brother Cornelius II, president of the New York and Harlem Railroad, chairman of the board of the New York Central, the Hudson River and the Michigan Central—the Crown Prince in short—and his wife, Alice Gwynne, took on 744 and 746, and in 1882 began to build the gigantic mansion that grew up to Fifty-eighth Street. The original idea was to imitate the chateau of brother William Kissam, considered one of the ten best houses in the United States, but the new house grew larger, more fortress-like, extruding a portico used only on state occasions, a high grillwork fence that allowed narrow glimpses of a small formal garden, restless white trim on long banks of windows relieved by truncated turrets and Gothic finials. The newspapers and periodicals, as breathless and prolix as Boswell reporting Dr. Johnson, recounted in awed details the splendors of the castle: silverplate to serve two hundred guests, thirty servants to dust and polish the vast reception halls and the grand ballroom, the cleaning to begin at 6:00 A.M. and be finished by 9:00 A.M. when the family emerged from its bedrooms.

Cornelius died in 1899, leaving a fortune of $72,500,000. His widow stayed on for a long time as *the* Mrs. Vanderbilt— Alva having given up the field for higher causes—continuing to design society's stratifications and exclusions. In 1908, daughter Gladys was married to Count Laszlo Szechenyi in her mother's baronial hall and went off to live in Hungary. In 1915, the same salons were used for a service for son Alfred Gwynne who had gone down on the *Lusitania*, a death that might have been avoided, it was said, if he had not given up his lifeboat to a distraught lady.

Regal Alice (regal except in her follies of advanced age) left her grandchildren, who had married prosperously as had her children (Gertrude, for one, combined her Vanderbilt inheritance of $7,250,000 with the fortunes of the potent Whitneys), generous portions of her estate, except for Cornelius IV who had gone into journalism, a profession of drunkards and liberals. To him she left a photograph of herself and nothing else. Alice Gwynne was easily displeased. Cornelius III had earlier angered her and his father by marrying, in 1896, Grace Wilson of the Southern house of Robert Wilson who had made his fortune by selling blankets to the Confederate army and for *his* Fifth Avenue mansion had bought the house of Tweed at 511. The Wilson tribe had a strong taste for the crème and were forceful in their drive toward it. The eldest son, Orme, had found Carrie Astor, the daughter of Caroline Astor, willing. May Wilson had married Ogden Goelet. Grace Wilson made a vivid social mark as a Vanderbilt, beginning with a house in Newport, creating rose-covered fetes around the casts of popular Broadway musicals invited to perform. No Wilson

was shy; Grace saw to it that on her lists of guests there were
titled and even royal names. Her son, Cornelius IV, describes,
in his *Farewell to Fifth Avenue*, tripping as a child on a long
ermine-trimmed cloak he was required to wear when Kaiser
Wilhelm boarded the Vanderbilt yacht; Edward VII was almost a family intimate, he suggests. When it appeared that
Grace was following the royal road of Caroline Astor and
Alva Vanderbilt Belmont, mother-in-law Alice relented, ac-
knowledging her existence, her enterprise and her social star-
dom.

Cornelius III and his family lived for a while at 677 where
Cornelius IV learned young to be bored with the platitudes of
big money talk as it issued from Morgan, Frick and, once in
a while, from silent Mellon. They moved across the street to
the ancestral house at 640 when it was willed to them by Uncle
George Washington Vanderbilt, who had inherited it and ten
million dollars from his father. George had leased it for ten
years, 1904 to 1914, to Henry Frick and sold the properties at
645 and 647, originally bought to prevent an office building
from facing his father's house.

George preferred to make his life at Biltmore, his estate
near Asheville, North Carolina, on 130,000 acres of forest land
whose gardens were designed by Frederick Law Olmsted; his
manor house was built by Hunt in the Vanderbilt chateau style,
the most astonishing American house of its time. Here George
carved out a complete life rather like that of Frederick II, the
thirteenth-century Hohenstaufen King of the Two Sicilies. Like
the Holy Roman Emperor, George learned languages, sciences,
literature, art and history from an entourage of learned men.
He built houses, schools and a hospital for his citizenry, taught
them scientific farming as Frederick did and forestry and established regulations by which they must live. His house contained
the largest single room in the United States, immense picture
galleries and courts and an imposing banqueting hall. He collected hundreds of thousands of books, Dürer etchings, tapes-

tries woven for the French court and adornments of kings. On his death in 1914 much of Biltmore was sold off, the forests given to the government as national park and the chateau available to the public for an admission fee and application to the Asheville chamber of commerce.

The age and atmosphere of her venerable house pleased Grace Vanderbilt; it made an appropriate stage for the old traditions she painstakingly maintained, the sharp scrutiny of calling cards, the careful examination of invitations, the strict supervision of her servants, the red carpets spread for guests, the tiaras for opera nights kept radiant.

Where the Vanderbilts left lacunae in the streets in the Fifties, other wealth filled them: Charles Harkness of Standard Oil, Benjamin Altman, several Guggenheims and their lawyer Samuel Untermeyer. Untermeyer was also chairman of the committee that devised the income tax and excess profits laws that came with World War I and very likely invented a few serviceable loopholes used by his friends and clients. The Edwin Goulds lived for a while at the northwest corner of Fifty-sixth Street in a building later used for his art *palais* by Duveen. The Charles B. Alexanders, related to the Rockefellers, settled in at Fifty-eighth Street; the Levi Mortons at Fifty-third. One Goelet in the neighborhood fancied mansards with elaborate chimneys, another Goelet preferred simpler Georgian brick and stone. Early in the twentieth century came the sybaritic hotels of long, varied menus, refulgent bars and stylish decor to parallel as well as they could the luxury around them.

For the decades between 1880 and World War I, these streets comprised, along with the houses being built to the north, a village of the greatest wealth and financial power in the world, the might reflected, as in the time of the great guilds, by the companion churches. St. Patrick's, which had slowly been spinning its spires and spirelets since 1858, was dedicated in 1879 and finished in 1888; it commanded a whole block. St. Thomas's had come uptown to Fifty-third Street in 1870.

In 1905, the brown Gothic structure was ruined by fire; it was rebuilt in the white limestone that accorded with several of its neighbors. Massive, impressively neo-Gothic, it served for the weddings and funerals of the truly chosen and drew comment from the less select. Over the Bride's Door there is a dollar sign carved in stone, a gesture carried over from the authentically Gothic where it was the habit of a carpenter or mason to leave his bit of social criticism on a high piece of stone or under a pew seat.

As private wealth gave over to corporate real estate and neighbors moved northward and to France and England, the Vanderbilts held on as long as they felt they could. After a sojourn abroad Alice Gwynne Vanderbilt found that the tax assessments on her town house had grown shockingly; the lower and early section of her house, once stables, was alone assessed for an annual tax of $130,000, and furthermore the boundless market of Irish and black servants had diminished markedly. She decided, in 1925, to be rid of the whole burden, sold the property, which Bergdorf Goodman built on, and moved to 1 East Sixty-seventh Street, formerly the house of the George Goulds. Cornelius IV, temporarily broke, lived at the time in a musty two-room walk-up across the street where he could watch the demolition of his grandmother's house.

The daughters of William H. who lived in sections of the original trio of Vanderbilt houses were also impelled to leave by rising costs and taxes that added up to several thousand dollars a day, and by the push of shops and office buildings. The first to move was Mrs. Shepherd of 2 West 52nd Street who took an apartment near the Metropolitan Museum, leaving her property to her sister, Emily Sloane of 642 Fifth, who sold both houses a few years before the 1929 Depression collapsed real estate values. The southwest corner comprised of these adjoining sites became an office building. For her visits to New York as the wife of Henry White, U. S. ambassador to France and Italy (her second husband), the former Emily Sloane

took over 854 Fifth Avenue, a not too large house, richly ornamented for its size yet graceful. The house at 680, owned by
another sister, Mrs. Seward Webb, went to trade as the Mutual
Benefit Building. The section numbered 684, owned by Mrs.
Hamilton McKown Twombly, yet another daughter of William
H., was sold to John Rockefeller II in 1926. She went to live
in an Italian Renaissance palace built for her at 1 East Seventy-
first Street, near Henry Frick's museum-palace.

The ladies lived a long time, Mrs. Webb rather quietly,
Mrs. Twombly as a lively antique whose corner was fair
grounds for platoons of maroon Rolls Royces, a corps of servants dressed to match, delivery wagons laden with choice foods
and flowers, and a constant flow of dinner guests fed by a master
chef who earned enough to conduct a minor Vanderbilt life of
his own. He had a Newport cottage and the necessary staff and
at least one car. Nothing, though, to match the cars of his boss,
who had Cartier install in one of them a vanity section that cost
in gold, gems and labor ten thousand dollars. She died in 1952
at the age of ninety-eight, a life span that saw the barriers
erected by Society in her youth eroded and razed by two wars,
hospitable speakeasies and cafe society, a depression and the
careless egalitarianism of the rich young. She lived it all with
curiosity and acceptance.

Despite the exodus, the churches held and hold, along with
stern Minerva, the University Club, at the northwest corner of
Fifty-fourth Street. Its patrician style, designed by Stanford
White, suited the commanding tones, the pilasters, the oriels,
the garlands, the ironwork, the copper fringes on triumphant
roofs of its 1899 ambience. It was a proud, careful job, with
the nobility of Italian Renaissance palazzi in its regal propor-
tions and amplitude of space, in the masks jutting out of broad
keystones, in the shields and their legends that band the upper
walls like the proclamations of ancestry and conquest that still
stud old Italian walls. Of a day when a college education was
a mark of a gentleman of means and breeding, and such dis-

tinction was made explicit, it was essential to carve college seals and names across the face of a club of educated men, and in Latin. Thus, the *sigilla* of COLLEGII GUILIELMENSIS, of UNIVERSITATIS BRUNENSIS, of HAMILTONENSIS, of CORNELLIANAE, of NOVI EBORACI and several others declare themselves, and decoratively, across the Avenue façade.

From its windows three generations of members have watched steel, concrete, glass, secretaries and shoppers displace the earthbound brown, the graceful light houses and the sables that issued from them to mount burnished carriages. They observed awnings hung by Cartier's at the southeast corner of Fifty-second Street to announce their new jewel case, a house in the French style sold to them—we are probably dealing with mythology again—by Mrs. Morton Plant for a million-dollar Cartier necklace of pearls. They saw lavish hotels come and go and the last remaining Fifth Avenue Vanderbilt house sold to Astor interests. That was 640, once a monument and then a vestige of the Age of Elegance (and Grossness) and finally a bewildered thing devoured in 1940 by the Age of Real Estate Speculation.

CHAPTER 7

ANNEX TO XANADU

t the turn of the century there were still a few reputable but declining hotels on Madison Square; the numerous new took uptown places, the Buckingham at Fiftieth Street, the St. Regis (built in 1904) at Fifty-fifth Street, the Plaza, the incomparable Ritz-Carlton, the Gotham, the Netherlands, the Ambassador, the Savoy and, between the old and new enclaves, the Vanderbilt and the Waldorf-Astoria. Many of them could not sustain the 1929 Depression and several, seriously threatened, were rescued only by corporate money domestic and foreign. The Plaza had its rich, permanently ensconced widows to help hold it together.

One of the hotels, the Pierre, a latecomer which chose as its opening year 1930, had one strong fiber in a history that tied it to Sherry's most glorious days. The dinners served Astors, Vanderbilts, the exigent Mrs. Stuyvesant Fish and the Pontifex himself, J. P. Morgan, were arranged by Charles Pierre who had come a long, studious way, his road not yet ended.

Ambitious and tenacious, like many of his fellow Corsicans, Charles Pierre Casalesco left his father's Ajaccio restaurant where he had been the busboy, to go as Charles Pierre to the brilliant Hotel Anglais in Monte Carlo. The new page boy was dazzled by the radiance of the jeweled geese that dropped golden eggs on the green baize of gaming tables; the Oriental potentate who couldn't be bothered estimating the mounds of chips the croupier raked in; the ladies with camellia-petal skin who bent over well-tailored shoulders, laving them in promising perfume; the scions of mad Russian houses, spraying millions of rubles like leaves on wild breezes. Charles also observed an exiled court as the deposed Empress Eugenie designed it; the aristocracy she had created in Paris, now in disuse, had still to follow her stringent rules, one of them that they not appear in gaming rooms without her, still their queen.

Charles Pierre, having learned a thing or two, moved on to absorb more restaurant and hotel training. On a job foray to London, he was picked out by Louis Sherry for a position in New York. Twelve years of Sherry's brought him to an impasse. Smart women were beginning to smoke in public rooms. Mr. Sherry forbade it in his restaurant, an irritating, old-fashioned prohibition, Pierre thought, and, after flights of heated words he left. A stint then at the Ritz-Carlton on Madison at Forty-sixth, followed by his own restaurant, first on Forty-fifth immediately west of Fifth Avenue, and later at 230 Park, a place equally famous for its cuisine and for its care of American heiresses who, it was seen to by M. Pierre (himself occasionally the escort) went directly home to Mama. Inevitably he became a conservative elder statesman, deploring the vast democratic size of World War I parties and the unrestrained Prohibition guzzling that followed after.

He soldiered on in this frantic new world that had lost its manners until a group of admirers and financiers, among them Otto H. Kahn, Finley J. Shepherd (who had married Helen Gould), Edward F. Hutton, Walter P. Chrysler, Robert Livingston Gerry (the son of Elbridge Thomas Gerry, lawyer, philanthropist and grandson of Elbridge Gerry, the inventor of "gerrymandering") and others decided to use the site of the Gerry mansion at Sixty-first Street and Fifth Avenue for a hotel to be managed and run by Charles Pierre.

Fifth Avenue at Washington Square showing a statue of Washington atop the temporary arch, 1889. When the arch was redesigned later by Stanford White, General Washington was brought down from his perch.

A gondola in the Central Park lake, 1880s.

The Central Park menagerie, 1895. The rudimentary zoo replaced the cages set into the Arsenal Building in the late 1860s.

Squatters' shacks in Central Park, early 1930s.

Skating in Central Park, 1894. Central Park West was just beginning to awaken; in the center background one of the early risers, the famous Dakota apartments.

a *Portrait of Otto Hermann Kahn, 1867–1934, New York's radiantly rich patron who fostered the arts.*

b *Mr. and Mrs. George Gould, 1908. Pearls, satins, smiles and domestic felicity ended in obesity for her and a younger, slimmer lady for him.*

c *Jacob Henry Schiff, 1847–1929, of the powerful Kuhn-Loeb banking house.*

a *Fifth Avenue looking north from Washington Square, 1909, when lower New York still had beguiling Old World manners.*

b *South Street, stereograph c. 1880s. The many masts piercing the sky and the streets evoke the vivid, busy East River port of a century ago.*

c *Bandits' Roost, 39½ Mulberry Street, c. 1888. Photo by Jacob Riis. Police feared the street; foreign visitors, especially writers, found its evil enticing.*

d *Slum interior, 1896, with mother, grandmother and four children.*

◄ *Henry Maillard's Retail Confectionery and Ladies' Lunch establishment in the Fifth Avenue Hotel, Broadway at 24th Street, 1902. With painted ceiling, polished columns and not one inch of undecorated space, it was designed to echo the elegance of the customers' houses.*

Mrs. Cornelius Vanderbilt is shown holding an electric light at the Vanderbilt Ball given by the William Kissam Vanderbilts. Her carefully planned gown flashed and glowed like the new electrical wonder.

Mrs. William K. Vanderbilt at the Vanderbilt Ball. When she was photographed in the costume of a Venetian princess, a small flock of doves was released to flutter about her.

Drawing room at 640 Fifth Avenue, one of William H. Vanderbilt's adjacent twin houses. Carolingian platelets, twisting and floating art nouveau flora and Greek drapery effect a bizarre charm rare in the salons of the time.

◄ *The Vanderbilt Ball. Bear, sled and snow were supplied by the photographer. The ladies' exquisitely embroidered Russian peasant garb, probably ordered from Paris, was enhanced with ropes of jewelry.*

Looking south on Fifth Avenue and 42nd Street at the reservoir which stood there between 1837 and 1900.

Fifth Avenue and 42nd Street, 1909. Several endearing old charms—the open double-decker bus, the decorous fashions, the old Temple Emanu-El at 43rd Street—and New York's immortal traffic.

The unhappy and ravishing Consuelo Vanderbilt, then the Duchess of Marlborough, with her father, William Kissam Vanderbilt, at the Paris races where he, at least, was always happy. (He died at a French race track.)

The drawing room of the Carnegie Mansion. This house, considered very advanced for its time with almost sybaritic plumbing, was simple compared to its contemporaries.

The intersection of Fifth Avenue and Broadway, looking south. The Flatiron Building later arose on the site, replacing the profusion of advertisements.

An 1876 photograph of Madison Square Park, Fifth Avenue and Broadway. To the right of the graceful street light, the arm and torch of the Statue of Liberty were placed to appeal for funds so that her parts might be assembled permanently on Liberty Island.

Madison Square about 1895. In the center is Madison Square Garden, Stanford White's fun house, and to the right the fun house of Leonard Jerome, Winston Churchill's merry grandfather.

The Flatiron Building on a rainy winter's evening photographed by Edward Steichen, 1909.

Fifth Avenue at 44th Street about 1900. The rural market and saloon held out against the citified buildings to the north and south of them.

A mansion at 126th Street and Fifth Avenue, with many of the downtown frills, 1904.

Fifth Avenue between 60th and 61st Streets, 1900, with the Metropolitan Club in the foreground. A Byron photo of a splendid site in an era of splendor.

The rich permanent decor was by Stanford White, the French Garden surrounded by dining tables the work of the staff of Sherry's for James Hazen Hyde's ball.

The Waldorf Astoria, at 34th Street and Fifth Avenue. This 1900 portrait gives the hotel its full due as indomitable repository of might and riches.

The C.K.G. Billings' Horseback Dinner at Sherry's, 1903. It was uncomfortable and smelly, but the point was to choreograph something novel, expensive and, above all, photogenic.

a *A 1912 study of H. C. Frick from whose shrewdness and wealth were distilled the pure gold of the incomparable Frick collection.*

b *The ardent Francophile, James Hazen Hyde, acting the perfect gentle knight with the actress Rejane who performed at a lavish ball he gave.*

c The *Mrs. Astor (the former Caroline Schermerhorn) who rigidly defined "Society."*

d *An 1853 Daguerrotype of August Belmont and his American wife, the beautiful Caroline S. Perry of the distinguished naval family, shown here with her sister Isabella.*

The Scene today: on the steps of the Metropolitan Museum of Art, where people congregate to watch the passing parade of street life.

The new structure, rising forty-two stories, could hardly keep the Richard Hunt chateau quality of the pink mansion it replaced, but a few old France touches were built into the hotel whose motto was "from this place hope beams." Hope beamed feebly that year and in spite of its appointments, its exquisite service and *feinschmecker* guests, the Depression almost strangled Pierre's dream. Not quite; he had clients like the nine-year-old Lucy Cotton Thomas whose guardians paid fifteen hundred dollars a month for a suite; and he took a good share, vying with the Ritz-Carlton, of the two to three hundred debutante balls that took place every fall. The use of the ballroom cost fifteen hundred dollars, the absolutely minimal meal three dollars, the orchestra one thousand dollars until two o'clock and a couple of hundred dollars for each musical hour thereafter. Nevertheless, there was a fall, to some degree pushed by the fact that very rich guests, not yet cured of glistening publicly, made the Pierre a target of hotel thieves who staged a conspicuous number of swift and rewarding robberies. Early in 1932, the hotel went into bankruptcy, limping along in spite of the debs and the gilded children, under Charles Pierre's management until his death in 1934. The fifteen-million-dollar hotel dwindled in value until it came down to the two and a half million paid for it by J. Paul Getty in 1938. What Getty did with it is a financial story to be dealt with later.

Talented as they were, none of the hotels of the day had quite the same genius for spinning shimmering veils of glamorous publicity about itself as the Plaza had. It attracted an opening guest list, widely published, of overwhelming names led off by Alfred Gwynne Vanderbilt. Behind the publicity there were real values for those who could afford them. The hotel's position, practically part of Central Park's skating ponds and carriage paths, set back from the street line on its own piazza, was picturesque as well as convenient; the food was exquisite, the service devoted, even tender. If you didn't know how to manage ship schedules or baggage checks or the intricacies of cabling, or were out of funds temporarily or needed sound advice about existing social hierarchies or a letter in Italian inquiring about a Florentine villa, Daddy Plaza took care of it. He safeguarded your jewelry and troubled himself about your pets. If you were inclined to retire now and then into your own jungle of eccentricities or perversions or drunkenness or vanity, this most permissive parent sent you a token of forgiveness and love to ease your sobered discomfort.

The greatest pleasure of living in the Plaza in its highest heyday, the years before World War I, was people-watching. There were, for instance, the ubiquitous and numerous Goulds. The oldest son of Jay Gould, George, his wife and their children lived in the Plaza while their house at 875 Fifth Avenue was being readied. Their daughter, Marjorie, came out at the hotel in 1909 at a cost of two hundred thousand dollars. Brother Frederick was also at one time on the register and later, Anna Gould; Howard Gould died there. The beautiful Edith Gould, George's wife, satisfied her longings for the theater she had left (and, incidentally, the hotel's constant drive for distinctive publicity) by staging a play in the ballroom. It was a short one-acter of infinite insignificance except that Mrs. Gould performed in a superb costume with a leading matinee idol, before a boudoir set purported to be genuinely invaluable French antique. The play, followed by tea, was performed on January 24, 1908, to an audience that was greatly augmented from the original guest list of two hundred. The increase was the result of the publicity devised by Frederick Townsend Martin, a younger and wittier brother of the Bradley-Martins of the Famous Waldorf Ball. He had money but liked the game of social manipulations and its entertaining results as well as his unique position in the Plaza.

Anna Gould, with no interest in the stage and certainly not a beauty, carried with her short, stout body an aura of drama that derived from her money and her bizarre, glamorous marriages. She lived in one of the grandest suites and although a widow, was never alone; she was always ringed by body-guards and nurses. In the gamut of their duties was the job of tasting her food, one of the effects of an upbringing that looked warily at all non-Goulds. The servitors probably didn't mind; the food was incomparably superior to home cooking and Anna tipped profligately.

The people-watchers and mythmakers had a nonstop royal progress to observe, expand upon and report, from Caruso to Scott Fitzgerald prototypes, from African potentates to Communist emissaries, from foreign writers to crowned heads of uncertain thrones and royal mistresses. One rewarding subject was a Latin American diplomat who carried with him a small treasury of gems from which he made gifts to passing females on a system so arcane that it landed him in the observation ward of a hospital. There were the closet transvestites—drag not yet a popular, open entertainment—whose luggage poured out brocaded evening gowns and splashy earrings. Occasionally they brought in maids to help them dress and play indoor games. There were the bacteriophobes (every hotel has at least one in its history) who wouldn't touch another hand or an object touched by another hand, who kept changing rooms to fool lurking bacteria, who used up countless piles of linens. The lands of Scheherazade sent chieftains who became enamored of the products of Western industry and shipped home great loads of expensive American cars and thousands of F. W. Woolworth items. One made his grateful farewell by giving a gold watch to every employee of the Plaza. Another was rumored to have brought with his tons of luggage a desert entourage whose toilet habits refused to accommodate to bathrooms.

The ladies seemed to have a subtle lead, if not in number in impact. The light of G. B. Shaw's life and of several others, the incandescent Mrs. Patrick Campbell, smoked a cigarette in one of the public rooms shortly after the hotel opened and roused a fury of morality and decorum. The reputations of

both actress and hotel were enhanced by the publicity and she
and an increasing number of dashing ladies went on smoking.
The restless Marie of Rumania, and the other royal Marie,
the Grand Duchess of Russia, stayed at the Plaza. Hetty Green,
awesomely rich and stingy, left her sleazy little room, the bags
of graham crackers she bought in cheap wholesale lots and
her dustbin wardrobe for a stay at the Plaza so that she might
show and marry off her daughter. According to Eve Brown,
the hotel's biographer, it wasn't an act of her own volition at
that. A friend, Annie Leary, who became Countess Annie
Leary by courtesy of the Catholic Church, nagged Hetty into
proper dressing and primping and hiring a suite where Sylvia
Green, already thirty-seven, could meet somebody, almost any-
body, who would make a reasonably acceptable husband. The
story runs that Hetty haggled over the price of the suite and
had it knocked down, an essential passage in the traditional
Hetty Green portrait. At any rate, she let Annie arrange a
luxurious dinner to be served on the Leary gold service. The
expenditure brought the reward of a husband, somewhat advanced in years but an Astor on his mother's side and quite
willing to marry. Maternal duty done, Hetty stripped off the
finery, put on the discolored skirt and returned to her tenement.

A popular fancy among foreign Plaza ladies was to keep
exotic pets. (Into the 1940s one could still see, in summer twi-
lights, a frail fawnlike lady in fawn-colored clothing, leading a
fawn on a leash in the Plaza area.) The most notable pet was a
lion cub who became a hefty, menacing adolescent. He lived
with his trainer in the suite of a Hungarian-Russian princess
who might have been created by an early film writer, when the
screen was romantic in the grand manner. She was, like many
audacious, imaginative spirits, a Hungarian, and a spendthrift
tipper, among a sterling number, who brightened the lives of
Plaza maids, waiters, doormen and desk clerks. She had married

and divorced a titled Russian whose name she combined with hers as Princess Lwoff-Parlaghy. The divorce settlement was rumored to have given her a million dollars a year, besides the gifts she was purportedly receiving from her lover, Germany's Kaiser. In keeping with her station she traveled with a complex entourage managed by a sort of medieval bailiff or "court chamberlain" and a suite of ladies-in-waiting, as she preferred to call her maids. She shuttled between the Continent and the Plaza increasing with each return the size and cost of her suite, decorated with her own rare art treasures, until her bill for rooms alone came to several thousand dollars a month, these sums paid in cash, the inside dope had it, by the German consulate in New York. The Plaza also paid dearly. Her lion once escaped into the hallway and was luckily lured back by an attractive slab of meat; she would not permit anyone but her staff and intimates to ride the elevators with her; she was exigent and explosively temperamental in the haughtiest Imperial Russian fashion. But her money and jewels were splendid, she gave the hotel great cachet and, furthermore, she was an artist, earning her pin money by painting portraits of royal personages and money barons at ten thousand dollars and more per portrait. In time the magnificent fabric of her life began to unravel. Other portraitists, less demanding, less expensive, began to make inroads on her trade, and then came World War I, the Revolution, a halt to transatlantic commuting, the collapse of the Kaiser and his house. When the unpaid bills mounted, the Plaza suggested she take a smaller suite, perhaps ten rooms rather than sixteen. Unthinkable for a great artist, a princess, a royal paramour. The unthinkable happened; the princess was forced out and took her retinue and accoutrements to a fashionable house where the bills piled up to reach into the hundred thousands. She died under a bombardment of sheriffs intent on taking over her house and possessions for the payment of debts. A remarkably fitting end for a Nazimova film, the Magyar eyes wide with fear and fever, the tempestuous hair a dramatic Medusa aureole, the slender agonized hand convulsively clutching a Romanoff bauble.

In the days when Consuelo Vanderbilt, as the Duchess of Marlborough, was accused by her Blenheim relations of being immodest and neglectful of family pride and tradition because she did *not* wear a tall, tight choker of row on row of pearls, the Plaza was a huge jewel box, its contents often lost, stolen, retrieved or shrugged off. The jewels for men were kept women and paintings, the latter hotly contested at Plaza auctions, the prices spurred to high flight by Sir Joseph Duveen who was for a time a resident of the hotel. The lead hawk, he usually reached the highest altitudes as the other hawks dropped away. One of them might have been Solomon R. Guggenheim, who lived in one of the most majestic of the Plaza suites, crystaled, marbled, plastered and painted in the French manner to show off his collection of Old Masters. (For the later abstractions which became the core of his Museum, some of the decorative froth was replaced by understated, costly modern.) Another remarkable collection, that of Chester Dale, moved into the Plaza during World War II when the safety and services of the hotel were more reliable than a private house could furnish. With the Dale Post-Impressionists in one suite, the Guggenheim paintings in another, a hidden masterpiece here and there and the art auctions, the Plaza played the role, yet another of its Protean guises, as dealer and curator of a distinguished private museum.

There was a Plaza before there was The Plaza. Projected on a strip of property that sold for $850,000 in 1883, it was meant to be the latest, most beautiful, etcetera, etcetera hotel in the country—the claim of every new wonder in the frantic growth of hotels, along with industry and commerce, throughout the country. (Gene Fowler spoke of these enormous gorgeous shelters as the temples of America.) The New York temple grew to four hundred rooms equipped with the latest com-

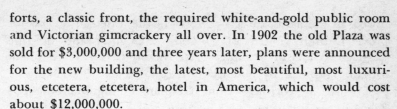

forts, a classic front, the required white-and-gold public room
and Victorian gimcrackery all over. In 1902 the old Plaza was
sold for $3,000,000 and three years later, plans were announced
for the new building, the latest, most beautiful, most luxurious, etcetera, etcetera, hotel in America, which would cost
about $12,000,000.

The grand opening of the French–American Renaissance
style Plaza took place on October 1, 1907, following a pre-
opening press dinner "in one of a series of elaborately decorated [rooms] with mirrors hung with brocaded old-rose satin
and lighted up with innumerable electric chandeliers." On
opening day, the New York *Herald* ran as headline, "Mr.
Vanderbilt Heads Plaza Register," and under that printed
photos of the lobby and the major dining room. One reporter
was overwhelmed by the foyer in Louis XVI style that opened
from the main entrance on Fifty-ninth Street. "There are floors
of Breche marble and carpets of illusive hue and chairs of
graceful forms, so much interwoven are the many beauties of
the hotel that it is a difficult task to analyze their charm." The
opening of the Plaza was clearly the smash hit of the day. The
hotel was twice as big as its parent, accommodated to millionaires waiting for new houses or those tired of the increasing
complexities of householding and the maintenance of vast ball-
rooms that were used once a year. Some rooms were reserved
for a choice few of the huge population of transients in New
York for business, for a fling and for measuring themselves
against challenges of the big city. For their ease in getting
around, there was a Plaza fleet of the new auto-cabs which
charged thirty cents for the first half-mile and ten cents for
each additional quarter-mile, an impressive price for 1907, as
was the cost of parlor, bedroom and bath: twelve to twenty
dollars a day.

The new owners of the property were the Fuller Company,
the builders of the first skyscraper in New York, the Flatiron
Building. Three of the planners of "the best for the best" fol-

lowed, in the main, success patterns of the nineteenth century: prove yourself worthy of the boss's daughter and use the Carnegie system of working where the air is full of useful information spilled by potentially useful friends. Ben Beinecke progressed meteorically from German immigrant butcher's delivery boy to owner of the store and on, to controller of wholesale meats, to supplier of ships and hotels, to owner of extensive stockyards and the large monies for financing hotels. Henry Black had worked for Fuller, married his daughter, an heiress of substance, and became president of the real estate and building company, broadening it to a value of over sixty million dollars. When he divorced Fuller's daughter, he gave her six million dollars, twice the sum she had brought to the marriage. Frederick Sterry started his career in an inconspicuous capacity at the United States Hotel of Saratoga Springs, the convivial meeting place for the racing set. With that experience he began to manage and improve the luxury hotels coming to life in a new resort, Palm Beach. In the process he learned to be the perfect suave and tactful hotelier and quite rich.

The École des Beaux Arts of Paris—no other school was to be trusted to produce architects with the appropriate knowledge of what was both majestic and smart—produced among its many disciples Henry Janeway Hardenbergh, of an old Dutch family. He was already much in demand, having built the extraordinary Dakota, one of the first grand apartment buildings, as well as the Waldorf-Astoria, the Copley-Plaza in Boston, the Raleigh in Washington. He was stylish, responsible and gifted, his work admired by later architects, among them Le Corbusier and Frank Lloyd Wright. An essential of his Plaza design was a tall temple of marble harmoniously combined with flourishes of Renaissance loggia, medieval turrets and the mandatory French roof. For the eight hundred rooms there were five hundred baths, an unusually lavish distribution in the first decade of the twentieth century. Two stories were

allotted to dining and tea-ing, meetings and balls, and the main floor was devoted to a sweeping entrance and courtly servitors behind distinguished desks.

Hardenbergh's agents did almost as well as White's in raping Europe for furnishings. They cadged the ormolus and polished curves suggestive of the tight waists and deep décolletages of the ladies of the French courts from French chateaux. Tapestries and Aubusson rugs were lifted from noble walls and floors. What couldn't be removed at a price was meticulously copied: oak paneling in the prestigious Old English style, hundreds of crystal chandeliers and fragile wine glasses ordered of the most skillful European craftsmen, marble chiseled and rubbed by dozens of imported Italian workmen to shine on the broad stairways. To match the resplendent tutti, an overture of liveried doormen bound in gold braid and buttons, and entrance greeters in silk knee breeches and pristine white gloves to welcome the first groups of American and European royalty.

Hardly had the great steamer trunks, nannies and art treasures settled in when a financial panic, as regular as summer plagues, clamped down on the city. Business fell and the liberal press clawed at the Plaza populace who swam in milk and honey while the rest of the city went cold and hungry. Unperturbed, the Plaza sent out its reports of groaning boards, with details that seemed to have been pulled out of the *Satyricon*.

The theater people and the idle beauties divided their time between the Waldorf-Astoria and the Plaza. They shone especially well at the Plaza tea dances and dinner dances and cut charming figures in perky ice-skating costumes, their parties succored by warming refreshment sent out by the solicitous hotel. In 1908, the front yard was improved as the Grand Army Plaza, designed by Thomas Hastings. St. Gaudens's equestrian statue of General Sherman was moved southward one block to grace the new plaza, the General shortly accompanied by a

Hastings fountain paid for by a fifty-thousand-dollar bequest from the estate of the publisher Joseph Pulitzer. The nude pulchritude of the Lady of Abundance in the fountain disturbed Cornelius Vanderbilt who lived in the one-hundred-room house next door to the hotel. He insisted she be removed. Clearly she wasn't. She stayed and the Plaza, not quite what it once was but still the Plaza, stayed, while the Vanderbilt mansion is remembered only in a few unusual shards. According to Wayne Andrews, a Vanderbilt biographer, a Moorish Room and a Colonial Room were bought by Marcus Loew for one of his movie palaces in Kansas City, but those, too, have probably vanished. The only fragment left in New York is a set of handsome gates, rescued by a daughter of the house, Gertrude Vanderbilt Whitney, the sculptress wife of Harry Payne Whitney. They now stand at the entrance of the Conservatory Gardens of Central Park, a memorial to the small but mighty Vanderbilt Empire that bordered and inspired by its very presence, the Plaza.

CHAPTER 8

IMPORT-EXPORT

s their husbands collected thoroughbreds and began to discard the spurious for the thoroughbred in art, the ladies—already sole commanders of armies of servants and court jesters and treasuries of diadems and historic bucklers—turned to the ultimate achievement, titles for their daughters. The towering purchase price was not difficult to get out of Daddy or an older brother, not always insensible to the raw passion, the compulsive "I want" that trembled on their women's faces. Besides, it was a form of appeasement to neglected wives and an intense preoccupation that absorbed considerable female time during which Daddy could play his own games more freely.

Parental consent and money assured, letters whipped off to key contacts in Europe, Mama galvanized the servants into preparing the luggage for an eight- or nine-day sea voyage. Voluminous dresses, to be changed several times a day, required dozens of trunks, shoe boxes, hatboxes, cases of jewelry and maids to guard them and to pull corset strings and close long lines of hooks and pearl clasps and to pin securely the elaborate puffs and coils of hair. Mama might have an entourage of secretaries and assistants to help attend to her exigent social duties and a personal physician to relieve bouts of mal de mer or to spoon out her special diet. She often brought her own linen and pieces of her own silver, distrustful of the quality and care available in public accommodations, although a suite cost as much as $2,000 per day; the need for her own luxuries was, as well, a symptom of her sensitivity and gentility. Should she want a private promenade deck she need only add to the bill four thousand dollars. Once across, fortune hunters among the other passengers eluded, the ladies went to the fashionable spas, carefully surveyed by yet other fortune hunters. On to Paris for clothing and titled beaux, and then to London to taste the nectar of real privilege, the superb, expansive kind, and to inspect the English market in husbands. Among the people they visited with were an enterprising tribe of vendeuses, women on the fringes of society who might, in later decades, have made successful careers in business and politics. Most of them had known high life in America and, as impoverished English noblewomen or adjacent to nobility, needed money to support their dependents—and that might include the mistresses and strumpets of the husbands. They earned their fat fees; entertaining, being entertained, alert, busy, compiling and comparing lists of European titles to yoke to American money, competing—but subtly—with one and other, often shaping a loosely bound syndicate. A foulmouthed generation like ours might call them procuresses, or at best rapacious marriage brokers, but they did have style, intelligence, wit and limitless aggressiveness. Assisting props for their business were the lists of selling prices of titles featured in newspapers and extensive coverage in *Town Topics* which, among its 1885 reports on great balls, ads for corsets and florists, and advice on correct dress, reported that Miss Eva MacKay's engagement to Prince Colonna had been authoritatively announced and that the list of American women who had married Italian noblemen was too long to be given in one issue.

The results often went awry but the initial motives were fairly balanced. Second and third sons of blooded families, resentful of their demeaned positions vis-à-vis titled older brothers and unwilling to settle for the army or the clergy, sought to buy back ego and power with American money; the scions of impoverished houses hoped to restore tottering chateaux, melting stately homes, and to shine up dimming titles with the golden infusions American girls and their mothers offered so willingly. Why should a nobleman waste time working when he might be cultivating his exquisite tastes? And who better equipped for learning from him than the American heiress, pliable and curious, wide-eyed for culture and polish, and the education in manners, art, decoration, style and carefree, aristocratic spending they could give her? Who else could provide reality for her fantasies of conversing with dukes and members of Parliament, of setting a dinner worthy of Edward VII and his entourage?

There had been, throughout American history, occasional marriages of heiresses to titles. Early in the nineteenth century, Elizabeth Astor, the daughter of the first John Jacob, had been persuaded to marry Count Vincent Rumpff, a respectable accomplishment for the family of a German butcher boy. The later line of glittering, eager girls that became a bargain-sale rush in the late nineteenth and early twentieth centuries was led off by Jenny Jerome, who married Lord Randolph Churchill in 1874, but she does not actually qualify for the high-stakes European gamble. She was, at the time of her marriage, virtually a European, and although Leonard Jerome supported his daughters generously, there was no remarkable exchange of ladyship for money.

It was not necessary, though it helped, that a girl have high social standing; many scions knew that their own titles derived from rough military prowess or, more often, from large loans, never collected, to a king. Her background could be grubbing in mines, driving herds of cattle, concocting useless elixirs, supplying the Civil War armies with shoddy blankets and putrid foodstuffs. It didn't matter much: the more numerous the millions, the worthier she. He might be dissolute, feebleminded, debt-ridden, homosexual, antique, decaying with venereal disease. It didn't matter much: the higher he stood in the Almanach de Gotha or Debrett's, the worthier he. Some marriages held, some dragged on unhappily for long years, some were monstrous but the *drang* for ancient names, preferably as labels for coronets, went on. Historians estimate that there were five hundred such marriages by 1909 and a thousand twenty years later. Ferdinand Lundberg pointed out, in his *America's Sixty Families* that American labor supported not only the ornate American estates from which the heiresses stemmed, but the many European castles they bought.

The heiresses came from all parts of the country, with Fifth Avenue, New York, a leading supplier. The Bradley-Martins of the famous ball had already, at the time of the big Waldorf bash, married off a teen-aged daughter to Lord Craven. The Guggenheims married into English gentry; so had the marrying Wilsons, the Astors and the Vanderbilts. The celebrations were dignified or bizarre, always lavish, always vividly publicized. When a Goelet girl married the Duke of Roxburgh in 1904, the newspapers ran purple descriptions of not only bride and groom but of the mob of thousands of women who grappled with each other to get into the church and cull a flower or a ribbon as souvenir—to the point where the police had to be summoned. Another ceremony was followed by a party for a thousand guests at Sherry's who had arranged to explode an immense bird from which shot ten thousand roses. One girl, the sister of Harry Thaw, was left standing at the church for almost an hour. She had been paired off with the Earl of Yarmouth who might, in time, become Marquis of Hertford. His only possessions were his title and debts which followed him to the United States and assaulted him—three hundred pounds' worth—just as he was about to be married. He refused to go through with the ceremony until the purchase price was raised to a million dollars.

That marriage took place in 1903, several years after the

two most momentous Fifth Avenue marriages, that of Anna Gould and, shortly after, of Consuelo Vanderbilt. One of the leading Susannas (there were Figaros as well) of the European brokerage chain was Minnie Stevens Paget, the daughter of the memorable Mrs. Paran Stevens of Fifty-seventh Street and Fifth Avenue. Herself enmeshed in a not too brilliant English marriage, Minnie became well ensconced in English society, was admired by the omnivorous Prince of Wales and tutored and encouraged by an old friend, the Duchess of Manchester, who had once been Consuelo Iznaga of 262 Fifth Avenue. One of Minnie's triumphs was maneuvering Anna Gould and Boni de Castellane into each other's orbits.

The fearsome Jay Gould had died in 1892 and his children were not making marked progress in society. The sons favored actresses while sister Helen immersed herself in good works. It was up to Anna, the younger sister, to paint a diadem around the shady Gould name. Whether she was engaged to one of the railroad Harrimans, as generally reported, or not, Anna was sent off in 1894 to visit in Paris with a refined lady relative of Minnie Paget. As if she were a valuable art treasure the thin-mouthed, heavy-jawed girl was put on display and the viewers came, a number more frequently and more warmly welcomed than the rest. The most serious contender was Count Boni de Castellane of a worn title and thin family fortune and the conviction that he was the repository of the best in French civilization. He pursued Anna back to New York, picking up the wherewithal for a dignified stay from a "good friend" (a closer meaning, "backer"), visited in Gould houses and, after a tour of the United States, returned to the Goulds and the courtship of Anna. During his visit he gleaned some idea of how boundlessly rich the family was and how "obsessed," to use Boni's word, they were with keeping their fortune in America. Nor was he too pleased, according to his story, when Anna turned down his suggestion that she convert to Catholicism. Although she was willing to be married by a Catholic archbishop, she wanted to preserve the right to divorce him should that become necessary. Furthermore, she rejected the rule of the Napoleonic code, which would give him control of her fortune. Both wary, neither romantic, although she was only nineteen, they were married in the early spring of 1895 in brother George's imposing house at Sixty-seventh Street and Fifth Avenue.

For days before the wedding the house was a busy, resplendent stage set, every scene traced by the newspapers: the money Anna gave to a thousand poor children for ice cream and cake; the details of the menu and the quantities of champagne served at the Waldorf in the course of a bachelor dinner Boni gave for his friends and new male relations; the arrival of his parents, the Marquis and Marquise, bearing a wedding present heirloom, a pearl necklace that was once the property of Marie de Medici; the coronet bought by eldest brother George from a Corsican prince to the tune of seventy thousand dollars. Sister-in-law Edith, a lover of nice things, was pleased to talk about the gifts. She and the awed papers (they usually added a tinge of criticism for spice and to conform with the approved muckraker stance) reported, exaggerating rapturously, that the famous coronet cost a half-million dollars, that among the floods of diamonds and pearls there was an antique gold necklace that had once been in the Spanish royal family, since presented to Anna by the de Castellanes. Brother George added to the coronet a many-stranded necklace of eight hundred pearls and seventy-two diamonds while his wife contributed a silver dinner set, service for twelve, touched with diamonds and rubies. Helen gave Anna a brooch built around a priceless diamond and young brother Frank came up with a chain of two hundred diamonds.

On the great day, played out for a crowd held back by several dozen policemen, the distinguished guests who included ambassadors and ministers, American and European aristocracy, were ushered into rooms that had been newly decorated with lush Oriental rugs, red damasks and velvets embroidered in gold and silver threads. To the strains of Victor Herbert's orchestra in a gallery above, the ceremony was held in the Moorish parlor, a romantic close of ebony, mother-of-pearl and sandalwood draped in Oriental silks. Anna wore a veil that cost six thousand dollars, her bridesmaids' dresses were trimmed in sable. After the ceremony, lunch was served by Sherry's who had arranged bowers of orchids and other rare blossoms brought down from the Irvington house and also saw to it that the guests had little golden boxes to hold the traditional souvenir pieces of wedding cake. The next day Anna made sure that her right to divorce Boni remained inviolate by going through a civil ceremony in Lakewood, and shortly blond, wispy, mannered Boni and darkish, round Anna and her large fortune took off for Europe and an erratic life conducted in a steady glare of publicity.

It is variously estimated that Boni spent, in the eleven years of their life together, between five and a half million and twelve million dollars of her money. He spent it on gambling, on a number of women worthy of Priapus, on paintings, on Gobelins, on entertainment, on country estates, town houses and their furnishings, on a yacht whose care consumed over one hundred thousand dollars a year—nothing but the choicest, the most remarkable, the most expensive. He fancied himself an organizer of royal fetes and for Anna's twenty-first birthday (some say to celebrate the birth of his first son) managed to reserve a large section of the Bois de Boulogne where he placed yet another version of that battered cliché, Versailles. The grounds were illuminated by eighty thousand Venetian lamps which, he said, were made exclusively for him on the island of Murano. (It might easily have been true.) He ordered built a ballet stage with special lighting effects. A leading Paris upholsterer arranged twelve miles of carpeting for the guests to stroll on. Several dozen men in red livery were spotted picturesquely here and there to prove it all Versailles. Although

the dinner attendance was small, only two hundred and fifty
and extraordinarily exclusive, the full guest list numbered three
thousand, entertained by fountains and fireworks and a cast—
dancers, musicians, living statues—of hundreds. Anna didn't
like it or the aristocratic company or the fact that one of its
titled beauties wandered off into the woods with Boni. He
complained that she had no sense of true elegance except that
taught her by Mr. Worth, the couturier. In this she was like
her crude brothers who were beginning to worry about their
sister and her fortune, particularly when a Paris dealer decided
he had waited long enough for the millions of francs owed him.
Boni was forced to pay, very resentful of the injustice done
him. Since he was broke only because he had purchased beautiful things to make a fairyland of art and culture for their sister
who would shine as the wife of a great connoisseur and collector, the brothers should bear the cost. They countered with
accusations of money wasted on women and gambling. Merely
hearths of refuge from the coldness of his wife, Boni answered.
The brothers, and Anna with them, held firm. The marriage
began palpably to dissolve and finished definitely in January
of 1906 when Boni came home to the marble palace in Paris
that had taken years and millions to complete, to find the
electricity cut and wife, three little sons and servants gone.
Much as it had cost her, Anna was not yet through with French
nobility. The next time around she married the rich Hélie de
Talleyrand-Perigord, whose mother was purportedly one of the
Prince of Wales's intimate *amies* and who was Boni's distant,
disliked relation.

Her niece Vivien, George and Edith's girl of the educated-
to-the-eyebrows tribe that inhabited the fifty rooms at Sixty-
seventh Street and Fifth Avenue and several other estates,
held to her bargain. She was a good-looking girl who had inherited some of her mother's famous beauty and might have
made a better choice than the one she did, or was saddled with.
In England she met a British officer, a younger son of a titled

family shackled by gambling debts and unpaid bills to the sup-
pliers of the liquor he consumed in notable quantities. He was
no longer young but impeccably an English gentleman, when
he wasn't too drunk, and a relentless suitor. When he became
the fifth Baron Decies on the death of his older brother, the
wedding was set and the same show put on in 1911 as had been
staged in 1895 for Anna: armies of dressmakers set to work by
Edith, a jeweled chaplet, coronet type, presented to his daughter by her father, crowds in the streets in front of St. Bar-
tholomew's where the marriage was performed, a grand reception at the Fifth Avenue house, the blaring display of gifts,
financial arrangements and off to a miserable life in one of
the stately homes of England which her husband later lost in
gaming.

Early 1895 was a nasty time for Alva Vanderbilt. The newspapers battened on the fact that she had been granted a divorce
decree from her husband who was living brightly in Europe.
Almost as irritating was the fact that the Goulds had achieved
a countess. Her own beautiful, intelligent Consuelo was ready
to be married to a title. In August, hordes of workmen transformed the grounds of the Marble House in Newport to re-
semble one of Le Notre's garden masterpieces; the footmen
were put into breeches and powdered wigs (extra pay for
powdering) to pour the best of champagnes. One of the guests
was the ninth Duke of Marlborough, of Blenheim and a
nephew of the Churchills. With Mama's heavy assistance, the
duke wasted no time—two weeks—in proposing to Consuelo.
The consensus of gossip was that Winthrop Rutherford, not
terribly rich, nor the descendant of a British military hero, nor
claimant to one of the most ponderous of stately homes, was
Consuelo's real choice for a husband, in time. She was only
eighteen and had hoped to continue her education at Oxford
but her aspirations counted for little. She was accustomed to
hearing from her mother, "I don't ask you to think; I do the

thinking, you do as you are told." The girl's view of herself, as she reports in her book, *The Glitter and the Gold*, was a product of her mother's "wish to produce me as a finished specimen framed in a perfect setting, and that my person was dedicated to whatever final disposal she had in mind."

The girl pleaded, protested, wept, but her mother forestalled acts of rebellion by having it published in the social columns of newspapers that Consuelo and the duke were formally engaged. Alva saw to it that there was no communication between Winthrop—or anyone else—and Consuelo; she threatened variously to kill herself and/or Winthrop and feigned serious illness. On the day that thousands gathered before St. Thomas's Church to observe yet again the carriages and costumes of the rich, Consuelo was imprisoned until the hour of the wedding ceremony (sparsely attended by Vanderbilts) which sealed the fashionable bargain. One of Alva's gifts to her daughter was a set of pearls that once had been worn by Catherine the Great, so the papers said. From Father Willie the couple received railroad shares valued at two and a half million dollars and a stipend of a hundred thousand annually for each. In toto, the marriage settlement amounted to over ten million dollars, the price for the privilege of shoring up and maintaining Blenheim and a palace in London and coping with relatives frozen in their aristocratic habits.

Consuelo was superbly dressed and bejeweled, well-educated and bright, a devoted mother to her two sons, an accomplished hostess, lovely to look at (not even the chic distortions of Boldini, who painted her like a breeze of expensive perfume, could deny her essential beauty) and cruelly unhappy. This hardly mattered to Alva in the early years. She had done her duty to her class and, as a loving mother, she had given her daughter the highest gift an affectionate mother could bestow and that was that. After eleven years, the Duke and Consuelo separated; divorce was too complicated a matter in Edwardian England. She moved to a house her sympathetic father built for her in London and organized a new life interestingly and fruitfully, cultivating supportive friendships and devoting herself to social welfare causes.

She had long before invited her mother into her life again and they became friends; Alva was sufficiently contrite to testify against herself in a complex divorce suit that involved the Rota of Rome. Consuelo was then free to marry an old friend, Jacques Balsan, in 1921, and live happily ever after into a handsome, dignified old age.

Consuelo's autobiography tactfully omitted many footnotes. One footnote must suffice to sharpen the portraits of Consuelo and her duke. In his Diary, Rene Gimpel mentions the fact that, even after the divorce, Marlborough had an income from his former wife. Nevertheless, he offered Gimpel a number of paintings to pay the expenses of his palace, especially "his apartment like those of the Great King of Versailles," furnished in the early years of his marriage with Vanderbilt money. Rigid and arrogant, he insisted on maintaining himself in the style to which he had become rapidly accustomed, the unquestioned right of the master of a great house, a ruler. As it was the instant right of Boni de Castellane and the barons and the princes—English, French, Montenegrin, German, Polish— the girls and especially their mothers eagerly bought as brilliant adornment of their lives.

The trade in golden girls for titles flourished until the dislocations of World War I, with suzerainties conquered and annexed, the titles empty paper bags. As the trade faded, one stalwart held on. She was Barbara Hutton, the granddaughter of Woolworth, who made an occupation of garnering, one after the other, princes and barons of obscure, used-up corners of Europe. The newspapers followed her marriages, but dryly, without a tinge of awe as in the old days and then forgot her as the once-lustrous transatlantic commerce died a small, feeble death to be revived, once in a while, in a startling obituary. On September 16, 1977, it was published that Anita Stewart Morris had died at the age of 91. The story goes on with all the classic ingredients. She was the daughter of one of the most Knickerbocker of Knickerbockers, William Rhinelander Stewart. She married, in 1909, a pretender to the Portuguese throne who promised her she might easily be Queen of Portugal although his connections with Portuguese royalty were extremely tenuous. He had a glorious name, Prince Miguel de Braganza, and was saddled with debts and a reputation for accumulating them royally. Like Anna Gould, Anita refused to become a Catholic; unlike Anna's family, Anita's mother supported the couple and their three young children for a good number of years until she could no longer bear the profligacy of Princess Anita and Prince Miguel. They wandered, they separated, they came together and the newspapers followed them. The story seemed much older than half a century or, from its beginnings, three-quarters of a century. It seemed to be a legend of an exotic, remote time, possibly a symptom of how thoroughly such patterns in Society are gone, at least publicly.

CHAPTER 9

FIFTY-MILLION-DOLLAR ROW

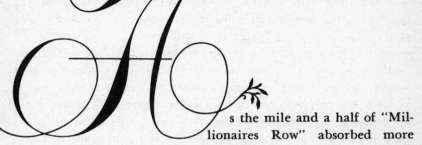

s the mile and a half of "Millionaires Row" absorbed more and more of the Avenue which faced Central Park and staggering sums of money (a lot worth three thousand dollars in 1852 was worth one and a half million in 1870 and thereafter soared upward), the mansion style seemed to grow, with a few dignified exceptions, more fanciful, more eclectic, gathering a bit of this and that to make inordinately expensive displays worthy of being photographed in guides exclusively devoted to them. These fantasies in this extraordinarily expensive residential area had an aggregate value estimated at seventy million dollars, unremarkable for a group of householders who controlled at least fifty million dollars each. A French visitor, Paul Bourget, found the Avenue bewildering and the money it represented unimaginable as early as 1895. "It is too evident that money cannot have much value here. There is too much of it. The interminable succession of luxurious mansions which line Fifth Avenue proclaim its mad abundance. No shops, unless of articles of luxury—a few dressmakers, a few picture-dealers . . . only independent dwellings each one of which, including the ground on which it stands, implies a revenue which one dares not calculate. The absence of unity in this architecture is a sufficient reminder that this is the country of the individual will, as the absence of gardens and trees around these sumptuous residences proves the newness of all this wealth and of the city. This avenue has visibly been willed and created by sheer force of millions, in a fever of land speculation, which has not left an inch of ground unoccupied."

Although it was generally agreed that palazzi and chateaux were the styles most suitable for the superrich, why not add a dome, a minaret, a curly, fat Victorian tower, or a Borromini lantern? And no architect disagreed to the point of walking off the job. Some of the houses were so thoroughly showpieces, inside and out, that ordinary living conveniences were neglected. A dealer who visited the steel magnate, E. T. Gary, in his house at 856 described Louis XV paneling perked up by Fragonards, a large marble staircase, quasi Renaissance furniture at its most stolid and a small, mean bedroom in which he visited with the white-haired man of seventy-three, "with the body of an old and poor clown on whom life has not smiled." Creature comforts were well seen to a couple of blocks to the south, at the north corner of Sixty-fifth Street, where Richard Hunt had built for Caroline Astor, her son John Jacob and his beautiful Wicked Queen, née Ava Willing, a chateau meant to rival any edifice in the Loire valley. The double palace, one for the young people, one for the Dowager Queen, was clasped in an ornate web of architectural ornaments. The joint gold-and-white ballroom was large enough to hold more than a thousand people and the kitchens were capacious enough to feed them. Although each of the show rooms enjoyed its own "period," with a nostalgic bit of Victoriana dragged in here and there, the elder Mrs. Astor clung to the traditional gold and white for her salon and brightened it with a rug woven of peacock tails.

Society had been changing for some time. The struggles of the society Amazons like Caroline Astor had been joined by young and livelier contenders more interested in fun than in decorum and sound ancestry—despite the dictum of the conservatives that there were actually fewer than two dozen families worth talking to in New York. Caroline took tentative steps into the shapeless new world: she dined frequently at Sherry's, began to entertain the Five and Six hundred and then over one thousand who spilled whiskey on the peacock feathers and ripped her brocades and velvets. Too old, too bewildered, she soon gave up. There were no more Metropolitan Opera galas after 1905, no more balls and drunken vandals; she retired to senility, a realm in which she queened it over other queens, and death at the age of seventy-seven in 1908.

The other part of the mansion was a house further divided by cruelty and inert passivity. Lady Cynthia Asquith described Ava Willing Astor, wife of John Jacob IV, as exquisitely dressed and "very beautiful in a decorative, Sèvres china way, but it is an applique, unventilated face and she doesn't look out of it and one cannot look into it." Out of this enameled face came unremitting contempt for her awkward, retiring and not very sharp husband; his one virtue was his money, which she spent with an almost vengeful passion. She enjoyed posing as a Bohemian, dashing off to odd, raffish corners of the city with rakish companions when she wasn't frozen for hours at the bridge table, leaving her husband to amble vaguely on his own or to tinker with this and that. He loved cars and accumulated a large number into which he invited lady passengers at whom he would make tentative passes. There was nothing tentative about Ava's lovelife; she might not have had as many lovers as she liked to imply, but lovers there were.

The money kept pouring in. Astor tenements grew more and more crowded, many of them enclosing sweatshops and grogshops that earned much higher rentals than the other rotting flats. With some of the vast earnings—exact sums and details were carefully guarded by the Astors—John Jacob IV built the St. Regis Hotel for the elite and the Knickerbocker Hotel for the ordinary rich. The St. Regis saw to every comfort and refinement of service and cuisine and did become a favorite resting and meeting place for a number of multimillionaires.

Ava, too, took time out for organizing a new enterprise. With the help of a few wealthy men, she hired Stanford White to build the Colony Club, ready for its exclusive female membership in 1907.

In the meantime they had somehow managed to produce two children, Vincent, whom Ava had little use for because he was so distinctly like his father, and Alice Muriel who didn't consume much of her time and attention, either. The dreadful marriage dwindled into longer and longer separations and, in 1910, divorce. With a settlement rumored to be ten million dollars, Ava went off to England and caught in marriage a great name, Lord Ribblesdale, once a dashing rake—which lured Ava—but now bored and aging, ready for country quiet by the time Ava got him. Calm evenings by the fireside were never for Ava, who went on her merry dance, merrier after Ribblesdale died in 1925. Fifteen years later she returned to the States, became again a citizen though she insisted on remaining Lady Ribblesdale; in attempts to retain the famous beauty she had herself cut, scraped, patched and colored countless times, the masklike face increasingly grotesque, the conduct more arrogant, the viperish tongue nastier.

The freed J. J. took to his yacht, his son, to partying and guiding the St. Regis on its exquisite way. His renewed happier energies found another outlet in rebuilding and redecorating the chateau at 840. Then he met a pretty, pliant young girl and married her. Madeleine Force was eighteen, he on the shadier side of forty. He took her to Europe, and brought her home, pregnant, on the *Titanic*. As the ship began to sink, he found space for her in a lifeboat and stayed behind, to die with an extraordinary number of other masters of finance and industry. He had left her the Fifth Avenue house and the income earned by a five-million-dollar trust, void if she remarried. Three million dollars had been settled on the child not yet born and the rest went to Vincent. Some provision for his sister Alice was wrested from the estate by Ava.

Vincent, a strange, friendless youngster, was only twenty
when he inherited nearly seventy million dollars and the positions on various boards that the fortune implied. Like his
father, he liked mechanical toys, whether the inherited fleet
of cars or advanced, sophisticated toy trains. Much of the rest
of his time was spent in refurbishing the stained family name
and assuaging a guilt new to Astors by establishing institutions
for mentally ill children, for helping immigrants settle in, for
the care of the indigent. To apologize to slum blacks, he built
a children's recreation area in Harlem; to make amends to
slum Jews he contributed to the relief committees established
by Schiffs and Warburgs. As generous as he was with the anonymous poor, just as mean he was with his stepmother Madeleine
and the loathed baby half brother, John Jacob VI, whom she
insisted on bringing up as a royal child, including all the costly
perquisites. She needed more money; Vincent wasn't giving
her any. Actually he gained back Madeleine's trust fund and
the 840 house when she remarried. Vincent himself was already
married to an old friend, Helen Huntington, who helped en-
liven, once again, his grandmother's house with big parties.
Besides giving free-form, exceedingly democratic parties, Vincent broke another Astor rule, "hold the holdings"; he sold as
if his properties were a burning cloak. In collaboration with
his English relatives he sold the Waldorf-Astoria Hotel for an
enormous profit and a few years later, on the site that had
belonged to Astors for more than a century, rose the Empire
State Building. 840 was sold, about 1925, for $3,500,000 to a
former peddler who turned it over to Temple Emanu-El. The
St. Regis was put on the market also, although he was reluctant
to relinquish it; the place was a steadily interesting home, as
it had been for his father, and fed him well. A sale was arranged, however, but default on the mortgage Vincent held
returned the hotel, with its fascinating details and kaleidoscope
of humanity from bellboys to magnates, to him.

As if to wipe out slurs, real and imagined, against him as a repository of unearned wealth and owner of a fleet of cars and a Leviathan of a yacht that consumed over one hundred thousand dollars a year, he aligned himself actively with Democratic and liberal causes and candidates, and when Mayor La Guardia launched his demolition of slums and building of housing projects, Vincent Astor turned over to the housing agencies his decaying properties at much less than the value of the land. Contributions to charities went on, as well as the Astor gifts to the New York Public Library and continued beyond his death in 1957 at the age of sixty-eight. As great fortunes often do, his proliferated almost of itself and he died twice as rich as he had been at twenty, leaving over one hundred twenty-five million dollars. He left his third wife several million dollars and a half-interest in the estate for her lifetime; the rest went into the Vincent Astor Foundation, a bequest that covered a wide gamut of charitable and educational activities. When *Newsweek*, on which he had spent $5,000,000, was sold and, finally, the St. Regis, the proceeds became part of the foundation. His real estate holdings were negligible, the remaining Astor properites having reverted to the English branch of the family.

Sister Alice, a darkly beautiful gifted woman, had died in 1956 in shrouds of Egyptian mysticism, her escape from an erratic, peripatetic life, and couldn't protest the dispersal of Astor property. The younger half brother, J.J.V, was enraged. He had been deliberately impoverished, his right to be a wealthy Astor taken from him by the vengeful older brother who had ruined the real estate investments initiated two hundred years before and since grown with the speed of binary fission into an infinitely large fortune, now gone.

In the row of architectural wonders that stood swollen cheek by jowl with the Astors, lived several particularly colorful colossi. In 1890, two associates of Louis Tiffany, Charles Coolidge Haight and Samuel Colman, began to build the strange

house that rose at the corner of Sixty-sixth Street, neither palazzo nor chateau, rather medieval in its broad, earth-hugging lines and Tuscan arches, no spires or Gothic frills. The interior, completed two years later, was the work of Tiffany himself, the most forceful exponent of art nouveau in America, a connoisseur of Japanese arts and a leading decorator to those willing to risk the romanticism and sensuality of his inventions. (Those who hired him for the chic of the name but hated the product had expensive regrets, like the Ogden Goelets who fought and suffered and paid the Tiffany company, Associated Artists, fifty thousand dollars nevertheless.)

These were sophisticated clients, Louisine and Henry Osborne Havemeyer, the Sugar King of the East. On Sundays they held musicales, using instruments from their collection of Strads and Guarneris, the host one of the participants; he practiced the violin every morning before he went to his office. Via a hall faced with mosaics around a fountain that trickled like the Alhambra's, the guests were ushered into the music room and the library. The furniture of the music room was light and delicate, set against Oriental panels on subtly tinted wallpaper, a most tactful background for unique Chinese vases and rugs and Oriental lacquers. Above, wondrous Tiffany chandeliers, clusters of bubbling glass of blossoms on slender floating branches of art nouveau metal. Tiffany devised, also, a suspended staircase of many frail elements, a fantasy from Arabian Nights, not unrelated to the fantasy of Whistler's Peacock Room. The adjoining lamps were bold, eclectic—Carolingian crowns studded with glass, supports in Chinese curves, suggestions of the Moorish—unparalleled in their inventiveness and dramatic effect.

The ceiling of the library was an arrangement of rich Japanese fabrics shot through with gold and silver; it shone like all the golden East. The furniture, some of it on Celtic and Viking themes, was carved and repeatedly stained and polished by Italian craftsmen until it had the patina of antique china. On fanciful tripods stood a priceless collection of Chinese bronzes. The Havemeyers disliked the usual red silks and velvets used as background for most pictures, and had these walls done in remote, soft-spoken Japanese tones. Against this bland background, illuminated by electric bulbs hidden behind lustrous arrangements of Tiffany glass, hung eight Rembrandts, two Halses, Holbein, Bronzino, Cranach and several of their equals.

The house and the advanced taste in furnishings that ranged the world—Byzantium, Ravenna, Venice, Morocco, Persia, the Far East—developed from several sources. First, the riches for it all. Henry Havemeyer was the son of a German immigrant who landed in New York and quickly found his way to sugar refining and Tammany power. Henry was born rich and eager to become richer. In the manner of his peers, he bought politicians of both parties and engaged in a series of sleight-of-hand refinery mergers that produced the Sugar Refineries Company in 1887, later disallowed by court order. It reappeared as the American Sugar Refining Company, which came forcibly to the public eye when its head was convicted of and fined two million dollars for cheating the customs on his sugar imports for many years. His was one of the first combines dubbed a "trust." Mrs. Havemeyer, more naive about industry than she was about art, thought trusts good, progressive entities: the presence of stockholders instead of partners, employees sharing profits, presidents and directors on salaries—and costs to consumers were lessened because of the economies conglomerates provided. "They were truly democratic," she said, "in the beginning, when the Rockefellers with the Standard Oil and Mr. Havemeyer with the sugar trust started the ball rolling. Every new form of industrial development has to have its pioneers and its martyrs as well as the profiteers in politics and blackmail. It is the history of the world from the days of Galileo to the present time."

Her Galileo, considerably older than herself (he had been

married to her aunt who had died), was as impatient and autocratic as she was patient and good natured. Along with his
harshness, though, grew an aesthetic sense that began to make
itself felt when, as a young man, he visited the Philadelphia
Centennial Exposition of 1876 and fell in love—as did Whistler,
Degas, Vuillard and other artists—with Oriental objects newly
burst on the Occidental world. He began to amass hundreds of
boxes of vases, bowls and ceremonial tea jars, becoming quite
expert in the process of searching for rarities that Louisine later
catalogued, stored and also became expert in. With the education in his Oriental objects as background, Havemeyer became
a quick study, and ready to spend, on the aspects of art which
were Louisine's field.

Louisine was a friend of the painter Mary Cassatt, the
sister of a Philadelphia railroad tycoon, who guided her, when
she was sixteen, to the Paris studios of several painters. Out of
her carefully allotted allowance Louisine bought her first Monet,
her first Pissarro; her first Degas cost her five hundred francs,
a group of Whistler pastels, thirty pounds. She was launched
on a life that left her happily free of the social struggle and
the competition for dazzling dress and jewelry. "I prefer to
have something painted by a man than something made by an
oyster." In 1901 the Havemeyers took their first European trip
together and, in the company of Mary Cassatt, began a series
of art hunts that Louisine reported later, simply and engagingly, in her book, *Sixteen to Sixty*. Tutored by Cassatt, who
had learned from Degas, they looked at Italian art and yearned
for it, chasing through Sicilian villages, lost hollows of hill
towns, in the footsteps of mysterious informers and their sub-
informers, to pick up a Lippi, a Veronese.

In Spain they were mesmerized by the art in the Prado,
particularly the portraits by El Greco, whom they studied carefully. They bought one El Greco for $250, turned down four-
teen for a total of $4,000 (because they were all on religious
subjects) and were offered Goyas that went for several thousand

dollars each. The Havemeyer purchases opened a market for Spanish art in the United States. "I found myself upon the crest of the wave in Spain for Grecos and Goyas," wrote Lou-isine, recalling the indefatigable and successful hunt for El Greco's *Toledo* and Goya's *Women on a Balcony*.

At home they continued collecting for Henry's immense storehouse of Oriental wares. The original gallery could no longer hold the Courbets, the Degases (ultimately there were fifty), the Manets that included the pastel portrait of George Moore and the larger *Mlle Victorine in the Costume of a Toreador*, a dozen Goyas, the El Grecos, the unavoidable Italian fakes and the antiques they picked up on their travels. An additional gallery was built and more paintings hung, except for nudes. Louisine didn't mind but Henry wouldn't have nudes around the house although he had the good judg-ment to buy some. Courbet's gorgeous, candidly sensual *Woman with a Parrot* he dispatched to the Metropolitan Museum im-mediately on purchase.

Havemeyer died in 1907. Louisine continued the musicales and the careful, judicious collecting she had practiced in her youth, broadening her repertoire with paintings like the famous *Third-class Carriage* of Daumier, with Hispano-Mor-esque plates, Chinese porcelains and incomparable prints. She arranged shows and lectured on Impressionist art, inspiring purchases in a new and suspect area, and when women's suf-frage became a vibrant cause, plunged in ardently. For the cause she staged a show of her Goyas and El Grecos at Knoed-lers who were threatened with a loss of patronage by anti-feminist customers. She was a good propagandist, speech maker, organizer and publicist and, crowning achievement, she man-aged to get herself thrown into jail. She was quite contented to stay with her friends but her children implored her to pay her fine and leave, and she did.

When she died in 1929, she left nearly 150 paintings to the Metropolitan Museum and permission for her three children to pick out others to give. They had been brought up in an atmosphere of connoisseurship and generosity (one of them, Electra Havemeyer Webb, was a collector of fine objects on her own) and their gift grew to almost two thousand paintings, prints and diverse objects of rare distinction. There was an ample supply left for an auction that ran more than a week, enough for the family and for later museum gifts, an abundant tree in short, fertilized by sugar, a passion for Japanese tea jars and an allowance not spent on French bonnets and kid gloves.

According to Ferdinand Lundberg who was fervently interested in Havemeyers, Goulds and robber barons in general, those whom the gods would destroy they seemingly first make rich, a statement out of a Depression book that has no validity for some families (see Rockefellers and Whitneys) and validity for others (see Ryans, one or two Astor lines and Goulds). While Helen Gould at Forty-seventh Street distributed great quantities of money and Bibles, Edith Gould, George's wife, was expanding her social horizons from her sybaritic estate, Georgian Court in Lakewood, and from the house at Sixty-seventh Street. With the help of the useful busybody, Mrs. Paran Stevens, Goulds finally appeared on the invitation lists of Mrs. Astor's ball although the Vanderbilts, still wincing at the memory of Jay Gould outfoxing their Commodore, were not quite ready for them. While Edwin went off on his own enterprises and young Frank studied engineering, particularly as it affected railroading, George and Howard ran the railroad interests their father had accumulated.

While George and Edith were building a family and entertaining sumptuously in New Jersey and on Fifth Avenue, Howard was pursuing an actress, Odette Tyler, despite the relentless objections of Helen. She won and Howard consoled himself by becoming, with George, a champion yachtsman; they were winners of most American yachting prizes. Then came another actress, Kathrine Clemmons, who didn't give a damn whether Helen liked her or not. Howard had found her in Buffalo Bill's Wild West Show, made her his "protégée," took her on travels with him and pushed her into the New York theater where she performed with no distinction. Edith thought the relationship disgusting—the woman couldn't even act—and Helen was beside herself with shame and rage; but Kathrine was tough and determined. Howard married her. It was a tempestuous marriage, Howard imperious, Kathrine half-mad with her new power. When a steward on a Gould yacht said that the fireworks Howard wanted set off were too old to use, Howard insisted and the steward was badly injured by the erratic explosions. He sued—one of the innumerable suits that involved Goulds—and collected fifty thousand dollars. Whether he liked it or not, Howard found himself featured in the newspapers, not only as a leading playboy, but as the husband of a woman with a talent for newsworthy trouble. She was sued by a variety of tradespeople because she capriciously rejected expensive items she had ordered. Lashing out at what she considered her inferiors—servants, craftsmen, seamstresses—she purred sweetly at her superiors, especially rich and famous men.

For a while the Howard Goulds lived in a rented house at 824 Fifth Avenue, awaiting the completion of a new mansion at Seventy-third Street and Fifth, on a large lot that cost four hundred and fifty thousand dollars, one of the choicest pieces of land in the city. Within a few years, Howard had had enough of house and wife. Since she would not divorce him, he gave her the house and a substantial allowance, sold his Irish castle on Long Island to Daniel Guggenheim and removed himself to England, where he stayed, and continued to pay the taxes on Kathrine's house at Seventy-third Street. He asked her to leave so that he might sell it. She said, not unexpectedly, no. The taxes on the house rose and stayed unpaid. Howard and George arranged a scheme by which George was to buy the tax lien, and then insist that the property, which he would buy, be put on the market to pay the lien. It worked well: George got his money back, Howard some of it, and Kathrine left the house, taking with her a fair chunk of the sales price.

The same year of Howard's departure, 1909, good-looking Frank divorced the young heiress he had married in 1901 and a year later took as wife a Broadway girl, Edith Kelly. They and his two little girls of the former marriage are listed as the tenants of 834 Fifth Avenue in a 1910 directory. Not for long, however, since Frank was not deeply concerned with the maintenance of the railroad empire that was beginning to slip from George's hands; horses and their breeding were his preferred metier. He moved to France and developed the famous Maisons-Lafitte stables whose horses carried off the most coveted prizes on leading European tracks. Either the French soil or his wife or both became inimical to Frank within a couple of years. He began to drink, went into a dissolute period in his life, and emerged to marry yet a third time, again following the family proclivity for actresses, Florence La Caze. Together they began to buy and develop areas in the south of France, establishing hotels and casinos. During the war they were accused of pro-Nazi activities but were, after a series of inquiries, cleared, and went back to developing the French Riviera where he died in 1956, leaving a wealthy widow and two rich daughters.

Back home, at Sixty-seventh Street and among the playing fields of Georgian Court, George, now the only brother active in the family enterprises, was having financial problems. He lost backers and was crippled by ferocious competition. He lost many millions when the price of Gould railroad stock dropped sharply during the 1907–1908 panic. He lost additional millions when he was frozen out by the combined forces of Union Pacific and Southern Pacific. His father's Western Union became the property of the American Telephone Company and Manhattan Elevated went to the Rockefellers, Ryan and company. There was a mountain of cash left though, and George took good care of it for his children, filling his new leisure with polo and riding to hounds and, shortly, with a fresh, young love. Edith, quite fat and growing fatter, rode, exercised, swallowed countless thyroid pills, tormented her abundant flesh with rubber underclothes to help her perspire the pounds off, but couldn't keep off champagne and festive dishes and, especially, sweets. While she grew more obese and avoided Society, George went hunting and found a showgirl, Guinevere Jeanne Sinclair, as appealing as Edith had been in her youth. He set the girl up in a spacious house in Westchester and there spent at least half his time. Since the Goulds that followed silent, private Jay had little care for secrecy, the affair became public knowledge, particularly stimulating when George bought Guinevere a town house and a rural estate and, about when he was to become a grandfather, sired a little boy, George, born in 1915, and a little girl, Jane, born in 1916.

As suggested, when not otherwise occupied the Goulds sued and were sued. Frank's wife sued him for divorce in New York; he sued for divorce through the French courts. In the spring of 1919 Frank and Anna sued George for twenty-five million dollars which, they said, he had mismanaged, and insisted that he be removed from the trusteeship of the Gould fortune. They accused him of not arranging the individual trusteeships their father's will had stipulated; of selling Western Union without consulting the family and, in addition, taking for himself a large sum as broker; of managing to lose over twelve million dollars of their father's railroad holdings, of destroying pertinent records. It was ruled by the Supreme Court of the United States that George no longer be in control and that a separate trusteeship be established for each of Jay's heirs. George appealed but it stayed established that his life was too full of pleasures (at a cost of a thousand dollars a day) to allow for the necessary unremitting watchfulness against the sharks that swam in his financial waters.

George died in 1923, money matters not yet satisfactorily resolved; Frank and Anna continued to sue his estate, which had developed further complications. Shortly after Edith died in 1921, George married Guinevere and legitimized his babies. But Jay's will had barred inheritance by illegitimately born offspring and the family en masse brought their heaviest legal batteries against Guinevere. After endless suits Guinevere got the interest on a million dollars' worth of securities George had given her and later, remarried as a titled English lady, one million dollars more. Anna and Frank managed to wring sixteen million dollars out of their sister and brothers in the course of a redistribution of family holdings. The third generation continued the family tradition: husband against wife, brother against sister, the estate dwindling under taxes and legal costs which amounted to almost three million dollars.

No later Gould was ever as rich as Jay and his children; the estate had flowed in too many directions. Some managed to stay, like George and Anna and Howard, in the papers: scandal stalked their lives; othere led reasonable and private lives. In time the name faded altogether except in the contributions by Helen and Frank to NYU and the Edwin Gould Foundation.

In 1900, William C. Whitney, "the grand seigneur on an epic scale," "a grandee of graft," reached one of his several apogees. A super–robber baron to his critics, he is linked with the Rockefellers, the Goulds, Thomas Fortune Ryan, Belmont and Morgan as despoilers of the public wealth and welfare. According to Ferdinand Lundberg, Whitney "was a prime example of those magnates who rose to peculiar eminence not through any economic contribution of their own, but through political positions and their willingness to use these positions for private gains." He was influential in nominating Grover Cleveland for the governorship and for the presidency later, and in keeping him there. For his efforts he was appointed secretary of the navy, a position which expanded his fields of financial and legal power. Out of office, he remained a dealer in politics and big money, reaching a peak of his wealth by manipulating the securities of the Metropolitan Street Railway whose collapse broke many small investors but not the team—including Whitney, Elihu Root, Ryan and Rockefellers—that gained control of major street transportation in New York City.

Adulators spoke of Whitney as a Warwick, the kingmaker, a none too flattering accolade since the fifteenth-century Earl of Warwick, Richard Neville, was as opportunistic and ruthless as a rapacious time afforded. (He proclaimed the son of the Duke of York, Edward IV, king, thereby becoming himself the acting king of England for a while. When he fell out of favor with Edward, he placed Henry IV on the throne, but hardly had time to enjoy his new eminence since he was killed by the forces of Edward IV a year later.) Warwick-Whitney is credited with improving a moribund navy, and with providing New York City, which had been grinding to a halt because its primitive transportation system was incapable of coping with the exploding population, with improved public transport. As a corporation lawyer and counsel to the city he helped establish a well-functioning fire department, gave sound advice on liquor licensing and slid out of and back into Tammany politics, mainly, admirers say, to promote reforms and assurances of honest government. The admirers do—they must—mention periods of disgrace over peculiar bond games and bribery ploys played with city politicians but stress unceasingly his role as city servitor and the promoter of "improved poliitcs," whatever that might mean. He was a worldly man, one of the founders and trustees of the new Metropolitan Opera and host, with his engaging and well-educated wife (the sister of Oliver Payne who was treasurer of Standard Oil), of artists, musicians and writers who frequented his salon as friends, not hired entertainers. His national prominence was such that Whitney was promoted as a presidential candidate but retreated before

Bryan's thundering free-silver convention speech of 1896, "and
you shall not crucify mankind upon a cross of gold."

At the turn of the century, the reshaped—into a fraudulent
knot that no one could understand or untie—Metropolitan Corporation spent a considerable amount in electrifying its tram
lines. (Cars pulled by cables were hard to control at curves,
frayed cables tore and riders were frequently injured.) Shortly
before the electrification began, the *World* under Joseph
Pulitzer pointed out insistently that the corporation had paid
little or nothing for franchises which earned forty million
dollars each for Whitney and his teammate Ryan in a few years.
Whitney fought a new Franchise Tax Bill then passed by the
state legislature but lost and the company paid a huge fine.
To add to the opprobrium, Whitney declared for the Tammany
mayoral candidate because, say his defenders, this was the only
way he could guard his company from the blackmail threats
of Tammany. Somehow the Tammany connection served not
only as safeguard but proved helpful in securing for Whitney's
company a monopoly of the rapidly expanding gas and electricity services in the city. At this point a large predator swam
in to roil the murky waters. August Belmont, the son of the
Belmont who represented the Rothschilds, was undermining
the future of the surface lines by subsidizing, with a bond of
one million dollars, a contractor ready to build a subway line.
Whitney's Metropolitan Corporation tried to force its way in but
was barred by Governor Roosevelt's opposition and Belmont's
as a member of the Mayor's Rapid Transit Commission. After
Whitney's death in 1904, Thomas Ryan conducted a titanic
struggle with Belmont to combine his surface transit company
with Belmont's subway. Both won; Belmont bought into Ryan's
company and they made money.

Armed with charm, amiability, an air of probity, intelligence, immense energy, acquisitiveness, a taste for power games;
working partnerships with partners who knew every loophole
in the frail law (and invented new openings), alert to faint

financial breezes before they began to blow, keen to be in anything that was commanding and profitable, Whitney was active in banking; in railroads along with Rockefellers, Vanderbilts and Carnegie; in mining with the Guggenheims; he controlled a steamship company and created, with James Buchanan Duke and cohorts, a tobacco monopoly. He bought a newspaper and hired Finley Peter Dunne, the creator of Mr. Dooley, as editor and entertainer, the king's jester. He was threatened by the feeble Sherman Antitrust Act, constantly assailed by the reform press, yet continued to flourish, enriched by the respectable fortune left him by Flora Payne on her death.

Henry Adams said of him, "Whitney had finished with politics after having gratified every ambition, and swung the country almost at his will; he had thrown away the usual objects of political ambition like the ashes of smoked cigarettes; had turned to other amusements, satiated every taste, gorged every appetite, won every object that New York afforded and, not yet satisfied had carried his field of activity abroad, until New York no longer knew what most to envy, his horses or his houses." In addition to two-million-dollar stables, the best in the world, a horse that won the English Derby, a notable yacht and his own private railroad cars, Whitney accumulated as many as ten houses and estates. One had been a steep-gabled, Romanesque-arched house on the southwest corner of Fifty-seventh Street across the street from the bastion with miniature rose windows that belonged to Cornelius Vanderbilt. When William C.'s son, Harry Payne Whitney, married Gertrude Vanderbilt, the girl next door, in 1896, the father gave his son and daughter-in-law the Fifty-seventh Street house and negotiated for the purchase of 871 Fifth Avenue, at the northeast corner of Sixty-eighth Street, to which he took his second wife, Edith S. Randolph, a vital social leader until she suffered a severe riding accident which killed her after a few tortured years.

Although it was fairly far uptown the house already had an old history, as "old" is defined in the race up Fifth Avenue. The site was bought originally by Robert Stuart, the sugar magnate, in 1880. He died before the capacious brownstone was completed but his wife stayed on until her death. In 1894 the house was bought for $562,000 by the head of the Asphalt Paving Company, a Mr. Amzi Barber. Having bought it, he chose not to use it but leased the house to Levi P. Morton, the banker and politician who had had several Fifth Avenue addresses earlier, at Forty-second Street and at Fifty-fourth Street. He, too, didn't last long in the Sixty-eighth Street house and it was sold to Whitney for six hundred and fifty thousand dollars. The indispensable team of McKim, Mead and White were called in for total remodeling and, after four years of planning and collecting, White declared himself satisfied with his new three-million-dollar creation. It was inspected by the newspapers which photographed it and judged it to be, with one exception, a well-integrated example of an Italian Renaissance palace, a loose flattering label attached to wealthy houses, particularly those with spindly columns at the windows and a "Tuscan" balcony. The exception was the addition on the Sixty-eighth Street side of a wing for the largest private ballroom in New York, whose carved, gilt-touched paneling came from a French chateau. The tapestries had been designed by Boucher, the gallery for musicians was a master work in wrought iron. The introduction to the house proper was two gates of ornate iron and bronze taken from a palace of the Dorias and a gateway made in the golden age of Florence. A floor of intricate Italian mosaics, a magnificence of tapestries—one for $10,000 bought of Duveen—an elaborately carved fireplace under a coffered ceiling and sinuous curves of rare white marble that shaped the entrance hall. Among authentic Attic marbles, and paneling carved by an unknown old master, paintings attributed to Van Dyck, Tintoretto, Raphael, Reynolds and illustrious company. Bathroom fixtures were, of course, gold on marble. In the extensive library, Whitney kept a distinguished collection of first editions, gathered by his agents. Like Henry Frick, though, he preferred lighter reading in his later years and left the rarities as untouched ornaments. To introduce his house and its splendors, Whitney arranged a debut ball for a favorite niece in January, 1901, and was acclaimed as the host of one of the most brilliant fetes in the annals of New York society, featuring the appearance of the elderly Mrs. Astor, cap-à-pie in royal velvets, diamonds and pearls. A year later, Whitney, then sixty, retired from active business to concentrate more assiduously on bright company and victorious jockeys and horses. The medicine of 1904, not always capable of handling efficiently an attack of appendicitis, helped cut short the life of the aging Golden Boy who had spent twenty million dollars or more in the last decade of his life and was still avid for pleasure.

The next purchaser of the house and a major portion of its furnishings, for a price of $1,600,000, was James Henry Smith, known as "Silent," probably shocked into silence by an unexpected great windfall from an eccentric uncle. He recovered sufficiently to throw big parties and marry. While on his honeymoon in 1907, Smith died. All the houses he had picked up here and there around the world were sold, including 871 Fifth. As it was about to go on the auction block, Harry Payne Whitney bought the house and its contents for three million dollars and established in it his sculptress wife and their family. Mrs. Whitney remained after Harry's death in 1930; her Fifth Avenue social life diminished as she concentrated on her sculpture and her Gallery, a pioneer exhibitor of contemporary American art. In April of 1942 she had it made known that the contents of the house were to be sold at auction and the house itself demolished. A week after the announcement she died, but the auction took place and the house was altogether gone by 1943, the end of an eventful and, considering its street and city, a venerable life.

The Social Register for 1910 lists at 864 Fifth Avenue a Mrs. M. H. Yerkes, the widow for five drunken years of the Chicago public transportation king, the satyr immortalized in Dreiser's novels of powerful men and their titanic lusts. Charles T. Yerkes was born in 1837 of a family of early settlers who became part of the prosperous community of Philadelphia Quakers. Uninterested in schooling, he devoted himself to making money, owned his own banking house when he was in his mid-twenties, and was considered a genius at dealing in municipal securities of the expanding city. By the time he was in his early thirties, he had become the financial ruler of the city. With the freedom of the city's funds he and friends in the city government began to invest heavily in the promise of Chicago. The Chicago fire created panic in the Philadelphia bond market and Yerkes and company could not deliver the city money they had gathered together and invested out west. Yerkes was arrested as an embezzler and sentenced to two years and nine months; he served only seven months. Out of prison, he recovered his personal losses, made money in railroad stock, divorced his wife and their six children, married a well-known beauty and moved to Chicago.

It required comparatively little time for Yerkes to take control of several Chicago street railway lines, which he undoubtedly improved but in so complex and arcane a way that his holdings were lumped as the "traction tangle." His principle was to "buy old junk, fix it up a little, and unload it upon the other fellows." "It is the strap-hangers that pay the dividends," was his response to complaints of bad service and breathless crowding. To discomfit the competition, he plagued it with meaningless lawsuits and false rumors of its shaky finances and probable collapse. His major activity was to buy

politicians at staggering sums. Those he couldn't buy he tried
to ruin. When Governor Altgeld refused both bribes and bills
designed to favor Yerkes, he was publicly accused of being a
dangerous Bolshevik and lost the next election.

As the profits piled up by methods and with a greed that
caused a Chicago journal to comment that "revolutions are
caused by just such rapacity," Yerkes moved some of his loot
to New York's Fifth Avenue where he built his extravaganza
of a house. By the late 1890s, Chicago, as corrupt a city as
there was, would no longer tolerate his sexual, political and
financial omnivorousness. Yerkes fell out of favor everywhere,
but not out of money, and moved to New York, bringing with
him his paintings, fifteen million dollars in cash and, quite
likely, a few young girls. His taste in girls was of the same
fashion as Stanford White's: the fifteen-year-old small-breasted
flower, innocent, yet trembling on the edge of depravity, and
in abundant supply. While White enjoyed himself with two
or three at a time, Yerkes bought up dozens—a shopgirl, a street
girl, the daughter of a minion, an inept little dancer with an
ambitious mother, not necessarily all American. On the annual
European tours with his second wife, the beautiful Mara, he
found time between amassing paintings and outrageously expensive furnishings, to visit and shower a bit of gold on the
nymphets he kept in key cities. Mara objected, drank, shrieked
and drank some more and shrieked more loudly, none of which
had any effect on *muy macho* Charles. He escaped her and the
scorn they both suffered in New York by busying himself with
building London's underground, where he, as always, was head
of the syndicate. Anyhow, he was ready to divorce Mara and
remarry, probably the lovely, poised, convent-bred girl of
brothel origin whom he introduced as a thoroughbred to the
guests she entertained in the Neronian palace he built for her
on Park Avenue. Before his plans could come to fruition,
cancer intervened. He gave his favorite a few hundred thousand dollars and a thick bundle of London subway shares and

also saw to it that a few other adorably affectionate girls need never worry. When Yerkes died in 1905 Mara had the mansion and the rest of the money. On her death, mansion, paintings, rare Oriental rugs and extraordinary objects were to be given to the city and the money to be used for a hospital for the poor.

It didn't work out that way. The fortune was depleted by the ten-thousand-dollars-a-week fund to keep his meshwork of lovenests, foreign and domestic, functioning happily. Mara made no attempt to conserve the rest. In spite of the luxurious overdecorated rooms in several styles, of the great galleries hung with distinctive paintings, of acres of marble and choice paneling, of historic fireplaces, columns and stairways; in spite of conservatories like tropical bird sanctuaries, in spite of the choice of beds designed for kings, despite the platinum door (platinum used to dull the original Venetian bronze, too brightly attractive to anarchists and other malcontents) or because of them, Mara spent little time at 864, preferring to entertain drinking companions in a suite at the Waldorf, where, ironically, her husband had settled in to die.

Mara remarried, her second husband one of the sporting-life Mizner brothers, Wilson. As Lucius Beebe tells it, both Mara and Wilson were drunk when they married and to keep him from fleeing, she held on to his trousers and underclothes. She must have moved him to 864 at some point because a central part of the story has Wilson imprisoned in an immense bed that once belonged to the Mad King Ludwig of Bavaria—or was it the eighty-thousand-dollar bed of the king of Belgium—drenched in drapes and frenetic carvings. He managed to send messages to his brother Addison who found him breakfasting in bed off solid gold plate. Since Wilson was under siege, he had brother Addison carry off for potential sale a good number of the great paintings—there were several Rembrandts and Halses and a stupendous Turner in the collection—by tying them around his legs under his trousers. In

time, Mara released and divorced Wilson and he returned to
the Waldorf, luxuriating in a suite he could now easily afford.
Mara auctioned off the beds, the Gobelins, the rugs, most of
the rest of the paintings, and went to live at the Plaza to
drink herself into an alcoholic's grave before she reached fifty.

The auction, an important one closely watched by collectors and their agents, came at a time when the art market
was extremely high, when a "name" painting which cost $30,000
fifteen or twenty years before could bring in over $130,000.
In toto, the Yerkes collection brought in between $20,000,000
and $25,000,000 and the house something under $1,300,000.
The city didn't receive the art, nor the poor their hospital, as
Yerkes had wished. The receipts from the arts sale were dis-
sipated by Mara and the merchants and legal advisers who
victimized her. The house stayed unused until swaggering
Thomas Fortune Ryan took it over and demolished it for use
as a garden adjacent to his fifty rooms.

By dabbling in diamonds with the Guggenheims, trams
with William C. Whitney, subways with Belmont; by organizing the monopolistic American Tobacco Company, controlling
a bank or several, a railroad here and there, the complex
Equitable Life Assurance Society, rubber plantations and coal
mines, the astonishing Thomas Fortune Ryan left, when he
died in 1928, an estate valued at $135,000,000 to $200,000,000—
more than Morgan left, it is pointed out by tycoon-watchers.
Shrewd and quick he certainly was, but the comments of
contemporaries give him other dimensions. Whitney added to
the words "adroit and suave," "noiseless," a curious word that
suggests slyness. One of the dealers who helped him collect the
costly medieval and Renaissance objects and bronzes he arranged
in the long gallery at the top of his house at 858 Fifth Avenue
and the late Rodins that stood in the open area next to the
house spoke of him as having, under the forbidding outward
aspect of magnate, "a delightful sense of humor and a deep

humanity"; the dealer admired his slender height and his skepticism of "news" since Ryan himself often manufactured it. He was spoken of as charming, as an innovator who hired a press agent long before the Rockefellers did, and as a devout Catholic; witness the private chapel in his house and the $20,000,000 he gave the Church. These gifts were inspired quite probably by the truer devotion of Mrs. Ryan, the boss's daughter, whom he married when he was the employee of a dry-goods merchant, both job and marriage lucky and smart breaks for a penniless Irish orphan. The Pope rewarded Mrs. Ryan by making her a Countess of the Holy Roman Empire. Ryan seemed to have cared less for the papal titles or even ordinary church approval: within two weeks of his wife's death after a long period of invalidism, he married a divorcee. He was then sixty-six years old.

Although his boss–father-in-law helped him financially, Ryan's life did not respond to the prophecy of his middle name until he became an acting and contributing member of Tammany. Coaxing, frightening, manipulating and bribing, he began to make big money during the street-railroad franchise struggle that joined him with Whitney and Widener, and Elihu Root for legal protection, as the syndicate named the Metropolitan Traction Company, organized in 1886. Ryan called it the "great tin box" which held the securities of the various companies the group had engulfed. Paid friends in City Hall advised Metropolitan of the frailty of a line; the syndicate bought it, watered the stock which they sold at inflated prices while they leased the line, and their others, at high rentals. Frequently they managed to make money by selling their own lines to their own syndicate. The profits were enormous and grew as stock was forced up and up until it reached over $250 a share in 1899, when it was dumped on a public entranced by the big profit potential of a giant company, ignorant of the fact that it was actually snarled in its own meshwork.

Three years later Ryan applied to Jacob Schiff of Kuhn,

Loeb and Company for help in financing with him one of several reorganization schemes. This was the Metropolitan Securities Company which included the participation of the Rockefellers and Tammany. Ryan and his associates continued to buy franchises low, sell them to Securities high and personally pocket the profits. In 1907 Metropolitan Traction, "the older tin box," went into receivership. In the course of an ensuing investigation it was discovered that a thirty-five-million-dollar bond issue had paid for twenty million dollars in political gifts and the rest could not be found or explained; books had been destroyed, large quantities of cash had disappeared. The loss to the public through Ryan and company's wheeling and dealing with the help of ten paid members of the state legislature, was estimated into the millions. During a Senate hearing in 1908, Robert La Follette said, "The Metropolitan Interborough Traction Company cleaned up at least a hundred million dollars by methods which should have committed many of the participants to the penitentiary."

During the years when Metropolitan Traction was gushing profits, Whitney and Ryan organized the American Tobacco Company, and reorganized and merged and recapitalized in their most talented juggling style, to the point where the banking community became wary of them. Their next logical step was to gain control of a few banks. Subsequent investigation of the banks revealed that funds entrusted to them were used to support Metropolitan Traction. A roaring scandal blew up and various regulations were imposed but that did not stop Ryan from taking over another line, gaining control of an insurance company in 1904, and another, the huge Equitable Life Assurance Society, at a third of its actual value (so eager was its principal shareholder, James Hazen Hyde, to be rid of it).

It was through Ryan, a major holder of their copper stock, that the Guggenheims came to the Belgian Congo, on invitation from King Leopold. The first effort in the reorganized royal properties was for rubber but the cost of extracting it proved too high. Copper, gold and diamonds (for which the American organization had exclusive ninety-nine-year rights) were infinitely more rewarding and Ryan held one-quarter of the stock of the awesomely fruitful enterprise. Never known to worry about ethics before, he somehow felt that he had to explain his imperialist presence in Africa: "I am interested not only in the industrial development of the Congo but also in its social and moral conditions." Conditions did improve but more probably as a result of the practices of the Guggenheims, who had, unlike Ryan, a long history of benevolent-despot labor relations, when it served them to be benevolent.

After 1910, Ryan began slowly to withdraw from his universe of enterprises, maintaining the power to buy political figures, to exalt or destroy them, and continuing to expand his collection, said at the time to be choicer and more artistically trustworthy than the treasures garnered by any of his American contemporaries. Admirers, carried away by the splendid show he always made, speak of his remarkable taste, untutored but sure, "intuitive," although the intuition may have been paid for, its source unacknowledged. Like his peers, he was easily made drunk and unwary by the words "Italian palazzo," especially if they were joined with ringing names, and like his peers, he needed an expert hand to direct or restrain him.

Much of the Medician splendor bloomed in its rich textures and lusters after the family left a commodious conventional house at 60 Fifth Avenue, near Washington Square, to move uptown. Ryan was then in his mid-fifties, still a handsome figure, soigné, vigorous, a reassuring wad of large bills in his pocket, a superb pearl in his cravat, ready to put his stamp on upper Fifth Avenue, at Sixty-seventh Street, in the garden of Whitneys and Goulds and wilder money plants like the house of Yerkes immediately next door. One entered the Ryan house through a fountained palm court; ballroom space became gallery hung over with old tapestries on heroic subjects; the private chapel had the size and opulent ornaments of a Counter Reformation church; ceilings were necessarily deeply and richly carved. To please his wife he built a church nearby on Lexington Avenue which cost him approximately a million dollars. Another million went into the purchase of Yerkes' house of which he saved only a few exquisite pieces of antique marble out of a Doge's palace, used to train the vines and flowers of his new garden, a sizable area and a piece of remarkably conspicuous consumption even for Fifth Avenue.

Like the mighty oak he was, Ryan overshadowed and impeded the growth of some of his saplings whose energies were poured into drunkenness, mindless profligacy, the pursuit of shoddy women, pursuit by unpaid merchants, divorce battles and law suits dirty and loud. Of his three surviving sons, Allen was the most offensive, the most implacable in his opposition to his father's second speedy marriage, Hamlet appalled by the wedding feast of funeral-baked meats. Allen's share of the family fortune when his father died was two black pearl studs worth a few hundred dollars. He was given fifty thousand dollars a year by his brothers, John Barry and Clendenin. Much of the money went directly to the grandchildren, bypassing the good-looking gaggle that survived of an original fifteen. John Barry was an artistic type who dabbled in literature and, like the princeling he was, enjoyed giving expensive little gifts—a bit of old ivory, an antique watch, a rare curio—and in the manner of aristocrats, forgot to pay. Tiffany, one of his creditors, reluctantly sued him for over seventy thousand dollars and collected. His son, John Barry, Jr., settled into a reasonable life, married to Margaret Kahn, the daughter of the arts-loving couple, Otto and Addie Kahn.

The line of Clendenin Ryan fell in a tragic collapse. Clendenin married well, had four children and at least one

affair with a show girl whose rent he neglected to pay and who sued him noisily. He was the executor of his father's estate which he expanded by five million dollars when he and his brother John Barry decided to sell much of the family's common stock at the peak of the 1929 market, immediately before the crash, and disposed of his father's outstanding racing stables. Then life began to run down. Divorced, he lived in seclusion, concentrated on collecting. Seriously diabetic, his weight dropped from a jovial 240 pounds to 150; he became nervous and depressed and then totally despondent.

On August 22, 1939, the *New York Times,* whose headlines carried the news of the nonaggression pact signed by Germany and Russia and New York's temperature of ninety-one degrees, printed a story on page three: "Clendenin Ryan Senior Ends Life By Gas. Favorite Son of Financier, 57, found dead in his Library with Head in Fireplace." He lived at 32 East Seventieth Street, with eight servants, none of whom would disturb him although they smelled gas. It was the disturbed neighbors who called the police. They axed their way through a two-and-a-half-inch-thick door to enter the library hung with Italian and Flemish paintings and found Ryan with his head resting on a book of etchings among four open fireplace jets; he had been dead for hours.

Clendenin, Jr., was a member of La Guardia's "secretariat," the deputy commissioner of sanitation, at the time of his father's death. Eighteen years later, apparently doomed by his father's fate—the same name, the same house, the same black depression—he locked himself in a bathroom and put a bullet through his head.

The original Ryan collection had been auctioned, bringing disappointing sums; a number of the Rodins found their way to the Metropolitan Museum. The original fortune was fragmented and trickled away. The house of the long gallery, of Renaissance bronzes, lustrous enamels and a garden of

Rodins, disappeared with its neighbors behind an anonymity of apartment walls, leaving not a trace of the old hubris and fall from high estate.

In 1911, the *New York Architect* published an article called "A Dignified Type of the City House," dealing with the house of Edward S. Harkness at 1 East Seventy-fifth Street. It detailed a number of the architectural problems involved in creating a feeling of large space on a city lot of thirty-five by one hundred feet, the dextrous manner of introducing window light while screening a room from an adjacent brick wall and commented on the intelligent designing that put a regal marble and bronze stairway into a side area to avoid cutting into reception space. "It was the wish of the client," said the article, "and the aim of the architect to design a dignified house that would not in an ostentatious way indicate its costliness, a feature unfortunately prominent in many of our pretentious city residences." It was referring to the frenzy of details that screamed at each other on the roof of Mrs. Cornelius Vanderbilt's huge house between Fifty-seventh and Fifty-eighth streets, and the stutter of mansards and spiky chimneys on the John Jacob Astor house at the northeast corner of Fifth at Sixty-fifth.

In its time the Harkness house was obviously a blue blood—and still is—set apart from its neighbors by the stateliness of its entrance pillars, the bronze meshwork fence like that around the Scaligeri tombs in Verona, its cool confident style. Unlike most of its peers, the house had, and continues to have, a long life: a wedding present to Mrs. Harkness, née Mary Stillman, shortly after her marriage in 1904, she lived in it until her death in 1950; it is now the seat of the Commonwealth Fund. Its base was Standard Oil, banking and railroads.

The Harknesses were early settlers in the Middle West, but it wasn't until the 1870s that Stephen, the father of Edward, began to amass capital as a partner in the booming oil refinery business whose petroleum was then mainly used for lamp fuel. Through periods of bloom and vicissitudes, Harkness held on to his shares while he broadened his industrial and banking operations in the Cleveland area and, like everyone else with money, invested in railroads.

His youngest child, Edward, born in Cleveland in 1874, was only fourteen when the father died. The eldest son, Charles, trained in the law, became administrator of the estate. He was a patient, astute holder and the investments that the father planted grew into a large fortune. After graduating from Yale, Edward joined his brother in the business of supervising the family investments, mainly in Standard Oil securities. Beginning to move around in New York, where the family office was now located, he met Mary E. Stillman whose father, a partner in a prestigious law firm, had also made canny investments and married a young woman whose family were shippers and shipbuilders. Mary Stillman and her three sisters were consequently left independently wealthy when their father died in 1906.

The serene and truly stately house, considerably altered for its present uses, still holds reminders of former beauties in outmoded styles. In the first-floor reception room, a superb rug and a double-ended desk carved deeply in the humanoid monsters of the late Italian Renaissance. Two pagoda-shaped cabinets that once held priceless jades are echoed in the light chinoiserie ceiling. Quality speaks not only from the painted and coffered ceilings, the arabesques of plaster work, the silky paneling but from the vaults, the trompe l'oeil and plasterwork that introduce the reception rooms and the marble staircase bordered in bronze acanthus circlets, still comparatively untouched and very handsome. Untouched, too, are the wonderfully painted ceiling and subtly colored walls of the library and the delicate porcelain flowers and graceful wall detail of Mrs. Harkness's boudoir.

Incomprehensible spaces like the dining and music rooms must be filled with images from photographs made in 1942. They show the music room focused on a beautiful medieval tapestry, the furniture in related design, and on the other walls, a lady by Lawrence and the Drummond children painted by Raeburn's cheery, swift brush. On the stairs an antique Chinese painting of a dignitary; on one marble overmantel, Constable's *Salisbury Cathedral*, on another, Guardi's San Marco arcades marching swiftly toward the luxuriant cathedral. A softly patinaed wooden panel holds an uncannily lovely Flemish head, another a Goya portrait. It was all superlative and much of it went to strengthen several sections of the Metropolitan Museum, which published Harkness donations in its bulletin of October, 1951, an impressive list accompanied by photos of several ineffable enchantments: an imperious African rooster; Coptic tapestry; seventeenth-century French lace with minute, perfect men and animals held in gossamer threads; small marvels of Egypt in faience, gold and marble; and, of ivory, small streaks of speed as gazelles and horses.

Upstairs, far upstairs, decor was limited to a white-tiled hallway, a large laundry room at one end of the corridor, a long row of tiny rooms at the other end. As in Victorian houses, where separate stairways were provided to reach the quarters of male and female servants, as distant as possible from each other, the Harkness maids slept on the fourth floor while the men servants lived in the basement, near the immense kitchen and its wide-hooded stove. Their cells were behind the roomy, pleasant servants' dining hall, quite large enough to accommodate the twenty servants Mrs. Harkness lived with as a widow.

The house is closed to casual visitors, but there is enough on the outside to reveal its character. The strong pillars, the strong bronze lace that politely but unmistakably excludes most of the world, the big windows supported by broad volutes, the bold shield above the entrance speak courtly Italian, the tones of the enlightened humanists, of the court of Montefeltro at Urbino perhaps.

When Senator William A. Clark of Montana wanted a

grand house at Seventy-seventh Street on Fifth, he wanted it truly grand, to demonstrate what a man worth an aggregate sum of one hundred million dollars or so, who owned most of the state of Montana—and its mines, its railroads, its politicians, its wood, its livestock and rivers—considered a comfortable habitat. New York architects lacked imagination and a sense of splendor so he went to Paris and found a maker of grandiosities whose plans were not altogether satisfactory either. It took him seven years to add and add again to a four-story rusticated and encrusted folly spewing an anthology of overblown detail taken from every county courthouse and Victorian city hall, plus a ridiculous steeple. The story goes that, reluctant to see anyone but himself make a profit, he bought and made profitable the quarries that yielded his twenty-one marble bathrooms and stairways, and the mills that turned out his big metal doors. It was estimated that he spent six million dollars on his house of one hundred thirty rooms, his several galleries of French painting, barbaric heapings of glowing rugs, dishes of gold, dishes of silver, objects of ivory, monumental fireplaces, a pool with steambath attached and a number of sybaritic etceteras.

Like other quick boys who followed the rush for silver and gold to the west, Clark found that mining did not pay much, but supplies at exploded prices did. In the common evolution of such apt learners, he became a prosperous merchant, moneylender and banker, still interested in mining, though. With enough money to afford a sabbatical year, he went east to learn what the Columbia School of Mines had to teach him and returned to Montana to work silver and then the floods of copper that made him a millionaire before he was forty. Montana was not yet a state (that came in 1889) when Clark, intent on controlling its destinies, fought a fierce, dirty-tricks battle with Marcus Daly, the owner of the fecund Anaconda Copper Mine, who wanted his own senator and henchman in Washington. (The enmity kept the adrenaline flowing all

their lives; when Daly was dying in a Fifth Avenue hotel, Clark
made loud daily inquiry: "Is the son of a bitch dead yet?")

Clark did not move into his Taj Mahal until he was in
his mid-sixties, his first wife dead and the children of that marriage quite grown. The Mrs. Clark who lived with him on
Seventy-seventh Street was in her twenties with two young
children. He had acquired her when she was in her teens,
given her some schooling and set her up in Paris, where the
children were born, circumstances that accounted for his frequent trips to France and his knowledge of French painting.
With a series of well-placed bribes he had French records doc-
tored so that it appeared he had married the young woman
several years before he actually did in order that the babies
be legitimate, although they never became major inheritors.

Society didn't bother much with Clark except to poke fun
at his house, nor did he bother much with society; he had what
he wanted, the showiest house, power, one of the biggest pots
of money, a respected collection of paintings and important
symptoms of virility—a very young wife and two young children still flatteringly young when he died at eighty-six in 1925.
The heirs would have nothing to do with the elephantine house
and sold it for three million dollars.

Seventy-ninth Street was a juncture of old money and new.
At the southern corner, a large chateaulike pile (now a center
for cultural matters Ukrainian) housed Augustus Van Horne
Stuyvesant, a bachelor descendant of peg-legged Peter, and his
spinster sister and their servants. Increasingly reclusive and
eccentric as he aged, he died a prisoner of mistrust and senility
in his tall, wide house. Across the street, stood the house of a
purist, Isaac Vail Brokaw, who had earned his palace in the
clothing business. He had examined, consulted, informed himself about architectural styles, when he lived at 528 surrounded
by Vanderbilt houses and their neighbors. He learned to
scorn the impurities of other Fifth Avenue structures and

settled on one specific Loire valley chateau to copy, that of a
sixteenth-century royal mistress. It was authentic, overstuffed
with French furniture and baronial fireplace mantels, and it
had a moat, shortly filled in because it was a hazard on a busy
corner that led to Central Park and the Metropolitan Museum.
One of the residents was Clare Boothe, later Luce, who had
married George Brokaw, the oldest son of the house. Neither of
them wanted the historic immensity or the costly maintenance
it required. But when George tried to sell it, his brothers instituted a lawsuit to restrain him. Back to the chateau for George
and his wife, and a few years later release by divorce, the house
playfully mentioned as corespondent. By this time, less demanding Fifth Avenue homes already had been boarded up
or demolished because taxes, the wages of servants and the
various services such houses required had become prohibitive.
The Brokaw house was a particularly difficult one to rent or
sell and it stood for a long time, a dusty anachronism between
the walls of multiple dwellings that in time absorbed it.

Immediately to the north on Eightieth Street, was the
house of Woolworth, built at the turn of the century. The son
of an upstate farmer, Woolworth got himself a job as general
factotum in a small varieties store. In order to move heretofore
unmovable stock of several kinds, the youngster gathered it
together in one section and topped it with a sign, five cents
for any item. The sale was a marked success and that rivulet
became the broad Five and Ten River. His monument was
the Woolworth Building, then the tallest in the world (1913),
built at a cost of fifteen million dollars. It was time, also, to
enlarge the homestead on Eightieth Street by building four
additional houses for his married children immediately off
Fifth Avenue. In one of them lived Mr. and Mrs. F. L. Hutton,
the parents of the conspicuous Barbara. It was rumored, although the plan never came to fruition, that Woolworth
planned to take over the whole square block bordered by
Fifth and Eightieth to create a kingdom to rival that of the

Vanderbilts', and he might have succeeded had he lived long enough.

Across from the Metropolitan Museum which, after a history of wandering had settled in to accumulate breathtaking art and broad stone wings invented by a succession of architects, lived William Salomon, a banker and collector who bore a special distinction: he was respected by art dealers. He had begun by learning from Duveen and Gimpel but soon did his own judging and buying, making very few mistakes in authenticity and quality, thus earning the reputation as the only American who didn't require dealers and their experts. As his collection grew he needed more gallery space, particularly since he anticipated buying the art accumulated by Charles I. He went to the old lady of ninety who lived in a little wooden house next to his, at Eighty-third Street, and offered her dazzling sums for her property. No, never. She had spent her childhood among the trees and rills and songbirds once there and intended to die among her memories of them. She was too old to care about a lot of money and, as far as yet another art gallery, there were plenty across the street and up and down the Avenue.

Salomon didn't get the royal collection because Duveen wouldn't sell it to him. The intransigent old lady died, the small wooden house died; neither left the faintest shadow on the forgetful Avenue.

CHAPTER 10

1900–1915:
THE ART BARONS

The five boroughs had been banded together as Greater New York. Brentano's books lingered on Union Square, contemplating the possibilities of Madison Square, while more generalized shops gathered around Thirty-fourth Street and Fifth. Their customers were abandoning hansom cabs for the auto-taxis, jaunty, low-wheeled and open for a show of dress and bonnet in good weather. Others were making it to new Fifth Avenue shopping on trains into the old Grand Central Station and its trail of open tracks that shot smoke and cinders onto Park Avenue, soon to be replaced by a new station of vast spaces over great arches. Tunnels under the Hudson and the East River had already been completed and work on Penn Station by the versatile McKim, Mead and White team was in progress to facilitate commuter travel in a city whose skies were already darkened by elevated lines, its streets crisscrossed with trolleys and pitted with new subway tunnels.

The car—the skin, love, toy and scourge of twentieth-century man—made marked inroads everywhere: fire wagons retired their horses and took to the motor and so did the mails and, soon, the sanitation wagons. Annual auto shows were becoming an institution that filled Madison Square. An auto parade chugged up Fifth Avenue annually for years, beginning in 1899. The domes and minarets of Luna Park, open in 1903, etched a fairyland sky at night, while by day Coney Island's sands supported daring gestures of stockinged limbs and bare arms. Fashionable houses were relinquishing the overstuffed and draping their mirrors and lamps and stairways in a new romanticism of shawls and languid hangings. Countless Gibson girls drawn by Charles Dana Gibson proved that the typical American girl had a tiny waist and swirls of hair caressing a ripe mouth and long, contemptuous eyelids. The Gibson male ideal had a sharp profile and strong jaw cut out of wood.

Between 1900 and 1910 the population of New York rose from 3,437,202 to 4,746,833. Marconi's wireless telegraphy was established between New York and England, and Wilbur Wright was startling the sky by flying over New York harbor. The city had forty playgrounds and a dozen or so bald squares and small parks that had been planned by Mayor Abram S. Hewitt, the civic-minded son-in-law of Peter Cooper. Long recreation piers were also built along the rivers. During the day there were kindergarten teachers to take care of the very young and at night the piers served as promenades, with band concerts, for the adults. A proposed child labor law was defeated because limiting a child's working hours was an infringement on his liberty.

To keep men out of saloons and the blandishments of free lunches with gin, the Women's Auxiliary of the Church Temperance Society maintained lunch wagons in several busy parts of the city. They served as many as 350,000 lunches a year at ten cents apiece, the money earned converted to free ice water fountains and winter coffee wagons for firemen, who tended to search for the booze nevertheless. More direct temperance means were the mission of Carrie Nation who worked with a Bible in one hand and a hatchet in the other to break windows and bottles and crack mahogany bars. The Five Points Mission, which had replaced the foulest of the local rookeries, was taking in needy children, and to put shoes on their bare feet there was established a widely publicized shoe club, each member to give a pair of shoes or a dollar a year. In spite of the provisions for play in fresh air and shoes, the child mortality rate remained high. Central Park which was valued in the decade before the Civil War at five million dollars was estimated in 1904 to be worth two hundred million. To the west, not far from the Hudson on Sixty-second Street, model tenements called Tuskegee had reached the full complement of colored tenants for whom they were built

Across town, too, significant changes. Although invitations to Mrs. Astor's grand balls still symbolized the acme of social prestige, society found her lesser gatherings dull and flocked to the livelier salons of other hostesses, among them her daughter-in-law, Mrs. John Jacob Astor IV, prettier and more playful. To whip things up there was Harry Lehr, like Ward McAllister, one of the grotesques of society history. For McAllister's worshipful Old World courtliness Lehr substituted wide-ranging gall, demanding and receiving free goods, services and money from the salesmen of luxuries to the houses whose entertainments he devised and very probably retainers from *Town Topics*, the blackmailing gossip sheet. "Blond, plump, petulant, waspish, with a fluty voice and a mincing gait," Lehr enjoyed appearing in drag and was enjoyed as a rare and stimulating novelty.

Lehr found himself a playmate in an imposing Stanford White house at Seventy-eighth Street and Madison Avenue, the home of Mrs. Stuyvesant Fish, who abetted him in spitting at the world they ruled, its only resemblance to the old "400" an unremitting anti-Semitism. Their insolence invented a large formal dinner in honor of a foreign dignitary, the Prince del Drago, who turned out to be an immaculately dressed monkey, his name a possible cruel reference to the Don Giovanni del Prago who lived at Sixty-second Street and Fifth Avenue. Dogs, circus animals, coarse and bubbly chorus girls as star guests, anything to pierce the usual social dullness, to shock and an-

noy. Few if any of Mrs. Fish's guests were offended; novelty was what they wanted and got, served on Mrs. Fish's three-hundred-piece gold service devised by Tiffany's to come apart for cleaning. (No social historian can resist the story, true or false, that a Newport butler, infuriated by the high-handed Mrs. Fish, took the whole set apart and left it in a disjointed heap shortly before a particularly important dinner party was to begin. The postlude to the tale relates that Tiffany's special Newport-in-season staff came to the rescue and put the golden service together again in good time to avert disaster and ignominy.)

As the Age of Elegance became confident enough to assume the willfulness and bad manners of old European families, it also began to buy world-renowned and very expensive art, an ultimate luxury. As undeniable proof of aristocracy, they gave it away, a habit that created superb museums. Although an interest in art among the informed public began to appear in the mid-nineteenth century spurred by worlds fairs and expositions, the questionable, large collections of A. T. Stewart and William H. Vanderbilt, and the paintings the first August Belmont picked up when he was minister to The Hague, there was little interest in the Old Masters. A few pioneers who tried to broaden American taste had failed. But while a 1904 show at the Metropolitan Museum, publicized as based on notable gifts and loans from several collections, clung to the nineteenth-century safeties of old furniture, reproductions of the Parthenon, the Pantheon and Notre Dame, battle scenes and pictures of well-fed livestock, solid masterpieces were beginning to cross the Atlantic, spurred on by English inheritance taxes and the decline of provincial European museums forced to free into a market of tempting prices a few of their coveted holdings. Along with these paintings, inlaid woods like those in the ducal palace at Urbino, eggshell porcelain, expressive bronzes, jeweled missals out of royal chapels and priceless tapestries, their flight stimulated by dealers, antiquarians, decorators, eager sellers and eager buyers. Having bested their competitors in industry and finance, the American barons were ready to do combat for art treasures, their swords and lances many-ciphered checks and blocks of valuable bonds. Dealers supplied battle calls, trumpets and fanfare. Among them they inspired a new collecting fever, an exploration of neglected paintings—Duveen is considered responsible for introducing eighteenth-century English portraiture, in generous display at the Frick Collection, for example—and within a few decades brought extraordinary quality to American collections.

An early, quiet collector, inclined to pay top prices rather than compete, was Benjamin Altman, who was initiated, or so they claim, by the Duveen brothers (not yet a divided family in 1882) several years before J. P. Morgan launched his hors de combat raids. The story goes that Henry Duveen, "Uncle Henry," invited the retiring bachelor merchant into his shop just before closing time one Saturday night. Altman said he knew nothing about art but was very much interested and Uncle Henry undertook to educate him in a series of Saturday night sessions, the only time Altman could spare. (S. N. Behrman, in his *Duveen*, flashes color on these meetings by describing them as held in Yiddish, and one wonders where, in that earthy shorthand, they found the words for Ming porcelains and Italian Annunciations.) Altman's first purchase was a pair of Chinese enamel vases that eventually went to the Metropolitan; he had held on to them all his life. As he grew more knowledgeable, he returned purchases to trade for something more desirable, always assured that the Duveens would buy up the discarded pieces at the original purchase price, millions of dollars worth of credit and debit passing back and forth between their hands. By the time Altman died in 1913, he had accumulated portraits by Dürer, Holbein and Velazquez; fourteen Rembrandts, a Vermeer; sculpture by Donatello, Rossellino and Mino da Fiesole; Oriental carpets of incalculable value; a singular group of Dutch and Italian painting of the

fifteenth and sixteenth centuries and a reputation among dealers for the keenest taste. Not all of these purchases were guided
by Uncle Henry since he and son James lost Altman to the
trickery, they complained, of nephew Joe, Sir Joseph the Magnificent.

Then came Morgan. He was especially fond of Uncle
Henry, from whom he bought the famous Garland collection
of Chinese porcelains, originally sold by the Duveens to Garland, and it was from the Duveens, when Joseph was still in
training with them, that Morgan bought several of his best
miniatures. Henry, sketched by Behrman as a "rotund, flat-
footed little man with a walrus moustache, who had never been
to school and spoke English with a guttural Dutch accent,"
was apparently trustworthy and winning enough to become not
only adviser but friend to the formidable autocrat who proved
his affection by bailing Uncle Henry out of a grave legal mess.
Henry had been for many years customs consultant on the
value of art imports; it was his job to calculate in dollars what
an import was worth and determine the amount of duty to be
imposed. No one doubted his word and for a long time the
family paid comparatively little duty on shipments addressed
to Duveens. The bubble broke when, in 1910, the competition,
or an angry employee, leaked accusations to the customs office.
They assessed past duty owed at ten million dollars. Morgan's
legal battery and Duveen's argued the sum down to not quite
a million, half of it supplied by Morgan.

J. P. Morgan fretted the lives of his fellow tycoons by
gathering the most expensive collection of the most remarkable
quality, an example to emulate and compete with. A few came
close, but no one quite matched him. Although he was inclined
to favor one dealer or another from time to time, the whole
world was the supermarket from which he bought large lots of
Tanagra figurines and medieval enamels, Gutenberg Bibles,
scores in Mozart's clear, elegant hand, incomparably illuminated and jewel-studded tomes, a Cellini cup and paintings later

ardently contested. There were fakes and peculiar attributions in the Morgan house and library on Madison Avenue but less than there were in several galleries of Fifth Avenue mansions. Protected by redoubtable assistants and corps of agents—and sixty million dollars to devote exclusively to collecting—Morgan rarely got anything but the best, a standard which also held, New York society quipped, for his dogs and mistresses, one of them the fascinating and talented actress, Maxine Elliott. After Morgan died in 1913, many of his gems, bearing the awesome and costly label, "From the Morgan Collection," were sold to the Metropolitan Museum and others to his most ambitious rivals, principally Frick and Jules Bache.

In spite of the prodigious exchanges of art and monies, there was no interest in contemporary art at the time, the art that was to produce momentous changes. According to Germain Seligman (the son of Jacques, who was a Morgan adviser and who supervised, for a whole year, the packing and listing of Morgan art and objects held in the Victoria and Albert Museum basements until the tax on art imports was relaxed in the United States) "modern" was a word used for nineteenth-century academicians and the Barbizon painters. "Advanced" was the label attached to Daumier, Delacroix, Gericault, Courbet and, almost dangerously advanced, Boudin and Manet. Monet, Sisley and Pissarro, certainly Renoir and Degas, were daringly risky. Very few people would venture into the realms of Cézanne, Toulouse-Lautrec, Van Gogh and Gauguin; and, Seligman goes on, the Carnegie International Show of 1911, designed for pioneering, showed no Picasso, no Matisse, no Post-Impressionist. One of the few intrepid millionaires, besides the Havemeyers, who ventured on unchartered seas was Adolph Lewisohn whose taste was guided by his son, Sam.

It was the Big Old Names that were earning, and deeply resented by American painters. One of their few bastions, a tiny bastion at that, was Alfred Stieglitz's Gallery of the Photo Secession, usually referred to as "291" from its address on Fifth

Avenue, swallowed long since by the Textile Building that uses Thirtieth to Thirty-first Street. Its dedicated business was to foster contemporary art and photography as an art form, publishing, for a short time, a magazine of the arts. 291 showed Marsden Hartley, John Marin, Arthur Dove, Eli Nadelman, Francis Picabia, Henri Matisse, and let it be known what was generally going on in European studios. Stieglitz and friends, including a useful and rich friend, Mabel Dodge, joined forces with the artists Walt Kuhn, John Sloan, George Bellows, Arthur Davies, and a number of other painters who organized the memorable 1913 Armory Show. Backed by interested friends of Arthur Davies, Kuhn and Davies scoured Paris and other European cities to bring back works too little known in the United States. With the help of supporters like the sculptress Gertrude Vanderbilt who sponsored many of them, they dressed up the large armory space at plebeian Lexington Avenue and Twenty-sixth Street (a neighborhood that still shows faded signs of the ribbon, underwear and tie manufacturers who once used its buildings) and hung their own work and that of their co-workers abroad. In all, the gathering totaled sixteen hundred paintings, sculptures and drawings, the work of three hundred artists, two-thirds of them American. The original purposes of showing American art and selling it was defeated by the startling quality of the Europeans: the machinelike people of Léger, the dark lyrical dreams of Redon, the whispered portraits of Marie Laurencin, the hot, simplified Matisses, the broken surfaces of Cézanne, the incomprehensible cubists and what was to become the caricatured symbol of the whole show, Marcel Duchamp's *Nude Descending a Staircase*. Seventy thousand people came to see the crazy art. Cartoonists ridiculed and lampooned the oddities; critics pro and con became for a short while important voices. The exquisite L. Tiffany loathed the show; James Stillman, banker, owner of a lovely Carrère and Hastings house and a few Mary Cassatts, and famous for having declared out of these surroundings that he had never had a happy moment in his life, vaguely declared for the artists, "Something is wrong with the world and these men know it."

Although the numbers of viewers and the heated comment in New York and other cities flashily introduced modern art, the brouhaha faded out and left few echoes. Seven years after the Armory opening, the Metropolitan Museum, urged by Mrs. Havemeyer, the collector John Quinn and several others of their advanced interests, opened a Post-Impressionist exhibition. It gathered a considerable number of viewers and many letters that protested a public display of art both decadent and Bolshevik.

Very few of the important dealers—Durand-Ruel an exception—bothered about this bizarre outback of the art market. The high patina of goods with tradition from old institutions and houses was more profitable, in spite of the extravagant expenses involved. A dealer with an inventory in the millions, European and American establishments to maintain, experts and agents to support, rare gifts and prayerful services to clients to pay for, secretaries, maids and particularly butlers to bribe —a persistent rumor had Bache's butler retired on one hundred thousand dollars, most of it rewards for warning Duveen of the advent of others dealers and fending them off—had to be as nervously on his toes as a foreign agent in wartime. Germain Seligman, again: "Visits were arranged to avoid conflicts, for certain clients could not be allowed to meet. My father had to prevent, if possible, any suspicion that he had first shown a work of art to someone else and that the present client was seeing the leftovers." When Frick was buying, other customers howled that dealers were giving him first crack at unique objects and, since it was often true, merchants had to be adroit in appeasing, assuaging and lying to other clients.

The dealer Rene Gimpel says of his father and the Duveens (as true of the Knoedlers and Wildensteins) that they were the pioneers of great art in the American home and that they deserve a place beside the men who made roads and rail-

ways, cleared the forests, built churches and schools. He does
not specifically say—implication is enough—that they used the
ruthless methods of the railroad builders in their dealings with
their clients and each other. They were a contentious continental family with half forgotten kinships that made them
cohere when the cause was large and stunningly fruitful, and
tear each other apart as competitors at other times. In 1907
Gimpel and his brother-in-law, Joe Duveen, pooled resources
to buy the remarkable Rudolph Kann Collection of which
three-quarters was sold at twice the purchase price two years
later. (The peripatetic Rembrandt, *Aristotle Contemplating the
Bust of Homer,* bought and sold by Duveen three times, almost
the property of Altman, once Arabella Huntington's and
finally, in 1961, entrusted to Parke-Bernet for a sale to the
Metropolitan Museum for $2,300,000, was originally part of
Gimpel's share.) To acquire the equally distinguished pieces
from the estate of Rudolph's brother, Maurice, the same arrangement held, and the profits were equally great.

Such occasional cooperation and close family ties did not
prohibit Gimpel from publishing his judgment that Joe "has
no knowledge of paintings and sells with the support of expert
certificates, but his intelligence has enabled him to keep up a
cracked facade in this country, which is still so little knowledgeable." With grudging admiration he adds: "Joseph Duveen
does business as he would wage war, tyrannically. He is an
audacious buyer and an irresistible salesman." John Walker,
onetime head of the National Gallery in Washington, neither
competitor nor brother-in-law, corroborates with, "My impres-
sion is that he knew very little about painting and sculpture.
He had the courage of other people's convictions—Bernard
Berenson's mainly." Walker, too, admires grudgingly, astonished at the supreme quality of an Italian group Duveen sent
to Washington. Whether it referred to the boss or the hand,
Berenson, who had teethed on the Gardiner Museum in Boston
to become an international authority on Italian painting, the

name Duveen meant to some clients Jove, whose thunder could not be disobeyed or even tempted. A troublesome bone in the lordly craw, for instance, was French and Company, headed by Mitchell Samuels, "one of the most formidable and knowledgeable merchants in the international decorative arts world," according to Seligman. It was Samuels who supplied Morgan and several others with important tapestries and provided Arabella Huntington's house at Fifty-seventh and Fifth with unique furnishings. Duveen favored other decorators; he ordered Arabella to throw the stuff out into the street. She didn't quite do that but Samuels lost the sale he thought was sealed.

Rivalries marked not only sales but care for reputations. Gimpel insists that it was his father who persuaded Benjamin Altman to buy pictures; Uncle Henry showed him only china. Thus, since it was the Altman collection that taught Frick and served as example to many Jewish amateurs who moved into the vanguard of collectors—Felix Warburg was collecting masterful prints and drawings, Mortimer Schiff bought a sixteenth-century jewel for $41,000 and a group of gouaches for $150,000, Otto Kahn and Guggenheims were developing reputations as connoisseurs—much of the expertise that followed Altman and enriched museums was to be credited to Gimpels, not Duveens. Gimpel, who was a Wildenstein partner for a time, could think of not one Berenson virtue; he considered him a fraud whose attributions were becoming woollier and woollier. Berenson hated Wildenstein and Wildenstein hated Berenson until "B.B." came over to him after a monumental quarrel with Duveen that cut an association of thirty years; they then united in hating Duveen. Jacques Seligman had had the French poet Apollinaire write a pamphlet attacking the authenticity of a Fragonard which the poet had never seen; it had been sold in America by Gimpel, whose reputation and sales Seligman was eager to ruin. Dealers bid against each other at auctions, driving a price high and hoping to stop at the proper moment for

bleeding the enemy. John Walker describes a sale that had the
raw quality of flea-market bargaining. The painting was special—the portrait of the child who became Edward VI painted
by Holbein and offered to Henry VIII as a gift. In the presence
of the director of the German museum which was offering it,
the august Duveen and Knoedler haggled for hours. Knoedler
exhausted Duveen and turned the painting over to Andrew
Mellon for $437,000. When Lawrence's *Pinkie* was similarly
contested, Duveen won. The assault of bribes on scrupulous
museum directors was unremitting and, to some, unbearable.
Roger Fry, the English painter and scholar, who had been hired
by Morgan, President of the Metropolitan Museum in 1904, to
become director of the museum, was forced to flee, not only
by the indigenous exigencies of the job, but by the importunities of dealers forcing checks on him.

In spite of certifications, often because of them, fakes were
persistent preoccupations with dealers and buyers, especially
as prices spiraled frantically until the crash. (In 1905 Altman
paid $120,000 for a Rembrandt, in 1927 a Rembrandt of like
quality cost Jules Bache $250,000.) Stung by earlier fakes,
Americans had begun to insist on certificates of authenticity.
These were sometimes as false as the works they swore to. A
horde of experts sprang up, creatures of ambitious dealers who
flooded the American market with "certified" meretricious art
that brought them millions on millions of dollars. Nor were
the fakes readily exposed: neither collectors nor museums were
eager to admit they had been gulled. Although the Germans
and their experts culled huge sums, it was the Italians, skillful
craftsmen, fonts of persuasive charm, born in the richest lode
of art, a knowledge of art purportedly enfolded in their genes,
who were the most colorful and adroit at the game of false objects and false testimonials.

A taste for masterpieces of Italian marble that were essential to American atria and galleries, quickened the ancient
Italian industry of reproducing antiquities, one of whose prac-

titioners had been the young Michelangelo. A dealer's description of an Italian swindle: "An Italian dealer will show you two busts and he'll admit one is a fake, a fact that is perfectly obvious. The one he'll show you as a genuine antique is equally fake but less visibly so." The most gifted of Italian forgers, treated with high admiration in the history of frauds, was Dossena, who early in life became a highly skilled stonecutter, capable of working in any style, classical, Romanesque, Gothic, Renaissance, baroque, rococo. Encouraged by a minor connoisseur, Dossena opened an atelier and went into production in a wide range from the pre-Hellenic to the Pisano, to the high Renaissance and, if the market urged it, later periods. He was meticulous and shrewd, using time-honored and still extant means of antiquing his material and never claiming specific provenance; a suggested period and "style of" sufficed. As Dossena's pieces wandered from local dealers to national and international dealers, they took on clear, ringing names which won them honored places in museums and important collections. The time ripened in the early 1920s for an expert here, a scholar there, to notice an unreconcilable oddity, a betraying detail. They remained a troubling family secret, no one in the world of art trading or exhibiting willing to acknowledge guilt or ignorance. Finally, after several years, Dossena opened the embarrassing subject publicly. He had learned how valued his pieces of sculpture were across the ocean, that they had earned over a million dollars, and he was furious with his local vendors who had given him a pittance of the huge sums. The story then becomes *vero italiano*: political accusations and counter accusations, Dossena's successful appeal to a "godfather" politico to speak his cause, the new light that shone on him because he was such a clever fellow to outwit American millionaires. He did little with his extraordinary skills and new glory but hold bibulous court and die a sot.

As Dossena was not the beginning, he was not the end of frauds. Not too long after Mrs. Havemeyer and the pioneer dealers Durand-Ruel made the Impressionists acceptable, they were faked. There were and are, as is generally known, dozens of false Corots wandering about, and semifakes of paintings begun by a "name" painter and finished by anonymous hands. It is estimated that several hundred canvases that Rosa Bonheur left incomplete were filled in by hired craftsmen and spilled on the market as authentic. No possibility could be left unexplored, no trick untried, when a John Rockefeller, Jr., would consent to pay Wildenstein almost three hundred thousand dollars for a Roger Van der Weyden; when Altman bought a Holbein whose cost to the dealer had been twenty thousand pounds for two hundred twenty thousand dollars; when Duveen paid three million dollars for Morgan porcelains; when Bache bought a bust of Marquise de Pompadour out of a titled house, via Gimpel, for a hundred and sixty thousand dollars, a Fragonard for a quarter-million and, some years later, a Van Dyck portrait for over three hundred thousand.

The quantity and quality of publicity surrounding such sales had to be carefully considered. There were collectors who were convinced that publishing names and prices would inspire revolution, and consequently their dealers celebrated major sales in muted whispers. Duveen liked his professional life fortissimo, eager to have the papers publish his star-studded lists of art just arrived from Europe at a cost of several million dollars. It was this Barnum approach that repelled some purchasers. Mellon, for one, bought mainly through Knoedler while Harkness never purchased from Duveen at all, although both were tempted by his repertoire. It has been suggested that the Duveen style discouraged the Soviet Union from inviting him when it selected Hermitage paintings for sales in 1930 to 1932: they preferred the tact of Knoedler. The more flamboyant publicity did, however, help create an interest in the general public and inspired ingenious methods of giving it fine art at little cost where no museums were available. At the close of World War I an enterprising American bought Millet's *Angelus* for eight hundred and fifty thousand francs. He toured the United States with the painting, earning two hundred thousand dollars in admissions and then sold the painting to a Paris dealer for a million francs, a Duveen-style gain.

High-class trade called for high-class quarters, increasingly exalted as attributions and prices became almost celestial. Fifth Avenue was dealers' row quite early. Long-established Knoedler's made stops at Madison Square and at Astor-Stewart country. Edward Brandus, a Parisian, kept a popular painting gallery near Thirty-seventh Street until he sold his business in 1904 when his Alma-Tademas and Corots were moved for showing to the Fifth Avenue Galleries at 366. The American Art Galleries, the Sotheby Parke-Bernet of its time, conducted a busy program of auctions and there were frequent auctions held at the Waldorf and the Plaza. The famous dealers made the common trade trek up Fifth Avenue, some of them, like the Duveens, moving from the tip of the island to Union Square before they settled into the shadow of the Waldorf, and later the Plaza. In 1918 Knoedler's took up quarters at 546, near Forty-sixth Street (it later became a showpiece of the dwindling Schraffts chain) where they offered all types of painting and art services in a baronial stone hall; below, a long gallery for quasi permanent exhibitions. Then the move, with several other dealers, to Fifty-seventh Street, and last to the current handsome space on Seventieth Street near Madison, today's art *souk*. The Wildensteins, considered the biggest and most active of the dealers still in business, found their way, via Fifth Avenue, to a graceful French building at 19 East Sixty-fourth Street in 1931 and stayed. In 1917, Gimpel took over 647, a distinguished private mansion of five stories with a marble façade, next to Cartier. The rental, paid to the Vanderbilts, was thirty-six thousand dollars while the cost of appropriate furnishings, lighting, transportation and setting of objects and paintings came to one hundred forty thousand dollars. When they were preparing to move, four years later, to Fifty-seventh Street at Fifth the rental quoted was a quarter-million. The Seligmans went from 303 Fifth to 7 West Thirty-sixth, then up to the former house of the railroad wizard, E. H. Harriman, at 705 Fifth, across from the Vanderbilt clan, in 1913. When that house was razed in 1926, the firm moved to 3 East Fifty-first Street, a large house which they gave up for smaller quarters at 5 East Fifty-seventh Street.

To earn fortunes they spent fortunes, Duveen most prodigiously. He had three establishments to maintain, in Paris, London and New York; Bernard Berenson, the richest of scholars, was on a generous retainer and commissions (competitors' gossip spread the word that he received 25 percent of the selling price of a painting; ergo, the astronomic Duveen prices); there were elegant brochures to prepare that accompanied the paintings, as often as possible mentioning previous royal ownership; there were expensive gifts to European museums whose directors and curators might think of him kindly and early when they heard of the dissolution of a major collection. Duveen laid out a good deal of money in his role as decorator—expert for perfect, perfectly appointed miniature palaces, according to Aline Saarinen. The money always came back and more: for the tiny exquisite palace models he collected twenty-five thousand dollars each. When he built himself a lavish new showcase of thirty rooms at Fifty-sixth Street on Fifth Avenue in the style of the buildings on the Place de la Concorde, he figured the cost would be covered by increasing the price of French objects 30 to 40 percent. The prices on Boucher cupids, Sèvres china, Aubusson rugs, Houdon sculpture and the works of their compatriots went up sharply with no diminution in sales.

The frenzied 1920s saw art, like commodities, buildings and bonds, purchased for speculation. The buyers of accredited, carefully researched works who, if they didn't truly like art, respected it as symbol of high achievement and as a means

of appearing on lists of museum donors—America's peerage—
found their ranks crowded with those who would buy anything.
The newcomers preferred bargains on schemes of deferred payment that profited from devalued European currencies, or
reached eagerly for the cellar discards stored by dealers for just
such an open, nondiscriminating market. The crash of 1929
brought back to the dealers many of the former discards as
well as great works offered at beggars' prices. The very rich,
as has been frequently pointed out, did not greatly suffer from
the Depression. Jules Bache, known as B.C. and A.C., Before
Chrysler and After Chrysler, rich to very rich, kept enhancing
his house at 814 Fifth Avenue with a collection that grew
under the wand of Mesmer Duveen. Although not as totally
dedicated to collecting as were Mellon and Frick, Bache competed fiercely and studied well, memorizing the pamphlets that
came with his paintings so that he could call off, by heart, the
lines of their wanderings. By paying extraordinary prices he
acquired a group of monumental paintings, among them a
Crivelli *Madonna and Child*, the Velazquez *Infanta Maria
Teresa*, a *Profile Portrait of a Lady* by Domenico Veneziano
(possibly) and Goya's *Manuel Osorio de Zuñiga*, the last bought
for his daughter, Mrs. Gilbert Miller, whose enthusiasm was
worth the $275,000 he paid for it. Her pleasure in the Little
Red Boy was so great, according to social chroniclers, that, in
order to have him close, she had a ring made that reproduced
the painting. It confused a number of her friends and visitors
who assumed the painting reproduced the ring. Around these
wonders the Bache collection kept growing, Depression or no,
to include in the first years of the 1930s, fifteen choice Rembrandts, five or six dashing Van Dycks and a host of supreme
Dutch, Italian and Flemish paintings.

A curious, latish collector in the old style was Samuel H.
Kress, the rival of Woolworth, Kresge and a number of others
who recognized the need for, and pleasure in, miscellanies of
cheap essential objects under one roof. Like other men of

means he made the European circuit and in time found it
dull. Urged by a lady he frequently traveled with (there was
never a Mrs. Samuel Kress), he found his way to an Italian
count who had a Renaissance collection and some experience
with Americans. Knowing the American faith in certification,
the count called on six experts to write histories and evalu-
ations of each of a group of paintings he suggested Kress take.
Bernard Berenson found most of the lot over-evaluated but
that did not deter Kress. He continued to collect in wholesale
lots, the way he was accustomed to buying sink stoppers and
electric bulbs. Like Morgan he bought from everyone, including intransigent Duveen who refused to bargain or give him
discounts, as toy merchants did. Duveen had art he found
irresistible and had the style to have made for him (as for other
Duveen big spenders) a large volume glorifying the Kress collection—limited, however, to Duveen's contributions to it.

John Walker's *Self-Portrait with Donors* offers a picture of
Kress's surroundings in the last bed-ridden years of his life;
it suggests more than a taste for the Italian Renaissance, rather
an addiction, an incapacity to stop buying in large batches. It
was Walker's mission to strengthen an interest Kress had expressed in possibly donating works to the National Gallery.
Armed with a carefully memorized knowledge of one thousand
paintings, a display that justifiably impressed Kress, he visited
with him in his penthouse apartment at 1020 Fifth Avenue,
across from the Metropolitan Museum. He found himself in a
Renaissance furnishings warehouse, uncomfortable, thronged
with unaccommodating Medici chairs upholstered in the inescapable red velvet, marble floors supporting heavy and densely
carved tables and wedding chests which supported, in turn,
crowds of bronzes and plaques. On the walls, Italian paintings
in velvet-lined shadow boxes, mainly primitives improved by
heavy varnish. Apparently he had similar arrangements of
paintings in his office in the Kress Building at the corner of
Thirty-ninth Street on Fifth. He had, says Walker, "the shop-

keeper's sense of order and conviction that merchandise should be well-lighted and attractively presented."

Walker's impressive knowledge, and the tact and delicate persuasion essential to his job, elicited just under four hundred paintings and sculptures, about a third of them still on display in the National Gallery. A note to Walker's account: a singular Nativity, attributed to Giorgione and expected in Washington for the opening of the gallery, appeared in the Christmas window of the Fifth Avenue Kress store surrounded by spikes of cloth poinsettia, tinsel, tin angels and shining tree ornaments. Clever merchandising? A gesture for public enlightenment? Perhaps it did impart the proper religious touch to the merchandise for those who saw the painting as a Christmas chromo. It certainly threw into startled dismay a few passing experts.

The Old Masters market began to dwindle. Via Duveens, Knoedlers, Wildensteins, Seligmans, Gimpels, Morgans, Fricks, Altmans, Harknesses, Havemeyers, Baches, Lehmanns, Warburgs and donors earlier and later, they came to rest at museums of world-famous quality. The new masters rose to prominence. Mrs. Havemeyer continued doing her enthusiastic best, as did the group readying to open the Museum of Modern Art. Chester Dale, who had earned his fortune in utilities and the municipal bonds of burgeoning Canadian cities, found modern French art attractive when he saw it in Paris and in Fifth Avenue auction rooms and bought eagerly. The two-million-dollar group that he amassed in the late 1920s was valued at fifty million dollars on his death in 1962 and went to Washington's National Gallery to fill incandescent room after room. The knowing and prosperous young fought the good fight for modern art as well; in the late 1920s, Lincoln Kirstein, Edward M. Warburg, and John Walker united as the Harvard Society of Contemporary Art, to hang a modern show in a Harvard Square gallery, not very large but influential.

The rest is current newspaper history, with American art

now in the foreground, worthy of export: a Jackson Pollock
to Australia for over a million dollars; the American art of the
Whitney Museum conspicuously extolled or slashed at by the
attentive critics; Rauschenberg, Warhol, Indiana, Stella, claiming the prices once the right of Velazquez and Turner. The
names change, the trade goes immortally on, for love of art,
for honors, for speculation, for holding like gold and diamonds
against a dour future, for the fun of a risky game. Its venue is
no longer Fifth Avenue but, as mentioned, on Madison Avenue and in extremely private galleries maintained in apartments with unlisted telephone numbers. A valiant attempt,
perhaps, to revive old-style exclusivity?

CHAPTER 11

SCHIFF TO KAHN

ome came as peddlers, some from German banking houses, some were born into cultivated, musical houses in the style of the Mendelssohns, some acquired cultivation with American wealth. The Seligmans, the Schiffs, the Warburgs, the Kuhns, the Loebs, to mention only the Founding Families, married each other, bred healthily, thrived financially and became a formidable clan spread along the upper reaches of Fifth Avenue. The formidability stemmed in part from unremitting cohesion among them and the proud knowledge of who they were, with no wish to change. They were German Jews of the latter half of the nineteenth century, achievers in finance, respecters of the arts, with a cool rational view of their religion appropriate to the reasonable upper echelons of Jewry. The aristocratic Sephardim, who had wandered into Holland and England and the Near East after their expulsion in 1492 from Spain, where they had, along with the Arabs, shaped a radiant culture never to be revived, spoke only to other Sephardim or to Gentiles, who accepted them as they did not the German Jews. The pecking order, uncomfortable from above, provided a large field of disdain downward.

There were, of course, traditional strictures: trust only your own people, find room for your sons in the business, don't claim attention, don't bother with land (too ephemeral a good for people repeatedly driven into exile), live and comport yourself at the height of respectability so that "they" might have no handle for criticism. The daily religious practices and prohibitions which filled many Jewish lives did not impinge on them; observances were limited to Saturday services at uptown Beth-El, High Holidays at the downtown Temple Emanu-El, Kosher Friday family feasts served by the older women and, from one patriarch at least, half-remembered, half-improvised blessings and graces. These rituals entertained some of the children, bored some others and troubled a few. James Warburg whose father, Paul, had come to America in 1901 to join the clan banking house, Kuhn, Loeb and Company, was one of those who wanted something more authentic. "Had I understood that the Jewish cultural heritage is perhaps more of a bond than Judaism, I would have better understood my half-conscious, quasi tribal feelings of loyalty. I had strong pro-Jewish feelings."

Kuhn, Loeb, the family fortress, had its beginnings in the German Jewish community of Cincinnati as the dry goods and clothing establishment of Abraham Kuhn. After the failed 1848 German revolution young Solomon Loeb, the son of a wine dealer in Worms, found his way to Cincinnati and the home and business of his distant relative Kuhn. They were ready with uniforms and blankets for the Union army when the Civil War broke out and emerged, at war's end, rich men. They brought their money to New York and established the banking house of Kuhn, Loeb and Company, which had jobs and partnerships for sons but no sons willing to fill them. The Loeb sons were more interested in the music fostered by their mother (the second Mrs. Loeb; the first, who died young, was Abraham Kuhn's sister) and other matters. Morris became a professor of chemistry and the husband of a Kuhn girl; James preferred the classics as art and literature, publishing the famous Loeb Classical Library. The younger James Warburg speaks of his correspondence with his uncle in Latin and sometimes Greek.

An overwhelming boy whom Kuhn, Loeb took on was Jacob Schiff of an ancient Frankfurt family of scholars and bankers. Abraham Kuhn on a visit to Frankfurt had made a proposal to Schiff to come to New York and enter the firm. Schiff accepted Kuhn's offer, entering the firm on January 1, 1875. Four months later he married Loeb's daughter Therese and shortly began to make the firm awesomely profitable, with a stellar reputation for sound advice in reorganizing railroads at a time when railroads were the favorite Wall Street toy.

Jacob Schiff, autocratic as he undoubtedly was, was described as a smooth, contained man, adroit in handling people, of baroque "Oriental" makeup, which often meant, as it meant in the time of August Belmont, "Jewish." He had the clear, cool, aggressive drive and imagination to become a master of finance, the admitted peer of Morgan, with whom he locked on control of western railroads. As a great lord, advising magnates, dragging children and grandchildren along Fifth Avenue for their dignified constitutionals, he was impressive. As a great lord, invited by the Guggenheims to help assess, with a view to financing, the possibilities of mining the Yukon, he dissolves into a lesser figure, petulant over the lack of respect and amenities for himself and his servants in the raw, cold land, making a quick turnabout after traveling over three thousand miles.

As patriarch and upholder of his version of the Old Religion, he was intractable and humorless. As head of his family and, in essence, head of the clan, he superseded God, the ever-present, demanding, implacable Old Testament God, according to the accounts of his daughter Frieda and her children and nephews. He had a heavy German accent and was quite deaf and impatient of other people's incomprehensible speech. (One grandson tells of a riddle he kept posing about the difference between a sea bath and a sea bass, pronouncing them both as "bass.") He was a man who gave away, with little fanfare and few commemorative plaques, fifty million dollars to charity (he supported Tuskegee College long before the black became a universal American obligation) and yet scribbled the destiny of railroad meshworks on used scraps of paper. He did not work on Saturdays but, when it suited him, ate nonkosher foods. Like a good Jewish father he weighed his children Frieda and Mortimer down with lessons in everything, including fencing lessons for Frieda in order that she become slimmer, more graceful, more soignée. Having prepared his good-looking, well-educated girl for the world, showing her her own possibilities in an alluring portrait ordered of Zorn when she was eighteen, he shut her in. And engaging mother Therese, born to be a lively, innocent ornament (she never did a stroke of work, never arranged a bowl of flowers, according to her daughter) wasn't of much help. She was the undereducated, submissive German wife of her times. And were she more independent, could she have coped so well with the stormy force of Schiff? Frieda was on a very short string financially—some of her meager allotment to go to charity—and on a short string socially. There were the opulent Loeb Sunday evenings at 37 East Thirty-eighth Street with wonderful spreads of food, music and lively discussions. There were the Tuesday afternoon "at homes," the Seligman feasts and, as the clan proliferated, other family houses to gather in; but it was almost always family. Visitors were likely to be mature professional or charity associates; the young were too often cousins. Weekend mornings were absorbed by Saturday services and Sunday walks in the park. Jacob would not permit his daughter to have a debut; a debut was an announcement to the world that here was marriageable goods. Schiff was not ready to let her go, nor would he be for a considerable time, no matter who the applicant.

The Schiff house of the 1880s and 1890s was at 932 Fifth

Avenue, at Seventy-fourth Street, a long, narrow house, crammed with hideous things Jacob had bought at auction, among them two huge Chinese vases into which the children vomited during a bout of whooping cough. (Frieda's sons vied with each other to see who could spit with more accuracy into their father's antique urn near the house entrance.) When Mortimer was married the house was given to him as a wedding present and the Schiffs moved to 965, between Seventy-seventh and Seventy-eighth, where they stayed until Schiff's death in 1920. There were improvements here, prompted by Sir Ernest Cassel, banker, art lover, adviser to Edward VII and Schiff's co-worker in international finance. Barbizon paintings began to appear on the walls and select objects of great value on taborets.

It was from 932 that Frieda was married, wearing a satin dress sewn with endless yards of Brussels lace sent from Europe by her mother-in-law and her grandmother. The reception was catered by Sherry who had artfully used tapestries to conceal laundering and heating equipment in the basement and turned it into a banqueting hall.

It started as a Grand Tour, including visits with European banking families, relatives, feasts and balls, music and the hiking and mountaineering that Schiff enjoyed (as his children and later his grandchildren did not, in spite of his efforts). At a dinner party given by relatives of the Loebs, Frieda, wearing her Zorn evening dress, met Felix of the considerable clan of German Warburgs. According to the family history and autobiography Frieda wrote in the twilight of her long life, that night Felix announced he had met the girl he was going to marry, a startling declaration from a handsome, life-loving young man, witty, a smart dresser, a sportsman, a frequenter of concerts and musicals, a man with a nice eye for women and the arts. He should have been the perfect candidate: of a cultivated old banking family and kosher, the son of the head of the Jewish community of Hamburg, Moritz Warburg, and

executive in the prestigious precious-gems firm of his grandfather, Nathan Oppenheim. But he was a lightweight, according to Schiff, too attractive, too playful.

The couple were to separate, each to return to his native
home; they were not to write to each other. The only letters
to be exchanged were letters from Frieda to Charlotte Oppenheim Warburg, Felix's mother, and from Felix to Jacob Schiff.
Some months later, toward the end of 1894, Felix arrived in
New York to sit out a difficult engagement. He was rarely
permitted to be alone with his fiancée and although he spoke
German with members of the family, his blithe spirit was
stifled by his halting English when he tried to speak with
visitors like James Hill, whose railroad chatter, accompanied
by the gentle clink of the handful of precious stones Hill
habitually carried, was disconcerting. Nor was it a limpidly
happy time for Frieda. She was in love with a man who was
pleasingly persistent and willing to undergo the trials her
father set him. However there were "facts of life," dark vague
whispers that frightened her. Her cheery, advanced grandmother offered to clarify one or two basic mysteries but Jacob
put his foot down: although his daughter might be chronologically and socially ready for marriage, her innocence must not
be darkened.

The marriage took place; the couple went to Italy on
their honeymoon accompanied by a termagant of a German
maid who insisted on treating Frieda as a child, dictating what
she might wear or not wear of her luxurious trousseau, getting
in the way of the couple as much as possible—as if on instructions from Jacob. They were as stubborn as she and before
their first anniversary they had a daughter, Carola, who was
born at 18 East Seventy-second Street, the first New York house
of Felix Warburg, now a member of Kuhn, Loeb. Within the
next twelve years, four sons, Frederick M., Gerald Felix, Paul
Felix and Edward M. It was time for a larger house, so one
was built in 1907–1908 at 1109 Fifth Avenue, on the corner of

Ninety-second Street, in French Gothic style. Schiff objected
to the style, it was too showy and might prick up a little more
of the anti-Semitism of which he was intensely aware. By the
time he made his protest it was too late to change to the
Italian Renaissance style he thought more suitable. His gesture
of protest was to turn his head away when he passed the growing house on one of his constitutionals. There were five grandchildren in the finished house; a devoted, obedient daughter,
although he did not always think so, and a son-in-law whose
tact, buoyancy and background made him a valued member
of the firm. Jacob's gesture of reconciliation with the house
was distinctly Schiff. He visited only because Frieda was ill,
made no comment about the house to her as they spoke and
the next day sent her a warm letter and a check for twenty-five
thousand dollars as a house gift.

Frieda Warburg's description of her house, now very much
changed as the Jewish Museum, had the formal arrangement
of its period on the lower stories: an entrance hall that introduced an inordinately space-consuming grand stairway, a small
gallery for the Warburg etchings, and beyond, the extensive
kitchen and pantries. On the Fifth Avenue side of the second
floor, the music room whose large pièce was the popular
Aeolian electric pipe organ which had buttons and stops to
push which gave one the illusion of performing music that
could be heard in every part of the house. Here, too, tapestries,
illuminated manuscripts, pieces of sculpture and, very probably, the house collection of Strads. The adjoining room held
Italian paintings, a cassone and a refectory table that held a
Raphael Madonna and Child. Via a conservatory with stained
glass which held a Botticelli and an ancient Bible, one entered
a tapestry-hung dining room. More intimate family rooms
occupied the third floor: the joint sitting room of the parents
where the children were blessed over the Friday night candles,
the master bedroom, Frieda's boudoir where they went for
prayers in German and Felix's dressing room where the boys

settled their father for a nap, then woke him and watched him dress. The fourth floor was the children's domain and the fifth was guest rooms, a squash court and, when he grew older, Edward's art gallery.

The grand stairway was a superb racecourse and offered challenging heights for spitting contests. The Aeolian pipe organ (advertised from its showrooms on Fifth Avenue as "Reproductive Organs") was there to be turned on at full blast, crashing on all eardrums at unexpected hours. The long haul of food from the kitchen to the breakfast room required impromptu stops for reheating, patience and improvisation. The play floor could be turned into a maelstrom of toy trains that threatened maids' ankles and cracked into each other with satisfying frequency. And Father, appropriately known as Fizzi, was not only glamorous—a spiller of gold-coin tips and a fancy dresser—but fun. He invented bicycle polo, entertained his children by singing Gilbert and Sullivan in German, encouraged his chauffeur to drive faster and faster to the great pleasure of the boys, introduced them to the joys of yachting and travel and, as in his family's house in Hamburg, stimulated them to use their wits and talents for home entertainment. He played squash with them and taught them tennis, swimming, skating and riding. Most of all he was fun because he found amusement and pleasure in his children and let them know it. One important sentence in the annals of the family is a statement he made to Frieda, "Your children may be spoiled, mine are fun."

The free-form, noisy atmosphere affected some of the servants as well. The butler, improbably named Congreve, entered the spirit of the house by devising an incubator in which he bred chicks and ducklings to use in a little farm scene that served as centerpiece for the children's parties. One of the boys brought a friend home from school; he stayed for three years. A young medical student invited in as companion-tutor, finished his schooling from the house and became, in time, a noted medical authority.

1109 Fifth Avenue held its people together for over thirty years, the children at school, the married children and their children returning for family parties and charity galas. When Carola married Walter Rothschild the latter found himself married to her young brothers who came to visit very frequently; when Paul was married, two of his brothers accompanied the couple on a portion of their honeymoon. In spite of the family closeness, everybody busily did his own thing or the clan thing, if he liked. Frederick joined Kuhn, Loeb; Paul went into banking—not with Kuhn, Loeb—and later into government work; Gerald's life was in music and improving the musical life of New York as one of the founders with Mayor La Guardia of the City Center and as organizer of music at the Metropolitan Museum where his Stradivarius Quartet (the instruments those of his father) often played. Edward was, by family tradition, destined for the arts because it was he who as a youngster showed visitors the impressive house collection of prints. Besides helping organize the Harvard Society of Contemporary Art, he became involved in founding the Film Library of the Museum of Modern Art and with Lincoln Kirstein and George Balanchine, the American School of Ballet.

"I am like Heinz's pickles. I belong to fifty-seven varieties of committees." This was Felix's way of summing up the multiplicity of organizations, primarily charitable, to which he belonged. As an admirer of Jefferson, he suggested that an ecumenical, rich trio—Protestant, Jew and Catholic—combine to buy Monticello for use as a scholastic center. When that plan fell through, he made a large contribution toward the restoration of the personable, unique house and its establishment as a national shrine. He was a trustee of Columbia's Teachers College, a lavish supporter of the YMHA and tangential organizations, of the Fogg Museum in Cambridge, of the Jewish

Theological Seminary and of a variety of musical organizations and individual musicians. He was the first president (1917) of the Federation of Jewish Philanthropies and although neither he nor Frieda—or for that matter the children—were Zionists, they made contributions to the financial and cultural life of Palestine.

After Felix died in the fall of 1937, Frieda wished to remain in the house, allaying the loneliness with the presence of the Max Warburgs, who had been driven out of Germany by Hitler. In spite of the constant attention of her family, it didn't work and she moved to an apartment at the corner of Fifth Avenue at Eighty-eighth Street. She would not sell the house although she agreed that its contents be dismantled in 1941 and the rarities sent, under Edward's supervision, to several museums, libraries and universities. Three years later, on the day that would have marked Felix's seventy-third birthday, Frieda turned the house over to the Jewish Theological Seminary for its Jewish Museum. For a while the displays were orderly and interesting cases of synagogue and ceremonial objects. Then for a few years the Museum became a stormy petrel of modern art; then with a new board, it subsided into ceremonial objects again with the addition of modern Israeli matter. Unfortunately, public use and age have dimmed the stained glass and dulled the meticulously carved woods. Frieda fared better than her house in their later years. She gathered honorary chairmanships and degrees, read voluminously in general matters and Jewish affairs, kept up her sizable contributions to institutions in the States and Israel and battened happily on her family and its accomplishments.

The Jewish version of Old King Cole spent many of his late years—not declining, rather rising—at 881 Fifth Avenue. Only one of several houses that belonged to Adolph Lewisohn, 881, was the preferred mise-en-scène for the New Year's Eve party he staged each year until he died at ninety. Having

wrested a good-sized fortune out of copper and lost his wife,
who might have been an inhibiting influence, Adolph decided
to live a little, creating his own small, fun-laden WPA arts
project during the Depression years, dispensing almost as much
money as did the government, in a much more cheerful, playful way. The entertaining, artistic, musical and literary, their
girl friends and sisters found him a sweet, generous old gentleman. When he moved from house to house or went on trips
abroad it was with a royal entourage that cosseted him, dressed
him, fed him, taught him elegant new skills, amused and titil-
lated him—and were all highly paid for their attentions. More
solid members of the Jewish community—those who weren't
falling into their own desuetude, no longer supported by the
strict mores of the clan—turned their heads away. In spite of
his many charities—the Lewisohn Stadium concerts, of course,
and his expenditures and efforts for prison reform—he was
spoken of as a ridiculous old fool.

One of the proofs of his dottiness was his art collection,
comprised of the "new" French art that few others gave house
room to. Lewisohn's original collection consisted of the usual,
approved Barbizon paintings. The legend says that a lady
friend advised him to sell these and buy, at very little cost, the
work of contemporary Frenchmen. Actually, the person who
persuaded Lewisohn to buy Degas, Monet, Gauguin, Cézanne
and Picasso at a few hundred dollars each was his clever, discriminating and affectionate son Sam who avoided the New
Year's bashes but saw no objection to an energetic, gleeful old
man spending his dotage learning to sing Schubert and Brahms,
to cut a soft-shoe caper in vaudeville style and perform at his
own huge parties which cost many thousands of dollars in
liquor alone. A reasonable man, and Sam was, might say this
was the best form of senility, if senility it was. Sam brought his
new wife, Margaret, of the populous Seligman tribe, to live in
881 and there they raised four daughters, none the worse for
having had an odd grandfather; according to Frieda Warburg,

they were a distinguished group of girls. And the old man had the best of two possible worlds, dinner at home with his son and amiable daughter-in-law, and the flattery, the whoopee and razzle-dazzle of his raffish court.

"Otto H. Kahn lived with infinite zest and no person who came really to know him escaped the fascination of his enthusiasm for ideas and his willingness at all times to promote them." This was part of the tribute paid by Olin Downes, the prestigious music critic, in the spreads of homage that the *New York Times* paid Kahn after his death on March 29, 1934. After sketching Kahn's rescue of the Metropolitan Opera by bringing in Gatti-Casazza as manager, persuading Toscanini to leave La Scala to conduct in New York, introducing Caruso and a star-studded company of singers, Downes continues, "The success of these years which inaugurated a period of unexampled prestige and prosperity for the Met, was due in large part to Mr. Kahn's clear-sighted appraisal of the situation, his judgment in supporting the right men to put artistic ideas into effect, and his policy, once these men had been appointed, of protecting them from interference in their work. . . . Mr. Kahn's mind was always restless, imaginative and sentient to whatever ideas were in the air. To use up every day all his energy; to come in contact with many minds and people in different walks of life, without self-consciousness and on equal terms, perpetually interested him." Elsewhere in the pages of encomiums, Downes again, describing a man on whom the Good Fairies had showered all possible blessings. "He lived at a very full tide with an astonishing capacity for work and play. He read new books voraciously and enjoyed them as he did food, people, thoughts. He could crowd an amazing amount of activity into a day, and had astonishingly the capacity to turn from occupation and topic, with complete concentration and freshness of approach. Artists and men of finance found him equally entertaining."

The King of New York, a favorite of Vanity Fair and the
bright op-ed page of the New York *World*, internationally
acclaimed as financier and—to a degree—political and economic
savant, passionate lover of the arts on whose international
facets he lavished millions eagerly, Kahn was born in 1867 of
prosperous merchants and manufacturers in Mannheim. Following the de rigueur pattern, they were interested in music,
literature and finance. Young Otto was encouraged to play the
piano, the cello and the violin, never to a point of mastery. On
his own he wrote two ponderous blank verse dramas that his
mother had him burn, which may explain his later passion for
writers and for writing. Since he was not to inflame the world
with his arts, the family sent him to train in banking, which
he combined stubbornly with courses in the arts and literature. In his mid-twenties he achieved an executive job in
the London branch of the Deutsche Bank and with it became
a London bon vivant and intellectual, a connoisseur of music
and the theater, a friend of artists and writers, an ornament to advanced salons. The next step was Wall Street,
which was somewhat put off by his German-English accent and
arts proclivities but nevertheless cognizant of his talents, elegance, poise and remarkable tact in handling stampeding railroad magnates. Though his tendencies were Edwardian Gentile,
his marriage was in the Jewish banking tradition, the bride
Adelaide Wolff, daughter of Kuhn, Loeb's Abraham Wolff, a
pretty woman, a woman of knowledge and sophisticated taste
in the arts. It was she who furnished a few of the several
Kahn houses and gathered the remarkable, wide-ranging Kahn
collection, from Gaddi, Cranach and Clouet to Botticelli, Rembrandt and Guardi, and into the modern French.

After his year abroad following the marriage, Kahn joined
Kuhn, Loeb and, aided by the tutelage of Schiff, frequent contact with Morgan, and the feared, brilliant railroad pirate
Edward Harriman, Kahn began to work boldly, releasing an
unprecedented flood of American railroad bonds in French

money markets and besting the omnivorous George Gould in their contests for control of major railway lines. After the older giants died, Kahn remained the most respected Kuhn, Loeb consultant to railroading interests and a prime mover in international finance.

Beside railroads to merge and pump life into at neat profits to Kuhn, Loeb, there were houses to build, an estate at Cold Spring Harbor, three town houses on Sixty-eighth Street off Fifth Avenue, a house at the corner of Seventy-ninth and Fifth and the noblest of them all, the Italianate mansion at 1100 (Ninety-first Street), considered the most beautiful house in New York by the cognoscenti of 1919–1920. The four Kahn children, two sons and two daughters, were brought up in the old Wolff house in Morristown, New Jersey. The New York houses seemed rarely to have settled in solidly for domestic use, possibly a reflection of Kahn's busy life, possibly a reflection of a faint lingering desire to return to England, where the Kahns had a house as well. (Before World War I he was urged by English conservatives to run for Parliament; he was not an American citizen and he tried, but the arcane complexities of British politics and persistent British anti-Semitism defeated him. He returned to the States and turned over the London house for a wide program in the instruction of the blind.) The splendid house at Ninety-first Street was hostel for entertainers and artists foreign and domestic. One of the houses on Sixty-eighth Street was the clubhouse—everything free—for French soldiers and sailors during World War I. The estate at Cold Spring Harbor seemed to serve largely for the weekends frequently reported by the *World*'s popular columnist Franklin Pierce Adams, known as F.P.A., as a gaudy fair of Kahn friends and acquaintances, from tattered writers to sleek financiers.

There was little time for domestic life. Kahn outdid his partner (and probably remote relative) in Kuhn Loeb, Felix Warburg, by a dozen committees, with the necessary enthusiasm and energy for attending to them all and the satisfaction of knowing that his public-relations man would take care of apprising the newspapers of the extraordinary range of his activities. F.P.A. summed it up in his couplet: "The sun it never shone upon a busier man than Otto Kahn." "Home" was for a long time the Metropolitan Opera, an expensive home which cost him almost five million dollars in thirty years of guidance and beneficence. He adored singers: Caruso, to whom he consistently lost in sharp Little Italy card games, and the queenly Jeritza, in legend his mistress. It was under his aegis that Chaliapin came to the Met. Kahn paid for lessons, and the rent, made investments and granted gifts to singers, composers, instrumentalists and extras in distress, and when he was pleased with an aria or two, he dropped a gift of several thousand dollars into the artist's pocket.

It was not only a question of being a good, rich, attentive friend. Kahn was convinced that America was ready to become a leader in the arts and his Metropolitan Opera was to help prove it. He subsidized a number of modern composers and insisted that their work be heard, staging more world premieres than New York City has seen since his time. The culmination of Kahn's ambitions for American music was an American opera, *The King's Henchman*, with libretto by Edna St. Vincent Millay and music by Deems Taylor, the critic of the *World*. Its reception was mixed but it was a landmark that encouraged American composers.

The Metropolitan Opera, absorbing as it was, still left time for exploring in other arts in other places. Pavlova and Mordkin were brought to perform at the Met in 1910 and then launched on a countrywide tour whose proceeds and the investments Kahn made for her left Pavlova a rich woman.

Several years later, the venturesome Ballet Russe, organized by Diaghilev and again sponsored by Kahn, came—sans prima ballerina, or Nijinsky. The Bakst costumes were spectacular, the Stravinsky music evocative, but what of the lead dancers? It was a fizzle, but Kahn was not through. Nijinsky's nonappearance was one of the chapters of an adventure story of confinement, harassment, escapes, threats, law suits and debts that drove the dancer to the borders of lunacy. Kahn put into action his full weaponry of money and friends in several embassies and royal courts. Ultimately Nijinsky arrived and was a stunning success. An extensive tour was planned for the next season with Nijinsky in charge of productions, a role he might just have been able to fill if the Russian government hadn't sent him a crescendo of messages inviting him to serve in the Russian army or take the consequences as a traitor. The delicately balanced, terrified Nijinsky let controls and plans slip from his hands and the season became a heap of disasters. It cost Kahn hundreds of thousands of dollars but he had brought ballet to the United States and it stayed and grew under the influence of dancers of the magnitude of George Balanchine.

The great ringmaster, in his opera cloak and meticulous mustache, moving in a low cloud of little dogs, continued to scour the world for culture and fun, heedless of the cost: the Moscow Art Theater, experimental French theater, the Washington Square Players, O'Neill's Provincetown Players, the Abbey Players, Germany's Reinhardt, the Hebrew Habima Theater, the advanced New Playwrights Theater, the Ibsen and Chekhov melange of Eva Le Gallienne's repertory theater. He helped Gershwin and Paul Robeson and Isadora Duncan and Hart Crane and sinking theater companies and publishers of gaunt, intellectual little reviews, and sponsored free and inexpensive concerts. He may even have given money to the Communist *New Masses* or the *Daily Worker*; Mike Gold, a writer for both publications, was one of his several thousand acquaintances and Kahn was a subscriber to *The New Masses* as well. (Although he was not alone among the wealthy to help the *New Masses*—Alva Belmont and Adolph Lewisohn made contributions, too—it makes a particularly interesting picture to imagine the silken dandy, complete to boutonniere and pearl stickpin reading polemics that called for his extermination and the end of his kind.)

There was the larger world's work to do also. His financial aid to Europe during World War I won him at least as many citations as Andrew Carnegie. He pressed for rational economic planning, for improved management-labor relations, which gave him a feeling that he might be almost a Socialist, and proud of it. However, when his friend Theodore Roosevelt proposed stiff inheritance taxes, Kahn asked him to reconsider; it would be better for business not to tie up quite so much money in taxes. He lectured and wrote on politics, economics, on the arts, on films as a potentially important art form, on jazz as basic to the development of American music, on socialism as a high goal of mankind. He liked to discuss the contributions of Catholicism (to which he was very much attracted though he declared himself unequivocally a Jew with the advent of Hitler) to music and art through the ages.

And there was still time for long yacht trips with friends to view indefatigably beauty and more beauty, and if the Parthenon needed shoring up, always the willing Kahn checkbook. Until the day of his impeccably tasteful swift death Kahn lived, as one commentator said, "as if the world were his oyster on which he fed intelligently and well."

CHAPTER 12

CENTRAL PARK

efore Central Park was laid out in the late 1850s Fifty-ninth Street was as sharp a dividing line between two cities as East Ninety-sixth Street is in the present. The march of brownstones northward thinned toward the Fifties, allowing space for institutions with abundant grounds, and for a few stubborn Dutch houses and farms east of the Avenue. The area now occupied by the Plaza, General Motors and the Sherry-Netherland was recreation ground in a hilly, rural setting. Brooks flowed into skating ponds which were haunted by engravers entranced with full swinging skirts and arms poised for flight across the ice. One pond was set aside for the exclusive use of the New York Skating Club which asked an annual fee of ten dollars from its members. Near the skating grounds, where the defunct Hotel Netherlands, built in 1893, stood in an enclave of its also defunct peers, there was a riding academy.

Above Fifty-ninth Street the Avenue was not graded and paved until long after the close of the Civil War. As late as 1875 a sick citizen out for an airing in the park had to give it up because the approach along Fifth Avenue was so badly paved that the bumping of his carriage caused him too much pain. North of Fifty-ninth Street the Avenue was a pitted path

between stone walls that kept the cattle driven into the city
from straying; westward, the vast squatters' city that became
Central Park and extended to within Mount Morris Park.
Among the dank marshes, the scummy ponds, the mattings of
brush and rocks that thwarted attempts at agriculture except
for a few scraggly farms, lived over five thousand people. Most
of the squatters made their houses of slats and lengths of tin
picked up here and there, at demolition sites, from a shattered
boat on a river shore. The least enterprising lived in an arrangement of trenches; the more prosperous, busy ragpickers
perhaps, whose industrious children cleared railroad tracks for
a few cents a day, paid rent for the use of frame hovels or space
in a brick or stone shanty. Among the hovels were rudimentary
barns and pigsties, a small quarry or two, bone factories and
packs of dogs—one hundred thousand dogs it was estimated—
who contested garbage pickings with goats, cats and chickens.
The population was a New York mixture: descendants of early
wanderers, freed slaves, a few bewildered surviving Indians, the
newer Irish and Germans. Their basic diet was the leavings of
prosperous households, carried off in dog carts. The boldest
resorted to stealing and victimizing their neighbors. Some of it
was honest, all of it tough, and the settlements were dangerously
unhealthy in their filth and the disease-laden ponds that bubbled noxious gases.

The noisome stretch was punctuated by two respectable
buildings. Near the lower end, the arsenal at Sixty-fourth Street,
the largest arsenal in the state, opened in 1848 after an expenditure of thirty thousand dollars. In less than ten years it was
sold to the city for nearly ten times the original cost, to become
the office of the Parks Department, the first American Museum
of Natural History, a police precinct with a menagerie in the
basement, the ur-Zoo. At the northern end near 106th Street
the school and convent of Mount St. Vincent had been established in 1847 by the Sisters of Charity of St. Vincent who had
taken over the site of a tavern of Revolutionary fame and six

surrounding acres for six thousand dollars. When their isolated quiet was shattered by the planners and diggers of Central Park, the sisters moved out to the Hudson River estate of actor Edwin Booth, soon to be replaced in the Park by the glossy horses and riders who had chosen Mount Saint Vincent as the terminal point of their races over newly opened paths.

The need for a large recreation ground in the exploding city had been a fervid topic since the end of the eighteenth century. Between 1820 and 1850 the population had more than tripled, from 125,000 to 450,000, producing the famous festering slums and quickly triggered anger among warring neighborhoods. The peaceable poor took their recreational ease in the quiet greens of cemeteries. The wealthy and civic-minded had, on their travels abroad, become enamored of European parks, particularly those of England. One of the most insistent propagandists for a big central park was Andrew Jackson Downing, a pioneer American landscape architect and editor of the influential *Horticulturist*. A second was William Cullen Bryant who, as co-owner and editor of the New York *Evening Post*, published in 1844, the first of many editorials calling for a park to be developed from a portion of the city's disappearing common grounds. After considerable discussion and dissension, legal ploys and counterploys, the state legislature approved the right of the city to use the area from Fifty-ninth Street to 106th (the land to 110th Street was a later addition) west of Fifth Avenue to what was then Eighth. In February, 1856, the Tammany-controlled city commissioners, led by the vivid and crooked Fernando Wood, "a scoundrel of special magnitude," made their usual move: they awarded their friends the sum of five million dollars for formerly cheap lots to be used as Central Park.

That year Society staged formal balls, like that of Mrs. Peter Schermerhorn in her house on University Place, a close annex of Washington Square and lower Fifth Avenue.

Robert L. Cutting, a founder of the Academy of Music and member of an anti-Tammany reform committee for civic affairs, offered a big reception, overburdened according to one guest with music, at his Fifth Avenue house. Mr. William B. Astor served forth tasty dinners on his golden plates.

Art aficionados went to the Academy of Design for a show dominated by a steaming, tropical landscape of Frederick Church, whose canvases were selling for ten thousand dollars and more. Art tasters and critics were talking about the plans for the new Roman Catholic cathedral on Fifth Avenue, "a combination of Cologne Cathedral and the Crystal Palace." They judged the grand size and scale potentially effective but had doubts about the use of iron ornamentation for spires and pillars; St. Patrick's couldn't last more than five years since the expansion and contraction of ill-matched stone and iron would tear the edifice apart. The musically minded went to Niblo's Saloon for symphony concerts, attended Theodore Eisfeld's chamber music recitals and saw at the academy the recently composed *Traviata* which one *feinschmecker* dismissed as utter drivel. Louis Gottschalk, a signal success, was offered twenty thousand dollars a year by P. T. Barnum for a series of piano recitals that would include his own compositions.

The third volume of Ruskin's *Modern Painters* had just reached America and was judged "full of life and brilliancy"; Dickens's *Little Dorrit* was reappearing in installments in the New York *Weekly Tribune*, turning the ladies into fountains of tears. Bronson Alcott, the transcendentalist and father of Louisa May, drew large crowds to his curious alternations of acuteness and fogginess in a series of "discussions," as he chose to call his lectures. The academic community which considered NYU and Columbia a sufficiency of higher education found amusing Peter Cooper's plan for a free university, his "Union"; they granted him good will and kindness but thought his conception of a higher school for working-class youth thoroughly impractical. Gentlemen of a scientific bent, stimulated by the giant steps all branches of science were taking, bought aquaria and microscopes and a variety of the magical machines that produced early photography. The search for anesthetics that would make pioneer changes in dentistry and surgery led to a vogue of sniffing chloroform and entering the "phantasmagorias" of hashish. The less venturesome attended spiritualist séances; the most timid settled for homeopathy and the cold baths and austere diets prescribed by a large tribe of homeopathic gurus.

For many it was a hard and nervous time. The economy was depressed, the winter very cold and there were thousands of unemployed freezing and mal-fed. Busy Broadway was a stream of cold black muck. Politically sophisticated unemployed German workers gathered in large numbers to listen to leaders immediately branded "demagogues." Threatened by agitators on the one hand and the volatile Irish on the other, more fortunate ladies took it upon themselves to alleviate the condition of the poor by arranging lavish entertainments for their benefit. "To a poverty stricken demagogue, the plan of feasting the aristocracy on boned turkey and pate de foie gras that the democracy may be supplied with pork and beans, and assembling the Upper Ten in brocade and valenciennes that the lower thousand may be helped to flannel and cotton shirting, would furnish a theme most facile and fertile," was the comment of one social critic.

In spite of the charity balls, charitable visits to the poor and the gathering in of homeless children, the streets swarmed with young prostitutes, and men were forced to carry guns in the evening to fend off the thievery and garroting that menaced the testy city. Gangs attacked firemen and vice versa in heady brawls that no one could quench because both gangs and firemen had strong political connections and were consequently unassailable.

Spurred on by the tensions and the rowdy drinking that usually marked July 4th, the brutal Dead Rabbits initiated in

1856 one of their most violent forays. They pillaged and killed, abetted by their women and young, who threw bricks and bottles off rooftops to maim the police trying to quell them. The mighty rival gang, the Bowery Boys, joined the police for a brief aberrant moment and then changed their minds and attacked the cops. As the violence mounted the police called out the militia and a rumbling, uneasy peace settled on the city. As if to exacerbate the nervous atmosphere, excavations for buildings on Gramercy Square caved in and killed several Irish laborers. Their women poured into the site to keen, "a wild, unearthly cry, half shriek and half song, wailing as a score of daylight Banshees, clapping their hands and gesticulating passionately," a fearsome sound in the new, frightened neighborhood which made guards of its footmen and petitioned urgently and fruitlessly for police protection.

In August, financial panic. Factories closed, banks failed, the number of unemployed reached almost forty thousand. By October, runs on nearly all the banks had caused a suspension of specie payments. The commercial streets were crammed with frightened, milling crowds and long anxious lines at the doors of banks. The two hundred thousand buildings which had begun to rise were stopped at one or two stories, their construction teams fired. Shops stayed open late and sent out broadsides about extraordinary sales to attract whatever money might be still around. Labor demonstrators waved inflammatory signs that threatened insurrection; corruption and lawlessness swelled, exploding to a climax when the Dead Rabbits took control of City Hall, manhandling those who opposed them, for a short terrifying time.

Above the city's tumult, the voices of ragged "Extra" boys heralding through the day and the night the extreme tension of national affairs. The regional passions that led to the Civil War were already at a boil. South Carolina threatened to secede if Fremont won the bitterly contested Presidential election and the New York *Herald* admitted that the "alienation of North and South is an unquestionable fact and a grave one."

Under these turbulent clouds, the beginnings of Central Park. Mayor Wood and his Street Commissioner gathered together a committee of seven reputable New Yorkers, for cachet rather than advice, among them the revered Washington Irving and Charles A. Dana, publisher of the *Sun*. Wood and Company already had a park plan begun three years before by a military gentleman, Egbert L. Viele, a graduate of West Point and the Mexican wars, who was appointed engineer in chief of the park works. Months passed and no work was done because there was no money for it. Mayor Wood wooed the working class by promising to put thousands to work in Central Park. His motives were political but it was a reasonable idea that provided the labor force, and innumerable continuing problems, for the man who was primarily responsible for devising the park.

Frederick Law Olmsted, the first American environmentalist, civic planner and organizer of major public projects, a leading force for rational and thorough medical services for soldiers during the Civil War, was born in Hartford, Connecticut in 1822, the son of a harmonious, sophisticated household that provided its children with skill in sports and dancing, languages and drawing, and if they liked, the right to wander.

After a brutal but interesting time as an apprentice seaman on a China clipper, Frederick returned, in 1844, to serve as an apprentice on a model farm and then to become an independent farmer. Life was good, the improvements he made in the farm attractive and profitable, the local girls lovable and he loved them all, singly and en masse. But childhood meanderings and the China voyage had opened glimpses of a larger and beckoning world. Amiable papa took over the farm and Frederick, Brother John and a friend took off for the young intellectuals' walking tour through England.

Frederick found the English countryside, as thousands before and after him, tender and gracious in spite of the appalling contrast of privileged wealth and the poverty of the peasant. He particularly admired the English parks: long slopes of lawn rising to one great copper beech, felicities of subtle tone and gentle rhythms joined by the slow amble of cows and the swift grace of deer. Olmsted was particularly taken with a Victorian park, Birkenhead, near Liverpool, designed by Joseph Paxton. "All this magnificent pleasure-ground is entirely, unreservedly, and forever the people's own," Olmsted recorded in the journals that were later published.

Soon after his return, already an established reporter, Olmsted was offered the job of examining and recording the South for the *New York Times*. He traveled in the South for a year, producing reports that became important eyewitness source books. Olmsted was not against slavery for its inhumanity; he pointed out that it was only one of a number of kinds of existing social immorality, citing the starving Irish tenant farmer, the seamen he had shipped with, the children slaving in the mills and dying in the tenements of prosperous Abolitionists who spent large sums on the rescue of slaves. His major quarrel with Southern slavery was its inefficiency and waste since slaves could not be expected to handle tools and the land with the respect that a free man might. The Abolitionists were mistaken, he said, because they refused to see that freed slaves, having so long lived in dependency, needed a long period of reeducation to come to their full capacities, which were not, he said, innately inferior but eroded by slavery. Nor was the white man in the South truly profiting—his power over human life must corrupt him.

After several other exploratory journalistic stints and an unsuccessful book business venture in Europe (not altogether a loss since he learned more of the landscapes and parks of England and the formal gardens and townscapes of Italy), Olmsted applied for the job of superintendency of the workers who were to reshape the mean area north of Fifty-ninth Street. Sponsored by respected names, Washington Irving and Peter Cooper among others, he got the job. The salary was fifteen hundred dollars a year, half the sum received by Viele, the chief engineer and planner. But jobs were scarce and this was a situation in which he could try out his principle that self-respecting and respected, disciplined labor produced maximum efficiency. One of the first shocks encountered in his work was confrontation by a mob that presented him with a list of many thousands of unemployed men who had been promised jobs by ward heelers. The force he actually used numbered about a thousand, soon organized in effective units that made rapid progress in the heavy work of crushing rocks and filling swamps.

Calvert Vaux, for many years Olmsted's partner, to whom he insisted equal credit for Central Park and later planning be given, was born in London in 1824, and quite young apprenticed to a leading architect who launched him on an exploration of English architecture which Vaux combined with a study of English parks and public playing fields. Andrew Jackson Downing was sufficiently impressed with the young Englishman to bring him to America as his partner. Vaux and other critics felt that the Viele project lacked coherence and style. Increasingly, informed interest led to a decision that a competition for a new design of the park be held. The competition was hedged with strict stipulations: space for a hall capable of adapting to exhibitions or music, three playgrounds of set dimensions, a big parade ground, a pond for skating, a romantic tower, an important fountain, extensive gardens and, absolutely essential, four major routes to carry traffic from east to west, the whole complex to be held within a cost of one and a half million dollars. Although both Vaux and Olmsted, who entered the competition jointly, would have preferred to plan many small squares scattered throughout the city, the early 1811 grillwork layout of streets hampered them and they had to content themselves with the one available central area. They submitted their winning "Greensward" design on the last day of the competition, April 1, 1858. In their presentation Vaux and Olmsted used "before" and "after" sketches in imitation of the noted English landscape designer, Humphrey Repton. The contrasts showed barren, scratchy reality juxtaposed with a dreamy sketch of soft cloudy trees bending gently over paths that led to a winsome lake, a wooded knoll soaring to the romance of a tower where dour emptiness had been. Both men planned the park not only as a recreation ground for all citizens, its soothing, leisured charms expected to exert moral influence on the often bellicose poor, but as a museum piece, a relic of the topographical variety of the city—the rills, the massive outcroppings of rock, the woodlands—they saw disappearing rapidly, erased to accommodate housing for future millions. Bird-laden trees were to enfold meadows whose serenity would smooth the abrasiveness of city living. A courtly overture to the natural beauties was the Grand Mall that led to the height that held the Belvedere Castle. A rectangular reservoir, later covered by lawn, was screened by trees, and the rills that ran among the bogs were drained and gathered to make lakes. The dramatic northern end was tempered to work with the picturesque overall plan and yet retained its own stronger character. The practical problems of keeping four lines of rumbling carts out of the way of walks and bridle paths and carriage roads was solved by taking a hint from London's Regents Park which introduced the underpass for through traffic.

Olmsted became architect in chief, a combination of superintendent and chief engineer. In spite of criticism, constant pressure for political patronage and threats of suspension of monies when Olmsted fought the pressures, work progressed rapidly in the atmosphere of the Olmsted principle that workers function best when they are trained through trustful, tactful discipline to be responsible men. Starting with one thousand men, his army of workers grew to two thousand five hundred within a few months and at times reached as many as four thousand. Tens of thousands of carts of earth were moved without mishap and, during a period of blasting when approximately twenty-five barrels of explosives were used daily, not one man was injured.

From the very beginning of his tenure, Olmsted educated the public to help him combat charges that the park would be unusable, overrun with thugs and vandals who would make it unsafe for gentler folk and their children. He selected guards and keepers who would understand that they must be polite and helpful and calmly authoritative. The public flocked in as soon as there were a few paths and responded to the raw park with exemplary behavior. The politicians' behavior was less exemplary. The exigent pushing for patronage jobs went on and a rival, Andrew Haswell Green, equally dedicated to the project but in a different style, a man much in civic matters and one of the commissioners who had become controller of park expenditures, made it his business to check every penny spent. (According to Laura Roper's biography of Olmsted, Green cut off supplies of draftsmen's pencils because Olmsted gave them out too freely and he berated Olmsted for an error of one dollar in the accounts.) Despite the nagging and gnawing, the park grew and bloomed. By September of 1859 a visitor, picking his way through long lines of earth-bearing carts and blasting areas, noted that "the ragged desert of out-blasted rock, cat briars and stone heaps begins to blossom like a rose," and that among the three thousand workers there were no idlers.

It was a monumental work that required troubled decades to complete, the continuity of planning threatened by Tammany encroachments, by the Civil War, by Olmsted's peripatetic life and work, his nerves and illness. No matter what the disruptions, the threatened incursions for loamier graft, the investigations that proved nothing but the strength of Tammany hands, the vision remained firmly fixed: "In all parts of the park I constantly have before me, more or less distinctly, more or less vaguely, a picture."

By the end of 1860, with the election of Lincoln, the southern states began to secede. Stocks fell in Wall Street, northern property in the South was destroyed, southern debts to the North cancelled, southern securities became worthless. Although "disunion" was, and had been for years a frightening word, the financial community flailed around in uncertainty, the political community had difficulty judging which way the wind would blow most advantageously, the newspapers were vehemently divided in their loyalties. "We are discordant, corrupt, and deeply diseased, unable to govern ourselves, and in most unfit condition for a war on others," was one disconsolate observation. A member of the influential Cutting family suggested that steps be taken to pull New York out of the fray: New York and the city of Brooklyn would combine as a free port, joined by Westchester and the county of Kings to form an independent principality. Suffrage in this new realm was to be limited to those whose financial worth was at least five thousand dollars. Fernando Wood proposed that the city itself secede to become an independent state with no minimum charge for suffrage—a prophecy of the "Fifty-first State" proposition of a century later.

In spite of its political preoccupations, New York went on enjoying itself. The big balls continued, the music lovers found their way to the plebeian Stadt Theater on the Bowery to hear Offenbach's *Orpheus in the Underworld*, readers were immersed in Wilkie Collins's *Woman in White*, an uncommon book that did not resolve its mystery until the very last pages. Lincoln haters demonstrated their sentiments with an evening parade illuminated with lanterns and torchlight and fireworks that spangled the sky. Their women swore to friends over the teacups that the Abolitionists were amassing great, lethal quantities of strychnine and arsenic for the slaves to slip into the dishes of their masters. The "plague-on-both-your-houses" business community concentrated on the improvements in ferry service to Morrisania, to Fordham Village and Kingsbridge, to

Staten Island and Long Island, and on buying lots for country villas. And Central Park was already a popular and appealing playground, work for its expansion moving rapidly. The courtly esplanade was complete though the trees that were to surround it were still frail saplings. The plantings in the Ramble had sprouted flowers and birds sang from their twigs.

In the spring of 1861, Fort Sumter in Charleston Harbor was fired upon and the Civil War began. New York tightened into fair unanimity. Afraid of a patriotic segment of the mob that might attack its office, the New York *Herald* changed its pro-South tune. Calls for volunteers elicited eager response from many quarters, although a portion of the working class, mainly Irish, wasn't having any, as the later draft riots would prove. Pro-Union fervor, however, put flags on every cart, every public and private building and every church, and in the hands of the two hundred fifty thousand who crowded Union Square and filled its side streets, their windows and rooftops in a great surge of united sentiment. Money was forthcoming and lives. A body of firemen who called themselves the "Zouaves," uncouth, independent and splendidly uniformed, went proudly and showily off to the wars to fall apart in battle because they were reluctant to submit to command and incapable of discipline. Military training, of a kind, commenced in a camp erected in the Battery and barracks went up in City Hall Park.

Soldiers were arriving in Washington exhausted and debilitated; many died of disease induced by poor sanitation and neglect, before they reached the battlefield. The Medical Department of the Army, mired in bureaucracy and indifference, heading by an elderly ailing man, did nothing for the men pouring into the capital. The healthy lay with the contagious; food was erratically supplied and often contaminated; there were no sanitary arrangements. Washington was a large, dangerous pesthole. Groups of women who banded together to collect money, and send medical supplies, food and clothing, organized as the Women's Central Relief Association. From this energetic group stemmed the famous Sanitary Commission, led by highly respected men from several fields. They asked Frederick Olmsted to become their secretary and he accepted eagerly the opportunity to be absent from Tammany, to participate in the war effort, to face the challenge of an immense, shapeless problem made more enticing by official opposition.

After the Confederate victory at Bull Run the army was demoralized, soldiers wandering about Washington dirty, hungry and in shock. This led to an historic report, one of a good number to which the medical department of the Army paid no attention. George Strong speaks of it as the Olmsted report, "queer and clever—probably the first study of causes of the loss of a battle ever made so thoroughly and so promptly." The office of Surgeon General Finlay stayed deaf and implacable but the commission persisted, gathering up by early 1863 two hundred agents and enough funds to spend forty thousand dollars a month, virtually running medical services for the army and hammering at the government to force the resignation of the ineffectual Finlay. One strong blow of the tireless battering ram was an Olmsted report that detailed hundreds of investigations of every aspect of the volunteer army, its weak spots, potential difficulties and suggested remedies. Finally the new bill to improve medical services for which the commission had fought was passed and an effective new Surgeon General, proposed by the commission, appointed.

As the new governmental body became more active, the work of the commission waned and with it the temper and health of Olmsted. The man who had been praised for his quiet tact and self-discipline, his inordinate capacity for work under trying conditions, became testy with exhaustion and immoderate in his criticism of other members of the commission. George Strong, a good friend and admirer and member of the commission, still valued his virtues and deplored the peculiar habits which fostered their collapse. He blamed the quarrelsome, irritable behavior on Olmsted's "most insanitary habits of life. He works like a dog all day and sits up nearly all night, doesn't go home to his family for five days and nights altogether, works with steady, feverish intensity till four in the morning, sleeps on a sofa in his clothes and breakfasts on strong coffee and pickles." Out of this disordered life he would return to the problems of Central Park, a brighter though still unfinished canvas, alive with carriages and strolling gentlemen, laughing girls and children rolling hoops.

During his returns to Washington, quarrels so troublesome that Strong removes himself from loyalty and reports remotely, "He [Olmsted] is an extra-ordinary fellow, decidedly the most remarkable specimen of human nature with whom I have ever been brought into close relations. Talent and energy most rare; absolute purity and disinterestedness . . . but, his appetite for power made him a lay-Hildebrand." The commission was relieved to accept his resignation and he as willing to leave as the commission was to have him go.

Already well known and sought after, Olmsted was offered planning jobs in many parts of the country, some exotic and doomed, others reasonable and accomplished. For President Lincoln he helped develop the first national park, Yosemite. For the College of California he designed the first totally planned American community, an idea that never took off, to be in time replaced by the patches of Berkeley. His exploratory reports constantly reiterated the Olmsted principles of planning for immense growth, for attractiveness that would lure and keep prosperous citizens and improve the health and morals of the poor, that would shape great cities which would, in spite of crowding and noise, become civilizing centers. Vaux, Olmsted and company had become the leading landscape architects in the country, their influence such that, as early as 1870, every significant city in the United States was tearing up lands for projected parks, a novel word in the American vocabulary.

The nucleus Zoo in the arsenal building wasn't much in the late 1860s. Like many early collections artistic and scientific, it was the dumping ground for collectors whose enthusiasm had deteriorated to encumbered impatience. The menagerie held twenty-three types of reptiles, alligators and tortoises predominant; a pair of American bears, two raccoons, two disconsolate camels, five prairie wolves, impressive populations of white rats, white mice and rabbits; a selection of elk, deer, sheep and buffalo. Birds made up more than half of the specimens: there were pelicans, peacocks, and fifty swans given jointly by the Worshipful Company of Vintners (a venerable guild of which Chaucer's father was a member) and the Worshipful Company of Dyers, also venerable, and both of London. An engraving in *Harper's Weekly* draws the animals with great vivacity, much livelier than they must have actually been in the impromptu, poorly organized quarters.

Like Currier and Ives, *Harper's Weekly* was thoroughly smitten with Central Park scenes. One of *Harper's* subjects, titled "Driving in Central Park" was a lady with a dramatic profile, tresses, feathers and collar flying romantically in the wind, her whip held like a royal scepter, her hand on the reins a ballet gesture, her face determinedly Amazon. Her gentleman companion in a placid round cap merely looks worried. *Harper's* was also interested in the minutiae of planting in the park, featuring details of imaginative patterns. The park was almost complete by the fall of 1869, well arranged and administered, laced with pleasant footpaths and lauded as a boon to the city and a great influence for improved civic life. It was judged "beautiful," "interesting," "lovely" for evening strolls with a stop for sherry at the casino, for exploring the Ramble and examining the busts of Humboldt and Schiller. In all, a priceless acquisition that would humanize and tame the masses. But in 1871 the park's wheel of fortune took another turn. The board of commissioners was pushed out by a Tweed Department of Parks. The parsimonious Andrew Green was fired and the new board took over not only all the city parks but also "street improvements," a portmanteau phrase that meant the

Ring could make profits from park lands as it liked. No one consulted the former planners and architects. All they could do was protest the destruction of carefully landscaped areas and stands of trees, the threatened invasion of a new opera house, a projected fast roadway for racing carriages, and a statue of Tweed, turned god as Roman emperors had, to stand among the poets.

After Tweed's arrest, the battered park went back to Vaux and Olmsted. In the spring of 1872 Olmsted was elected president and treasurer of the Department of Parks. Though the old business partnership was dissolved, Vaux stayed on as consulting landscape architect and Olmsted as both landscape architect and superintendent. The old bone in the throat (only, it appears, to Olmsted who had a *mauvaise langue*) Andrew Green, reappeared, sponsored by Tammany as the money man. Once again Olmsted tendered his resignation; once again he was cajoled into staying. Green blocked all moves to increase funds for the park and in 1874 the estimate of costs for the coming year was severely cut. Faced with renewed struggles, Olmsted made the prophetic remark that under the circumstances then prevailing—the lack of understanding of the park's original purpose, of monies for proper supervision and guarding—the park could "become a nuisance and a curse to the city." Soon it was Green's time to be pilloried by opposition politicians. In the course of that battle, Olmsted and Vaux's work was further crippled and Olmsted's office abolished in spite of vehement public protest. He was forced to sue for his salary and twenty years after he first walked into the morass north of Fifty-ninth Street and saw in its bogs and rocks the dream of the splendid park that pulled him back and back again, he walked out, vowing he was through, forever through, with Central Park.

In 1881, Vaux became superintendent architect of the park and wrote his former partner of the several vandalous incompetents who had filled the job in the preceding years. They had removed the screens of trees that set the park apart; hidden nooks and shaded dells designed as picturesque surprises were flatly opened to immediate view; they had sponsored a bullfight with native bulls who were no braver than the men pitted against them. There was talk of promoters planning a big exposition in the park and renewed plans for a fast roadway. Matters grew worse when Viele was resurrected and appointed architect in chief in 1883. Again, a desperate call for Vaux and Olmsted to rescue Central Park. Vaux returned as landscape architect; wary Olmsted consented only to occasional consultations. No one followed their suggestions and the park deteriorated, portions of it almost shambles by 1885. Very quietly a bill was passed in 1892 permitting the disputed racing road to be built on the west side of Central Park. The public was furious and so was Olmsted, who issued a statement pointing out that Central Park was paid for by the earnings of the people of New York, not the owners of fast trotters, and any diversion of this public property to the enjoyment of the few was unjust and immoral. Vaux also fought the speed track and was outshouted and humiliated but returned to his thankless, torturesome job. Both men were leaders in a rapidly expanding field, both were prosperous and no longer young; they could earn more money more peaceably in any number of places, but they held on, as Olmsted expressed it, with "a degree of devotion that no greed and no selfish ambition would have induced."

After a long absence, Henry James returned to New York early in this century. Reporting in *The American Scene*, he finds the magnificent Fifth Avenue houses basically insubstantial, transient in quality. His Washington Square is badly marred, only its churches solid in their gray stillness. The Lower East Side was vivacious, its foreign intellectuals stimulating and Central Park a wonder and delight—the vindication of Vaux and Olmsted's Herculean efforts. "The perception comes quickly, in New York, of the singular and beautiful but almost crushing mission that has been laid, as an effect of time, upon this limited territory, which has risen to the occasion, from the first, so consistently and bravely." James compares the park to a "cheerful, capable, bustling, even if overworked hostess of the one inn whose hospitality is unfailing." He goes on to another female simile, the park as the only actress of a destitute company who "assumes on successive nights the most dissimilar parts and ranges in the course of a week from the tragedy queen to the singing chambermaid. The valour by itself wins the public and brings down the house—it being really a marvel that she should in no part fail of a hit." He was enthralled by the "sweet ingratiation" of the park, by the variety of accents and the brilliance of the polyglot show, "the great and only brilliancy worth speaking of, to my sense, in the general American scene—the air of hard prosperity, the ruthlessly pushed-up and promoted look worn by men, women and children alike."

Entranced by the incandescent lady for whom he could find no one name, James must also have been enchanted by the romantic Victorian touches—gems from the matrix England—that were ornate little bridges, a Mineral Springs Pavilion designed by Vaux after the bubbles and lace of the Brighton Pavilion and Victorian Gothic embroidery on arches. A bow to English romanticism appeared as a mysterious, alluring cave at the side of the lake; and medieval banners, as in the courts of the powerful barons, danced on tall poles. There were canopied little boats attached to images of swans, a curvaceous bandstand adorned like a ceremonial cake, rustic crosswalks over rustic rills and the innocent countryness of thatched shelters. For the less contemplative, gliding in sleek sleds, and when the weather changed, shining carriages. For New York's photographers and painters—Stieglitz, Glackens, Prendergast, and a host of others—the park was an infinity of rewarding subjects and moods.

The total work of art that Vaux and Olmsted had planned, the unity of landscape and recreation, was maintained with difficulty, but maintained, by Vaux and Samuel Parsons, Jr., trained by Vaux and after Vaux's death superintendent of parks and landscape architect. After Parsons resigned in 1911, the park deteriorated sadly according to Henry Hope Reed who was a later curator and historian of Central Park. The vegetation died, not cared for or replaced; guarding was lax and the park seemed up for grabs, the grabbers often impeded by the public who put a stop to some of the fancier schemes. The sly act that opened a speedway for trotting was repealed and a law passed to bar the park to fairs, circuses and racing. Every once in a while it was suggested that this piece of park land or that, all of soaring value, be sold. The Zoo had not been included in the original plan, nor had the Metropolitan Museum, but animals and art were not inimical to public enlightenment and recreation; Olmsted himself was a member of the Metropolitan Museum committee and Vaux one of its first architects. Then came the automobile, forced out of the park in its early years. Admitted in 1899, it began to consume first one road and then another; paths and greens were covered with asphalt, plantings asphyxiated by fumes, trees ripped out to make parking lots. Twentieth-century progress finally managed to distort the image that years of political corruption, financial starvation and chicanery had never been able to mar quite so thoroughly.

CHAPTER 13

THE GOLD, SILVER
AND COPPER MUSEUM

he earliest begetter of the Guggenheim Museum, the founder of a corporate entity that controlled the lives of thousands of Mexicans, Chileans, Amercans and Africans, that played rigged roulette with finance and atoned with philanthropies, was Meyer Guggenheim. He came to Philadelphia from a Swiss ghetto in 1847, accompanied by his father, his stepmother and a gaggle of their children. He became a peddler of small household necessities and a few cheap adornments in the villages of Pennsylvania. He couldn't very well wing his way on the small sums he collected from the wives of miners and farmers but he thought of duplicating, perhaps improving, the stove polish they all used, a product that earned dollars for its manufacturer and pennies for him. The formula turned out to be quite simple and the investment minimal, particularly since Meyer and his father, Simon, could make and stock the polish at home. The profits enabled Meyer to abandon his petty miscellany for a lucrative partnership in a wholesale business of household products.

He married his stepsister, Barbara, and immediately began to accumulate sons. He had a total of seven in fourteen years: Isaac, Daniel, Murry, Solomon, Benjamin, Simon and William, in that order. Not only God but the Civil War was good to Meyer, offering him opportunities for speculation in foodstuffs as well as an army contract for a strong coffee essence, heavy in chicory and easy to use.

Born to a shrewd man who had found it easy to become rich and a respected member of a synagogue community organized on relaxed lines (their Jehovah closed his eyes to Saturday moneymaking), the sons were soon launched onto possibilities for becoming richer still. In 1878, silver was discovered in Leadville, Colorado, and Meyer found himself three years later in the rowdy, shapeless town where vast monies might be shoveled up for the taking. Meyer bought into two mines, struck a loaded vein and in spite of labor difficulties and flooding became one of the instantly superrich "Bonanza Kings." By 1890, the two mines, the Minnie and the A.Y., were totally Guggenheim controlled and valued at $14,556,000.

Erratic and extortionist freight rates charged by the railroads were a constant problem, and so was the sabotaging hatred of poorly paid miners who worked twelve-hour shifts. The most irritating problem, though, was the high cost of smelting, the smelters taking large profits on the process and then selling the metal, no longer the property of the mine owner. That business had to be scrutinized and a piece of it taken. The younger sons were dispatched to the West to concentrate on smelting and refining as the newly formed M. Guggenheim's Sons corporation. The older boys took upon themselves the acquisition of mines in the Southwest and in Mexico.

The agents of Porfirio Diaz, Mexico's dictator, were not averse to dealing with the sophisticated, well-traveled Guggenheims, who had some Spanish among them and continental social graces, as well as the wisdom to evaluate the actual power of the *Científicos* who shored up Diaz. Dan and Murry made the deals while Sol stayed—revolver in belt to guard against assaults from underpaid Mexican miners—to supervise the works near Monterrey. More smelters, more mines in Mexico, more refineries in the States, and although no financial reports were published, it was generally known that M. Guggenheim's Sons was making over a million dollars a year in profits by 1895. Resisting the overtures of American Smelting and Refining Trust (organized by the Lewisohns and Standard Oil) to merge with them, the Guggenheims decided to concentrate on Latin America, inviting as associates men who had a taste for risk and the money to withstand it. One such man was William C. Whitney, who was looking for adventure and money for his son, Harry Payne. They organized the Guggenheim Exploration Company which would "prospect, explore and deal in lands, mines and minerals." When the eight-hour-day law was passed in mid-1899 and the American Smelting mines and smelters tried to outwit it by arranging piecework on a lower scale, plus overtime, which made a total of a twelve-hour day for unimproved wages, the workers closed down every Trust smelter in Colorado. The smarter Guggenheims acceded, temporarily, to the eight-hour day, pending hearings on the constitutionality of the new law, and went on working. It cost them nothing and profits rose because of the inactivity of the competition. Now was the time for a favorable merger with American Smelting and Refining which left the boys the largest factor in the Trust. They had thirty million dollars in smelting stock, total control of the mines in Colorado and Mexico, a Mexico–New Jersey steamship line to serve their smelters and refiners, and the Exploration Company.

With the hiring in 1902 of the fabled mining engineer John Hays Hammond, the Exploration Company became the greatest of all mining ventures, a burrowing animal with tough skin and sure instincts that furrowed the American continents to the far north and south. European capital, avid for a piece of American industrial expansion, swallowed up a Trust bond issue eagerly, increasing the capitalization to seventy-seven million dollars. With that and other holdings the Guggenheims bought up additional companies until their Trust controlled almost all the silver output of South and Central America,

British Columbia, Mexico and the United States. The Trust held ninety-three properties, having wiped out many smaller operations, whose collapse helped create the ghost towns of Colorado and Nevada.

In 1906 a call for help and a challenge came from across the waters. The aging King Leopold II of Belgium who used the Belgian Congo (called a Free State) as vast private properties worked by slaves who were mutilated, assassinated, and spent their lives and deaths chained together, was threatened by his own citizenry, which was ready to nationalize his territories and their fabulous yield. He was in a hurry to organize a more acceptable company for exploiting the rubber and gold of the Kasai River. His agent, sent to America to defend the king against criticism of his brutality and to find investment money, came via the influential Thomas Fortune Ryan, to the Guggenheims. Late in 1906 they were given the concession—a quarter-interest remained with Leopold—to control all prospecting for minerals in an area forty-five times the size of Belgium. Instead of the notorious lash, gun and barbed-wire camps maintained by the Belgians, the American company built villages, moved in immense stocks of cattle, kept store prices moderately low and paid its workers a couple of dollars a month plus small bonuses. A minimal amount of intelligent observation among diamond miners showed that they cared little for diamonds, and they were no longed subjected to inspection of their feces for swallowed gems. When reports came in that the diamond take was very promising in Angola, the Ryan-Guggenheim team extended their activities across the border.

Africa yielding satisfactorily, it was time to discover the American north, the Yukon and Alaska, which required a great deal of money to reach, to make livable and profitable. Time also to get a Guggenheim into Congress where he might help quash madmen who were objecting to the rape of the country by trusts. The U.S. Senate, generally referred to as

the "Millionaires Club," made seats available for purchase by
the highest bidders, and Simon of the Guggenheims could certainly afford any price. In spite of sharp criticism of the man
and of Colorado, which had so eagerly sold itself, Simon stayed,
wearing the Guggenheim indifference to criticism, his ties to
political life severed only with the inauguration of Woodrow
Wilson.

Exultant and invulnerable, the family took on the far
north and its promise of hundreds of tons of copper, offering
J. P. Morgan and Jacob Schiff part of the bounty of their
Alaska Syndicate in exchange for financial help in making a
new world that required a railroad line to run between ice
peaks, steamship companies to transport the ore thousands of
miles to smelting plants, coal mines to provide power, and
odds and ends like fisheries and canneries. The Syndicate practically owned Alaska though other frenetic financiers and speculators were also building Alaska railroads with the help of
gunmen to guard their property. Icy storms destroyed "Gug-
gen-Morgan" structures; one of their gunmen was convicted of
maiming a man for life, and the papers screamed about the
omnivorous Syndicate and its extermination of Alaskan seal
and salmon.

Halted for a while by Roosevelt, the purportedly Great
Trust-buster, and helped by Simon and his Washington
friends, the Syndicate was cleared of charges of exploiting public lands and using monopolistic practices, in spite of an enraged public and poison-penned muckrakers. After a series of
lawsuits (an important component of Guggenheim lifeblood)
to clear titles, they began to build toward the new El Dorado,
the Bonanza mine near the Kennecott glacier. In the fearsome
cold and paralyzing snowdrifts railroad workers drove thousands of piles deep into the frozen earth to make a railroad
bridge, lashed cables to the houses that they might stay anchored and blasted tunnels to reach the mine four thousand
feet above the valley. The first yields carried ore that was 75

percent copper, many times purer than that of the mines in
the Southwest. In spite of the great cost of reaching and shipping Kennecott copper, it was the cheapest in the world, under-
cutting the price of competitive mines. In 1911, with work
just begun, the Syndicate made one million, six hundred fifty-
eight thousand dollars in Kennecott, and by the end of 1912
approximately twice that amount.

Not as pure as Alaska copper but certainly easier to extract was the product of Utah Copper, a promising enterprise
which needed backing. Guggenheim Exploration moved in and
took a quarter-interest in the gigantic spread of earth and its
possibilities, mainly supported by the public who had invested
in the company's shares. More mines to explore, fields of copper in Nevada, millions spent for railroads to carry off the
yield. As the empire grew, and militant unionism with it,
strikes became more numerous and aggressive under leaders
like Eugene Debs and Bill Haywood's Wobblies. To counter
strike action, the company closed the plants and cut off wages,
rationalizing the steps with one of Sol's autocratic statements:
"I believe the wage earner is more extravagant in proportion
to his earning than the millionaire." A western newspaper
countered by pointing out that the extravagance of the poor
was to give up a large part of their incomes to Guggenheims,
Morgans and Rockefellers, and maybe if they stopped supporting capitalists they would feel better. The limelight was
turned on Utah Copper, accused of maintaining intolerable
living conditions in its work camp, styled "a long sewer," the
filthiest, most depressing place in America. The newspapers
collected and published telling statistics: Guggenheim earnings were between eleven and twelve million while their employees were crushed by rocks, crippled, died of lead poisoning,
were made chronically ill by fumes; one man of four in their
American Smelting was disabled by accident each year.

Meyer's boys gathered themselves together and established

housing, hospitals, accident compensation and a rudimentary welfare system that caused their friend Adolph Ochs of the *Times* to praise them for enriching the lives of their men. At hearings of the Industrial Relations Commission during Wilson's administration, Meyer's son, Dan, was most impressive and surprising with his statement that workers were justified in organizing. Though increase in labor turbulence was at bottom a primitive matter of envy, improved working and living conditions should be a part of industrial progress. Dan rolled on, to a gaping crowd, deploring the lack of legislation that might protect the workingman. There should be, he said, cooperation among the government, the employer and the employee to provide more comforts for the worker; he was entitled to them. Jaunty, confident Dan also proposed that the state furnish work for the unemployed, the money to be raised by taxing the rich, and that captains of industry devise profit-sharing plans. One blot in this workers' Eden: no organizer puts foot into a Guggenheim open shop.

The lucky Guggenheims hit a rich lode when World War I broke. Much of the abundance of their copper mines would soon be bought up by the Allies, financed by Morgan's half-billion-dollar Anglo-French war loan. As Europe swallowed immense quantities of copper and pleaded for more, the public became increasingly keen for shares of the valuable metal. Why not issue stocks and bonds on the aggregate wealth of all the mines and help compensate for the cost of the expensive Alaskan venture, productive as it was? Dan, Sol and Murry, with the help of legal and financial experts, erased Guggenheim Exploration, heaped all the copper in one shining mountain and announced dazzling assets and profits, the opening gambit of an elaborate put-and-take game which would, again, evoke fruitless criticism and calls for trustbusting. As World War I went on, the government challenged the price of copper; the Guggenheims countered by challenging taxes and asked for increased prices. There were hearings before the Senate and the Federal Trade Commission but no one was too eager to rock the boat of wartime effort.

Life settled back to Guggenheim normal after the war— satisfying profits and strikes weakened by the importation of thousands of Mexicans willing to work at low wages for crippling hours, preferably ignorant of unions. It was not until 1937 that the Mine and Smelter section of John L. Lewis' CIO forced its way into the Perth Amboy refinery, one scene of the family Götterdämmerung. By that time profits were dwindling; law suits, accusations of illegal manipulations and successive reorganizations sapped Guggenheim power. American Smelting and Refining still listed Dan, Sol and Murry on its board but important decisions were in other hands. The gods lived out their twilight, nevertheless, in a sunset glow of wealth generally compared to that of the Rothschilds in Europe. Isaac, for instance, left an estate of ten million dollars after taxes in 1922, and when Murry died in 1939 the inheritance tax paid by his two children was three and a half million dollars.

The Guggenheim name began to fade, except in the unforgiving West, where it kept reappearing in divorce court reports (the younger Guggenheims set a record) and a variety of benefactions musical, aeronautic, botanical, medical and literary. Harvey O'Connor, the Guggenheim biographer, points out that John D. Rockefeller had to pay millions to whiten his image and Carnegie gave away a considerable portion of his monies to erase his "Scottish pirate" label while the Guggenheims, with comparatively small investments in public favor, managed to leave a benevolent family portrait of kindly uncles and aunts. The Grand Duke uncle was Solomon, who had been painted by Sir William Orpen, owned several estates and had a daughter who became Countess Castle-Steward. As lord of all he surveyed, wherever he happened to be, he had occasional annoying encounters with other authorities. Immovable object met irresistible force when Robert Moses, then Commissioner of

Parks—and much else—in New York, tried to drive a road through Guggenheim property to Jones Beach. For five years Solomon R. would not permit it because the marsh in which he shot duck, property that had cost him one dollar an acre, might be disturbed. Moses of the honed tongue had many strong words for Guggenheim but it took a state edict to break the oceanfront lease. The insult of heavy postwar taxes drove Solomon from a house at 743 Fifth Avenue to a suite at the Plaza, that suite the Fabergé egg that hatched the Solomon R. Guggenheim Foundation.

The catalyst who turned Solomon from factual Dutch genre and Italian opulence to nonobjective painting (whose charms made home life a constant pleasure, he said) was a young painter, Baroness Hilla Rebay, a champion of avant art in Germany. In 1926 he commissioned a portrait of himself from her and she, volatile, appealing and a zealot, introduced Guggenheim to the work of artists she knew, among them Kandinsky, Léger, Chagall and Rudolf Bauer. She was forceful—called the Catherine the Great of her school—and he was willing to take a chance on her recommendations. He changed the decor of his suite to accommodate a cork wall for the dancing Kandinskys and a field of somber taupe to show off the many Bauers, a particular enthusiasm of the baroness (for their sexual charm, was the judgment of several critics); his conversation on art turned from praising the expressive rendering of Corot trees to extolling the triangle, square and circle as spiritual forms of absolute purity and beauty. He opened his collection for viewing by the cognoscenti, now and then sent some of it out for shows and in time opened an office from which Miss Rebay supervised the collection.

In 1937, the Guggenheim Foundation, with the capacity for creating a museum, was established, and in 1939 it opened a public showcase at 24 East Fifty-fourth Street. The collection increased and was shown in several cities on the east coast, providing knowledge, if not always acceptance, of leading contemporary painters. The strict nonobjectivity of the paintings was stressed and confirmed in the name of the institution, The Solomon R. Guggenheim Collection of Non-Objective Painting, which expanded its repertoire to include the works of American painters if they cleaved to the rules.

Things were moving oddly but fairly steadily when out of the wings stepped Frank Lloyd Wright, who was commissioned to build a museum for the collection in 1943, when Solomon was eighty-two (he died long before the project was completed, at eighty-eight). It is reasonable to imagine that the building of Nero's Golden House, the raising of Brunelleschi's dome, the roaring yeahs and nays that accompanied Michelangelo's work on St. Peter's attracted watchers and commentators, those who lauded and those who snarled. But they were aesthetic conflicts among fewer people in small cities with no newspapers to keep the public eye and ear filled with an interminable vaudeville of praise and blame, suspicion and hope, voiced by a large cast of impassioned, voluble characters with a talent for the ornate and sometimes incomprehensible strophe. The star was always —from beginning to end, from 1943 to the time of his death in the spring of 1959, six months before the Guggenheim Museum opened—Frank Lloyd Wright. He wanted the site to be at the tip of Manhattan or near the Morgan Library and finally accepted the use of Mr. Guggenheim's land south of Eighty-ninth Street on Fifth Avenue.

In the sixteen years between the original commission and the actual opening, through overt dissent from city officials, more covert dissension among directors, and Wright's mysterious silences and absences, traditional in the lives of heroes, the public presses flowed luxuriantly. There were always a few reliable museum subjects to dwell on, the best inevitably Wright himself, ensconced at the Plaza whose architect, Henry Janeway Hardenbergh, he respected: "I like it almost as well as if I had built it myself." For his own suite he discarded the chastity of the open desert spaces he admired and crammed it with the savage colors of a gypsy camp.

The incomparable Wright arrogance was established quite consciously in his youth. "Early in life," he said, "I had to choose between honest arrogance and hypocritical humility," and he chose the former, abetted by his towering talent and the accompanying skills that made him, at the age of nineteen, the best draftsman in Chicago, a city that was building busily and inventively. When the Guggenheim commission came his way Wright was in his seventies and universally acknowledged to be one of the greatest twentieth-century architects. The Guggenheim was his first New York building but he was not impressed; it was a measure of the backwardness of the city and its repetitious, cliché-ridden skyscrapers that it had not been ready for him before.

One of his opening numbers was a display of his model for the museum, an occasion he wreathed in slightly mystical cadences probably imbibed from his father, a circuit preacher. He called his projected work "organic" architecture as opposed to the ordinary modern, which was capable of increasing in height with technological advances but essentially no different from the convention of building layer on layer that went back to Roman insulae. His structure would have the smooth, balanced forms of nature, the wholeness and serenity of the egg, the quiet tones of sand and shell, and, like plants and trees, would enrich itself and its contents with nature's light. It would be a temple of harmonized arts where Bach and Beethoven might appropriately sing—but not Verdi of that "ponderous anachronism," the opera. As if in response to the common criticism that the building would be nothing but a giant snail, Wright built, in 1949, a ramp-snail inside an appealing neo-Romanesque gift shop in San Francisco, the snail's spiral designed to carry customers gently through an evanescence of sparkling glassware.

After intervals for such work and the renowned research center for the Johnson Wax Company, in Wisconsin, Wright returned to New York to discuss, among other problems, revisions of the Guggenheim plan after the acquisition of the corner at Eighty-eighth Street which, finally, gave the whole Fifth Avenue front to the museum. Although glass dome, uninterrupted ramp and continuous picture space were still the basic design, Wright could now set the building in roomy space to make it "a temple in the park on the Avenue." This Pantheon with a conch core troubled New York's Building Commission and the Board of Standards and Appeals, which doubted that the building could go up at all, it violated so many regulations. Wright was disdainfully airy about the whole thing. Surely, New York's building regulations were antiquated and the board should know that his building prophesied inevitable new codes. While the board bent a bit, he corrected, still protesting. Why did people refuse to understand that here was something truly new, a building that served paintings as none had yet—and that was true of all the museums they might mention.

Meanwhile, the Collection of Non-Objective Painting had moved to a six-story Guggenheim mansion at 1071 Fifth Avenue. More Klees were bought, many more Kandinskys, more Feiningers, swelling the collection by seven hundred items within a decade. The walls were draped with discreet gray, the paintings contained in massive frames and soothed by the music of Bach that flowed through the house. It was very like a European private collection forced by taxes and the cost of upkeep to admit the public. However, the collection enjoyed freedom from taxes as a foundation and had pledged for this privilege to foster the taste, education and enlightenment of the public, as a museum preferably, and to sponsor lectures, scholarships and a program of publications. It did mount exhibitions and issue sumptuous catalogues, but said Aline

Louchheim (later Saarinen) in a *New York Times* article, the
foundation had not quite met its promises. Although there had
been several impressive shows—the exhibitions had been "dominated in a somewhat immodest fashion by paintings of the
museum's own director, Baroness Hilla Rebay, and those of
her once close friend, Rudolf Bauer," and, "it is the consensus
of most qualified critics that the work of neither would receive
this emphasis in any other museum." Such shows were accompanied by the baroness's mystic-snob prose that was capable of
phrases like "cosmic reaction" and "genius is the special gift of
God to the elite of a nation."

Another objection to the museum was its rigidity in ruling
that *no painting might ever, ever show an object*, no matter
how stylized; no Picasso guitar, no Redon bouquet, no Léger
woman. They existed among Guggenheim treasures but were
kept out of sight. Whether this policy would be maintained or
relaxed in the Wright building was a subject no one in control
would discuss, nor whether there would be an expanded board
with more permissive standards to run the new house, whose
site Solomon Guggenheim had given—plus two million dollars
for the building and six million to maintain it as a museum.
In 1951, fresh winds blew away the egocentricity; the baroness
became emeritus, and James Johnson Sweeney became director.
He was once director of painting and sculpture of the Museum
of Modern Art, and before that, propagandist for new art,
football player and Irish poet. Under Sweeney the paintings
were removed from their somber frames and given light and
air, the term "nonobjective" lost its iron casing, young American artists began to bring their work for consideration and
possible showing. Sweeney was free to select from the remarkable collection to create small stimulating shows and, with the
trustees, arrange for new important acquisitions. Among the
trustees were two of Solomon's daughters, his nephew, Harry
A. Guggenheim, who was chairman of the board, and Harry's

wife. The Museum took on dash and stature, its international awards closely contested by artists and closely observed by critics.

In those halcyon days there was still Wright, his plans, his quarrels, his sprays of insult; there were the artists who didn't want a ramp to cut off the bottoms and tops of their paintings, already bewildered by a slanted wall, and Mr. Sweeney, whose sympathies were with the artists. Up to the day of the opening in October, 1959, and after, sour criticism and ecstatic praise clashed in the air above upper Fifth Avenue. It was a bun, a clothes washer, a marshmallow, an insult to art. It was a splendor of modern architecture, a masterpiece. One critic managed to combine the pleasures of praising and finding fault simultaneously: "The building is so spectacular that it overwhelms the painting." To Wright, the building was a "liberation of painting by architecture," a place that would, for the first time, put "20th century arts and architecture in their true relation." To the staff it meant unaccustomed problems in placing paintings and difficulties that ensued from the cavalier treatment Wright gave to storage and restoration space. The public loved it: the quarrels, the clarion publicity, the novelty, and flocked in great hordes to examine the source of all the excitement. On the first Sunday, ten thousand people queued up, held back by five policemen. Only six thousand and a few more got in that day but they kept coming. What they saw was not pristine Wright; Sweeney had instituted changes to make the building more workable for paintings. The Wright-Sweeney creation, the intrinsic quality of the collection of three thousand works, the interest of a growing public which the museum had helped educate in modern art and the typhoons of publicity in which it had lived for years made the Guggenheim a lodestone for native and international visitors.

Over the years, nudged by necessity, the Wright scheme has been considerably modified; the once princely endowments, one for the building which was much more expensive than anticipated, and one for the upkeep, diminished by rapidly rising costs, allow little money for new acquisitions. Fortunately, there is a good stock of valuables to cull from for auctions. In 1962, Sotheby's auctioned off a number of Solomon's Old Masters and two years later, it sold off fifty of the one hundred seventy Kandinskys. The sums realized helped enhance and modernize the collection and extend its purchases to younger artists.

An international classic in its twenty years, this extraordinary building is now rarely if ever severely criticized. The tendency is to take pleasure in its light tones, in the curves repeated on the sidewalk, in the niches off the ramp and the elevators, and to admire, in the graying light of the end of day, the varicolored ribbon of hats and hair and shoulders as it slips along the pale edge of ramp.

CHAPTER 14

CARNEGIE AND FRICK

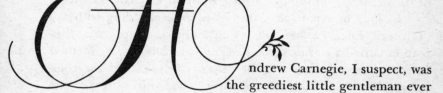

ndrew Carnegie, I suspect, was the greediest little gentleman ever created," opens John K. Winkler's biography of *Incredible Carnegie*. A quote from one of Carnegie's superintendents of steel adds, "Andy was born with two sets of teeth and holes bored for more." He was devious and ruthless and given to moral homilies while he broke men to splinters. He was a stellar example of an industrial time that interpreted the principles of Herbert Spencer and Charles Darwin to mean that he who ravaged his way to the top was merely obeying a supreme edict of God and nature.

The short, stocky "little Scotch pirate" was the son of a poor weaver in Dunfermline, Scotland. When Andrew was thirteen the family emigrated to Pittsburgh, where the father did little better. The mother, Margaret, found a job sewing shoes and also took in washing while the children found a variety of small jobs. Andy became a telegraph messenger boy and showed such quickness and skill that at sixteen he was an operator handling foreign news and at seventeen, when the Pennsylvania Railroad reached Pittsburgh, became the clerk and operator to the superintendent of the Pittsburgh division. He was in an excellent spot to give information and take payment for it, to make influential friends and money and to move up in position until, at twenty-four, he became superintendent of the division. To turn a phrase of Andy's favorite, Shakespeare (next to Bobby Burns, that is), all occasions did inform in favor of him. First, the Civil War broke out. With adroit, convincing misrepresentation, Carnegie had already acquired an iron works to profit from the war boom, but it needed capitalization and expertise. It was his brother Tom's idea that the small company join with a better equipped, prosperous firm, Kloman & Phipps, of which Andrew Kloman was head.

In spite of a postwar slump, matters kept riding with the "Carnegie Luck." When labor would not take a pay cut, Kloman imported a German who had devised a laborsaving method of rolling metal plates and the improvement earned the company millions. By the time Carnegie was thirty-two, in the fall of 1867, he could look with immense satisfaction at the records of Kloman & Phipps, his Keystone Bridge works and a few other enterprises. He was ready, also, to try himself on New York. In the evenings, attended by his mother, he expanded his meager education with the help of tutors. During the day, from his office on Broad Street, he dealt with the staid financiers, the swindlers, the con men, the sneaky silent, the energetic talkers, who mobbed the financial streets for slices of the measureless pie promised by the postwar expansion of industry and finance. As usual, Andrew bested the best as he wove and interwove his expanding meshwork. Orders for bridges from his Keystone Bridge Company gave work to his Union Iron Mills and increased the value of the bridge company's bonds. On the side, he handled big Pennsylvania Railroad money in profit-splitting deals that were to be kept secret. On another side, he joined, with his old Pittsburgh boss, Tom Scott, and with George Pullman, to become an important stockholder of the Pullman Company. When it was rumored (a story possibly floated by Carnegie himself) that Union Pacific needed six hundred thousand dollars Carnegie arranged to raise the money through Pennsylvania Railroad securities

and thus achieve control of Union Pacific. Carnegie and Pullman became directors of the railroad and Scott the president.
Part of the deal was custody of three million dollars in Union
Pacific shares placed in a vault by Carnegie with the understanding that they would stay until the six-hundred-thousand-
dollar loan was repaid. Shortly, great quantities of the sup-
posedly sequestered stocks reached the market and were sold,
at startling profits. Union Pacific demoted the Carnegie-Pull-
man-Scott trio although Carnegie protested he was blameless;
it had all been Scott's idea.

By 1880 the Carnegie mill and the smelting plant organized ten years before was turning out ten thousand tons of
steel per month at a profit of about 140 percent, not yet
enough for the Scottish dervish, who hurled insults at super-
visors, pitted them against each other, inspired competition
poisoned by hatred and chopped down directors—always, he
assured them, breaking his own heart in the process.

In the late 1880s the huge Homestead plant alone, a segment of the expanding empire, was reporting earnings of
three million dollars and American steel was shoving England
out of the market. To sell his products—railroad parts, bridges,
beams and girders for ironclad houses—Carnegie returned to
New York with his mother and settled her and himself into
the fashionable, lavishly decorated Windsor Hotel at 571 Fifth
Avenue (later destroyed by fire, leaving only a Windsor Ar-
cade). He entertained, was jolly and generous, recited Bobby
Burns, acted scenes from Shakespeare, made friends and
amassed orders. He also managed to rid his companies of
brother Tom's father-in-law, William Coleman, who had
helped them financially during hard times. Between cracking
the whip in Pittsburgh and selling steel, Carnegie got around,
making sure to meet every Name, if not for business, then for
social enhancement. He liked to feel he was an intellectual, a
lover of art and music, a craftsman of letters. For the socialists
he occasionally met in advanced circles he turned on the egali-

tarian spout: "He who dies rich dies disgraced." There was no way of charming several Wall Street giants, though. Having played hidden Byzantine railroad stock games with him, they knew and feared him; Morgan flatly despised him.

In 1882, enter Henry Frick, aged thirty-two and already a millionaire, accompanied by his young heiress wife, to lunch at the Windsor Hotel with Andrew Carnegie. Then and there began a momentous partnership that created and maintained a combine so efficient and profitable as to be unique in the annals of industry; unique in the history of labor relations for the months of mayhem at Homestead; unique in the grotesquery of the ultimate Frick-Carnegie divorce suit.

A graduate of a rudimentary business college, Frick became an accountant, as efficient, neat and controlled as he would be—with a few rare explosions—throughout the rest of his life. Like the Carnegies, the Fricks worked as a family unit in their modest beginnings, acquiring by thrift and shrewdness an extent of Pennsylvania coal lands. To build ovens for baking coke of the coal his properties yielded, Henry went to a leading Pittsburgh banker, Judge Mellon, for loans. (Judge Mellon's son was the Andrew Mellon who became Frick's friend. Both were sparse of words; both, tightly and protectively bound around themselves; both, in their later years contestants for costly Old Masters; both, in an association of over forty years addressed each other as "Mr.") Judge Mellon's agents found that, as Frick had claimed, he could produce an unusually high grade of coke and that he was selling it rapidly and profitably. He kept straight books and was reliable in his person and practices, except for one eccentricity: he liked pictures. This was a minor fault, however, and Mellon subsidized him to the extent of twenty thousand dollars, which bought Frick 100 ovens.

Surviving the panic of 1873 with the help of Judge Mellon's banking firm, Frick kept adding to his holdings and by the time the postpanic depression subsided his H. C. Frick

Company controlled 80 percent of the coke production of the rich Connellsville area. Coke had leaped from its panic price of less than a dollar a ton to five dollars, more than half of that profit. First million achieved, Frick was ready for the Grand Tour of Europe, marriage with a young woman from a prosperous home and, the next step, a leading role in industry. Beginning with a minority interest they bought from Frick, the Carnegies soon had a half-interest in the Frick coke company which was provided capital by the larger firm to increase the number of its coke ovens to five thousand. They were capable of roasting six thousand tons a day, snapped up by steel works which churned out worked metal for the insatiable railroad, shipping and building industries.

In 1886 Tom Carnegie, font of balm and reasonableness, mediator between Andy and his victims, died at the age of forty-three. Shortly after, indomitable old Margaret died and Andrew, who had promised mother never to marry while she was alive, married soon thereafter. He was past fifty when he married Louise Whitfield in 1887, and ready to cap his career with an effulgent house on Fifty-first Street, immediately west of Fifth Avenue.

The business conflicts with Frick were many. Carnegie issued prolix critical notes; Frick sent back sharp, terse answers. Most irritatingly he disregarded advice about running his coke company, the H. C. Frick Company, in which the cool ex-book-keeper had managed to regain a two-thirds interest in addition to his total control of the extensive Connellsville holdings. As czar of the region he ruled with a spiked fist. When his men struck in the winter of 1889–1890, Frick imported Central Europeans to supplant them, initiating months of warfare; armed gangs stormed the ovens and pits, inflamed marauding mobs terrorized the whole community. The dead and wounded carried off and dissenters forcibly closed out, the Frick books were re-examined. Losses had been considerable but Carnegie admired Frick's steely strength and, on credit, turned over to

him a 2 percent interest in Carnegie Brothers and gave him
the job, as chairman, of combining the Carnegie interests into
one organization. Carnegie didn't like Frick, whom he couldn't
seduce with Bobby Burns or funny stories; Frick disliked Carnegie's cant, his homilies and his jester's cap. Inconsequential
considerations, since each appreciated the moneymaking genius
of the other. The metal presses that stamped out bridges and
armor-plate for ships, rails, beams and pillars, were supplied
by materials from the company steel mills; the steel was tempered by the company's blast furnaces, which were fed by company coke from company mines and transported by company
railroads and company ships. No middleman earned a penny
from Carnegie and Frick. Under Frick's organization, production and profits increased forty-fold in a dozen years.

With a little time on his hands, Frick bought a plant,
Duquesne, where he introduced sophisticated and profitable
methods of turning out rails. Carnegie used his spare time to
write one of his books, to travel, to voice his opinions on anything that came to mind, with a concentration on social in-
equities. Life was jolly; lots of attention, shooting and hunting
with obedient guests at his huge Skibo estate in Scotland, its
ancient dour castle awash in organ music, meals accompanied
by the skirling of bagpipes. In New York, more entertaining,
courting the leaders of the arts and thought, marching to dine
to the mournful nasalities of imported pipes, acting the laird
at any place he chose to be.

Business soared, reaching a peak with reorganization, in
1892, as the Carnegie Steel Company, Limited, the largest producer of steel and coke in the world, capitalized at twenty-five
million dollars. It employed over thirty thousand men, many
of whom spoke no English and some of whom were misty about
the role of unions, although the militant Homestead plant had
a union contract that forced improved conditions—and consequently increased production costs. In 1892 Frick reminded
the workers that their contract would run out early in July and

that thereafter the salary scale and working hours would be those he chose to establish. Carnegie, who had mapped out the campaign to demolish the union, was safely holed up in Scotland, but he was—hadn't he repeatedly said so?—the worker's friend, the adulator of honest labor. Under the illusion that Uncle Andy would come to the rescue, the Homestead men turned down Frick's terms. Frick declared the plant closed as of July 1, and brought in three hundred armed men from the Pinkerton National Detective Agency. The barges that carried Pinkerton men and their ammunition toward Homestead in the dead of night were detected by union men. There was an exchange of fire and the infamous Homestead war was on. Workers in other Carnegie plants who sympathized with Homestead went on strike when Frick refused to meet with union leaders. He was going to run his business as he saw fit, supported by private communications from Carnegie, who publicly disclaimed any control of the works, now surrounded by eight thousand guardsmen.

Though both were now excoriated by liberal forces, some of the weight of blame and loathing was taken off Frick by the anarchist Alexander Berkman, who tried to assassinate him. He shot Frick twice and stabbed at his legs with a sharpened file. While the bullets were being extracted the industrialist issued a statement that the incident would not change his labor policies, nor would he accept a bodyguard. So much red-blooded American machismo was irresistibly admirable. The shafts directed at Carnegie doubled; *he* was now the Homestead murderer and was hanged in effigy. Five months of conflict cost the company two million dollars but the net profits for 1892 still managed to total four million.

Two years later there came a new flood of scurrility, cartoons, invective. The newspapers had uncovered a neat piece of work that gave the government low-grade, defective Carnegie armor plate for high-grade prices. The steel barons were endangering the lives of our naval men and cracking the supremacy of our navy, the papers roared. Hearings, astonishment, contrition, promises, a political contribution where it might most matter, and the wheels went on revolving and sparking. On stage, soon, Henry W. Oliver, who controlled a major plow and shovel manufacturing firm and had founded the Oliver Mining Company, the first to dig for the invaluable iron ores of the Mesabi Range in Minnesota. In need of money to develop his ore fields, Oliver offered the Carnegie Company one-half of his capital stock for a loan of five hundred thousand dollars. Carnegie, absorbing the culture and clear skies of the Continent, didn't like the idea, but Frick was interested and with Oliver turned to John D. Rockefeller, who had made sizable investments in the distant, almost inaccessible range. Rockefeller leased them his lands at a low royalty in exchange for a guarantee that 1,200,000 tons of ore would be shipped on his steam and railroad lines to Lake Erie at a rate that would profit Rockefeller and yet save the Oliver-Frick alliance five hundred thousand dollars a year. Carnegie found this pleasing and the arrangement by which his combine controlled five-sixths of Oliver Mining. Furthermore, other mining stocks were slipping and the ensuing selling panic gave Oliver and Frick an opportunity to buy options at low prices. Before the century was out, the coalition would own two-thirds of the highest-grade ore in the world. Carnegie Company profits were twenty-one million dollars in 1899, more than five times the four million of 1892, with anticipated profits of forty million dollars by 1900.

Frick and Carnegie inevitably found reason for an acrimonious, undignified and closely watched law suit that concerned the value of Frick's interest in the company. The contested sums evoked memories of the Homestead conflict and investigations into the low wages of men who worked twelve hours a day and often on Sundays. The civic-minded, the liberal clergy, the cartoonists attacked en masse, aiming particularly at the Carnegie philanthropies, ceremoniously bestowed

out of a bottomless well of money which his laborers did not
share. The once invulnerable reputation of the company
began to suffer; reports of dissolution were rumored in the
banking and industrial communities. It was better to take the
legal mess out of the public eye so a compromise was arranged.
Carnegie lost nothing; Frick got fifteen million dollars for his
disputed interest, and under a short-lived new consolidation,
both men, as major shareholders, came away with many millions in stocks and bonds. Still an emperor, Carnegie was, however, becoming aware of flourishing competitors. A solution
was to merge them with Carnegie Steel. The negotiating team
consisted of J. P. Morgan and his partner, Judge Elbert H.
Gary, with Charlie Schwab representing Carnegie. The Scots-
man sold his empire for five hundred million dollars in the
most monumental industrial sale yet. The newly organized
United States Steel thus became the largest trust, capitalized at
nearly one and a half billion dollars and feared by many for
the power that could make paper dolls of government leaders
and move the country in whichever direction it dictated.

Carnegie, worth four hundred million dollars and retired,
went on another binge of philanthropies. Belatedly, he established a relief and pension fund of four million dollars for the
forty-five thousand workers in his former plants. New York
City received over five million dollars for sixty-eight branch
libraries, the city to be responsible for the sites, books and
maintenance. In 1904, the Carnegie Institution of Washington
was established to encourage investigation and learning "for
the improvement of mankind," with the income from over
twenty-two million dollars to spend. Pittsburgh was presented
with the Carnegie Institute and the Carnegie Institute of Tech-
nology, a scholastic and cultural enclave that includes a distinguished picture collection. Twenty million dollars went to
universities in the States and Scotland. He transformed his poor
hometown of Dunfermline into a paradise of playing fields,
music and model tenements, and placed a statue of himself, as

Hadrian might, in a newly conquered and improved town. All in all, he gave away over three hundred fifty million in his lifetime, always stipulating that only the income of a bequest be used. For more immediate pleasure, Carnegie accrued medals, Grand Crosses, degrees and, traveling fast, accumulated the freedom of fifty-four British and Irish cities.

Recorded dates differ, but sometime early in this century, Carnegie wandered far uptown on Fifth Avenue and, envisioning the place without its resident shanties and bedraggled children, he saw on Ninetieth and Ninety-first streets the site for a mansion which would also serve as his office. The house, completed in 1905, cost $1,500,000 to build and had sixty-four rooms and careful, complex plumbing (the bathrooms were judged by experts to be "models of artistic sanitation"). Since there was never a Carnegie enterprise left unsung, the house was abundantly covered in newspapers and periodicals. "The house," said one, "is one of the grandest and most imposing in the United States, and yet how simple its lines." It was praised for being a residence rather than a palace; for being as gracious as an English house sitting calmly in garden and iawn where Sir Walter Scott might have been a happy guest. It was worthy, too, of the important social event that was Mrs. Carnegie's annual meeting called in aid of the Students' International Union.

The pacifist views Carnegie came to during his short direct contact with the Civil War were unchanged during World War I; they attracted a federal commission hearing ostensibly called to question his charitable foundations, one of them the Peace Palace at The Hague. He testified brightly, told his funny little stories, avoided all possible barbs and hooks—not severely menacing, in any case—and bounded back (he was then eighty) to continue work on his autobiography. There were other matters also to take care of: a new estate in the Berkshires, the quality of the organ for the huge new country house and pipers to hire. In 1919 he married his daughter off to the lilt of Scottish airs and, having done all he could for the world, died at the age of eighty-four.

While Carnegie was opening his house uptown, Henry Frick leased 640 Fifth Avenue, William H. Vanderbilt's house. It had taken him twenty years to get there, since the time he and Mellon had examined the luxurious houses on the Avenue and estimated costs of upkeep. They had figured that Vanderbilt's house, then the most splendid in the city, would require an income of about one thousand dollars a day—at 1880 values —or 5 percent on six million dollars, which young Frick thought might suffice him. During his tenancy of 640 Frick acquired the site of the Lenox Library on Fifth Avenue between Seventieth and Seventy-first streets and had Hastings of the accomplished Carrère and Hastings team build him a French house with Italian overtones suitable for the family and its imposing collection. Art and family moved into the cool palace, beautiful and remote, in 1914. The main salons were decorated by an English firm appointed and supervised by Joseph Duveen who also supplied objects and paintings, a good number of the best acquired from the estate of Morgan, who had died in 1913.

The second floor was decorated by the first successful woman decorator, Elsie de Wolfe. With an assist from Stanford White, who vouched for her capability, she had been commissioned to do the Colony Club, at the time (1907) a scandalous institution that gave rich and modish women license to gather and amuse themselves as men did in their clubs. That well-done job vaulted her into prominence, and Frick called for her. He was tired of the assaults of dealers and wanted her to act as buffer. She was to accept no percentage from the international vendors but take a chance on 10 percent of whatever he purchased. She accepted. Jacques Seligman had in his control in Paris part of the famous Wallace collection of London, a collection that Frick admired. Seligman invited Elsie de Wolfe to visit and have the first glimpse of his Wallace pieces.

She convinced Frick to see them too and in half an hour he bought many million francs' worth of furnishings, leaving her speechless and 10 percent of the vast sum richer.

Unlike many of the Barons, Frick always had some interest in art. Like them he bought at first largely French paintings and mainly of Knoedler, then at 355 Fifth Avenue near the Waldorf-Astoria. A contemporary dealer tells the touching story that Frick saw there a Bouguereau painting of a little girl who resembled Frick's dead daughter. The purchase of that painting was purportedly the beginning of Frick's intensive collecting. A good number of the early purchases were disposed of as his tastes became more finely honed, his dealings with dealers more canny, his rivalry with other collectors increasingly triumphant. He had distinct advantages over them: he concentrated almost all his time on his collection and he was a favored customer because he was openhanded, willing to make payment immediately, occasionally to the tune of several million dollars in one meeting.

Shortly after Morgan died a famous set of Fragonard panels, *The Progress of Love,* was exhibited at the Metropolitan Museum along with other Morgan gems. The coy, rosy-bottomed angels and the dignified distant temples had been painted on order from Madame du Barry but she changed her mind when they were finished in 1773; she wanted something more stylish, less dimply and more classical. Fragonard took them back to his house in southern France whence they, in time, issued forth to find their way to the omnivorous Morgan and the Museum. On a visit to the exhibit Duveen bumped into the Knoedlers, who were also examining the Fragonards. It took no leap of acumen to surmise that they would try to buy the panels for Frick. Duveen quickly called on Morgan's son, the heir of the unrivaled collection, and offered him first a million dollars, and when that was refused, one and a quarter. He then asked Morgan to call Frick to vouch for the authenticity of the price and to add that Duveen would sell the panels

to Frick at no increase, no commission. Duveen had Frick and
kept him, educating him in the puerile qualities of the fashionable acres of Bouguereaus rampant and bellicose Meissoniers,
revealing the deeper, transcending beauties of Rembrandt,
opening the golden flood of Italian Renaissance genius, pointing out the high skills and charms of English painting.

Frick was careful, methodical and determined to have the
best hang on his walls and that best became better, encouraged
by Duveen and in emulation of the Wallace collection. It
makes revealing page-turning to look down the list of art purchases as they appear chronologically in George Harvey's biography of Henry Clay Frick. The acquisitions of the first fifteen
years, 1881 to 1896, bear no star, indicating that they do not
hang in the final collection. Of the forty or so bought between
1897 and 1901, only ten are starred, while the years 1902 to
1911 show half the items starred. Of the last years, until 1919,
the pages are thickly sprinkled with stars and awesome names—
Dürer, Rembrandt (seven in this period alone), Van Dyck, Vermeer, Duccio, Titian, Turner, El Greco, Goya, Ingres, Piero
della Francesca, Laurana, Michelangelo, Bellini, Corot, Velazquez, Constable, Whistler, Rubens, Hogarth, Gainsborough, to
mention only part of the Frick roll call, which numbers about
one hundred artists, accompanied by excellence in French
furniture, in Renaissance bronzes, in Chinese porcelains and
Limoges enamels.

Handsome, the master of the most dignified house—his
servants all wore somber black—and a supreme collector, he
and his wife still bore marks of the raw provincial. The most
commonly repeated vignette depicts Frick sitting on a papal
or ducal throne of the Renaissance, surrounded by his masterpieces, reading a popular magazine while the huge ornate organ
at the head of the marble stairs pours out the treacle of sentimental popular songs. The story may stem from a dealer; dealers not only enjoyed educating in their particular direction
American millionaires, but exchanging stories about them. Du-

veen liked to tell of the Van Dyck, a portrait of two young men,
he had hung for approval and potential purchase in the Frick
house. Mrs. Frick objected strongly to the painting; she couldn't
live with two such markedly Jewish noses (this was a time when
hotel advertisements still carried the legend "No Jews, no
dogs"). The noses belonged to two young Stuarts, the nephews
of Charles I. Rene Gimpel reports a strange scene, surrealistic
and naive. When he visited the house, Frick proudly showed
him that he had put his extraordinary Italian bronzes, once
Morgan's, on ball bearings so that they might be seen in the
round. Gimpel was both amused and appalled at the desecra-
tion and completely thunderstruck as their owner turned one
and then another and another and faster and faster until he
had them spinning simultaneously, delighted with his whirling
tops. But, whatever he did with it in his time, his twenty-
million-dollar legacy to the city of New York remains, as Rene
Gimpel called it, "a royal gift."

CHAPTER 15

CODA

ifth Avenue is increasingly a Kermess: a revival of medieval fair of pilgrim-tourists, and vendors to gull them with overpriced souvenirs as their ancestors of the Middle Ages sold rosaries and amulets blessed by themselves alone; and mimes, jugglers and musicians, a raggle-taggle of beggars, third-rate troubadours and twelfth-rate limners.

Washington Square entertainment led off with respected chamber music. Some of it gave way to a hundred guitars plangent and raucous; banjos, hoarse blues and rock voices and elixirs to strengthen them wrapped in brown paper bags. McKim, Mead and White's Judson Memorial Church at the southern end of the Square, trailed the disorganized dissidents of many years, from the restless beat poets through the beatific flower children who tried for Fra Angelico angels, the "outrageous" painter who later had Madison Avenue and its galleries at his command. It held the spontaneous, incomprehensible little explosions of "happenings," the dreary despair of drug programs—always distinctly "with it," or ahead of it. The spring and fall art shows, once confined to the square with a tangent for crafts, has sprawled into the Avenue, surrounded New York University and is overwhelming the Italian coffee houses with its cute kiddies and harsh African heads. Poetry accompanied by music, a specialty of Village clubs some years ago, has moved into the square as one of its stops in City parklets.

The Old Row and its neighbors to the north were long ago sliced into apartments and reshaped again for use by New York University. The only Fifth Avenue house left of the building rage of the 1850s is the Salmagundi Club, at number 47, a conservative art group—although it doesn't like that label—and school, the tone often set by an association with the United States Navy whose activities, mundane and majestic, are recorded by Salmagundi painters. In spite of its musty purple-brown color and no great nobility of design, the building has been cited for its architectural distinction, possibly because it still manages to exist and hold on to its chandeliers exploding from foaming plasterwork ceilings, anaerobic Victorian window drapes and marble fireplaces strong enough to support fruits, flowers, putti and maidens.

Portions of the brownstone that once belonged to Thomas Fortune Ryan, at number 60, are still embedded, completely hidden from public view, by the businesslike walls of the Forbes Building. The old houses west of Fifth on the side streets are cherished and well cared for—when they are not destroyed by bombs—and the solid churches that entice visitors with unusually good music grow more handsome in their long dusk.

In late 1976 the head of that bedraggled phoenix, New York restoration, once again rose to announce that pushers and whores were to be removed from Fourteenth Street, that Union Square was to be scrubbed, clipped and beautified with new trash cans, fresh paint for its railings, neat plantings and weekly noonday concerts. The required $1,500,000 was to be contributed by businesses in the quarter, eager to pull their habitat out of its mire, sodden here, a bit too bubbly there. At this writing, the winter of 1977–78, no overt moves. From another source, a revival of the square's political days, a meeting of elderly socialists in a hall near the square to honor the memory of Eugene V. Debs and Meyer London, who shaped the Socialist Party. One possible ornament, the green market that brought fresh fruits and vegetables and homemade breads to Union Square on Saturdays, may be removed. It blocks traffic they said; the dismay of Village merchants who cannot compete in price or country charm is probably a closer reason.

An ornament that has lasted for a while, is a Union Square branch of Rizzoli's book shop of the Fifties on Fifth Avenue, less high-Milanese in design than its parent, more seriously devoted to foreign books and periodicals. It is the most recent of the book shops filling the quarter that, for over a century, never quite stopped being book and publishing row. Among office listings of firms devoted to sentimental memorabilia, research in heraldry, addressing and mailing, agencies for medical workers and many men's clothing manufacturers, not far from Brownie's wholesome restaurant and Shackman's kewpies and doll-house nostalgia, there is one building, 101, that houses a Jewish periodical, a Croatian publishing house, Africana Publishing, International University booksellers and the original publishers of the Peter Rabbit Books. One of this group was, and may still be, the firm of Albert Boni, engaged in microfilming early American newspapers and the three million pages that comprised the collected British Government Publications, the publications of the New York Library and, best known, the two-volume compact Oxford English Dictionary, its monumental contents meant to be read with a magnifying glass. The company was once the adventuresome publishers, Boni and Liveright, and for old times' sake, the offices in 101 keep a few of its publications around, Joyce's *Dubliners* (bought in 1919), for instance, and dozens of titles in the innovative Modern Library series. In telling of the Fifth Avenue of his youth, Mr. Boni described a vanished neighborhood: the New York Hospital that ran between Fifteenth and Sixteenth west of Fifth Avenue; the Salvation Army shops on Fourteenth Street off Fifth that took the discards of publishers and booksellers and sold them to the used-books stalls of Fourth Avenue. On the Avenue, at the southwest corner of Fifteenth Street, there was an art-loving book shop that gave work space among its shelves to painters and etchers.

The international book market that is further helping displace compounds of lighters, umbrellas, vitamins and recording tape—everything cheap—is led off by the two sections of Barnes and Noble at Eighteenth Street, the annex of remainders a strong lure to Sunday bargain hunters. (In mid-1977 another bargain annex was opened at Forty-eighth Street and Fifth.) The Four Continents shop at 149 concentrates on Turgenev, Tolstoy, Dostoevsky and Chekhov in attractive editions; the records of Russian artists; and the beguiling wooden dolls within dolls. A few paces away, at 125, China Books and Periodicals, passionately Left. Under a large display of posters whose benign dignitaries walk among Chinese children as plump and beautiful as good apples, are heaps and piles of Maoism, Marxism and Leninism in German, Persian, French and Spanish, and, in English, books on the problems of blacks and Puerto Ricans. It is a charged, stentorian place, doing an ecumenical job in its way. The music from the loudspeakers is often a Mexican folk song, the young man at the cash register a Harlem black, the Saturday customers intense and skinny white girls in ineptly knitted long shawls shopping with their consummately bearded silent young men.

Another type of fervor streams from the windows of the combined Librería Hispánica and Librairie de France at the southeast corner of Nineteenth Street with a sign that announces, "*Todo lo que usted siempre quiso saber sobre el sexo,*" the last word in red letters. There are also spates of home medicine, and general self-improvement in Spanish, and French paperbacks as well as records, art books and a wide range of guidebooks. To encourage the Hispanic customers— of which the shop may not yet have enough for its vast quarters and great number of books—a well-designed poster of a boy who says he is *"bilingüe, bicultural y orgulloso de mi raza."*

In its new optimism, the interesting slattern of a neighborhood takes on weekend light opera (called Broque) across from the Flatiron Building. While uptown neighbors decay, the obscure area seems to be lifting its head to the arts and inviting the young, who respond to its inexpensive attractions. Long after the Metropolitan Life Insurance Building, built in 1908, stopped playing Handel on its chimes and the night glow that Sara Teasdale called "its tower of amber light" had become a commonplace, after the house of Catherine Lorillard Wolfe and Samuel Morse's Venetian Academy were long gone, the Jerome mansion still held on as the Manhattan Club, into the 1960s. The last Madison Square Garden carried its name and boxing matches uptown in the mid-1920s. The saddest loss among the floating minarets and Stanford White frosting that vanished was that of St. Gauden's Diana, apostrophized in her short life as "huntress of pleasure," "restless Diana," "New York's proper deity because she exulted in life." When the lithe girl, poised for flight, was brought down to earth it was discovered that she had been put together with rivets large enough to hold the plates of a battleship. New York would have nothing to do with the hulking creature and shipped her off to the Pennsylvania Museum of Art. In the late 1960s, a sudden yearning for her gnawed at the hometown; Mayor Lindsay pleaded for her return but Philadelphia had grown fond of her. She reappeared to New Yorkers as a much reduced model from the storerooms of the Metropolitan Museum, to shine in a Whitney show of American sculpture in 1976, then back to the storerooms.

Insurance swallowed up not only Diana but White's Madison Square Presbyterian Church, a splendor of pillared porticos and classical dome, adorned by the neo-Byzantine and Louis C. Tiffany. Such luminaries and their coteries gone, the nannies and decorous children removed to Central Park, the square decayed rapidly. In spite of the cheeriness of a tall, broad tree surrounded by carolers through many Christmases, the park returned to the paupers it had served in its beginnings. As early as 1917, it was described as a place of derelicts who were combed out for the parades and celebrations. It is still a listless park, mainly a mortuary of disregarded post–Civil War statues. At the westward corner with Twenty-third Street, stands William Henry Seward, Lincoln's Secretary of State. This was to be a statue of Lincoln. Before the head was ready, the money ran out, so a homeless head of Seward was attached to Lincoln's body, a not uncommon act in the history of commemorative statues. (Rheumy Roman emperors, if they lasted long enough to be rheumy, had their heads placed on the knotty musculature of Hercules or the smooth androgynous beauty of Apollo.)

At the Madison Avenue end of Twenty-third Street, Roscoe Conkling, the contentious post–Civil War Senator, stands bearded, keen-eyed, saved from total immobility by a hand gesture. Behind him the movement around the Metropolitan Life Building and the richly columned and pedimented marble building that houses the appellate division of the supreme court, swarming with hortatory, law-linked statuary and a splendor of architectural detail that brought its cost, in 1900, to three-quarters of a million dollars.

Their own sort of impressive monument are the several old trees protected from an inimical world by tall metal fences. Besides the molestation of trees, the Park has other problems: dogs are not to enter, "Pigeon Feeding Prohibited," "All alcoholic beverages prohibited in this park." On a bench facing the courthouse sits a man dispensing grain and peanuts from a plastic bag. His terrain is impassable for the restless pecking, the jerky strut and thrust of dozens of pigeons, the quick hop and swoop of sparrows. Nearby two dogs dart and dance with each other in an inner, barred section of lawn.

Except for animals and birds, and rush-hour bands of peo-

ple running between office and bus, the park's inhabitants are
as inert as the statues. One of the city's homeless ladies, in an
ill-fitting, matted wig she has picked out of a discard bin,
slouches on her bench peering out at nothing from her fortress
of lumpy plastic bags. Her neighbor is happier. No bags, no
impedimenta except an oily cap that tries to slip off his supine
head, and a rag of sweater that leaves his midriff bare for easy
scratching. A student from nearby Baruch College pores over
his notes, a pair of lovers coo and murmur at each other, a
squirrel brushes through a fall of brown leaves. It is all very
quiet and private, as private as if the square were thickly
walled, disconcerting to be in and a great relief to emerge from,
into Fifth Avenue and the laughing pizza and Coke world of
young bus drivers ending their Fifth routes at Twenty-sixth
Street.

Where the Hotel Brunswick stood—in its front yard was
the first publicly exhibited electric light, placed on a tall tree
pole—and then Brentano's, which in time ceded to Woolworth's, there is now the large gift center at 225, almost im-
pregnable for those without buyers' credentials. During gift
fair weeks it is a frenzy of puffy coiffure, big pocketbooks, intense faces speaking a variety of regional accents—the more
remote the accent, the heavier the pancake makeup and the
rouge. The buyers rush through the windowed halls, notebooks
at the ready, to select saleable items for hometown shops: flowers waxy or silken, music boxes, baskets and buckets, salad
bowls, corn-husk dolls, chess sets, sweet boykins and girlkins
in pottery and papier-mâché, poor reproductions of bad sculpture and reasonable reproductions of Gauguins and Van Goghs,
bird cages, furry red toilet covers, soap like fruits and large
peanuts, like candy and shells, huge ceramic penguins and orang-
utans, curly glass and linear, ethnic and period heads—Mexican, Spanish, Moorish and Elizabethan—and for those to whom
the past is lovely, old cuspidors and toy trolleys. It is all very
serious (two women discussing a hard-boiled egg platter with

a salesman might be participants in a grave medical consulta-
tion) and a little frightening as testimony of American tastes—
if it weren't for some good museum reproductions, the English
china and the Waterford that occupy, as they might have in the
turn of the century Madison Square shops, the Fifth Avenue
windows. With the gift center as mother hen and the toy center
diagonally downtown, a large scattering of gift chicks: silver,
glass, lamps, general decor and the crafts of Poland and Israel,
Viennese art publishing and a bazaarful of Indian saris, of huge-
eyed dancers, radiantly embroidered camels and well-fleshed
bronze gods.

In the jumpiness of international souvenirs, two churches,
oddly placed in their present surroundings and yet vital. A
century ago they sat in leafy serenity and later among faint
echoes of Holland House jollity (Thirtieth Street) and the
dignity of the Calumet Club, the Knickerbocker Club and
brownstones flat, pimpled, or studded that housed their parish-
ioners. From the Avenue at Twenty-ninth Street, the low
green roof of the litch gate of the Little Church Around the
Corner (more formally, the Episcopal Church of the Transfig-
uration) built in 1849 and now a grateful intrusion of the
picturesque on a meaningless street. Enclosed in its garden, the
church casts a Wordsworthian image, its mild exoticism enhanced by the fact that this has been the "Actor's Church" since
1870. The celebrated actor Joseph Jefferson had tried to arrange
the funeral of a friend at an elite Madison Avenue church and
was refused because the dead man was an actor. The church dignitary suggested that Jefferson try the "little church around the
corner." Hence the name, and the presence of actors and the
sentimental who choose the church for their weddings, and
the many who sketch its modest appeal. A solid, enduring comfort is the Marble Collegiate Church on Fifth Avenue and its
preacher of "positive thinking," Dr. Norman Vincent Peale,
who has been spreading the wholesome word for forty-five years
and still draws large crowds with his recipes for peace of mind.

During his services, the rather solemn church shines in the brilliant lights provided for television and the punching, folksy virtue of his unalloyed optimism.

Relics of the times of the churches sit high above the street uniformities of modern glass and cement. The upper stories of number 256 are terraced, arched and embroidered in a playful greed that borrowed from the Italian Renaissance and Spanish plateresque on a layer of Moorish. At 306, above a coffee shop, crusty brown boils with rosettes and circlets while Polk's hobbies and electric trains next door sit in bays held by pillars rising to a massive cornice. The broad windows of a number of these houses and the decorative initials like royal shields indicate that they were once the showrooms for select merchandise, now supplanted by "To Let" signs.

The northeast corner of Thirty-second Street bounces cushions in a wholesale storefront where once the august Knickerbocker Club, organized to guard members of old families from the intruding new, lived among jutting bays and balconies on a big dour house. The club was within easy reach of an impeccably authentic Knickerbocker, Johnston Livingstone, who lived across the street. Next door to him the Countess de Laugiers-Villars, one of the numerous American heiresses who married titles. A few elderly houses amble up the Avenue to meet the Tokyo Trust Company in good-looking Occidental dress. And then 350, the Empire State Building.

Past the doorman and under the canopy, into the marble vestibule—rather like the long nave of a church, its altarpiece an Empire State in metal relief shedding dense rays of glory. At its side a small, three-dimensional image and the legend of the donors and the builders and when they wrought, March 17, 1930 to March 1, 1931. Were it picked out in early mosaics and labeled "Jerusalem" or "Bethlehem" it could not be more churchly. The spell is broken by music and the high, hot voices of school groups and visiting families massing in the arcades to buy candy and hot dogs and to assault the elevators that fly to the observation platforms. Sharpened to the one adventure, they miss the architectural ornaments around them, styled in the geometrics of Art Deco, worked decoratively into the floors, the elevator doors, and in plaques that celebrate concrete, tools and the dignity of machines and men.

This most spectacular, expensive, advanced, and so forth, building of its time was planned by a combine of DuPont money, Heckscher money, Altman money and the money of a number of other investors led by John J. Raskob, who had organized Alfred E. Smith's presidential campaign against Hoover in 1928 and who, in spite of that failure, stayed on as chairman of the Democratic National Committee. They bought the Waldorf-Astoria and a few attached lots for seventeen and a half million dollars and appointed ex-Governor Smith president of the new project. They estimated that the building alone would cost about five million dollars. Money was no problem; there was lots of it everywhere and it was particularly easy to find for investment in the greatest, most advanced skyscraper of them all. Almost too apt a symbolic coincidence: the Waldorf was demolished in October, 1929, the month of the crash that led off the 1930s depression. Estimated building costs were reduced to two and a half million dollars and the original blocky design thinned to a tall shaft.

The Empire State design was not altogether determined by the owners and architects; it was strongly influenced by the developing rival, the Chrysler Building, one of the boom-baby skyscrapers that managed to grow up during the Depression. Raskob was the most ardent Chrysler watcher. The Empire's limit of eighty stories had to be raised, he insisted, because the Chrysler was threatening to go higher. So, Empire went to eighty-five stories, taller than the Forty-second Street building by a scant four feet, and then there was the danger that some-one—Walter Chrysler—might just push a thin tall needle up from its spire. Thirty-fourth Street erected a two-hundred-foot dirigible mast that raised it to 1,250 feet, the tallest building in the world until the World Trade Center lifted its girders to 1,350 feet forty years later.

It was a wonder of efficient building, planned for saving time and labor so that complete standard units could rise four or five stories in a good week. The vital statistics, in superlatives, poured out and still do: The miles of elevator shaft laid end to end would stretch for seven miles; seventy-three elevators, more than any other building in New York contained, willing to zoom up and down at speeds from six hundred to twelve hundred feet a minute at any time of the day or night. Nine hundred tenants from six continents, cared for by sixteen thousand persons; two hundred women who clean up the trash—100 tons a month—left by two million visitors in each year. You can buy an airline ticket, eat in one of several places, fit a suit, get your shoes and teeth repaired, send flowers, leave a stock order, cash a check, find a messenger or a stenographer—everything but a bed and love. This almost complete life within the fortress-castle, a reminder of medieval living brought to the inhabitants of skyscrapers, is now a commonplace, but the Empire State and its uptown contemporary, Rockefeller Center, were the modern innovators in these convenient and companionable uses of inner space.

The first Empire State years were dour. The tallest white elephant in the world, meant to be a world center for many industries and mired in a depression, had very few tenants. The agents, unable to lure concerns with a rental of only $3.50 to $5.00 per square foot of space, began to concentrate on the singular réclame of the building with its unparalleled views across the city and the rivers and out to sea, with dirigibles like friendly dolphin smiling in at your window—the utter uniqueness of it all. In spite of the blandishments only one-third of the building was in use from the time of its ceremonious opening in 1931 till 1941 when the pre–World War II boom began.

The growing international fame of its observation decks,

which stretched an unbelievable New York at a tourist's feet, curious enterprises and accidents and adroit publicity joined to wreathe the building in an aura of legends, a few tentatively perched on fact. A few weeks after the building was completed, an attempt was made to try out the dirigible mast deck as a small depot for airmail parcels. A squadron of celebrities waited high in the building to watch the blimp and its packages arrive and settle at the mast. Crowds below, stretching for several blocks, watched breathlessly as the blimp tried and tried again, touching, retreating, menacing the distinguished assemblage as the wind pushed and pulled it from the building. The crowds on the street were rewarded with a shower as ballast was released from the blimp and it gave up. A few months later, another try, more successful, less exciting. In 1945, a tragic event. Seven persons inside the building and three in an Army bomber were killed when the plane, confused by fog, crashed into the seventy-eighth floor. A persistent piece of Gothic-novel apocrypha says that the elevator shafts howl, partitions make grisly cracking noises, window frames groan, and the whole building sways like a reed when storm winds whip the building. The disappointing facts are that, with no nearby protection, the higher sections are buffeted by high winds, but according to gyroscopic experiments the shaft sways only an uneventful one-quarter inch under the most severe storm.

In time, the novelty and adventure drained away. A top-floor cafe no longer exists and the number of suicides has diminished with improved fencing on the observation decks. The building is fairly full of tenants, gathered as marts of women's hosiery, representatives of more than one hundred shoe manufacturers, offices of the "notions" industry and of the leading names in the giant man-made fabrics industry. While the offices were filling with samples of shoe models and the bright bits and pieces of notions, the building continued to modernize, stimulated by changes in ownership and rises in value. In 1951, Raskob's estate realized thirty-four million dollars from one purchaser while the land beneath the building went to Prudential Insurance for seventeen million. Three years later the Empire State was sold to a group of Chicago developers and sold again in late 1961 to an investment firm for sixty-five million dollars, the highest purchase price for a building to that time.

The world-famous views are trimmed by a frail Gothic dart on one building, a frill of copper on another, the long teeth of empty piers far below, cowering under predator planes. At the very top, FM music wafted by a delicate web of transmission from seventeen stations, simultaneous and ungarbled; from the TV tower twenty-two stories high, placed in 1950, the enlightenments and mediocrities of nine local television stations. At night the illumination turns the upper stories and tower into an art deco gem, a diamond brooch sitting on a dark velvet pedestal, tiny twinkling rubies on its slender clasp. The gem's glow is subdued only when the Audubon Society advises that thousands of migrating birds are arriving and it would be kind not to blind and confuse them in their flight.

By the opening of World War I, Fifth Avenue was, as mentioned, one of the most expensive streets in the world, for the goods in its shops and the value of the ground on which they stood, as well as its houses. The little shops that now line the Thirties, nervously dashing around the queenly feet of Altman's and Lord & Taylor's, began their accelerating encroachment when more stable shops, led by Saks Fifth Avenue in the mid-1920s, moved up to the area of the great hotels. Gresham's Law, the bad driving out the sound, appears to apply as well to Fifth Avenue as to Lombard Street in Elizabethan England, particularly in the Thirties and Forties Streets, where a huge, fragmented flea market spreads variegated, suspect wares. A few shops are elderly descendants of itinerant Middle Eastern peddlers, sitting among their "rare Orientals" and "banquet linens" and "genuine jade" and heavily encrusted flatware, wailing through the decades that inimical forces are closing them out, they must fold their tents and flee. A newer breed has joined them with members of efficient fast-food chains and brashly lit fairs of transistors, calculators, radios, cameras, luggage, sunglasses, binoculars and racks of skyscraper postcards for the tourist trade. On a mysterious system of preferment or an erratic do-si-do of supply and demand, one shop will concentrate on cheap watches, fountain pens and lighters while another finds its happiness in a jammed populace of china ballerinas, goose girls, shepherds and shepherdesses and their twee pets. Like cuckoos they invade empty stores on short leases when earlier businesses disappear into the suburbs or dissolve altogether. CLOSING OUT they all weep loudly—handkerchiefs, dishes, hand-painted vases, plates, paintings, tablecloths, porcelain flowers, chalky Italian figurines, onyx elephants, ivories and jades, chess sets, flatwear, big ashtrays, little ashtrays—and then the eye refuses to see any more. When Tiffany's took its clock, gems, craftsmen and customers up to Fifty-seventh Street, what was there to do with its Venetian edifice at Thirty-seventh Street? In the late winter of 1975 there were signs on the dusty windows to announce floors to sublet, or a corner to rent. By the spring, the signs pleaded for a lessee or buyer to take the whole of the dignified derelict; the most recent real estate rumor (1978) is that it may be razed and rebuilt in the style that incorporates, like the Olympic Towers, shops, offices and apartments.

Staring into the local miscellanies, an occasional, somberly dressed lady may be heard to say to her companion in the tones of the Middle West, "Is *this* Fifth Avenue?" She had grown up believing that the "longest retail street in the world" was also the most beautiful and most stylish. Heaped warehouse discards hardly match the fixed image built from her mother's and her grandmother's reports of visits to New York. She will find vestigial fragments of that Fifth Avenue in the dashing Lord & Taylor signature and the discreet, "Founded 1826." She will

find them in a limestone building, once a townhouse, that carries pretty plaster ornaments and, when charging past the desperate chorus of MUST RAISE CASH, in the plaque that
remembers the Wendels in a bronze niche immediately north
of Kress's window. It bears a relief of the four-storied house
and a passing carriage, then goes on to say in mannered letter-
ing that the house stood here for seventy years. On the death
of Rebecca Wendel Swope and Ella V. von E. Wendel, the last
survivors, the property, the plaque goes on, was willed to the
Drew Theological Seminary of Madison, New Jersey, "which
By This Tablet, Makes Grateful Acknowledgment of the Gift."
(The plaque may or may not last beyond the fall of 1977 when
Kress's, which beamed on the street for forty-two years, turns off
its shine.) The confused visitor might look into the windows
of erstwhile Arnold Constable which, after 150 years of New
York merchandising, gave up the ghost in the mid-1970s and
yielded its space to the New York Public Library. She might
admire the indomitable longevity—seventy-five years—of Lane
Bryant's outsize Athenas and Junos, who smile at their stone
counterparts on the pediments of the library across the street.

To a non–New Yorker, it comes as something of a surprise
to see the steps of a revered institution like the Central Branch
of the New York Public Library used as a meeting place for
anyone, everyone, a few tinged with passion on its way to madness. The man in pink rags and headcloth, white stripe painted
on his nose, exhorting, teaching, forcing pamphlets of an obscure religion of the East on passersby as insistently as only the
newly converted can. A black lady in a blond wig, wearing
white boots and pocketbook, sits on the lowest steps on the rise,
smiling, gently swaying to her own secret music, smiling and
swaying for hours. Behind her, the incessant popping of Puerto
Rican Spanish and the purposeful stride of solitary young Japanese scholars.

In contrast to the restless front-steps agora, the library's
inner halls mount orderly, handsome shows that display the

institution's treasures, among them antiques garnered by the
Astors and Cogswell: the first history printed in England by
Caxton in the fifteenth century, an immense hand-painted engraving that recorded the ornaments used by Raphael in the
Vatican *stanze* and the Audubon prints that old John Jacob
bought and paid for slowly. Another exhibition displayed artifacts of the most satisfying of literary romances, the courtship,
marriage and elopement to Italy of Robert and Elizabeth Bar-
rett Browning. To preserve its multilingual eight and a half
million books and keep adding the half-million it acquires
yearly, the library tries for public funds to add to its steady
bequests, a gift here, another there, a search for "friends" to
make small, steady contributions; and it bows to the times when
all institutions must charm, with a fashion show. In the general
enterprise and rejuvenation, even the guardian lions have undergone freshening.

The backyard, Bryant Park, that flows from the distinguished western end of the library now leads a schizophrenic
life. An engaging oasis of lunch time concerts for several years,
it still tries with flower shows, with drawings of projected city
planning, with poetry recitals—these interspersed with threats
to close the park because of an invasion of drug dealers, gamblers and men desperate enough to kill. The struggle between
art and dereliction has not, however, seriously depressed local
values. The rental on a set of offices at Forty-fourth Street was,
in early 1977, eighty thousand dollars a year.

Leading off with the penny-whistle tunes of frilly figurines
giggling and pouting, the area stumbles through men's suits,
and costume jewelry to stop in a gathering of Circes called
Aeroméxico, Air Panama, Polish Airlines, Hawaiian Travel,
British Airways and Qantas living in pinched space while the
adjoining banks are broad, high, expansive, serene. One of the
first of the banks to use candid glass and metal was the Manufacturers Hanover Trust Company, at 510, built in 1954 by
Skidmore, Owings and Merrill, who opened a clear vista of lush

greens and a huge safe of gilt and nickel as well-designed bold ornament.

A short distance up the Avenue, a set of contrasts to the clear reason of glass. The Scribner Building, at 597, remains in its 1913 exuberance of curly plaster, slender pillars, a many-paned glittering façade, putti and garlands that waft in faded breezes of La perfumed Belle Epoque. Built fourteen years later, the Fred F. French Building, at 551, stems from another and interesting architectural universe, restricting most of its ornamentation to lengths of ceramic designs arranged as bands and studs of red and green on the dark background of its slender setbacks. A third and different curio in this group is a building that burdens shoe shops, airlines and the ubiquitous cameras, etcetera, with a massive appliqué of everything the neo-baroque could possibly bear in the way of triumphal arch and convulsed statuary, a return to bygone Fifth Avenue effluvia.

The Elgin Gardens property held by Columbia was shelter for conveniently located speakeasies in the early Depression years. As leases expired, a number of proposals came forward for the use of the land. The most seriously considered was Otto Kahn's suggestion that a new opera house be placed in the area. The leading backer was John D. Rockefeller, Jr., who arranged with the university to hold a twenty-four-year lease, with renewal options extending into 2057, at an annual ground rental beginning at $3,000,000, escalating to $3,600,000 in 1952 and in 1977 to $9,400,000. A new opera house was not paramount in a troubled time; plans rusted and collapsed, and what was Mr. Rockefeller to do with a large block of expensive land that was bringing in little revenue? Rockefeller Center then began to take shape on the streets from Forty-ninth to Fifty-first bordered by Fifth Avenue, covering an area not quite three blocks square. The work of wrecking and excavation began in 1930, ridding the space of a million tons of building shards. Two years later the broad craters began to fill with millions of bricks and thousands of tons of cement. In the years of building, and even before the first speakeasy fell (one remained, to be reconstructed years later as a pub not unlike a speakeasy), the center was criticized vehemently, more rarely and less vehemently defended. Although it gave much needed employment to architects, engineers, unskilled laborers, masons, bricklayers, plumbers, sculptors, painters and decorators, there were those who thought the buildings unnecessary and dull. Further dissension was kindled by the roaring, stamping disputes among architects, artists and decorators who worked in a storm of mutual disdain.

Reappraisal, acceptance, adjustment and ultimately admiration took their usual course. Now Rockefeller Center is a source of New York pride as a unique example of urban planning, for its good-looking functionalism, its integration of forms to make the satisfying whole, planned by the architectural firms, Reinhard and Hofmeister, Corbett, Harrison and Mac-Murray, and Hood and Fouilhoux. Such extensive space planned as a unit around a vast inner court was a singular idea in a time when skyscrapers were placed to face the street and the only measures to prevent them from charging at each other and keeping pedestrians in permanent twilight were setbacks in upper reaches.

Though both the Chrysler Building and the Empire State, precursors by a few years, had freed themselves of a number of traditional gestures, they could not quite relinquish the sky-piercing spire. Rockefeller Center contented itself with subtle variations in textures and tones in the body of the building, its bow to cathedral architecture in the statues, panels, murals and bas-reliefs placed close to intimate eye level, decorative elements repeated more modishly in recent westward extensions of the center. To a New Yorker of the late 1970s, parklets, benches and broad ledges for lunching, and sculpture in skyscraper at-

riums have become accustomed pleasures. It was Rockefeller
Center's Channel Gardens, the attractive sunken skating rink,
the cafe tables and clusters of shops that first introduced the
urban townlet, the place for a half-hour vacation, for calm
staring, for recollecting the leisured welcome of European
plazas.

The presence of foreign buildings and their shops in
Rockefeller Center—an English building; a French building
carrying the lovely robust figures of Janniot; an Italian building which bears the same bronze vine and grain that Manzu
designed for a door to St. Peter's in Rome (a subtle gesture
of kinship, it might seem, with St. Patrick's across the Avenue)
may have been the invitation for the foreign shops and airline
offices that surround the center. The predominant accent is
Italian, the Italian of merchant princes, like the ancient silk
merchants of Lucca and the goldsmith-bankers of Lombardy,
now come to show their treasures in a small market already
comprised of the best and most costly shops in the city. Like
the old traders, some of the new have settled into shades of
older palazzi. Lower Gucci lives in a hauteur of exquisite silks
and princely leathers set into a corner that once belonged to
William Rockefeller, he who provided that his fifty grandchildren would be millionaires by 1950. Upper Gucci occupies a
place left by a Dodge who had a firm hold on Mexican copper
for a while. The Buccellati, of the via Condotti in Rome, installed their baroque jewelry where in 1928 Vincent Astor
tacked a new dining room onto his father's honored hotel, the
St. Regis, now the St. Regis Sheraton. Alitalia sits squarely in
Vanderbilt country. Rizzoli placed its books and records in
good-looking Italian functionalism encased in the remains of
a Gallic confection with swinging festoons that was built for
Cartier's in 1907. There are others and more to come, very
likely, as long as expensive Italian equates with exclusive chic,
as it has on and off for centuries. A number of non-Italians sit

in stately shadows as well: Air France in the empty shell of the Criterion Club, in its day dressed in brick and white stone and a pillared portico; Eastern Airlines on a Harkness site; the chirping cards and cheery party dishes of the Hallmark Gallery was once the royal court of Sir Joseph Duveen; Tiffany's of the enchanting windows and the conservatism roaring from boxed space bought of the *New York Times*, is haunted by the twice-Huntingtoned Arabella.

The old frills and arabesques banished by the shops still dance in the sky. From the ledge near the fountain of the distinguished Corning Glass Building they compose a particular New York view, not as dramatic as the skyline from Brooklyn nor the God's eye view from the Empire State or the World Trade Center towers; nevertheless indigenous, unexpected and engaging: an enormous green cornice, the copper green of a French roof with surging popeyed windows and, at the crest of the slope, a lonely little gazebo. Then, a potpourri of Italianate tower, Tudor chimneys, oriel windows held together by an immense potcover. The nineteenth-century scene pauses for a long endless shaft of modern darkened glass then returns to the furbelows on the roof of the Plaza Hotel, lording it over fountained space, a relic of a luxurious expansive time and reminder of Cornelius Vanderbilt who turned his back on its immodest female statue. Few Vanderbilts, once rich grist for reporters, now reach the news. Gloria Vanderbilt, in her childhood the center of a long custody suit dripping salacious details, and subsequently married very young—though already once divorced—to the conductor, Leopold Stokowski, then in his sixties, reappears as a designer, mainly of household textiles. In the fall of 1976 Saks Fifth Avenue, taking on like many large shops the artistic and cause fetes that once belonged to hotels, staged an exhibition of her works, the proceeds of admission tickets to help the invaluable Museum of the City of New York. Another Vanderbilt, Cornelius IV, made the obit pages on July 8, 1974. The lengthy feature reviewed his immediate ancestry—son of Cornelius II and Grace Wilson Vanderbilt and grandson of Alice Gwynne Vanderbilt—and his rebellion, choosing to make his life of journalism, publishing and writing books. One of them, *Farewell to Fifth Avenue,* cut him out of the Social Register and sent him back to the social ignominy of his great-great-grandfather, the Commodore. Alfred Gwynne Vanderbilt, the owner of famous racing stables and their legendary horses, resigned as chairman of the board of the New York Racing Association in 1977.

In the spring of 1976 two moviegoers searching to sweeten a rueful French film dashed across Fifty-eighth Street to the newsstand of the Plaza for candy. No Chunkies, no M&Ms, no Almond Joys, no Fruit and Nuts in sight, and the childish avidity soured to childish heartbreak. The man behind the counter said, "Wait," went to a secret cache and brought out a small heap of assorted goodies. "I have to hide them," he said, "too many people rip 'em off."

This the fabled, courtly, abundant urban garden whose trees were gold, the fruits rubies? Guidance counselor to kings and tycoons, to duchesses and princes authentic and inauthentic? The great landmark—with a plaque to prove it—as capable of invasion, as vulnerable as a poor little grocery store? Why not? The Plaza's longevity (seventy in 1977 and, for New York, as old as Notre Dame) is a history of adjustment to the times and their ills mutable and immutable.

Whatever remained of conservative resistance, the Curia of old ladies kept alive almost forever by the restorative airs and services of the hotel, died off. With Prohibition the favorite oasis, the Oak Room Bar, sobered to stockbroker's office, and the charming Rose Room went into auto sales. With relief from Prohibition, the Oak Bar was resurrected and the Rose Room changed to the Persian Room, unusually durable as a night boîte of star performers. The Palm Court refurbished itself and brought in an appealing and popular combination of Edwardian ruffles and Viennese schmaltz.

The 1930s Depression seriously marred one basic Plaza characteristic, the manorial suites. The rentals were prohibitive, spacious empty apartments elsewhere were going for considerably less and there were, again, large pools of unemployed servants eager to work in them. Many of the suites were cut into single rooms and that opened the Plaza to a different clientele, more frequently transient and middle class, for whom the hotel represented a rare step into luxury or a permissive expense account. The old obstreperous queens and princesses were replaced by Elizabeth Taylor and Zsa Zsa Gabor, who married Hiltons, later controllers of the hotel. With each change, the Plaza shrugged and submitted to what was making the world turn that day. In the 1950s it celebrated wise-eyed, six-year-old Eloise, a concoction built of an entertainer's repertoire and sunbursts of publicity, the best stunt an "Eloise" room, set aside and decorated by the hotel as if she were truly a legendary figure—Alice in Wonderland perhaps. In early 1964 came the Beatles, when they owned the world and all its young. Although the reservation was made in a false name, well-disseminated advance whispers churned up masses of ululating youngsters trying to charge the police barricades at the entrance. The next year, a blonde film star, all French, all breasts, pout and public-relations men, came to stay in the enormous suite once used by Anna Gould. Through those years, the Plaza was threatened with extinction, to be replaced by office buildings. But it was rescued by the Municipal Art Society and other experts who designated it a landmark.

Long gone is the intense, personal supervision of Harry Black and Ben Beniecke; far-flung, impersonal Western International Hotels has taken on their cares. Gone are most of the room decorations of Hardenburgh and Elsie de Wolfe, the Guggenheims and Frank Lloyd Wright. And would the Goulds have ventured into the popular restaurant, Trader Vic's, or stand on line for Sunday brunch in the Palm Court, or permit their children to wander in a lobby crowded with the hearty accents of Chicago, Broken Bow, Oklahoma and the *souks* of Tangiers? And would their children, bound to nannies and governesses, have swiped packets of Lifesavers and bubble gum?

John Jacob Astor's and son Vincent's St. Regis is now the St. Regis Sheraton, its King Cole Room brought in from the old Knickerbocker Hotel downtown and still playfully muraled, the Caen stone Colonel Astor required still on the lobby floor and the staircases. Some of the Waterford crystal chandeliers and the original fireplaces adorn a good number of suites, the revolving doors retain their rich bronze patina under graceful metalwork runs and trills, and the glass cab call box in its bands of bronze has become a rare antique, the only one of its kind in the city. Not all the chinoiserie, the lacquer tables, the plasterwork pediments over doors and period wall paintings and furniture in several of the commodious and most expensive suites date from 1904, but are careful replacements. In spite of its distinctions, the hotel finds it necessary to expand its trade with fashion brunches attended by the designers, as well as an advertising campaign that stresses the "kingly" quality of the hotel and its antiquity, ergo exclusivity; but it seems unlikely that it will ever again be exclusive to the same degree that brought out the gold-plated Tiffany service when an Astor client-friend arranged an especially elegant bash.

The Pierre? J. Paul Getty, who had paid two and a half million dollars for the hotel in 1938, made a tenfold gain on his investment by selling apartments on a cooperative arrangement, leaving space for restaurants and accommodations for transients. The Pierre perked up, its roof a favorite place for stylish weddings in the 1960s, and continued to thrive under new lessees who took over in 1967. In 1973, the British-based Trust Houses Forte Corporation, in control of several leading

European hotels, took over. The roof has been closed for a
number of years, its functions taken over by other public rooms.
The Pierre very little resembles Charles Pierre's hotel except
as an elderly unit in a strip of ornamental skyline and a place
with a reputation for reliable cuisine.

For many years, Avenue strollers, watching for a glimpse
of millionaire emerging from J. P. Morgan's Metropolitan Club
on Sixtieth Street, or a movie star from the Hotel Pierre, found
their eavesdropping eyes stopped by a high fence topped by
trees that held the corner of Sixty-first Street and continued
deep into the street. The leisured starer might have looked up
at the windows of the enclosed house, 800 Fifth, and in the
silent, shuttered rows, find one open, a curtain blowing, a sil-
houette passing. These might be the figures of two women care-
takers or a guard. No one else had steadily inhabited the house,
set on an extraordinarily valuable strip of land (in close proxim-
ity to the Plaza, the Sherry Netherland, Bergdorf Goodman's,
elderly clubs and Central Park) for almost fifty years. The plain
Georgian house was built late in the development of Millionaire's Row, 1922, by Ethel Geraldine Rockefeller Dodge, the
niece of John D. Rockefeller and the wife of Marcellus Hartley
Dodge, the grandson of the man who established the Reming-
ton Arms Company. It was one of the most expensive pieds-à-
terre extant; the Dodges preferred to live on an estate in New
Jersey that gave them the space they needed for dog breeding
and their annual dog show. Although the thirty-five-room house
was rarely used, Mrs. Dodge kept buying and demolishing surrounding properties for yard room to exercise the dogs she
meant to keep in the kennels on the fifth floor but the dogs
also lived there infrequently. Neither dogs, except for one
who was companion to the caretaker, nor Mrs. Dodge came
to Fifth Avenue at all after the mid-1950s. Mr. Dodge died
in 1963. Shortly before his death his wife was adjudged mentally incompetent and became the ward of a trust company

that took care of her property until her death in 1973 at the age of ninety-one. The dozens of dogs continued to flourish on prime beef that cost fifty thousand dollars a year, and so did the trees and bushes in the Sixty-first Street jungle.

In the spring of 1975 the *New York Times* turned a small battery of reporters architectural, financial, and editorial onto news of the prospective sale of the "mysterious" Dodge site for ten million dollars. It was sold to real estate developers, the paper reported, for something less (eight to nine million) and raised a welter of plans, counterplans, murmurs of disappointment and voluble protest; projects designed and redesigned, frequent noisy meetings with influential neighbors and zoning boards—the sort of small storm that had not swept Fifth Avenue since Frank Lloyd Wright fought for his version of the Guggenheim Museum. There was a complexity of problems to consider (typical of New York with its helter-skelter, patchwork development) in building on the most desirable spot in the city: satisfying the regulations of the several sets of zoning agencies that controlled different parts of the block, and proving the impossible, that a thirty-three-story apartment building equipped with a large parking garage would not altogether immobilize the traffic on streets that could bear no more. Aesthetically, would the proposed building harmonize with the ornamental skyline etched by its neighbors, would its frontage live easily with surrounding façades? Plans were adjusted and, more importantly, zoning regulations, as they had been before and will be again; no investor in buildings spends millions without the knowledge that boards are sensible businessmen and their dicta pliable. Whatever eventually rises to thicken the open, loose area, Central Park will gain. According to a recent ruling, developers in the region must, in exchange for design concessions permitted them, donate a sum for the improvement of the park. Thus, dead Mrs. Dodge, who probably never entered the park and rarely looked at it, becomes by a remote, legalistic thread a donor of new zoo cages, a stand of young trees or revived grass patches of Olmsted and Vaux's memorable Greensward.

The Roaring Twenties meant, for the middle and working classes, the skinny flapper in the skinny dress and the sexiness of stocking rolled just above the knee; it meant a hip flask of bathtub gin, it meant Pola Negri and Valentino, Peaches Browning and Lindbergh. For those with money it meant a wild market when gold seemed to rush out of the ground like oil, according to foreign visitors. With Andrew Mellon, sponsored by Henry Frick, as secretary of the treasury, interpretations of the tax laws relieved the burdens on the very rich. Mellon himself managed a substantial tax refund and saw to it that U. S. Steel was refunded twenty-seven million dollars. Inside information from the top gave financiers the opportunity to buy aviation stock, as important as railroad stock had once been, in large lots at much lower prices than the general public paid. The families of influential bankers and directors of monopolies were finding ways to spend the money which came in faster than it could be used. The obvious was more yachts, more cars, more jewels, more estates and houses. One artistic gesture was a hundred-thousand-dollar theater to house amateur performances that took place no more than five or six times a year. According to European observers, the almost universal occupation of the rich was drinking. An art dealer, looking around at his prospective clients, became speechless; all he could say about alcoholism among the upper class was that it was beyond anything one could imagine. He found himself suffocating in fumes of alcohol during art sales and saw flasks in every hand at a funeral. Several wealthy women of his acquaintance died of alcoholism. The young drank as well but managed to wear some of it off by energetic dancing, introduced earlier by Vernon and Irene Castle, in hotels and nightclubs.

When the boom of speculation fell apart in the fall of

1929, it was usually the smaller speculator who was ruined.
By the winter of 1929, the most exclusive restaurants were
crowded; the theaters played to full houses; new limousines as
well as the vintage Rolls Royces rolled down Fifth Avenue;
dealers in antiquities, authentic period furnishings and paintings were thriving. It was at this time and in the immediately
ensuing years that Jules Bache, for one, collected some of his
most valuable paintings. Rentals on Fifth Avenue were one
to two thousand dollars a room and apartment furnishings
averaged one hundred thousand dollars, sometimes exclusive
of bathrooms fitted with semiprecious stones and gold. (An historian mentions a tub made of one chunk of onyx that cost
twelve thousand dollars.) Within the space of a few blocks in
the Forties and Fifties on Fifth Avenue there were three shops
that supplied Old English silver, two that sold imported French
lingerie and linens, the French *bottier* Pinet, an English company of custom-made boots and shoes, several exclusive tailors,
two noted furriers, the toys of F.A.O. Schwarz, objects from
Imperial Russia, and at least ten jewelers, all survivors of the
crash and functioning in 1934. Private railroad cars whose
average cost was one hundred thousand dollars were still in
use; the Vanderbilts maintained a dozen yachts. One of Woolworth's daughters, Jessie Woolworth Donohue, found comfort
in her matchless collection of emeralds and a seventy-five-
thousand-dollar sable coat as she watched her husband gamble
away not quite one million dollars in less than a year. One
thousand guests were invited to the debut of her niece, Barbara
Hutton, at the Ritz Carlton. Two cases of champagne were
provided for each guest and part of the decor devised by a
leading designer consisted of over five thousand dollars' worth
of flowers. The total cost of Barbara's coming out was one
hundred thousand dollars, a sum that would have bought a
good many Depression apples and apple stands from New
York's streets.

Some of Barbara's peers felt pinched, for real or imagined

reasons. Jules Bache's granddaughter, Muriel Richards, tried to become a model as some of her friends did, while others endorsed cold cream and cigarettes. Mrs. W. K. Vanderbilt, Sr., earned five thousand dollars for extolling the virtues of a bed. A number of society women had gone into the business of selling the clothing their husbands had paid for; one descendant of the Whitneys became a nightclub singer. Poverty was rarely the cause of this blossoming of female enterprise. It may have been a question of debts the women did not want their men to know about, but probably also stemmed from a wish to join a broader and more amusing world than the one into which they were born.

Directories of 1933 and '34 list Jules Bache still at 814. Those were years when his neighbors were gone and going, their Millionaire's Row, which had changed its part of the city from desultory to breathtaking, reduced mainly to apartment houses. These had their own splendors, triplexes and roof gardens, paintings, tapestries and servants and, when it leaked out, drama. Monied lives were much less public property; fashion and high-life magazines were occasionally given a well-rehearsed short scene, but that was all. Except for the descendant of 840, John Jacob Astor VI, who spent much of his life in the newspapers. The fact that he took a nine-to-five job was news; that he quit shortly because working left too little time for fun was news. His attempts to get more money out of Vincent were news. When he was young, John's mother had enriched the tabloids with mouth-watering stories. When she lost 840 Fifth, the compensation was marriage to the wealthy William Dick. She divorced him when she was forty for love of a poor and handsome Italian prizefighter, aged twenty-six and also married. After the necessary arrangements were made in Italy and New York, Madeleine and Enzo Fiermonte were married. The bizarre marriage, a cornucopia of tabloid fodder, ended in divorce five years later but that did not put a stop to the publicity they both liked and needed since they were fairly broke. Enzo told all about the marriage in articles for a true-confessions magazine and tried his hand at moviemaking—again all about his romantic marriage—but one of his stars, Madeleine, died in 1940 and the project with her.

A few years earlier, in the thirties, John Jacob had reached his majority and the five million dollars left by his father. The limelight became his, beamed on his Newport cottage, his long row of new cars, the twenty-five servants he kept in his house at Ninety-first Street, immediately east of Fifth Avenue. The limelight rarely left him; he was *the* playboy with a marked talent for trouble with women, induced by what is most kindly called "naiveté." He married; he divorced; he was married again in 1946 to Gertrude Gretsch, one of the characters in an incredible marital and legal jumble that cost many thousands of dollars to resolve, and then peculiarly. When John was over forty, separated from Gertrude and ready for love, he met Dolly Fullman. Without Gertrude's consent he got a divorce decree in Mexico and rushed Dolly to Gretna Green so that they might be married as fast as possible. Dolly was a grievous disappointment and the marriage lasted little more than a month. She asked for support on a legal separation; he countered, following Gertrude's argument, that there had been no marriage since the Mexican divorce was not legal. But, it was ruled, Dolly was not culpable while John J. was and therefore he had to pay her legal fees and was responsible for supporting her modestly. Gertrude and her daughter by Astor were allotted millionaire sums, three thousand five hundred dollars a month for support.

Who was his wife, though? The question went from court to court to Supreme Court. The common judgment said both women were Mrs. John Jacob Astor and he a bigamist until Gertrude, no longer amused, divorced him. But Dolly was still his wife in some states and not in others, mainly because of different property rights laws, and he was forced to live a bachelor in the apartment he had taken at 998 Fifth Avenue. Now and then he tilted against Vincent's will, claiming his brother was insane. He managed to squeeze a pittance out of the Astor Foundation, and after many years resigned himself to a worth of thirty million dollars rather than the many more he felt were his due.

McKim and Mead's 998, considered the finest apartment building in New York, in which Murry Guggenheim also chose to live, left a number of 1910-style badges of distinction on apartment houses. They still wear iron and glass canopies, volutes, shields and sculptured heads in one combination or another; they bulge at one section, recede under pediments at another; the vast lobbies are based on Vespasian's shining marble halls. The younger houses, however, indulge themselves in a canvas canopy or none and seem to come out of the same flat, dignified mold. Of the town houses left a few are derelict and threatened with demolition, or changed from private to public service, or, as in the side streets, cut into apartments. The pleasing curve, graced by putti, masks and ladies, of the Payne Whitney house at 972 is now used by the French Cultural Services. The house of Señor Carlos de Heredia at 973 belongs, ornate door and all, to the Eastern States Mission of Latter-day Saints. Under the festoons and plasterwork gaiety of 854, bought by Mrs. Henry White, one of the daughters of William H. Vanderbilt, a sign that says "Socialist Federal Republic of Jugoslavia." At the south corner of Sixty-fifth Street, there lived in 1918 William Watts Sherman, two houses away from William Guggenheim and Frank Gould. The Union of American Hebrew Congregations now holds the corner. The Heart House of the New York Heart Association, at the south corner of Sixty-fourth Street, occupies the place once owned by Edward J. Berwind, the coal magnate and a noted collector. The Knickerbocker Club at Sixty-second Street holds to the structure it had built in 1915.

And on it goes, in the same style northward on the Avenue: the American Irish Historical Society at 991, where Daniel

Crawford Clark lived side by side with Frank W. Woolworth and his daughters. Across from the Metropolitan Museum next to the Benjamin Duke house (unique in that it is tenanted in part by a member of the Duke family) an apartment house that swarms with 16th Arrondissement Paris detail. Then, the Goethe House, and the unexpected Stanhope Hotel, whose outdoor cafe adds to the animation around the museum. Up the street at 1026, 27 and 28, is Marymount School, once a row of private houses that shared a style of bowed windows and metal balconies, thick cornice teeth and forbidding doors barred with swings and swags of metal. The National Academy of Design is at 1083, the address in 1918 of Archer M. Huntington, son of Arabella and adopted son of Collis. The adjacent house, 1082, belonged to a Gould. At the corner of Eighty-sixth Street, the massive house in a non-style called "French Classic Eclectic" that was built by Carrère and Hastings in 1914 for William Starr Miller, in 1944 the residence of Mrs. Cornelius Vanderbilt. When she died in 1953 the property was bought by the present tenant, the Yivo Institute for Jewish Research (a few Vanderbilt houses have had unusual destinies; one to the Jugoslavs, one to the Jews, one on East Sixty-third Street bought and lived in by Gypsy Rose Lee). Otto Kahn's ineffably dignified Italian Renaissance landmark palace at Ninety-first Street is now the property of the Society of the Sacred Heart; the Warburg house continues to function as the Jewish Museum. In 1976 the Carnegie Mansion became part of the Smithsonian Institution as the Cooper-Hewitt Museum, an encyclopedic and wittily displayed collection of fabrics, wallpapers, furniture, fashion prints, birdcages, keys and locks, ornaments, tools, needlework, ceramics, architectural drawings and a wealth of allied material in the decorative arts accumulated by the granddaughters of Peter Cooper and originally installed as part of his Cooper Union, downtown.

At the corner of Ninety-fourth Street, a red brick Georgian

house with black shutters announces itself as the International Center of Photography, an institution opened in late 1974 with plans to be not only repository and display ground, but a teaching center with workshops, lectures and meetings of photographers, illustrators and people working in tangential fields; in short, to have photography fully recognized as a major art. In spite of necessary changes, the center maintains some of the spaciousness of the town house built in 1915 for Willard Straight, financier, acting chief of the Far Eastern Affairs section of the State Department and later adviser to American financial interests in China. Straight was well connected: his wife was the daughter of William C. Whitney, the sister of Harry Payne Whitney and consequently the sister-in-law of Gertrude Vanderbilt Whitney. Among them, they created two liberal entities: the Straights founded the *New Republic* and subsidized it for decades while Gertrude Vanderbilt Whitney established an influential showcase of American art, the Whitney Museum.

After Straight died in 1918, the house went to Elbert Gary, one of the heads of U.S. Steel, and later became the property of Mona Williams, the best of the "Best Dressed," exotic and independent, very attractive to society-page editors. When Mona was growing up in Kentucky during World War I, opportunities for advancement for bright, ambitious girls were few unless they were fairly well educated, and her horse trainer father hadn't much use for educating girls. She found a quicker way to advance herself by marrying at eighteen a rich Milwaukee German and within a few years divorcing him. He gave her two hundred thousand dollars; she gave him their son and shortly thereafter married a supremely good-looking Manhattan banker, James Irving Bush, whose means helped launch her on an inventive and unremittingly conspicuous career. This marriage lasted no longer than the first. Mona then became the wife of middle-aged Harrison Williams, the gentleman friend of one of her lady friends, who had become

superrich on public utilities. Traveling between New York and
Long Island and their estate in Palm Beach, Mona Williams
entertained generously and cleverly, surrounding herself with
the bright people of cafe society. She had her portrait painted
by Dali who was smitten with her strange blue-green eyes and
her delicate other-world quality. The English accent she acquired on trips abroad, her distinctive taste in house furnishings, in clothing and jewelry won her supremacy as a leader of
fashion and the role of heroine in a popular novel of her time.
The Sunday rotogravure sections never neglected her and rarely
forgot to mention that she had one of the most valuable collections of emeralds in the United States. The quiet, hard-
working husband, one of the richest men in the world, whose
money created this total work of art, died in 1953 at the age
of eighty. Mona then acquired the one thing her life had
lacked, a title. She married Count Eduard von Bismarck and
her former town house became the New York seat of the
Audubon Society. After the society left, the house led a dusty,
near-derelict existence until photography rescued its good pro-
portions and oriel windows.

At 104th Street is the Museum of the City of New York,
a flexible institution that plays several roles. As community
center it flings out a great red banner to warn its neighborhood against VD; as entertainment center it stages concerts
for adults and puppet shows and "Please touch" exhibitions
for children; as historian it arranges an informative "Cityrama"
that explores all the ages of New York; as remarkable collection it displays skillfully New York matter, from Dutch soldiers
guarding their port, to the Duncan Phyfe furniture and Rembrandt Peal portrait in an early-nineteenth-century drawing
room, to a beguilingly preposterous picture of the Crystal
Palace worked in oil on glass with mother-of-pearl inserts. A
photograph of an opium den of the 1880s; an earlier lithograph
of a group of prostitutes who, in their bonnets and shawls,
look like girls designed by Jane Austen; a dolls' house of the

mid-nineteenth century modeled on the Goelet house that stood at Nineteenth Street and Broadway; an architect's model—furniture, paintings, beautifully dressed family and all—of the Frick mansion library; an expensive collection of toys, photographs, engravings and books—in short, a fine and affectionate gathering that documents, it would seem, every breath the city takes.

Early in the nineteenth century Eighty-seventh to Ninety-sixth streets was called the Harlem Commons; at about Ninety-first Street a hilly stretch which rose quite high (consequently called Observatory Hill) spilled a creek now contained as the Harlem Meer at the northern end of Central Park. The creek fed the Benson Farm, along Fifth Avenue from Ninety-sixth to 121st Street, supplying locals with fishing and rowing as it meandered into the Harlem River. The one height left untouched in the progressive leveling of the city was the rocky mound long known as Mount Morris, now Garvey Park, in Dutch days called Snake Hill for obvious reasons and still spired by a fire beacon, the last in the city. An early settlement, as the Dutch name indicates, of a mixed population including Negroes, Harlem was New York's first suburb, served by Hudson River boats, by horse-drawn trams and, toward the end of the nineteenth century, by elevated trains. Before the easy accessibility (though it had decent roads, farms and respectable houses, and the earliest public library) remote Harlem developed a whispered fame for sporting houses, the most notorious the "Red House" whose owners battened on blackmailing vulnerable and prosperous citizens, like Cornelius W. Lawrence, Mayor of New York in 1834 and 1835. There were those who saw Harlem growing swiftly while the high hills southward stayed barren; as for the land to the north, that would not be developed for centuries. The optimistic yet wary city watchers hoped for great improvements, especially after the opening of Central Park. "New boulevards and avenues north of the Park will be magnificent someday, if New York not be swindled to death."

As every New Yorker knows, the swindling neither stopped nor killed the city or Harlem. In spite of noxious Goatville, an Irish squatter settlement at the northern edge of Central Park, the end of the nineteenth century saw spacious, costly houses— one row built by McKim, Mead and White—springing up in Harlem, mostly for white owners. A photo taken in 1905 shows Temple Israel at the corner of 125th Street and Fifth Avenue and next to it, the Harlem YMCA. Neighboring the houses on 125th Street near Fifth, were the beginnings of Harlem's main shopping center and musical entertainment at Oscar Hammerstein's Harlem Opera House. Shortly after came hordes of blacks, from the South, from the Middle West, from the slums of New York: Black Bohemia on the far west side of midtown, San Juan Hill in the West Sixties and in the Nineties, around Columbus and Amsterdam avenues. White reaction to the influx of blacks was divided between renting them apartments at highly profitable rates and holding on until they were later forced out, with the help of shrewd real estate agents, by collapsing values, the worth of a house not much greater than the moving costs.

By 1915, the section of Fifth Avenue leading into Harlem had been abandoned. A report published that year speaks of Carnegie (Observatory) Hill at Ninety-first Street as tenements, empty lots defaced with billboards and thriving saloons which replaced a number of well-built earlier houses. For several blocks around and beyond Mount Morris Park and lining Fifth Avenue near 125th Street were solid, neatly ornamented houses. Beyond, tenements again, "swarming, from 127th to 139th with foreigners and negroes," and, according to the report, dirty lots and runnels of garbage flowing toward the Harlem River. The great showcases for white audiences lured by the hot, novel, seductive and socially forbidden, were Small's at 135th Street on Fifth, Connie's Inn and, most famous of all, the Cotton Club, whose policy dictated no overly black blacks in either audience or chorus line; a deep gold tinge was about enough.

Above the voices that sang the blues and the "race" songs that created a thriving record industry, soared the voices of black poets, Claude McKay and Countee Cullen keening black agony, Langston Hughes singing the same tunes more wittily. They were encouraged and sponsored by older writers, like W. E. B. Du Bois and James Weldon Johnson whose anthology of American Negro Poetry spread their voices far beyond Harlem. They found material and inspiration in the Schomburg Collection, the largest gathering of material concerning the Negro in the United States now housed in the Countee Cullen Branch of the Public Library and an unexpected assist from Carl van Vechten whose *Nigger Heaven* introduced to the white world a version of the black quite different from the accustomed stereotype.

Throughout these years and before, from the time Harlem had become a cohesive community, there were steady blasts of protest: against lynching, against discriminatory schooling, against Jim Crow restrictions, against the Klan, against the menial jobs open to blacks. As early as July, 1917, Harlem's sense of mission was strong enough to stage one of the most impressive Fifth Avenue parades of the myriad that have enlivened or bored the Avenue. In the course of a race riot earlier in the month, whites in East St. Louis had, while driving thousands of Negroes from their homes, maimed, killed and lynched about two hundred of them. In response, Harlem's intellectuals organized and led off a silent parade of fifteen thousand people, not a sound but the low throb of funeral drums, nor a word spoken except by accusing placards.

New and exceedingly alluring propaganda took much of Harlem with the advent of the West Indian, Marcus Garvey, and his Back to Africa movement: blacks to respond and be responsible to blacks only in a black world; there was nothing for the black in a white man's world. Garvey inspirited countless blacks and collected immense sums of money from them for his organization and the ships for his Africa-bound convoys.

He loved bombast and had a developed sense of theater. For the religious, he staged an awesome ceremony in 1924 that recreated Christ as the universal suffering black man and Mary as the black Mater Dolorosa. For the most devoted and worshipful, he created a court on whose nobles he conferred high-sounding, exotic orders, in the style of Cristophe of Haiti. For his enemies, including the NAACP, who thought that the field of black progress was and should be the United States, damning polemics in his popular newspaper, the *Negro World*. He became quite rich, suspect, and was arrested for using the mails to defraud. His bookkeeping was found to be exceedingly careless and one of his ships unseaworthy. He was jailed and then deported.

Although Garvey had stimulated a great interest, especially among writers and artists, in African backgrounds and an evolving respect for their ancestry, he had both disappointed and divided Harlem. The Harlem Renaissance began to fade and although the Savoy Ballroom still glittered and the great choirs still rang out and Langston Hughes spoke his sharp pieces and Harlem publications issued protest, the divisiveness created by the Garvey movement and the grinding poverty of the Depression turned off the brilliant light.

One of the last witnesses and participants of the Harlem Renaissance, Lewis H. Michaux, died in 1976 at the age of ninety-two. For forty-four years he ran a Harlem bookshop that was a meeting place for black writers. His stock of books, grown from a dozen to two hundred thousand, by and about blacks primarily, was a valued adjunct to the Schomburg Collection. From his window at 1270 Fifth Avenue he observed the rise and fall of his neighborhood, the high-stooped houses become hungry, cramped tenements, windows broken and toilets dead and stinking. He heard noisy rent parties in apartments that lent themselves readily to prostitution. He felt the anger that marched on 125th Street in 1935 to destroy the shops of white

merchants and saw a recrudescence of pride in the establishment of the Studio Museum in Harlem.

Periodically there are announcements of rehabilitation
programs for Harlem with specific statistics of housing units,
school and hospital facilities, sums of money to be contributed
by the city, the state, the federal government. For over forty
years, there have been rosy dawns for Harlem that never quite
bring full day. In the meantime, grim houses continue deteri-
orating, the ambitious young leave, while the elderly, the
violent young and the listless young stay.

Those who can manage optimism draw magnificent arches
in the sky at 110th Street and Fifth Avenue which will be the
gateway to a new, grand Harlem. The present gateway is Arthur
A. Schomburg Plaza, twin octagonal towers of thirty-five stories,
a lower building east of these and, connecting them, a spacious
plaza of planters, wooden arcades, benches and trees. The building to the east houses the prestigious Northside Center for
Child Development conducted by Dr. Kenneth B. Clark and
Dr. Mamie Phipps Clark. Nearby, a less luxurious yet attractive new housing project.

Within a short distance, a vista of 1950s public housing,
monotonous and undignified; the closets had no doors, the
toilets had no seats, "instant slum" was stamped on the first row
of bricks. Beyond, a wasteland of empty lots and houses marked
for demolition. Those still inhabited display scabby, fat cats,
howling dogs in the windows and, in the front yards, mattresses,
discarded cabinet doors and piles of fallen brick and refuse. An
exquisitely delicate set of iron gates guards a deep yard of garbage and two well-fed large chickens. This was part of an area
that was to have undergone renewal but never did. At about
117th Street rehabilitation had begun but the money ran out
while the well-designed Canaan House, a middle-income project,
managed to get itself built and subsidized. From 118th Street
a surprising, lyrical view of Mount Morris Park and its old
watch tower. The rest is burned out, leaving here and there

vestiges of broad bay windows and good door ornaments. West of the park, on 122nd Street, a rather miraculous double row that keeps its houses as they were early in this century, comfortable, impeccably neat and decorative.

Above 125th Street, several side streets with well-kept brownstones and brownstone reminders on the Avenue, sometimes burned out, sometimes trying to hold themselves together around street-front churches. There are echoes of grandeur in the fine doors, the window detail and mansards of number 2080, which might be worth as much as $350,000, even in its poor condition, were it downtown. On 2066, masterful plasterwork and wood carving in a palatial door. Number 2100 repeats the flowing detail, the women's heads, the ironwork and immense lobby—this one totally wrecked—of 1915 apartment houses in the vicinity of the Metropolitan Museum. Much of the rest is despair and garbage until one comes to the middle-income projects that line the rest of Fifth Avenue.

Hardly a seductive neighborhood except for the Studio Museum at Harlem above the corner of 125th Street and Fifth Avenue. Number 2033 is a loft building that serves as a big, easy, disorganized studio for black painters and, downstairs, has two large exhibition rooms for the work of black artists on black themes, not limited to Harlem but gathered in Harlem, the spiritual capital of Black America.

Founded in 1968, sustained by the New York State Council for the Arts, the city and private gifts, the Studio Museum has become a vital community center. One month it shows the works of an Ethiopian painter; another month, the masks, ritual objects, instruments of Africa, felicitously displayed in an air of African music; a group show of Harlem artists in 1969; later a "Symbols" show by Benny Andrews and the accomplished prints and sculptures of Elizabeth Catlett. Two months were devoted to the Toussaint L'Ouverture series of Jacob Lawrence and a similar period for Joseph Delaney's work. There are exhibitions of remarkable photographs culled

from black centers all over the world and a ceaseless program
of concerts, lectures and films that explore the African and
Afro-American experience as folk medicine, as blues, as poetry.
To keep the pot boiling attractively, instruction at no charge
in the studio's Graphic Workshop, a steady flow of brochures
and catalogues and a quarterly newsletter that keeps the community informed of exhibitions of black interest in other parts
of the city.

The art frequently consists of angry posters and cartoons,
shouts of defiance charged with primitive strength and the
alluring and frightening patterns of voodoo. In one manner
or another, it usually harks back to Africa, particularly during
the Kwanza harvest and fertility celebration that runs from
December 26 through January 1. The purpose of the festival
is to instill in black youth pride in the richness of his heritage,
to give him the cultural roots from which he has for centuries
been severed. Whether the effort is fruitful or not is difficult to
know but the Studio Museum makes a lively, intelligent try
at it.

One additional seduction in the grim neighborhood: the
courtly old ladies and gentlemen who greet passersby with a
gracious nod and "Good morning, good morning" on their way
to church while their neighbors sleep.

CHAPTER 16

THE SCENE 1975–1977

In spite of what Ada Louise Huxtable, the architecture critic of the *New York Times*, justifiably called "the trashing of Fifth Avenue," citing clumps of ugly airline offices and the mediocrity of design placed over distinguished Beaux-Arts buildings and the spread of junk at dishonest prices, there are a few shreds of the distinctions that cause Fifth Avenue to be referred to, still, as "the finest street in the city." After a long pause the double-decker bus is back, in sparse numbers, but present. Celebrity-watching is still an important Fifth Avenue sport, as witness the gatherings at 1040 to catch a glimpse of Mrs. Jacqueline Kennedy Onassis. The Olympic Towers has foreign tenants who spend two million dollars on remodeling an apartment, as in the carefree old days. The Plaza conducts the venerable Debutante Assembly and New Year's Ball. The jeweler Bulgari, in the Hotel Pierre, occasionally sells emerald necklaces for two million dollars. Tiffany ranges the field, from comparatively inexpensive trinkets and watches to one diamond at a quarter-million dollars and, in a sequestered private place, jewels whose price, in these irritable times, is discreetly whispered.

Although the show of money and luxury hasn't abandoned the Avenue altogether, its presence becomes more sparse and may, in time, be totally erased. A number of large companies and airlines which considered a Fifth Avenue address indispensable to their image and well-being have been relocating on Park and Madison avenues, no mean streets by any measure, at half the rent they had formerly paid. In order to stay on Fifth and pay its enormous rentals, designers have—like apartment dwellers in similar circumstances—begun to share space. In spite of these comely international boutiques and accompanying attractions of the Fifties streets, anchored by Rockefeller Center to the south and the Plaza to the north, the newly emptied spaces may go the way of the Thirties and Forties, slipping into what is too politely called "tourist-oriented retail" goods. (The greatest wonder of these goods, other than their undeviating ugliness, is their capacity to pay incredible rentals. Where does the money come from? Or are all these innumerable stores actually segments of one vast multinational with factories in Hong Kong dedicated to the meretricious?) And whatever space calculators and china flowers don't use will undoubtedly be filled with the grinning bonhomie of quick hamburgers and fried potatoes, also exceedingly succesful enterprises to judge from their eagerness to pay Fifth Avenue rentals.

In some not too distant day Fifth Avenue may be a street of limited interest except for the pioneer skyscrapers to be studied as we now study Borromini churches, and for its handsome breadth and length (the whole much handsomer than the sum of its parts), hospitable to the all-purpose theater it is fast becoming. London has street entertainers and so do Paris and San Francisco. New York will have no less, though, than its most awesome avenue (erstwhile, if you like) laden with some of its most awesome institutions, for playground, rehearsal theater, circus, camp meeting tent, political forum, madhouse lawn, splendidly replete in almost all seasons with the tireless New York Scene.

New York expresses its immutable need for a densely filled

stage, away from which it feels abandoned, in a new, freed Fifth Avenue, closed to traffic from Thirty-fourth Street to Fifty-seventh on Sundays of the Christmas season. Given the lavish gift of the whole wide avenue to walk on, New Yorkers stroll as if it were May. The ambling starts at Altman's whose windows full of large animated storybook characters bewilder the littlest children distracted by the many people, the clarion voices of older brothers, the shiny balloons within balloons overhead, the forest of legs closing around them.

At Lord & Taylor's, the decorum of a roped line, proper to viewing a stylish show, sometimes nostalgic, always chic. One year the scheme was based on Christmas engravings of a century ago by Thomas Nast. The jolly fat Santa Claus, the fine velvet clothing of the little boys and their sisters, a creamy baby with lovely tendrils of hair, urged a return to an untroubled, plump time when life was upper middle class, steaming plum pudding, willing, careful servants and enchanting storybook children.

Wallowing in the pleasure of the wide street as if it were broad prairie, a group saunters toward the public library, its lions wreathed in greenery and big red bows. On the platform of the library, a group of young singers from Fordham University, led by a young man who has carefully studied the professional manners of TV announcers, clear voice, friendly smile and profound sincerity. The songs, all barbershop classics, are sung with good will and little style but the audience is eager to seem pleased.

Above Forty-second Street the Skatemobile, manned by good-natured young men. Using gray barrier trestles provided by the Police Department, the Skatemobile crew has blocked off a street to make a roller skating rink. The system is efficient and just. A child takes off his shoes, and standing on cold, shoeless pavement, hands them into the huge wagon and is given, in turn, a pair of high shoes with attached skates. The skate shoes are scuffed and streaked, the size is not always perfect, but the wheels roll. The intrepid adventurer starts at the top of the subtle slope, rolls down and stomps heavily up again, swooping and stomping repeated ad infinitum with a solemn air of conquest. There are the little girls who have to be supported by both parents, mewling, exclaiming, kicking daddy's ankle, yanking mommy's arm as the little body bends backward, bends forward, pulled by the unruly wheels. There is the faller-down who likes falling down, or maybe she thinks this is the way the game is played. She rises only to collapse willingly, eagerly; she is quite happy. And there is the small round mother encouraging her large son, a head taller than she, to skate. He clings, clasping and towering over her. She pushes a little. He clings. She begins to laugh and then he does and so they stand embracing, tears of laughter rolling down her face, he immobile with laughter and fear.

Up the street a dragon and a castle and the busy doings of a group of puppets, invisible to those of normal height because fathers have grown taller with children on their shoulders. Unable to see, one listens to voices; "Daddy, what's the man doing?" "You'll have a hamburger later," "If you don't leave Joey alone, I'll smack you," "Mary, where's Annie? I told you to hold on to her." Annie, who has dug her way forward among several big, hairy-sweatered backs, calls and signals her position among fathers explaining princesses and dwarfs to their staring young.

The Gothic portals of St. Patrick's frame a group of madrigal singers, who sing an unusual group of songs to an entranced audience. Across the street, in the arms of a Rockefeller Center doorway, a handsome Jamaican plays two steel drums softly, producing variations on a Xmas carol rich in rubatos and trills, as if it were transcribed by Chopin. St. Patrick's, in the meantime, has changed its madrigals for a group of middle-aged gentlemen in yellow Russian blouses who sing Slavic carols and liturgies. It is stately music, somberly beautiful and listened to in awe by solemn babies and their elders.

Down the sidewalk above Saks swoops a towheaded, red-bearded stout man on a bicycle, hell bent for something, heedless of the crowd which stops to stare at the unblinking large parrot on his shoulder and another on his handlebar. The thickets of people force him down a side street where he melts into the hordes streaming toward the Avenue. Saks has decided, again, to go for splendor, gallon bottles of perfume, fragile art nouveau fans, king's-ransom jewelry and, for extra show, small lady acrobats and dancers, silvery, sequined, as sinuous as Indian goddesses. The kids don't care much and the fathers allow themselves only one displeased look, but the women stay, immune to the cooing of other ladies mired behind them, "Please, other people want to see, too."

Across the street, almost total immobility in the crowd trying to look closely at the Rockefeller Center tree. Because they have been tactfully edged off the Avenue proper by comely young cops, the vendors of large inflatable footballs, the sellers of twisted zeppelin balloons and the pretzel and chestnut men gather here. Also discreetly whispered off the Avenue into the swaying mass, a group of eight-foot *fantoches*, with dark, grim papier-mâché heads and long burlap bodies hung with signs that cry the plight of Mexican labor in California.

A platform set between Fifty-fourth and Fifty-fifth streets thuds and bounces to the full bright skirts and swift feet of Polish-American folk dancers and the light point-and-step patterns of Irish dancers. Some of the kids like it, some don't. They have been looking for Mrs. Santa Claus, listed on the program sheet as one of the party's hostesses. A policeman with the broad-winged mustache of a Gay Nineties barber doesn't know where she is. His companion cop says, "She probably had a nervous breakdown in this crowd." The explanation doesn't satisfy the children, but distraction comes easily from balls and bodies flying in the air near Fifty-seventh Street where a basketball board and a trampoline have been set up to dizzy the broad windows of Doubleday's with unaccustomed reflections. Tiffany's jewel box windows are lost among tweed coats, serapes, Afghan cloaks, white, yellow and red wool caps and pompons and a high frieze of swaddled infants now as sleepily remote as Buddhas.

At four the entertainment folds up, automobile traffic begins to nose its way through the crowds reluctant to be penned on sidewalks. There they continue their bright parade of tall and short, in boots, moccasins, sandals, in winging capes and embroidered sheepskins, beards, cascades of hair, jackets like small zeppelins, serapes and ponchos, a few minks, a few greatcoats of slim waists and high collars designed by Beau Brummel, savoring the waning pleasures of this biggest and best of all block parties. (Late note: the party is still entertaining but the Fifth Avenue shops have decided to stay open those Sundays and the atmosphere is less intimate and carefree.)

Another opportunity for warm, cozy crowding combined with staring are the parades that absorb numerous weekends from spring into fall—in spite of discomfort and protests and the prodigious costs of cleaning up after parades—to a degree that the Fifth Avenue Association calls "nightmarish." St. Patrick's Day, the Easter Parade—less parade than milling around in rococo hats—and military parades lead off. The Germans then begin to whirl and march on their Steuben Day. Jews come out in dedicated numbers on Israeli Day; Latins march and dance for Christopher Columbus as do the Italians. Contagious rhythms spice up the Avenue on Puerto Rican Day. The Greeks propel their classical floats and emphatic music on their special day and in early October the Polish thump and twirl. Hare Krishna followers pull their tall, bright chariots down the Avenue, and a less brilliant group that wants marijuana altogether legalized oozes down the same path.

During the course of one of its annual conventions the

Veterans of Foreign Wars, which meets in August, decided to hold its twenty-thousand-strong parade late on a Tuesday night, rousing with its bands, drums and high spirits hundreds of irate citizens who let the police know just how angry they were. The defense was that "This is good, clean Americana" and only the Russian embassy would be expected to complain about a parade that carried two thousand American flags. Almost every organization with a cause to protest or celebrate or, as the Rolling Stones did, to advertise, feels it has a right to the Avenue. In response to complaints from shops and from Fifth Avenue apartment owners who object to the noise, the mess left on their streets, and the deterioration of the value of their property as undesirable, the Fifth Avenue Association has been campaigning for parades to be limited to the stretch from Fourteenth Street to Fifty-seventh and to be held only on Sundays. It has been a long, weary battle, nowhere near won and possibly never to be won as long as there exist the large ethnic groups that make up the city and the blocs of voters they represent.

More decorous entertainment is supplied by the big shops to celebrate their birthdays with clowns, music, games, handicrafts demonstrations. Or, they arrange celebrity parties, or hold black-tie suppers to introduce a refurbished department, or stage a revival of street games to sell a book of echt-nostalgia to children who have no streets to play on. They support city causes, singing the praises of the Big Apple and its cultural centers in their newspaper ads. When Italian week, which seems to be shaping up as an annual, comes around, it brings Sicilian carts and Renaissance wedding processions; Botticelli Primaveras who speak flowers and the agonized Adam and Eve of Masaccio who weep over the gloves, sweaters, shoes, scarves and boxes brought from la bell'Italia.

The busiest and most Protean of nonstop theaters and playgrounds, in spite of its myriad faults from dirt to gambling to violence, is Central Park, no more finished than it was one hundred years ago, always open to depredation and improvement. Enthusiasm for popular sports introduced tennis and baseball to the park shortly before World War I. In the 1920s scallops of park edge were furnished with the slides and swings of playgrounds. Essential as these were, they dried up strips of lawn, unrooted trees, obliterated remaining bits of lyricism. It was not until the Depression of the 1930s that the park came to fresh life. Echoing its origins, it took on large numbers of the unemployed, supervised by the Civil Works Administration and the Works Progress Administration. The sheep left their meadow and their shelter, built in 1870, became the Tavern on the Green restaurant. Part of the lake disappeared, old structures were razed, wildfowl were lured to the pond to wade among pelicans and swans. The hovels of squatters whose "Hoovervilles" filled the empty old reservoir were cleaned out as they had been eighty years earlier. The Mall, where children once rode in goat carts, became the open hall for WPA concerts of unemployed musicians, for folk dancing exhibitions and free-form styles of dancing on summer evenings. Behind the Arsenal there grew a plaza flanked by new Zoo buildings to replace the unsafe cages that once required armed guards. A short distance north of the Arsenal, there later came the Children's Zoo, as sweet as penny candy.

Periodically, a shocking event—attacks on the Zoo's frail deer, for instance—brings on waves of reexamination and reform. Animal lovers, appalled at the tight cages of the larger animals, insist that they be sent to the Bronx Zoo and that all zoos be phased out eventually. Someone thinks well of one large area for societies of small animals; another prefers a butterfly forest in an enormous landscaped room or the iridescence of tropical fish in large tanks. Everyone has an opinion on what to do with the park. Almost always, among complaints and projected reforms, are calls for revival of the Olmsted-Vaux Greensward plan. As late as December, 1974, the *New York Times* asked City Hall to open its purse just a little to restore "that neglected and ravaged masterpiece of design and delight on its way to total ruin."

Whether that masterpiece can be restored or should be restored is an interesting problem. Rebuilding the lost Eden is a pleasing idea but how useful would the restored museum piece be and how many would it deprive of free or inexpensive entertainment? It is conceivable that Olmsted and Vaux, planning now, would include a soccer and baseball field and a zoo in their design, and weekend freedom from traffic. Their plan for recreation might easily include a cafeteria that looks out on seals, strollers, cracker jacks and balloons. They would hardly object to Shakespeare or dance recitals at the side of their castle or to waltzes, fireworks and tall fantasy figures celebrating New Year's Eve in the park. Nor to the jugglers and clowns and storytellers, the tottery senior citizens making merry, the Festa Italiana, the reunion of elderly Jewish actors. The septuagenarian Olmsted, who insisted that the Chicago World's Columbian Fair adorn itself with singing gondoliers, vendors in colorful costumes and strolling musicians, would welcome the impromptu music combos, the bicycle riders, the sketchers, the magicians, the youngsters who set up a few pieces of plywood for improvised theater, the opera, symphonic concerts, Gilbert and Sullivan, jazz from Ellington to punk, the picnickers and intrepid dawn bird watchers. It is a great plenty, admittedly badly marred, that might with refurbishing and vigilance return, not to the original Greensward plan, but to a workably modern fascsimile of the "first real park made in this country —a democratic development of the highest significance."

Saturday, September, 3:00 P.M. Sherman's Bucephalus lowers over a fat girl, a slender girl and a boy, all in top hats and blue jeans, watching from the flower-decorated carriages they tend, the goings on of a Hare Krishna group, nestled in the shadow of the horse. His head and behind are garlanded with rows of sparrows; one sparrow sits on the outstretched hand of Victory (or is she Peace?) and one on the peace frond she extends. A girl in a sari is humbly—so humbly that it is theater—cleaning up after people who have been invited to eat spiritual food set forth on a large table spread with India print cotton. The collation is pure and innocent—a milky fruit juice, pieces of watermelon, chopped apples and raisins served by a Ceres in pristine long white robe and covered head. A board of text and pictures explains the meanings of the movement and extols the calm purity a Hare Krishna life holds: no sex outside of marriage, no drugs, no alcohol, no meat and, yes, you can hold a job and still be a member in good standing. A few feet from the table, a musical group—squeeze box, sitar, flute, gourd drum, cymbals and castanets—plays and chants while its fellow devotees sway, beatified. Some of them look particularly odd, not only because of the shaved heads and the long thin topknot, the white streaks down the center of forehead and nose, but because of the prevalence of thick-lensed spectacles and thick gray American sweaters under the orange veiling. The leader of the chanting group is a good-looking man who talks to the camera-clicking audience about the word of God and "the way" that leads to the highest spiritual life, "the bliss of true, blissful reality." He invites the assemblage to come the next afternoon to a meeting hall in Brooklyn, carefully repeating the exact address and hours, for a big ten-course vegetable dinner and chanting. And to come back here next Saturday, same place, same time. He is engaging, and his dark, warm face well suits the bright, gold-draped little shrine nearby and its gaudy images and the gentle monotony of the chanting. What is askew are his heartfelt "wonderful," "beautiful," in Bronx cadences closer to Odets than Krishna.

An August day at 4:00 P.M. between Forty-seventh and Forty-second streets: one bagpiper in kilts, one accordionist, six pretzel vendors, all Greek; one girl in a loose halter threatening to shake out her substantial breasts; moving downward, a bumpy navel and farther downward, heavy, lined ski boots. In

that brief stretch of street, in a few minutes, come two people
talking to themselves, one blind man with a dog and a cup of
pencils, five boys and six girls distributing handbills for the
monster uplift meeting organized by Dr. Moon, two portly
black-clad gentlemen wearing the long beard of Abraham and
the sidelocks of David, discussing the diamond business, locally
centered on Forty-seventh Street west of the Avenue.

Rainy evening. A lady *clochard,* one of the growing number that sleeps on street benches and in the subways, dangles a
cigarette from her lips, her hands too full of shapeless bundles
tied in black plastic and cardboard. She is small and thin, possibly drunk, certainly mad. As she staggers across the sidewalk,
she bumps her bundles into a passerby and in a baleful voice,
fixing him with a malevolent eye, rasps, "You'll turn into a frog
for that. I'll make you turn into a frog, you bastard." Suddenly
Fifth Avenue turns into a haunt of enraged, frenzied menads.

Late spring, Sunday afternoon. At Sixtieth Street and the
park, a magician in a pirate's headkerchief held down by a
Robin Hood hat. His blouse is bright, his small beard red, his
mustache curved like a scimitar, his eyes bright green; he is
very picturesque and not a very good magician. He makes a
piece of rope longer and shorter, plays tricks with small
amounts of water and fancies himself a comic. "If you didn't
like my rope trick, please just applaud my mustache." The
magic words for lengthening the short rope are "down with
pay toilets" and his request for contributions—"nothing over a
hundred please"—are "a break for commercials." The smart
kids aren't much impressed but he keeps trying—in the park,
outside, and on that favorite Fifth Avenue stage, the steps of
the Metropolitan Museum—and he is pleasing to look at, classy
in his presence, if not in his work.

Oblivious of the magicians, traffic, pretzels, pearly hotels
to examine across the Avenue, pedestrians zany and sober, people chomping on hot dogs, children wailing over dropped
ice-cream cones, an ambulance banshee shrieking in the dis-

tance and the Loreleis of Tiffany's and Van Cleef's and Bergdorf's down the street, the books searchers take on their habitual
mute, bent stance among the metal boxes that become book-
shelves across from the Hotel Pierre. They seem enviously
cocooned, away from the Mexican bark painting and trinkets
below, the portable radio blasting country music above and the
whirr and bells of bicycles all around.

Outside Doubleday's near Fifty-seventh Street a lively old
drunk mouths a harmonica; his music is the meaningless scoop-
ing up and down the scale of a child exploring the instrument
for the first time. A black friend holds out a hat for contributions, both team and hat ignored by a neat, plain girl who is
selling God's word a few feet away.

5:15 P.M. Threatening Tuesday sky. Under Tiffany's elderly clock stands a man with a boxful of umbrellas, two
dollars for ladies, two fifty for the men's, no tax. Obscuring
the radiance of one perfect Tiffany diamond attached as shield
on a toothpick castle, the vendor moves as restlessly as a bird,
watching for the looming blue of a cop, calling to customers,
arguing with one who insists on testing too many umbrellas.
As two customers threaten to walk off, he mutters consent to
inspection, still crying his wares, still wary of the dark blue cop
cloud, making fast change, protesting a twenty-dollar bill. (He
has the change but it takes too much time to count out.) Trade
is brisk; the small crowd indifferent to the buffetings of the
homebound rush, dips into the big box, pulls umbrellas out,
pops them open and closed, adroitly avoiding a neck here, an
eye there. The activity attracts another fast-moving vendor, a
hefty young man with a box of roses in paper-wrapped bundles.
He tells his umbrella friend that he was going great until a
cop chased him off the street near the General Motors plaza.
Undiscouraged, rather fired by the perpetual chase, he shouts,
"American Beauty roses, two dollars a dozen." Between shouts,
a cautious purchaser asks if the stems are attached to the heads
by wires. The vendor pulls himself up to his heavyweight height

and proclaims to the crowd, "Honest to God: no crooked stuff. This is the real goods." The paper bundles fly from the flower box, the umbrellas balloon open and snap shut, dollar bills stream from hand to hand.

August, noon. A Hallmark show featuring a variety of patchwork quilts: orderly, eccentric, explosive, serene. Framed by the folk murals, a lady in old-fashioned rural costume demonstrates their making. Outside, a young chamber group of flute, violin and recorder plays Corelli with high skill. The musical competition, a block southward, is an old man playing a tottering Lehar tune on the violin. The visual arts are represented on the steps of St. Thomas's church where a stout black man paints practiced small watercolors, three dollars each. Accusing St. Thomas's, a flash of graffiti complains that Christianity died in the Middle Ages and urges passersby and the church to THINK.

A bagpipes player in kilts, with the narrow face and short red beard that suggest D. H. Lawrence, performs a skirl or two and to a small herd of loiterers and strollers displays a sign offering his services at weddings, wakes, testimonial dinners and bar mitzvahs.

July, Sunday in the Piazza Maggiore before the Metropolitan Museum. The summer navel punctuates the space between halter and shorts, or is covered by a long swinging skirt in old-fashioned calico patterns, in Indian paisley designs, in strong African colors. Foreign tourists pick their way among ice-cream eaters, puzzle-solvers, sunbathers, radio-listeners, arguments and desultory conversation on the steps. The Japanese clutch their cameras, the French their Michelins, the Dutch their raincoats, although the sun is steadily refulgent; the Spaniards and Italians trust themselves entirely to their leaders, flocking to calls of "por aquí" and "diritto, diritto."

At closing time, the foreigners leave, dragging themselves to yet another sight-seeing requirement; the indigenes keep to the steps for the next acts of the nonstop weekend show. Yesterday it was a juggler and an unemployed actor reading Shakespeare's sonnets; today it is a pantomimist working on a midway point of the steps. He is in tight, skinny black, his face piercing white. He paces out mechanical, precise steps, jerking his head like a robot in a mad, angular ritual. The crowd finds his death dance too macabre and turns its attention to a group on the street level. A long-haired man in red, white and blue pants and a deep cap, and a companion in black are the acolytes for a young man in a loose white pantomimist's costume, the "Children of Paradise" kind. The attendants pass him crystal balls and a skull with which he dances slowly, in vaguely Oriental gestures. He might be a dancer working out, with a little help from his friends, an improvisation on a new theme, it might be part of a drug trip or a private joke or the result of a bet. No one much cares; the audience is young, a television generation and anything that passes before its eyes is entertaining.

No matter who is doing what at the bottom of the museum steps, the hot dogs, pretzels and sweet sodas stay, one vendor joining the vaudeville by wearing a tall green hat marked "Mexico" and playing Greek tunes on his radio. South of the open-air theater, a street market of earrings made of fishing lures, of twisted copper, of silver wire; carved trays made while you wait; Mexican mats; pendants of stone, of metal, of African beads and of tiny cloth dolls. A primitive Near Eastern fiddle and shallow parchment drum call customers to crude burlap bags, very ethnic. Tall waves of cushions threaten to crash on pre-Columbian pottery made last week; pools of finger rings glint from every corner of the *souk*. And there is art, gluey with varnish, of cute little dogs, wistful, big-eyed children, timid landscapes and movie posters and instant portraits for three or four dollars. Coney Island appears as a large canvas painted with Mae West and a strong man on a beach, both lacking heads; the joy and joke is to be photographed with one's head

atop either body. On an adjoining bit of ground, two dogs jump through hoops to an accompaniment of pale quips.

A small duchy surrounding Seventy-ninth Street belongs exclusively to Italian Baroque music, sounded by a woodwind trio, by a lone and unusually competent fiddler, by a cello duo, on one open case a sign, "Our Ambition Is Exceeded Only By Our Lack of Tuition." Immune to their music, to Mexican and Afghan crafts, to piles of dashikis and quezquematls and tinsel jewelry, an extremely stout lady, hair, face and flesh melting benignly, sits with her rows of belts, making no attempt to sell them, just smiling into Fifth Avenue traffic and the hordes leaving Central Park for baths and supper.

When crowd and vendors have gone, when the sidewalks are empty and quiet and the long light pales, when St. Patrick's spires cast shadows like Van Gogh's black-flame cypresses on the glass wall of the Olympic Towers, from the darkened doorway of the Squibb Building comes the lonely farewell call of one trumpet on a slow, blue journey. A farewell, perhaps, to splendors gone and a last few going?

BIBLIOGRAPHY

Allen, Frederick Lewis. *The Lords of Creation*. New York and London: Harper & Bros., 1935.

———. *Only Yesterday*. New York and London: Harper & Bros., 1931.

Amory, Cleveland. *The Last Resorts*. New York: Harper & Bros., 1952.

———. *Who Killed Society?* New York: Harper & Bros., 1960.

Andrews, Wayne. *Architecture in New York*. New York: Harper & Row, 1969.

———. *The Vanderbilt Legend*. New York: Harcourt, Brace & Co., 1941.

Balsan, Consuelo Vanderbilt. *The Glitter and the Gold*. New York: Harper & Bros., 1952.

Barlow, Elizabeth, and Alex, William. *Frederick Law Olmsted's New York*. New York: Praeger, in association with the Whitney Museum of American Art, 1972.

Beebe, Lucius Morris. *The Big Spenders*. Garden City, N.Y.: Doubleday, 1966.

Beer, Thomas. *The Mauve Decade*. Garden City, N.Y.: Garden City Publishing Co., 1926.

Behrman, S. N. *Duveen*. New York: Random House, 1952.

Birmingham, Stephen. *Our Crowd*. New York: Harper & Row, 1967.

———. *Real Lace*. New York: Harper & Row, 1973.

Bourget, Paul. *Outre-Mer*. Paris: A. Lemerre, 1895.

Brown, Henry Collins. *Brownstone Fronts and Saratoga Trunks.* New York: E. P. Dutton, 1935.

Burnham, Alan. *New York Landmarks.* Middletown, Conn.: Wesleyan University Press, 1963. Published under the auspices of the Municipal Art Society of New York.

Churchill, Allen. *The Improper Bohemians.* New York: E. P. Dutton, 1959.

————. *The Upper Crust.* Englewood Cliffs, N.J.: Prentice-Hall, 1970.

De Leeuw, Rudolph M., compiler. *Both Sides of Broadway From Bowling Green to Central Park.* New York: De Leeuw Riehl Publishing, 1910.

Dickens, Charles. *American Notes for General Circulation.* New York: Harper & Bros., 1842. London: Chapman and Hall, 1842.

Duveen, James Henry. *The Rise of the House of Duveen.* London and New York: Longmans Green, 1957.

Eliot, Elizabeth. *Heiresses and Coronets.* New York: McDowell, Obolensky, 1959.

Fifth Avenue Association. *Fifty Years on Fifth, 1907–1957.* New York: Fifth Avenue Association, 1957.

Fifth Avenue Bank of New York. *Fifth Avenue Events.* New York: Fifth Avenue Bank, 1916.

Fiske, Stephen. *Off-hand Portraits of Prominent New Yorkers.* New York: G. R. Lockwood & Son, 1884.

Gimpel, René. *Diary of an Art Dealer.* Translated by John Rosenberg. New York: Farrar, Straus & Giroux, 1966.

Goldstone, Harmon H., and Dalrymple, Martha. *History Preserved: A Guide to New York City Landmarks and Historic Districts.* New York: Simon & Schuster, 1974.

Harvey, George. *Henry Clay Frick.* New York and London: Charles Scribner's Sons, 1928.

Havemeyer, Louisine. *Sixteen to Sixty.* New York: privately printed for the family of Mrs. H. O. Havemeyer and the Metropolitan Museum of Art, 1961.

Hirsch, Mark D. *William C. Whitney, Modern Warwick.* New York: Dodd, Mead, 1948.

ᴐok, Stewart Hall. *The Age of the Moguls.* Garden City, N.Y.: Doubleday, 1953.

Hone, Philip. *The Diary of Philip Hone, 1828–1851.* Edited, with an introduction by Allan Nevins. New York: Dodd, Mead, 1936.

Hoyt, Edwin P. *The Goulds.* New York: Weybright and Talley, 1969.

James, Henry. *The American Scene.* Bloomington: Indiana University Press, 1968.

Johnson, Allen, ed. *Dictionary of American Biography.* Under the auspices of the American Council of Learned Societies. New York: Charles Scribner's Sons, 1928.

Johnson, James Weldon. *Black Manhattan.* New York: Arno Press, 1968.

Josephson, Matthew. *The Robber Barons.* New York: Harcourt, Brace & Co., 1934.

Kavaler, Lucy. *The Astors.* New York: Dodd, Mead, 1966.

Koch, Robert. *Louis C. Tiffany: Rebel in Glass.* New York: Crown, 1964.

Kouwenhouven, John A. *The Columbia Historical Portrait of New York.* New York: Harper & Row, 1972.

Leslie, Anita. *The Remarkable Mr. Jerome.* New York: H. Holt, 1954.

Luhan, Mabel Dodge. *Intimate Memories.* New York: Harcourt, Brace & Co., 1933.

Lundberg, Ferdinand. *America's Sixty Families.* New York: Vanguard Press, 1937.

Lynes, Russell. *The Tastemakers.* New York: Harper & Bros., 1954.

Maher, James T. *The Twilight of Splendor.* Boston: Little, Brown, 1975.

Matz, Mary Jane. *The Many Lives of Otto Kahn.* New York: Macmillan, 1963.

Maurice, Arthur B. *Fifth Avenue.* New York: Dodd, Mead, 1918.

Mayer, Grace M. *Once Upon a City.* New York: Macmillan, 1958.

Morris, Lloyd R. *Incredible New York.* New York: Random House, 1951.

Mumford, Lewis. *The Brown Decades.* New York: Dover Publications, 1955.

New York as it is (1833–34), and Citizens Adve York: J. Disturnell, 1833–40.

Nichols, Mary E. [Eve Brown]. *The Plaza*. Ne Press, 1967.

O'Connor, Harvey. *The Guggenheims*. New York: 1937.

O'Connor, Richard. *The Scandalous Mr. Bennett*. Ga len City, N.Y.: Doubleday, 1962.

Osofsky, Gilbert. *Harlem: The Making of a Ghetto*. New York: Harper & Row, 1966.

Ottley, Roi, and Weatherby, William J., eds. *The Negro in New York*. New York: The New York Public Library, 1967.

Pulitzer, Ralph. *New York Society on Parade.* New York and London: Harper & Bros., 1910.

Pember, Arthur ("A.P."). *The Mysteries and Miseries of the Great Metropolis*. New York: D. Appleton, 1874.

Reed, Henry Hope, and Duckworth, Sophia. *Central Park: A History and Guide*. New York: C. N. Potter, 1967.

Roper, Laura Wood. *A Biography of Frederick Law Olmsted*. Baltimore: Johns Hopkins University Press, 1973.

Ross, Ishbel. *Charmers and Cranks*. New York: Harper & Row, 1965.

Saarinen, Aline B. *The Proud Possessors*. New York: Random House, 1958.

Scheiner, Seth M. *Negro Mecca*. New York: New York University Press, 1965.

Seligman, Germain. *Merchants of Art, 1880–1960*. New York: Appleton-Century-Crofts, 1961.

Social Register, New York, The. New York: Social Register Association, 1888–1930.

Still, Bayrd. *Mirror for Gotham*. New York: University Press, 1956.

Stokes, Isaac Newton Phelps. *New York Past and Present: Its History and Landmarks, 1524–1939*. New York: Plantin Press, 1939.

Strong, George Templeton. *The Diary of George Templeton Strong, 1835–1875*. Edited by Allan Nevins and Milton Halsey Thomas. New York: Macmillan, 1952.

Tompkins, Calvin. *Merchants and Masterpieces*. New York: E. P. Dutton, 1973.

Frances. *Domestic Manners of the Americans*. London: Whittaker, Treacher & Co., 1832. Barre, Mass.: Imprint Society, 1969.

Trow's New York City Classified Business Directory, Boroughs of Manhattan and the Bronx, 1922–23. New York: R. L. Polk.

Walker, John. *Self-Portrait with Donors*. Boston: Little, Brown, 1974.

Wallace, Irving. *The Square Pegs*. New York: Knopf, 1957.

Warburg, James Paul. *The Long Road Home*. Garden City, N.Y.: Doubleday, 1964.

Wecter, Dixon. *The Saga of American Society*. New York: Charles Scribner's Sons, 1937.

Wharton, Edith. *The Age of Innocence*. New York: D. Appleton, 1920.

Wharton, Edith, and Fitch, Clyde. *The House of Mirth: a Play in Four Acts*. New York: Rosenfeld, 1906.

White, Norval, and Willensky, Elliot, eds. *The AIA Guide to New York City*. New York: Macmillan, 1968.

Who's Who in America. Chicago: A. N. Marquis Co., 1899–1931.

Winkler, John K. *Incredible Carnegie*. New York: Vanguard Press, 1931.

Worden, Helen. *Society Circus*. New York: Covici, Friede, 1936.

Works Progress Administration. *W.P.A. Guide to New York City*. New York: Random House, 1939.

The following photographs were obtained through York Historical Society, New York City:
Fifth Avenue at Washington Square
Central Park lake gondola
Jacob Schiff
Otto Kahn
South Street seaport
Fifth Avenue and 42nd Street, 1909
Mrs. Cornelius Vanderbilt
Broadway and Fifth Avenue
Madison Square about 1895
Madison Square Park, 1876
Fifth Avenue and 44th Street
Mansion at 126th Street
Waldorf Astoria Hotel
Mrs. William Astor
The Belmonts and Caroline Perry

The following photographs were obtained from the Byron Collection of the Museum of the City of New York:
Central Park menagerie
Central Park skaters
Maillard's Confectionery
Mr. and Mrs. George Gould
Slum interior
Metropolitan Club at 60th Street
Hyde Ball: Dining Room at Sherry's
Billings' Horseback Dinner
Mme. Rejane and Hyde

We wish to thank the Museum of the City of New York for permission to use the following photographs:
Squatters' shacks
Bandits' Roost
Bear, sled and ladies at Vanderbilt Ball
Mrs. William K. Vanderbilt
Vanderbilt's drawing room
Carnegie's drawing room
H. C. Frick

We wish to thank the Bettmann Archive, Inc. for permission to reprint the photograph of Consuelo and William K. Vanderbilt.
The Edward J. Steichen photograph of the Flatiron Building is reprinted through the courtesy of the Metropolitan Museum of Art, gift of Alfred Stieglitz, 1933.

The photograph on the last page, The Scene today, is by James McGuire.